Working With Families in

M000249823

Working With Families in Medical Settings provides mental-health professionals with the tools they need to figure out what patients and families want and how, within the constraints imposed by twenty-first century healthcare settings, to best give them the care they need. Psychiatrists and other clinicians who work in medical settings know that working with a patient with a chronic illness usually entails work with that patient's family as well as with other medical professionals. Some families need education; others have specific difficulties or dysfunctions that require skilled assessment and intervention. It is up to the clinician to find productive ways to work with common themes in family life: expressed emotion, levels of resilience, life-cycle issues, and adaptation to illness, among others. Enter *Working With Families in Medical Settings*, which shines a spotlight on the major issues professional caregivers face and shows them how to structure an effective intervention in all kinds of settings. Psychiatrists, particularly those in psychosomatic medicine, and other clinicians who work with the medically ill will find *Working With Families in Medical Settings* to be an essential resource and guide to productive relationships with patients and their families.

Alison M. Heru, MD, is an associate professor of psychiatry at the University of Colorado Denver, School of Medicine and an associate professor of medicine at National Jewish Medical and Research Center. She is a coauthor of *Working With Families of Psychiatric Inpatients: A Guide for Clinicians* and *Clinical Manual of Couples and Family Therapy*.

Working With Families in Medical Settings

A Multidisciplinary Guide for Psychiatrists and Other Health Professionals

Alison M. Heru

Routledge
Taylor & Francis Group

NEW YORK AND LONDON

First published 2013
by Routledge
711 Third Avenue, New York, NY 10017

Simultaneously published in the UK
by Routledge
27 Church Road, Hove, East Sussex BN3 2FA

Library of Congress Cataloging in Publication Data
Heru, Alison M., 1953-
Working with families in medical settings : a multidisciplinary guide for psychiatrists and other health professionals / Alison M. Heru.

pages cm

Includes bibliographical references and index.

1. Psychiatric hospital care. 2. Family psychotherapy. 3. Mentally ill--Family relationships. I. Title.

RC439.H477 2013

616.89'156--dc23

2012038651

ISBN: 978-0-415-89700-6 (hbk)
ISBN: 978-0-415-65648-1 (pbk)
ISBN: 978-0-203-80457-5 (ebk)

Typeset in Minion by Fakenham Prepress Solutions, Fakenham, Norfolk NR21 8NN

Certified Sourcing
www.sfiprogram.org
SFI-00453

Printed and bound in the United States of America
by Edwards Brothers, Inc.

Dedication

To the patients and their families who so generously share with us the most intimate details of their lives, in the hope that they can receive the best care. This book is also dedicated to trainees; that their aspirations keep them hopeful, generous and brave.

Contents

List of Contributors

Nora Cavelli ND, MA, RN, CNS
Psychiatric Consult Nurse
Department of Case Management, University of Colorado Hospital, Aurora, CO

Kamryn T. Eddy, PhD
Assistant Professor of Psychology
Harvard Medical School, Cambridge, MA

Staff Psychologist
Massachusetts General Hospital, Boston, MA

Ellen H. O'Donnell, PhD
Staff Psychologist
Massachusetts General Hospital, Boston, MA

Instructor
Harvard Medical School, Cambridge, MA

Paula K. Rauch, MD
Director, Marjorie E. Korff PACT Program
Massachusetts General Hospital, Boston, MA

Associate Professor of Psychiatry
Harvard Medical School, Cambridge, MA

John S. Rolland, MD, MPH
Professor of Psychiatry & Behavioral Neuroscience
University of Chicago Pritzker School of Medicine

Co-Director
Chicago Center for Family Health

Frederick S. Wamboldt, MD
Co-Director
Center for Health Promotion

Professor of Medicine
National Jewish Health

Professor of Psychiatry
University of Colorado School of Medicine

Marianne Z. Wamboldt, MD
Chair, Psychiatry and Behavioral Sciences
Children's Hospital Colorado

Professor and Vice Chair of Psychiatry
University of Colorado School of Medicine

Preface

Families have a powerful influence on health, equal to traditional medical risk factors (Campbell, 2003). Campbell reviewed the literature on family factors and medical illness and concluded that the quality of the marital relationship was the most influential family relationship on health for adults and emotional support was the most important and influential type of support that families could provide. However, negative, critical, or hostile family relationships have a stronger influence on health than positive or supportive relationships. Since Campbell's review in 2003, the evidence that family functioning influences health behavior and illness outcomes continues to grow.

Family research has historically focused on white middle-class nuclear families mostly because they have been the easiest to recruit and therefore study. Families in the real world are more diverse, frequently with a more complex structure, such as single parents with a kinship support system that includes neighbors and local communities. LGBT families and multigenerational families are also more commonly identified in our current times. Little research has been done on families of different or mixed ethnic and cultural backgrounds. There is a substantial gap between family research and the real lived experience of many families. Family researchers must extend their reach out into the real world.

Families are more prominently considered at either end of the life cycle, where dependency needs are highest. At the beginning of the family life cycle, pediatricians and child psychiatrists focus on ways of helping families manage childhood illnesses. At the end of the family life cycle, geriatricians and palliative care specialists focus on helping family members support patients as their life skills diminish. Family perspectives are therefore frequently shaped by the discipline where the patient receives care.

Families of patients do receive attention in this process but no single medical discipline "owns" the family concerns. No single medical discipline attends to the needs and assessment of families. Family Medicine attends to the needs of individual family members, but does not address the needs of the family unit as a whole. Typically, physicians make diagnoses and then inform the patient and family about the diagnosis and the prognosis. Physicians answer questions asked by the family but rarely enquire in depth about how the family is functioning. Social workers talk with family members as part of their routine assessment of patients, focusing on the health and safety of the home environment and the adequacy of resources for the patient. Nurses instruct the primary caregiver in hands-on patient care issues such as home wound care or illness management. Psychologists may focus on interpersonal problems such as communication difficulties. Marriage and family therapists have developed a Medical Family Therapy (MedFT) that helps families cope with chronic medical illness. Hospital administrations balance the requests of families with the many regulations and standards required to provide safe, effective patient care. Each discipline touches the family in their own specific way. This book promotes an encompassing and systematic approach to families, for all disciplines.

History of Family Factors in Medicine

Family factors were first recognized in psychosomatic medicine by Alexander and French (1948) who described how families "transmit" illness. The first notions about families identified the "affective hypothesis" where repressed negative feelings cause physical symptoms. (See page 157 for further discussion of repression.) This hypothesis was in line with the psychoanalytic thinking of the mid-twentieth century and was based on clinical impressions rather than scientific study. Early research articles include "Is there a psychosomatogenic family?" (Loader, Kinston, and Stratford, 1980). Families have also been differentiated into types e.g. Minuchin's enmeshed over involved families.

Parentectomy was popular in the treatment of asthma for about 50 years. How did parentectomy "an inconceivably harsh and invasive family-based intervention for asthma became the reigning treatment?" (Wamboldt, 2008, p. 131). Wamboldt describes the historical background to this story and concludes that parentectomy "co-opted three potent metaphors that fueled its dangerous seductiveness and longevity, these were: (1) the decisive (incisive?) action of surgery (who would not want limbs cut off if it saved you certain death from gangrene); (2) the double-barreled mysteries of allergy and the unconscious (what lives in the dark eventually will come to get you); and (3) the risk of data-based myopia (in today's words, it was "evidence-based," and like today, inferences and policies are very often made from shockingly incomplete datasets). His moral is that even though there is considerable evidence that something in some families' emotional environment worsens some children's asthma, until all of the "somes" are removed from the preceding sentence clause, we must never jump to conclusions (especially if they lead to invasive interventions), with the greatest danger residing in the "simplest" conclusions (Wamboldt, 2008, p. 134). Parentectomy is an example of a family intervention where families were "blamed" for causing illness. This cautionary tale reminds us that our involvement with patients and families must first be governed by the principle: Do No Harm.

Current Status of Family Factors in Medicine

Family research has progressed significantly over the past decades. We have a more detailed understanding of how family factors affect biological processes, which in turn affect health and the expression of disease. A recent meta-analysis has documented the association between child abuse and increased risk of poor physical health in adulthood (Wegman and Stetler, 2009). The magnitude of the risk is comparable to the association between child abuse and poor psychological outcomes.

Some health care systems include families in the care of patients with chronic medical illnesses. In the UK, the National Institute for Health and Clinical Excellence (NICE)

(2004) has guidelines that recognize the needs of caregivers and children of persons with multiple sclerosis (PWMS). The NICE guidelines include suggestions for family physicians on the best ways to include caregivers in their practice (http://www.nice.org.uk). The document states: "Family members (including any schoolchildren) living in the same house as the person with MS, and any family members delivering substantial support even if living elsewhere, should be supported by:

- Asking about their physical and emotional health and well-being, especially in the case of children aged 16 years or less, and offering advice and referring on for additional support if necessary.
- Providing them with general factual information about MS; this should only be extended to include more specific information related to the person with MS with the permission of that person.
- Ensuring that they are willing to undertake support of personal activities of daily living (such as dressing and toileting), are safe and competent at such tasks, and that the person with MS is happy for them to provide such assistance.
- Informing them about social services carer assessment and support procedures.

In the US, the American College of Physicians in conjunction with ten other professional societies offer ethical guidance to physicians in developing patient, physician and caregiving relationships (Mitnick, Leffler, and Hood, 2010). The AMA has a self-report questionnaire that can be made available in the waiting room (see Appendix, p. 230). A national organization of family caregivers offers a virtual library of information and educational materials ranging from national educational campaigns to Tips and Tools for family caregivers, information on agencies and organizations that provide caregiver support, to workshops on communicating effectively (http://www.thefamilycaregiver. org). In 2010, an American Psychological Association Presidential Task Force on Caregivers developed a Family Caregiver Briefcase. The Briefcase is a web-based resource that includes: caregiving facts and figures, strategies for reaching family caregivers, research opportunities and considerations, assessment tools, and resources for psychologists and caregivers (http://www.apa.org/pi/about/publications/caregivers/index.aspx.) Physician recognition of the value of the caregiver role contributes to a positive caregiving experience and decreases rates of patient hospitalization and institutionalization.

We are closer to defining the family interventions that are protective, promote health and prevent illness. When illness is present, we are clarifying what types of family intervention maximize resilience and minimize the illness experience. The importance of social and family support is undisputed. However family support may not be enough. When parents of children with cancer were studied, the presence of support was not associated with less parental distress (Gerhardt et al., 2007). When family support is not enough, family interventions must be considered.

Contribution of this Book

This book is written primarily for physicians who practice psychosomatic medicine. This includes general psychiatrists, general psychiatric residents and psychosomatic medicine fellows. Physicians in palliative care, primary care and internal medicine as well as practitioners in nursing, social work, and marriage and family therapy will also find this book useful. Administrators and members of hospital patient and family committees will find a rationale and practical suggestions for developing family-oriented patient care.

This book provides the knowledge and skills needed to provide family-oriented care, regardless of discipline. This book organizes current family research and presents it in a practical way that is useful for clinicians in office practice. This book emphasizes family assessment **before** family intervention. Several models of family systems assessment and treatment are discussed, but the main model used is the McMaster model (Epstein, Bishop, and Levin, 1978) and its associated treatment model, called the Problem-centered Systems Therapy of the Family (Epstein and Bishop, 1981). The McMaster model emphasizes a detailed and thorough assessment prior to intervention and, as many family systems experts have remarked, a good assessment is therapeutic in itself. A good assessment points out in a clear manner to families, how their functioning affects symptoms and illness behavior. High functioning families frequently progress to making the necessary changes on their own.

Three levels of family intervention are described: first is family inclusion which requires minimal training for the health care professional, second is family psychoeducation, which requires family skills training and third, family systems therapy which requires training in specific family concepts and intervention techniques. These three levels are derived from Doherty's 5 levels (1995). Family systems therapies share common factors, regardless of the original brand name of structural, strategic or narrative. The common factors include conceptualizing problems in relational terms, disrupting dysfunctional relational patterns and expanding direct treatment to include family members of the index patient (Sprenkle, David and Lebow, 2009). Each chapter differentiates between these 3 levels of interventions, emphasizing research and treatment outcome results and providing guidelines for clinical application.

Part I, Chapter 1 reviews family research, providing the rationale for including families in the care of the medically ill. In Chapter 2, Drs Fred and Marianne Wamboldt present highlights from their family research in childhood asthma. They make important recommendations for involving the family and the community in the clinical management of asthma. In Chapter 3, John Rolland presents his integrative model of family adaption to chronic medical illness and disability. He illustrates his model with several case examples.

Part II focuses on the involvement of the family in the health care system. Chapter 4 discusses the work of the Institute of Patient- and Family-Centered Care. Chapter 5 is written by Nora Cavelli, an experienced nurse on the psychosomatic medicine service at the University of Colorado Hospital and is illustrated with richly detailed case examples. She provides tools for the multidisciplinary team to work effectively with challenging family situations in the hospital setting. Chapter 6 presents the caregiver's perspective, including cultural aspects of the caregiver experience and caregiving across the life cycle. Chapter 7 is authored by Drs O'Donnell, Eddy and Rauch and highlights the Marjorie E. Korff PACT (Parenting at a Challenging Time) Program. This program was founded and developed by Dr. Paula Rauch, at Massachusetts General Hospital (www.mghpact.org) in 1997. This unique parenting program addresses the common challenges and needs of parents with cancer.

Part III provides guidance on how to complete a family systems assessment, followed by guidelines for family interventions. Chapter 8 reviews coping skills, differentiating between individual, couples and family coping skills. Cultural variations in coping styles are considered. A case example brings these concepts alive and shows how to use these concepts in practice. Chapter 9 describes family systems assessments and outlines the common factors of family systems assessment. Two clinical cases are described. Chapter 10 describes three levels of family intervention: family inclusion, family psychoeducation and family systems therapy. A case example shows how initial family inclusion progresses through family psychoeducation to a full family systems assessment. While this progression is not much discussed, it may actually be how things work in the office as the family becomes more comfortable with participation in care. Chapter 11 follows a couple in detail through the assessment and treatment process. This case shows how adaptation to illness consists of solving family problems and a real shift in family functioning. Lastly, Chapter 12 outlines multifamily group (MFG) interventions, differentiating between the family support, psychoeducational and family systems approaches. The evidence base for MFG's is presented and several examples illustrate how to develop and run MFGs. With changes in the health care system on the horizon, MFGs promise a cost effective way to improve health care outcomes.

In summary, families want to be included in patient care. Families recognize that an adjustment in the family's way of functioning is needed in order to live well with chronic illness. Families want to be educated about illness management. Families are key in maintaining continuity for patients as they navigate the complexities of the health care system. Families are our best allies in ensuring that patients are in good compliance with treatment and have the best possible medical outcomes. We must do our best to educate, support and help them solve family conflicts that arise during the care of their relatives with illness.

Important Resources

This reference list includes key texts that are influential and promote family-oriented health care. A list of prominent family journals, with their date of first issue, shows how family research and family intervention have progressed in the past decades. Generally, these journals are discipline specific, although several journals are inter/multi-disciplinary e.g. Family Process, and the Journal of Family Theory & Review. Families, Systems, & Health is the only family journal dedicated to publishing clinical research, training, and theoretical contributions in the areas of families and health, with a particular focus on collaborative family healthcare. The Collaborative Family Healthcare Association (CFHA) was developed by a group of family medicine educators to advance integrated care in the community. Their focus is on Primary Care Behavioral Health and the integration of behavioral health into the family medicine clinic setting.

Key Texts

Crane, D. R., and Marshall, E. S. (Eds) (2005). *Handbook of families and health: Interdisciplinary perspectives*. Thousand Oaks California: Sage Publications.

Linville, D. and Hertlein, K. M. (Eds). (2007). *The therapist's notebook for family health care: Homework, handouts, and activities for individuals, couples, and families coping with illness, loss, and disability*. New York: Haworth Press.

McDaniels, S. H. (1995). *Counseling Families With Chronic Illness*. Alexandria, VA: American Counseling Association.

McDaniels, S. H., Hepworth, J., and Doherty, W. J. (1992). *Medical Family Therapy: A Biopsychosocial Approach to Families*. New York: Basic Books.

—(1997). *The Shared Experience of Illness*. New York: Basic Books.

McDaniels, S. H., Campbell, T. L., Hepworth, J. and Lorenz, A. (2004). *Family-oriented Primary Care: A Manual for Medical Providers*. Second Edition, New York: Springer.

Rolland J. S. (1994). *Families, illness, and disability: An integrative treatment model*. New York: Basic Books.

List of Prominent Family Journals

Australian Journal of Family Therapy (1979–2008), became the Australian and New Zealand Journal of Family Therapy (2008)

Contemporary Family Therapy (1986)

Families, Systems, & Health (1983)

Family Journal (1993)

Family Process (1962)

Family Relations (1951)

Journal of Family Counseling (1973–1976), became International Journal of Family Counseling (1977–1978) became The American Journal of Family Therapy (1979)

Journal of Family Issues (1980)

Journal of Family Psychology (1976)

Journal of Family Social Work (1994)

Journal of Family Theory & Review (2009)

Journal of Family Therapy (1979)

Journal of Marital and Family Therapy (1974)

Journal of Marriage and Family (1940)

One article of note: Families and Health: An Empirical Resource Guide for Researchers and Practitioners (Proulx and Snyder, 2009). This annotated bibliography reviewed articles published in the past decade and includes articles emphasizing contemporary research findings, theoretical contributions, and their application.

References

Alexander, F. and French, T. M. (1948). *Studies in Psychosomatic Medicine*. New York: Ronald Press Co.

Campbell, T. L. (2003). The effectiveness of family interventions for physical disorders. *Journal of Marital and Family Therapy*, 29(2), 263–81.

Doherty, W. J. (1995). Boundaries between patient and family education and family therapy. *Family Relations*, 44, 353–8.

Epstein, N. B. and Bishop, D. S. (1981). Problem Centered Systems Therapy of the Family. *Journal of Marital and Family Therapy*, 7 (1), 23–31.

Epstein, N. B., Bishop, D. S. and Levin, S. (1978). The McMaster model of Family Functioning. *Journal of Marital and Family Therapy*, 4(4), 19–31.

Gerhardt, C. A., Gutzwiller, J., Huiet K. A., Fischer, S., Noll, R. B. Vannatta, K. (2007) Parental Adjustment to Childhood Cancer: A Replication Study. *Families, Systems, & Health*, 25(3), 263–75.

Loader, P. J., Kinston, W. and Stratford, J. (1980). Is there a psychosomatogenic family? *Journal of Family Therapy*, 2, 311–26.

Mitnick, S., Leffler, C., and Hood, V. L. (2010). Family Caregivers, Patients and Physicians: Ethical Guidance to Optimize Relationships. *Journal of General Internal Medicine,* 25(3), 255–60.

National Institute for Health and Clinical Excellence (2004). Multiple Sclerosis: National Clinical Guideline for Diagnosis and Management in Primary and Secondary Care. London: HMSO; 2004.

Proulx, C. M. and Snyder, L. A. (2009). Families and Health: An Empirical Resource Guide for Researchers and Practitioners. *Family Relations*, 58 (4), 489–504.

Sprenkle, D. H., David, S. D. and Lebow, J. L. (2009). Common Factors in Couple and Family therapy: The Overlooked Foundation for Effective Practice. Guilford, NY:

Wamboldt, F. (2008). Asthma theory and practice: it's not too simple. *Family Process*, 47(1), 131–6.

Wegman, H. L. and Stetler, C. (2009). A Meta-Analytic Review of the Effects of Childhood Abuse on Medical Outcomes in Adulthood. *Psychosomatic Medicine*, 71:805–812.

Part I

Family Theory and Research

Overview of Part I

Chapter 1: Family Research

This review of family research provides the rationale for including families in the care of the medically ill. The field of family research is vast, and studies and reports are scattered throughout many books and journals. The research presented in this chapter is described under the headings of family factors influencing biological processes, family health beliefs and behaviors, social support and marital quality, and family protective and risk factors. The evidence-based family interventions are described under the headings of promotion of healthy behaviors, family interventions in acute illness, and family interventions in chronic illness. Three meta-analyses of family treatment outcomes are presented. The examples of family research given in this chapter are chosen for their ease of application to the clinician's daily practice.

Chapter 2: Family Factors in Promoting Health: The Case of Childhood Asthma

In this chapter, Drs Fred and Marianne Wamboldt present highlights from their family research in childhood asthma. This chapter identifies the family factors that influence self-management behaviors. The authors state that special attention should be given to families whose illness narratives and stories suggest they are not confident in their plan to manage asthma. The community and broader sociocultural context of the family is an equally important factor in influencing asthma outcomes. The authors make recommendations for involving the family and the community in the clinical management of asthma.

Chapter 3: Family Adaptation to Chronic Medical Illness and Disability: An Integrative Model

Dr John Rolland describes his integrative model of family adaption to chronic medical illness and disability. He presents a normative model for the psychoeducation, assessment, and treatment of families living with chronic illness. Dr Rolland describes psychosocial types of illness and the time phases of illness. In his family assessment section, he introduces the importance of multigenerational legacies and the inter-weaving of illness, individual, and family development. Health/illness beliefs serve as a road map for families as they struggle with adaptation to illness and engage with the health-care system. He illustrates his integrative model with case examples.

1   Family Research

- Family research outcomes depend on who, what, when and how families are studied.
- Family factors influence biological processes, disease onset and course.
- Good quality relationships are associated with better illness outcomes.
- Family interventions prevent disease, hasten recovery, and improve patient functioning.

Introduction

Family research encompasses many topics: family factors that influence biological processes, family health beliefs and behaviors, social support and marital quality research, and evidence-based family interventions. Family research includes the study of healthy couples in the community, families with loved ones who are recruited from hospital settings, and patients and their families at the end of life. Researchers in these different fields use their own definitions and conceptualizations of family issues, which makes it difficult to generalize from specific studies to families in general. It is a significant undertaking to assimilate the diverse findings into a coherent body of knowledge that can be useful to the busy clinician. Nevertheless, when the body of evidence is presented, it becomes clear that family factors have a significant influence on health and that family interventions can prevent disease, hasten recovery from acute illness, and improve functioning in chronic illness.

WHO to Study

The easiest family group to study is a family dyad. This dyad is usually an identified patient and their significant other, such as a parent and their ill child, or a patient and their caregiver. Rarely are whole families studied, although there are notable exceptions, such as Kazak's interventions to reduce the emotional impact of the effect of childhood cancer on mothers, fathers and siblings (Kazak et al., 2007). An area of growing interest to family researchers is the transition of children with chronic illness into adulthood (Claessens et al., 2005). This transition involves both individual and family developmental stages, as well as the transition from a supportive pediatric care environment to a more independent adult care environment.

Most family research has been carried out on white middle-class couples who volunteer through outpatient clinics, support groups, or posted advertisements. Much less family research has been carried out with families in poverty, minority families, single parent families with or without extended family support, blended families or lesbian, bisexual, gay, transgender (LBGT) families. Families in different cultures can have very specific caregiving concerns (see Chapter 8). Research constructs may need to be modified or constructed de novo in order to accurately assess and address these diverse family constellations and structures and the specific family concerns in different cultures (Bernal and Domenech Rodriguez, 2009).

WHEN are Families Studied?

Adaptation to illness unfolds over time. The family has specific and different adaptive needs depending on the stage of the illness and the developmental stage of the family (see Chapter 3). Families are "in crisis mode" when coping with an acute stressor and routine family tasks can be neglected. Families develop strategies over time to manage the stress of coping with chronic illness, although these strategies may develop without much contemplation or forethought. Researchers should take into account this developmental and adaptive process when assessing families and testing interventions. There are only a few longitudinal studies of families coping with chronic illness and only a few prospective studies of families where the impact of illness has been studied from its onset through the family life cycle. End of life is a particularly difficult time to study families, as grief inhibits the family's ability to engage in research (see Chapter 5). Families may be more receptive to family interventions at earlier stages in their adaptation to illness. Clinical experience suggests that families are more likely to engage in treatment at the time of crises.

WHAT to Study?

Family researchers study a vast range of topics, from individual biological factors to the whole family adaptation to illness. Early family researchers focused on the importance of good social support (Revenson and Majerovitz, 1990). However, initial attempts to measure social support consisted of simply asking patients if they had good family and social support. Over time, researchers have found that good support influences illness outcome through many different pathways e.g. medication adherence, lifestyle changes, and relationship quality. The study of family support has become more sophisticated with specific measures of family functioning being linked to patient outcome.

Key aspects of family relationships that affect patient outcome include the family perception of illness demands and individual, dyadic, and family coping styles. Family conflict more commonly occurs at transitions in family life stages, For example, family conflict during adolescence is linked to difficulties managing diabetes (Anderson et al., 2002). Adaptation to illness is an important process and the target of many successful family interventions.

HOW do we Study Families?

How to study the family is determined by what the researcher wants to measure. Individual biological processes are measured in the laboratory or hospital setting. The subjective experience of individual family members is measured through self-reports or interviews. Family interactions are measured using structured family interviews or family observation. Family interactions are complex to measure and require specific training to identify dysfunctional family patterns.

As manipulation of data becomes more sophisticated, the association between variables can be examined more closely. For example, for many years, no clear association between marital quality (MQ) and patient illness outcomes was found. However, when researchers began to differentiate between good and poor marital functioning, improved illness outcomes, especially for women, became apparent for patients with good MQ (Heru, 2010).

Family Assessment Tools

Many family assessment tools are useful for studying families with medical illness. One family assessment tool that measures the family emotional environment is the Camberwell Family Interview (Vaughn and Leff, 1976). This two-hour interview tool assesses expressed emotion (EE). EE is a construct made up of three components: the number of critical comments, the expression of overt hostility and the degree of emotional over-involvement in the family. EE has been well researched in different cultures. In Latino cultures, a related construct of family warmth is more predictive of good outcome than the EE score (Lopez et al., 2009). In Western countries, patients with medical illnesses who live in high EE families have poorer outcome (Wearden et al., 2000).

McCubbin's resiliency model of family stress, adjustment, and adaptation (McCubbin et al., 2002) describes how families' experience of stress is modified by their strengths. After working through the adaptation phase, the family works together to perform the roles and responsibilities to meet the challenges of the illness. The family stress theory, based on Hill's ABC-X model, provides the underlying theory for the resiliency model (Ingoldsby, Smith, and Miller, 2004). According to Hill's model; A represents the stressor event; B represents resources, or the family's capabilities in adapting; C represents the definition the family gives to the situation, or the "meaning-making" of the illness; and X represents the degree of crisis the family experiences. Families with limited resources and negative "meaning-making" will experience a greater crisis, whereas families with resources and positive "meaning-making" will experience less of a crisis. The resources that individuals and families have to cope with stressful events are an important component of family stress theory (Hobfoll and Spielberger, 2003).

The Family Environment Scale (FES) assesses family cohesion, conflict, and control (Moos, 1986). Cohesion measures the level of family commitment and provision of support. Conflict measures the degree of discord and expressed anger in the family. Control measures the rules and rigidity within a family. The Family Relational Index is an associated brief screening tool that can be used in families with medical illness (Moos and Moos, 1981).

The Dyadic Adjustment Scale (DAS) (Spanier, 1976) and the Abbreviated Spanier Dyadic Adjustment Scale (ADAS) (Sharpley and Rodgers, 1984) measure perceived agreement regarding philosophy of life and aims, goals, the frequency of stimulating exchanges of ideas, and of working together on a project. Asking patients to rate their level of satisfaction with their marriage, on a one-item Likert scale, was found to have a sensitivity of 86% and a specificity of 86% when tested against the thirty-two-item DAS (Bailey, Kerley and Kibelstis, 2012). This one-item screen has been used in the primary care setting to identify the patient's satisfaction or dissatisfaction with their marriage. Knowing which families to refer for family assessment and family treatment is an important clinical need.

The Family Assessment Device (Epstein, Bishop, and Levin, 1978) is a self-report tool that has been translated into over twenty languages. It assesses family functioning in six family dimensions: roles, problem-solving, communication, affective involvement, affective responsiveness, and behavior control. There is an associated McMaster Clinical Rating Scale (MCRS) and an associated McMaster Structured Interview of Family Functioning (McSiff) (Ryan, Epstein, Keitner, Miller and Bishop, 2005). The "McMaster model" and its associated treatment model, the Problem-centered Systems Therapy of the Family (Epstein and Bishop 1981), are used to assess and treat families with medical illnesses and are described in depth in Part Three of this book.

Measurements of Coping

There are various models of coping that measure individual, dyadic and family coping. Dyadic coping styles are ways that couples "share" illness stressors (Bodenmann, 2005; Berg and Upchurch, 2007). The questions that clinicians would like researchers to ask and resolve are: what is the relationship between individual family members' adaptation to illness and the adaptation of the family as a whole? Is it always optimal for the family to adapt as a unit? What is the implication for the family when each member adapts individually? Is a mixture of individual and dyadic coping styles acceptable? Researchers and clinicians continue to learn about the process of the family's change and adaptation to illness. For example, avoidance has generally been seen as a negative coping skill, however being able to temporarily push away thinking about a stressor and focus on something else, is now considered good adaptive coping. This is an example of adaptive avoidance and is to be differentiated from maladaptive avoidance. The DBT-Ways of Coping Checklist (DBT-WCCL) is a new assessment tool that measures adaptive avoidance (Neacsiu, Rizvi, Vitaliano, Lynch, and Linehan, 2010).

Individual coping styles vary with the stage and severity of illness. Emotional coping is more common at the beginning of the illness. Avoidance of emotional processing prolongs emotional distress, even though it may help manage distress acutely. Emotional processing is measured with the Acceptance of Emotions Scale, which assesses the extent to which patients are accepting, friendly, and nurturing toward their feelings (Politi, Enright, and Weihs, 2006). Acceptance of emotions has a protective effect, which is associated with decreased mortality in breast cancer patients (Politi et al., 2006; Reynolds et al., 2000; Cunningham et al. 2000). At later illness stages, emotional coping is frequently replaced by problem-focused coping. Chapter 8 discusses the measurement of coping styles in more detail.

The following sections describe family research that is most useful for clinical practice.

Family Factors Influencing Biological Processes

Family Stress

Acute marital conflict is associated with increased blood pressure and pulse (Kiecolt-Glaser and Newton, 2001). "Normal family arguments" cause an elevation in blood pressure (BP) in patients (24 women, 19 men) when they and their partners discuss a threatening topic for ten minutes (Ewart, Taylor, Kraemer, and Agras, 1991). In women, hostile interaction and marital dissatisfaction are associated with increased BP; while "supportive" or "neutral" exchanges are unrelated to BP changes. In men, fluctuations in BP are related only to their partner's speech rate. Women have more sustained autonomic, neuroendocrine, and immunological stress reactions following negative interactions with spouses, than men (Kiecolt-Glaser, Glaser, Cacioppo, and Malarkey, 1998). This gender difference in biological reactivity to conflict has been replicated (Bloor, Uchino, Hicks, and Smith 2004) and may contribute to poorer outcome for women with cardiac disease (Heru, 2010).

Acute marital conflict is associated with changes in T cell subsets and natural killer cells (Dopp, Miller, Myers and Fahey, 2000) and increased IL-6 production, indicating an increased sensitivity of the immune system (Kiecolt-Glaser et al., 2005). Increased IL-6 production is associated with the development of the following age-related diseases: cardiovascular disease, osteoporosis, arthritis, Type 2 diabetes mellitus, cancers, and Alzheimer's disease. In couples with high attachment avoidance i.e. mistrust and avoidance of intimacy, acute marital conflict was associated with an 11% increase in total Il-6 production and heightened physiological reactivity. Whereas couples with low attachment avoidance i.e. trust and comfort with intimacy, had a 6% decrease in Il-6 production (Gouin et al. 2009).

Good social support moderates physiological reactivity to stress. Volunteers recruited from a newspaper advertisement completed three tasks in response to a social stressor. Subjects with good social support showed less cortisol reactivity, reduced neuro-cognitive reactivity and reduced neuroendocrine stress response (Eisenberger, Taylor, Gable, Hilmert, and Lieberman, 2007).

Chronic family stress is associated with persistent stimulation of cytokine production, thus accelerating the risk of age-related diseases, especially in the elderly (Kiecolt-Glaser, McGuire, Robles, and Glaser, 2002). Increases in proinflammatory cytokines are associated with depressive disorders and anxiety, suggesting a mechanism linking depressive and anxiety symptoms to illness (Glaser, Robles, Sheridan, Malarkey and Kiecolt-Glaser, 2003). Dementia caregivers have a 4 × increase in IL-6 and have poorer health outcomes following illness, compared with non-caregivers (Kiecolt-Glaser et al., 2003). Even several years after the death of the spouse, IL-6 changes remained high.

Acute Family Stress

- Associated with acute changes in physiological status
- Social support reduces physiological reactivity
- Low social stress is associated with higher oxytocin levels
- Good marital quality is associated with better cardiovascular profiles.

Chronic Family Stress

- Associated with worsening of longer term health markers and higher mortality rates
- Caregivers experience premature aging of the immune system.

Altered immune function is also found in adult daughters whose mothers have breast cancer (Cohen and Pollack, 2005). Norepinephrine levels mediated the relationship between the daughters' distress and their immune functioning. Cortisol levels mediated the relationship between daughters' distress and IL-2 secretion. In the daughters, stress hormone secretions and immune functions were related to both their own and their mothers' psychological distress.

Low stress is associated with higher oxytocin (OT) and vasopressin levels, providing protection from illness. Couples who received nasal OT prior to a structured conflict discussion, had lower cortisol levels and improved communication (Ditzen et al., 2009, Heinrichs, Baumgartner, Kirschbaum and Ehlart, 2003). In a study of wound healing, higher vasopressin levels were associated with fewer negative communication behaviors (Gouin et al., 2010). Couples with more warm contact had higher OT levels compared to couples with less warm contact (Grewen, Girdler, Amico and Light, 2005). OT's cardioprotective effects on sympathetic activity and blood pressure may be greater for women.

Unlike adults, children exposed to chronic stress have enhanced immunity. Children who live with parents who have psychiatric symptoms, were noted to have more total number of illnesses, and specifically more febrile illnesses, than controls (Wyman et al., 2007). Elevated chronic stress had enhanced rather than decreased natural killer-cell functioning, suggesting that chronic stress may have enhancing effects on the developing immune system.

Growing up in a family with unstable relationships is a key variable associated with increased childhood illness. In a nine-year study, biological, psychological, and health outcome data were measured in 264 infants, children, adolescents, and young adults, ages 2 months to 18 years, residing in a rural Caribbean village. Household income, land ownership, parental education, and other socioeconomic measures were only weakly associated with childhood illness. There was no evidence that higher socioeconomic status such as improved housing, diet, workloads, and access to private health care, had any direct effect on child health. However, unstable mating relationships of parents/caretakers and household composition were associated with abnormal glucocorticoid response profiles, diminished immunity, and frequent illness (Flinn and England, 1997).

- Illness affects all family members through direct biological processes and indirect behavioral effects

Family Health Beliefs and Behaviors

Family health beliefs influence family health-care decisions. Beliefs about pain control contribute to decisions about if and when pain medication should be taken. The beliefs of parents of children with cancer pain influence their decisions about managing their child's pain (Forgeron, Finley and Arnaout, 2005). Many parents of children with persistent pain believe that coping well with pain and managing stress well, helps their children in the long run (Claar and Scharff, 2007). Similarly, spousal beliefs about disability, emotion, control, and medication are correlated with partners' pain severity and pain adjustment (Cano, Miller, and Loree, 2009). When a couple has congruent beliefs about the women's ability to control her pain in rheumatoid arthritis, the women have better psychological adjustment (Sterba et al., 2008). Health beliefs are an appropriate focus for family treatment (Levy, 2010; Levy et al., 2010) (see Chapter 10, p. 189 for further discussion).

- Health beliefs and health-care utilization patterns run in families.
- Cognitive-behavioral therapy and family therapy can change health beliefs and behaviors.

Social Support and Marital Quality

Social support can be measured by assessing the patient's integration into a social network. Social integration improves outcome for patients with diabetes (Griffith, Field and Lustman, 1990; Zhang, Norris, Gregg, and Beckles, 2007), cardiovascular disease (Lett et al., 2009; Luttik, Jaarsma, Moser, Sanderman and van Veldhuisen, 2005; Rodriguez-Artalejo et al., 2006), hypertension, arthritis and emphysema (Tomaka, Thompson and Palacios, 2006). Social support includes providing practical support which helps patients keep appointments, adhere to medications, a healthy lifestyle, and the recommendations of the physician, thus reducing hospitalizations and mortality rates (Di Matteo, 2004, Sayers, Riegel, Pawlowski, Coyne and Samaha, 2008). Emotional support improves patient outcome in many medical illnesses (Reblin and Uchino, 2008).

Perceived and actual supports are variables that can be measured independently (Lett et al., 2009). In a study of social support in rheumatoid arthritis (RA), social support both perceived and actual, were measured with the Impact of Rheumatic Diseases on General Health and Lifestyle (IRGL) social functioning scale (Evers et al., 1998). Perceived support is the measure of perceived availability of emotional and practical support (availability to share sad and pleasant events, obtain support when faced with stress and pain, get help for casual work). Actual support is the measure of the number of relatives and friends in a patient's support network. Poor actual social support at the time of diagnosis predicted functional disability and pain at three- and five-year follow-ups in patients with rheumatoid arthritis (Evers, Kraaimaat, Geenen, Jacobs and Bijlsma, 2003). It is important to note that patients do not always recognize having received support even when they benefitted from it (Bolger, Zuckerman and Kessler, 2000).

Spousal support can be measured with well-known family assessment instruments such as the Dyadic Adjustment Scale (Sharpley and Rogers, 1984), although many researchers construct their own scales. In the Healthy Women Study, MQ was measured by assessing the amount of time spent together, quality of communication, sexual activity, agreement on financial matters, and similarity of interests, lifestyle, and temperament. This prospective study assessed MQ in 493 females, over an 11 to 14 year time period. The subjects had their cardiovascular health assessed with serial ultrasound measures of intima-media thickness and plaque in the carotid arteries and serial CTs assessed calcification in the aorta and coronary arteries. Women with good MQ had better cardiovascular risk profiles and illness trajectories, with lower levels of biological, lifestyle, and psychosocial risk factors, when compared with women who had moderate or low MQ or women who were single, divorced, and widowed (Gallo, Troxel, Matthews and Kuller, 2003).

In a study of survival of 189 patients with heart failure, MQ was assessed using measures of marital satisfaction (six items), marital routines (ten items), and useful illness discussions (eight items). Good MQ was a substantially better outcome indicator than individual risk and protective factors, such as psychological distress, hostility, neuroticism, self-efficacy, optimism, and breadth of perceived emotional support (Rohrbaugh, Shoham and Coyne, 2006). Improved survival continued during an eight-year follow-up period (p < 0.001), especially for female patients. The marital components that were found to be most predictive of good outcome were the frequency of the couple's "useful discussions" about the patient's illness and the ratio of positive to negative exchanges identified during a videotaped interaction.

Up to this point, MQ research has focused mostly on heterosexual white middle-class couples. Families in the real world are more diverse, frequently with a more complex structure, such as single parent families with an extended support system, LGBT families, families that include three generations, and families of different ethnic or mixed cultural backgrounds. Family researchers need to make efforts to include more diverse families in research protocols. Clinicians must remember this caveat and consider how the reported research might be applicable to the family in their office.

- Social and emotional support improve illness outcome.
- Good marital quality is associated with better cardiovascular risk profiles and illness trajectories, especially for women.

Family Protective and Risk Factors

In a review of the literature, Weihs and colleagues found specific protective and risk family factors associated with medical illness outcome (Weihs, Fisher, and Baird, 2002). Improved medical outcomes are associated with protective family factors such as good communication, encouragement of individual family members, expression of appreciation, having clear family roles, and spending time together as a family. Healthy families minimize the disruption that the illness has on normal family developmental tasks. Family factors that are considered risk factors are intra-familial conflict, blame, rigidity, and high levels of criticism. Criticalness and hostility are considered the most influential risk factors on disease outcome. Several possible protective factors, where the evidence is only suggestive, include the ability to talk about emotional issues, the integration of ritual and routine in family life, secure attachments for children, good problem-solving ability, and family recreation time.

Chapter 2 provides a detailed discussion of how family factors influence health in childhood asthma. The family factors that negatively impact treatment adherence are: a non-white race/ethnicity, older children (adolescents), high criticism and poor advice quality (Wamboldt et al., 2000). Family factors that influence adherence to home environment recommendations such as avoidance of tobacco smoke and exposure to pet allergens, are less clearly understood. The family's experience of traumatic stress related to life-threatening asthma attacks is raised as a possible influence on treatment adherence, with the family avoiding triggers such as the use of inhalers and doctors' appointments. As a consequence, the asthma worsens, leading to a self-fulfilling prophesy of life-threatening situations, when the experience of traumatic stress gets reinforced. Traumatic stress symptoms might be more prevalent in poor and minority families where there is less access to health care. Overall, treatment adherence is better in families with a daily routine (Wamboldt, Bender and Rankin, 2011). Importantly, family adherence behaviors consist of different family factors, and how a family performs on one adherence measure may be different from how they perform on other adherence measures.

Family Protective Factors in Medical Illnesses

- Good communication
- Adaptability
- Clear roles
- Achieving family development tasks
- Supporting individual members
- Expressing appreciation
- Commitment to the family
- Religious/spiritual orientation
- Social connectedness
- Spending time together.

Family Risk Factors in Medical Illnesses

- Family conflict
- Rigidity
- Blame
- High levels of criticism.

Evidence-Based Family Interventions

Family interventions in medical illnesses can promote health, prevent illness, hasten recovery in the acute phase, and improve adjustment and management of chronic illness. Family interventions that are most applicable to the clinic setting are presented. This is followed by summaries of three recent meta-analyses of family interventions. Chapters 10, 11 and 12 provide detailed examples of family interventions in medical illnesses.

Promotion of Healthy Behaviors

Behavioral interventions for couples show promise in treating nicotine dependence (H. La Chance, personal communication, 2011). A small pilot study of patients with nicotine dependence (n = 11) and their non-smoking romantic partners participated together in smoking cessation treatment. During the treatment phase, 100% of the smokers made an attempt to quit and 91% were smoke free at eight weeks post-quit. By six months post-quit, 73% were smoke free. This is a significant improvement over traditional smoking cessation treatment in which typically 25–33% of smokers remain quit at six months.

A family systems therapy model of treatment, called the family consultation (FAMCON) model, has also been used to help couples quit smoking. Using the FAMCON intervention, twenty couples reached a 50% rate of stable abstinence of at least six months (Shoham, Rohraugh, Trost and Muramoto, 2006). This model is especially helpful for female patients who are less likely than men to achieve stable one-year cessation, especially if the couple rate their baseline partner support as coercive or unhelpful (Rohrbaugh, Shoham and Dempsey, 2009).

FAMCON treatment proceeds through a preparation phase (Sessions 1–3), a quit phase (Sessions 4–5), and a consolidation phase (Session 6+). Sessions 1–3 assesses smoking-related interactions, past quit attempts, other complaints, and couple strengths. These sessions emphasize indirect intervention using solution-focused questions that imply the possibility of change, such as "what they will most appreciate after quitting." In Session 3, the consultant gives observations about how smoking fits the couple's relationship, why and how quitting will be difficult, reasons to be optimistic about success, and issues for the couple to consider in developing a quit plan. The couple is asked to consider a quit date. Cessation is most successful when partners work together and accept a communal coping frame: meaning that smoking is "our problem," rather than the individual's problem. Cessation is successful when couples find satisfactory ways to enjoy the quit phase and when the partners jointly choose and prepare for a quit date. See Chapter 9, p. 170 for details on the FAMCON family assessment and Chapter 10, p. 189 for details of the FAMCON intervention.

Supportive family intervention programs can prevent caregiver illness. Spousal caregivers (n = 406) of patients with dementia who participated in an enhanced counseling intervention, had a reduced incidence of depression and perceived burden at follow-up. The patients were living in the community and the caregivers were studied over a nine and a half-year period (Mittleman, 2005). The intervention consists of six sessions of combined individual and family counseling, and a support group, followed by *ad hoc* telephone counseling.

Family Interventions in Acute Illness

A family intervention in acute illness can simply be a brief family psychoeducational intervention. For example, spouses (n = 296) of patients who had coronary artery bypass graft (CABG) surgery, watched an educational videotape after the surgical procedure. Three situations were compared: a *mastery* videotape that was optimistic and supportive, and depicted couples as calm and confident; a *coping* videotape that showed ups and downs in the recovery process; and a control group that did not watch any videotape. The videotapes featured real patients who had undergone CABG and their spouses. Spouses, especially male spouses, were found to be able to master the situation better after watching the *mastery* psychoeducational videotape (Mahler and Kulik, 2002).

In the control group, female patients had significantly more problems that required office visits at the three- and six- month follow-ups, compared to female patients whose spouses had viewed the *mastery* tape ($p < 0.05$ at three and six months). Patients whose spouses were in the control group were also rehospitalized more during the first month than patients in the other conditions ($p < 0.05$ for all comparisons). Spouses who viewed the *coping* tape were more likely to have conflicts with the patient regarding diet, trying to stop the patients doing "too much" ($p < 0.05$) and were less likely to expect that the patient's recovery would move steadily forward ($p < 0.05$). Overall, female patients had more postoperative problems than male patients ($p < 0.01$). It is worth speculating why the mastery group did better than the coping skills group, which showed the difficulties as well as the successes.

- Female CABG patients had better outcomes when their spouses watched the "mastery" videotape.

Family Intervention in Chronic Medical Illnesses

Chronic illnesses require families to develop long-term coping strategies. Patients with systemic lupus erythematosus SLE and their spouses who participated in a six-month psychoeducational support group developed improved coping (Karlson et al., 2004). The intervention was led by a nurse and consisted of a single one-hour session, followed by monthly telephone sessions. A problem-solving approach, which taught the specific stages of problem solving, was used. These steps are: problem identification, generation and evaluation of alternative solutions, choosing a solution, and making concrete plans. Couples were encouraged to generate their own solutions, based on past successful behaviors. A second aim was to identify discordant patient and partner beliefs about patient self-management abilities, and to help couples reach a common understanding of the patient's actual abilities. This led to improvement in their communication about lupus management. The control group received an attention placebo, a 45-minute video presentation about lupus and monthly telephone calls. At twelve months, social support ($p = 0.03$), self-efficacy ($p = 0.02$), and couples communication ($p = 0.03$) were higher and fatigue was lower ($p = 0.02$) in the treatment group. Teaching patients and their families the steps of problem solving is an important component of psychoeducation that emerges from the coping with chronic illness literature.

Emotional distress is a major obstacle to rehabilitation in patients with chronic low back pain. In a controlled, prospective study of the effectiveness of couples therapy for patients with chronic low back pain ($n = 56$), Saarijärvi (1991) found that marital communication improved in patients who participated in couples therapy, whereas it worsened in the control group. Couples therapy consisted of five monthly sessions conducted by two family therapists. Outcome measures included self-reported psychological distress, marital satisfaction, and reported pain and disability. In a five-year follow-up, psychological distress was decreased in the treatment group and increased in controls ($p = 0.005$) (Saarijarvi, Alanen, Rytökoski, and Hyyppä, 1992). No difference was found in other self-reported or clinical outcome measures. Couples therapy prevented the psychological distress that accompanies the usual experience of managing chronic pain.

Palliative care integrates the needs of the family into the patient's end-of-life care, and family members who receive palliative care services describe benefit. In a telephone interview with 190 family members of patients who had recently died, 65% of family members reporting that their emotional or spiritual needs were met, as compared with 35% of usual-care patients' family members (p < 0.004) (Gelfman, Meier, and Morrison, 2008). Among the palliative care patients' family members, 67% reported greater self-efficacy, compared with 44% of usual-care patients' family members. Palliative care integrates the needs of the family into the care of the patient, without the use of a specific assessment or treatment protocol. End of life issues for families are described in more detail in Chapter 5 (p. 88) and Chapter 6 (p. 109).

Meta-Analyses of Family Interventions in Medical Illness

Meta-analyses give us a broad overview and highlight strengths and weaknesses in family research. Studied variables include patient, family and illness variables. Patient and family variables include the age of the patient and caregiver, the type and quality of the caregiver relationship, the perception of illness demands, illness appraisal, and individual, dyadic and family coping styles. Illness variables include the type and stage of the illness and actual illness demands.

Family interventions are described as family support groups, psychoeducational interventions, and family systems therapies. Outcome variables are both patient and family outcomes. Measurable patient outcomes include physical and mental health, quality of life, and illness behaviors. Measurable family outcomes include caregiver depression, caregiver burden, quality of life, and relationship quality. Three meta-analyses of family interventions are presented.

Meta-Analysis of Family Interventions: Martire, Lustig, Schulz, Miller, & Helgeson (2004)

Studies were divided into dementia and non-dementia studies and required to be randomized, controlled trials (RCTs), with a comparison to treatment as usual (TAU). Inclusion criteria were: an assessment of the marital/family relationship, and the marital/family interventions had to target **both** the patient and the family caregiver. Family interventions that addressed relationship issues were analyzed separately. All studies had to report data for patients or family members, or both, on one or more of nine non-illness-specific outcomes. Of the 235 studies identified, 29.8% met the criteria for inclusion. Effect sizes were calculated for each study and then combined to arrive at an aggregate effect size for each outcome.

Identified patient outcomes were depressive symptoms, anxiety symptoms, relationship satisfaction, physical disability, and mortality. Identified family member outcomes were depressive symptoms, anxiety symptoms, relationship satisfaction, and caregiving burden. Family interventions were defined as psychologically, socially, or behaviorally oriented. Some family interventions were excluded if they did not meet the above criteria. For example, studies of at-risk families rather than ill populations were excluded. The number of family members enrolled had to be at least 90% of the number of enrolled patients. Most family interventions (86%) were psychoeducational.

The results of this meta-analyses found that family intervention marginally improved patient mortality in five studies of patients with heart disease. In these studies, 53.5% of the patients who received family intervention were living at follow-up, compared to 46.5% of those in TAU. Family interventions decreased mortality when they involved a mixed group of family members but not when they only involved spouses (p = .001). There was little evidence that family interventions improved patients' depressive symptoms, anxiety symptoms, enhanced their relationship satisfaction, or improved their physical disability.

For family members, family interventions reduced depressive symptoms only when the intervention was addressed to them specifically and when relationship issues were addressed. Likewise, family interventions relieved anxiety among family members only when the interventions addressed relationship issues. Family interventions did not enhance their relational satisfaction. However, family burden was lessened by family intervention, and although the aggregate effect size was small (d = .10, p = .00, k = 40), it was uniform across all studies.

Meta-Analysis of Family Interventions: Hartmann, Bazner, Wild, Eisler & Herzog (2010)

All studies were required to be RCTs, and include a TAU comparison. Trials were excluded if the intervention was solely based on informational brochures or films without additional education or discussion, or if the comparison group was another psychosocial intervention. Hartmann and colleagues examined three outcomes: patient physical health, patient mental health, and family member health. The authors identified 52 RTCs, involving 8,896 patients with diseases including stroke (n = 27), cancer (n = 15), arthritis (n = 2), diabetes (n = 2), AIDS (n = 2) and systemic lupus erythematosus (n = 1). The duration of treatments ranged from 30 minutes to 54 hours (median = 6.25 hours). Family interventions were categorized as "psychoeducational" or "relational-change focused."

Patient physical health measures were patient dependency, clinical symptoms, self-rated physical health, and disease management. Patient mental health measures included depression, anxiety, quality of life, general mental health, and self-efficacy. Family members' health measurement included assessment of burden, depression, anxiety, general mental health, and self-efficacy.

Patient physical health improved with all family interventions compared to TAU (OR = 1.81). The effect size remained significant (p = 0.001) for the twelve studies that reported follow-up. When the involved family member was the spouse, the overall effect was higher compared with the involvement of other family members. Patient mental health was improved with family interventions compared to TAU (OR = 1.72). Family members showed improved outcomes in 18 studies (OR = 1.84). In the four studies showing follow-up, family member outcomes had only a small effect size of 0.43 (p = 0.12).

Despite the many variables across the studies, the effect size was stable, although small (OR of 1.72– 1.84). This effect size means that patients who received family treatment had a 72–84% higher chance of improved health compared to TAU. The mean overall effect sizes were 0.32 for the patients' physical health, 0.28 for the patients' mental health and 0.35 for the family members' health. The effect sizes are not large, but were significant and stable over time. Overall, there were higher effect sizes for relationship-focused interventions compared to psychoeducational interventions.

Meta-Analyses of Family Interventions for Patients with Medical Illness

Patient Outcome

- Improved mortality rates for patients with heart disease, especially when mixed group of family involved, not just the spouse
- Better physical health for the patient, especially if spouse involved
- Less patient depression
- Stronger effects with relationship-focused interventions than psychoeducational interventions

Family Members' Outcome

- Better physical health
- Less caregiver burden, depression, anxiety, especially when relationship issues addressed

Meta-Analysis of Couples Interventions: Martire, Schultz, Helgeson, Small & Saghafi (2010)

This meta-analysis specifically examined couples interventions. The authors identified 50 studies and subjected 25 studies to meta-analysis. Most couple interventions were psychoeducational and disorder-specific. Three studies used a partner-assisted approach where the partner's role was to help the patient meet cognitive or behavioral objectives of the intervention, e.g. pain management or relaxation. Eight studies used a telephone intervention. Fourteen studies used a multifamily group format.

Patient outcomes included physiological outcomes in four studies: viral load and CD4 cell count in HIV, glycosylated hemoglobin and fasting blood sugar in Type 2 diabetes, erythrocyte sedimentation rate in rheumatoid arthritis and blood pressure in hypertension. Patient health behaviors were measured in four studies: adherence to medication, diet, or exercise. Three patient outcomes were measured in sufficient numbers to qualify for meta-analysis: depressive symptoms, marital functioning, and pain.

The meta-analysis showed that couple interventions are successful in reducing patients' depressive symptoms, enhancing marital functioning, and reducing pain. All effect sizes were small. Patients who received a couple-oriented intervention showed greater improvements than those receiving TAU or a patient psychosocial intervention. Partner benefit occurred in one third of studies, with improvements in their psychological and marital functioning.

Meta-Analysis of Couples Interventions for Patients with Medical Illness

- Reduce patient's depressive symptoms and patient's reports of pain
- Improve patient perception of marital functioning
- Improve partner perception of psychological and marital functioning in one third of studies

Conclusion

Family research in medical illness is a complex enterprise. A consistent finding is that family factors influence health and disease, and that family interventions are of some benefit to patients with medical illnesses and to their family members although the effect sizes are small. There are clear priorities for improving family research.

The first priority is the inclusion of families that are more diverse in terms of income, family structure, and cultural and ethnic backgrounds. This includes validating screening and assessment measures for different populations. Simply translating English language tools may not be adequate when assessing illness beliefs and behaviors in non-English speaking cultures. The acceptability and efficacy of family interventions need to be tested for specific family types, structures, and ethnicities.

A second priority is for clarity about theoretical models used for family assessment and family interventions. Current models include the coping and stress paradigm used to study caregiving, and the psychoeducational and family systems models used in family interventions. Chapter 3 details the Family Systems Illness Model which deserves further empirical study. This is an integrative model that addresses three dimensions: psychosocial illness types, the developmental phases of each illness type and key family systems variables. The model emphasizes the match between the psychosocial demands of the illness over time and the strengths and vulnerabilities of a specific family at a specific point in their life cycle.

A third priority is to gather naturalistic data about families and illness. Just as all families are dysfunctional for a few months after the birth of a baby (Gustafsson, Björkstén, and Kjellman, 1994), all families may be dysfunctional for a short period of time after the diagnosis of a serious illness. The "trauma of diagnosis" is pertinent for the whole family after a diagnosis of cancer (Kissane, 2012). How long does the "trauma of diagnosis" persist? What factors help the patients and families diminish the effects of trauma?

A fourth priority is to assess the mechanisms of change. What factors promote family resilience? Does individual resilience drive family resilience? What do we know about how couples move from individual to dyadic coping? What are the characteristics of couples that decide to do this? There is further discussion of this process in Chapter 8, p. 153. Is a mixture of coping styles helpful? How should families manage when each person has a different way of coping? If one person displays perceived unhealthy coping, how should the other family members deal with this? Should therapy promote a dyadic or communal coping style or can each individual have his or her own coping style?

A fifth priority is to match family interventions to the family's needs. Most interventions do not take into account the stage of illness or the family stage of adaptation. Families with educational and support needs are more likely to benefit from psychoeducation. Families with relational or family conflict are more likely to benefit from family systems therapy. If you do not screen adequately, then interventions are less likely to meet the needs of the patient and families and the results will not accurately reflect the efficacy (or not) of the intervention. The development of good screening tools for use in the clinic is a priority.

Lastly, can family research develop a preventative agenda? Can we develop psycho-educational programs that focus on improving problem solving, communication and management of emotions BEFORE family conflict arises? We know what good family functioning is and we know the protective factors that promote good outcomes in medical illness. Perhaps public health programs will see the wisdom in strengthening families as a way to improve patient and family health outcomes.

References

Anderson, B. J., Vangsness, L., Connell, A., Butler, D., Goebel-Fabbri, A., and Laffel, L. M. (2002). Family conflict, adherence, and glycaemic control in youth with short duration Type 1 diabetes. *Diabetic Medicine*, 19, 635–42.

Bailey, J. Kerley, S., and Kibelstis, T. (2012). A brief marital satisfaction screening tool for use in primary care medicine. *Family Medicine*, 44(2), 105–9.

Berg, C. A., and Upchurch, R. (2007). A developmental-contextual model of couples coping with chronic illness across the adult life span. *Psychological Bulletin*, 133(6), 920–54.

Bernal, G., Domenech Rodriguez, M. M. (2009). Advances in Latino Family Research: Cultural Adaptations of Evidence-Based Interventions. *Family Process,* 48, 169–78.

Bloor, L. E., Uchino, B. N., Hicks, A., and Smith, T. W. (2004). Social relationships and physiological function: the effects of recalling social relationships on cardiovascular reactivity. *Annals of Behavioral Medicine*, 28 (1), 29–38.

Bodenmann, G. (2005). Dyadic coping and its significance for marital functioning. In T. Revenson, K. Kayser, and G. Bodenmann (Eds). *Couples coping with stress: Emerging perspectives on dyadic coping* (pp. 33–50). Washington, DC: APA.

Bolger, N., Zuckerman, A., and Kessler, R. C. (2000). Invisible support and adjustment to stress. *Journal of Personal and Social Psychology*, 79, 953–61.

Cano, A., Miller, L. R., and Loree, A. (2009). Spouse Beliefs about Partner Chronic Pain. *The Journal of Pain*, 10 (5), 486–92.

Claar, R. L., and Scharff, L. (2007). Parent and child perceptions of chronic pain treatments. *Child Healthcare*, 36, 285–301.

Claessens, P., Moons, P., de Casterlé, B. D., Cannaerts, N., Budts, W., and Gewillig, M. (2005). What does it mean to live with a congenital heart disease? A qualitative study on the lived experiences of adult patients. European Journal of Cardiovascular Nurs*ing*, 24(1), 3–10.

Cohen, M., and Pollack, S. (2005). Mothers with breast cancer & their adult daughters: the relationship between mothers' reaction to breast cancer and their daughters' emotional and neuroimmune status. *Psychosomatic Medicine*, 67, 64–71.

Cunningham, A. J., Edmonds, C. V., Phillips, C., Soots, K. I., Hedley, D., and Lockwood, G. A. (2000). A prospective, longitudinal study of the relationship of psychological work to duration of survival in patients with metastatic cancer. *Psycho-Oncology*, 9, 323–39.

DiMatteo, M. R. (2004). Social support and patient adherence to medical treatment: A meta-analysis. *Health Psychology*, 23, 207–18.

Ditzen, B., Schaer, M., Gabriel, B., Bodenmann, G., Ehlert, U., and Heinrichs, M. (2009). Intranasal oxytocin increases positive communication and reduces cortisol levels during couple conflict. *Biological Psychiatry*, 65, 728–31.

Dopp, J. M., Miller, G. E., Myers, H. F., and Fahey, J. L. (2000). Increased natural killer-cell mobilization and cytotoxicity during marital conflict. *Brain, Behavior and Immunology*, 14, 10–26.

Eisenberger, N. I., Taylor, S. E., Gable S. L., Hilmert, C. J., and Lieberman, M. D. (2007). Neural pathways link social support to attenuated neuroendocrine stress responses. *NeuroImage*, 35, 1601–12.

Epstein, N. B., Bishop, D. S., and Levin, S. (1978). The McMaster Model of Family Functioning. *Journal of Marital and Family Therapy*, 4(4), 19–31.

Epstein, N. B., and Bishop, D. S. (1981). Problem-centered systems therapy of the family. *Journal of Marital and Family Therapy*, 7 (1), 23–31.

Evers, A. W., Kraaimaat F. W., Geenen, R., Jacobs, J. W., and Bijlsma, J. W. (2003). Pain coping and social support as predictors of long-term functional disability & pain in early rheumatoid arthritis. *Behavioral Research Therapy*, 41(11), 295–310.

Evers, A. W. M., Taal, E., Kraaimaat, F. W., Jacobs, J. W. G., Abdel-Nasser, A., Rasker, J. J., and Bijlsma, J. W. J. (1998). A comparison of two recently developed health status instruments for patients with arthritis: Dutch-AIMS2 and IRGL. *British Journal of Rheumatology*, 37, 157–64.

Ewart, C. K., Taylor, C. B., Kraemer, H. C., and Agras, W. S. (1991). High blood pressure and marital discord: not being nasty matters more than being nice. *Health Psychology*, 10, 155–63.

Flinn, M. V., and England, B. G. (1997). Social economics of childhood glucocorticoid stress response and health. *American Journal of Physical Anthropology*, 102, 33–53.

Forgeron, P. A., Finley, G. A., and Arnaout, M. (2005). Pediatric pain prevalence and parents' attitudes at a cancer hospital in Jordan. *Journal of Pain Symptom Management*, 31, 440–8.

Gallo, L. C., Troxel, W. M., Matthews, K. A., and Kuller, L. H. (2003). Marital status and quality in middle-aged women: Associations with levels & trajectories of cardiovascular risk factors. *Health Psychology*, 22, 453–63.

Gelfman, L. P., Meier, D. E., and Morrison, R. S. (2008). Does palliative care improve quality? A survey of bereaved family members. *Journal of Pain Symptom Management*, 36, 22–8.

Glaser, R., Robles, T. F., Sheridan, J., Malarkey, W. B., and Kiecolt-Glaser, J. K. (2003). Mild depressive symptoms are associated with amplified and prolonged inflammatory responses after influenza virus vaccination in older adults. Archives of *General Psychiatry*, 60, 1009–14.

Gouin, J. P. et al. (2010). Marital behavior, oxytocin, vasopressin, and wound healing. *Psychoneuroendocrinology*, 35, 1082–90.

Gouin, J. P., Glaser, R., Loving, T. J., Malarkey, W. B, Stowell, J., Houts, C., and Kiecolt-Glaser, J. K. (2009). Attachment avoidance predicts inflammatory responses to marital conflict. *Brain Behavioral Immunology*, 23, 898–904.

Grewen, K. M., Girdler, S. S., Amico, J., and Light, K. C. (2005). Effects of partner support on resting oxytocin, cortisol, norepinephrine, and blood pressure before and after warm partner contact. *Psychosomatic Medicine*, 67, 531–8.

Griffith, L. S., Field, B. J., and Lustman, P. J. (1990). Life stress and social support in diabetes: association with glycemic control. *International Journal of Psychiatry and Medicine*, 20(4), 365–72.

Gustafsson, P. A., Björkstén, B., and Kjellman, N. I. (1994). Family dysfunction in asthma: a prospective study of illness development. *Journal of Pediatrics*, 125(3), 493–8.

Hartmann, M., Bäzner, E., Wild, B., Eisler, I., and Herzog, W. (2010). Effects of Interventions Involving the Family in the Treatment of Adult Patients with Chronic Physical Diseases: A Meta-Analysis. *Psychotherapy and Psychosomatics*, 79, 136–48.

Heinrichs, M., Baumgartner, T., Kirschbaum. C., and Ehler, U. (2003). Social support & oxytocin interact to suppress cortisol and subjective responses to psychosocial stress. *Biological Psychiatry*, 54, 1389–98.

Heru, A. (2010). Improving marital quality in women with medical illness: integration of evidence-based programs into clinical practice. *Journal of Psychiatric Practice*, 16(5), 297–305.

Hobfoll, S. E., and Spielberger, C. D. (2003). Family stress: Integrating theory & measurement. In P. Boss (Ed.). *Family stress: Classic & contemporary readings* (pp. 142–57). Thousand Oaks, CA: Sage.

Ingoldsby, B. B., Smith, S. R., and Miller, J. E. (2004). *Exploring family theories.* Los Angeles: Roxbury.

Karlson, E. W., Liang. M. H., Eaton, H., Huang, J., Fitzgerald, L., Rogers, M. P., and Daltroy, L. H. (2004). A randomized clinical trial of a psychoeducational intervention to improve outcomes in systemic lupus erythematosus. *Arthritis Rheumatology*, 50, 1832–41.

Kazak, A., Rourke, M. T., Alderfer, M. A., Pai, A., Reilly, A. F., and Meadows, A. T. (2007). Evidence-based Assessment, Intervention and Psychosocial Care in Pediatric Oncology: A Blueprint for Comprehensive Services across Treatment. *Journal of Pediatric Psychology*, 32(9), 1099–110.

Kiecolt-Glaser, J. K., Glaser, R., Cacioppo, J. T., and Malarkey, W. B. (1998). Marital stress, immunologic, neuroendocrine, and autonomic correlates. *The Annals of the New York Academy of Sciences*, 840, 656–3.

Kiecolt-Glaser, J. K., Loving, T. J., Stowell, J. R. Malarkey, W. B., Lemeshow, S., Dickinson, S. L., and Glaser, R. (2005). Hostile marital interactions, proinflammatory cytokine production, and wound healing. *Archives of General Psychiatry*, 62, 1377–84.

Kiecolt-Glaser, J. K., McGuire, L., Robels, T. F., and Glaser, R. (2002). Psychoneuroimmunology and psychosomatic medicine: back to the future. Psychosomatic Medicine, 64, 15–20.

Kiecolt-Glaser, J. K., and Newton, T. L. (2001). Marriage and health: his and hers. Psychological Bulletin, 127, 472–503.

Kiecolt-Glaser, J. K., Preacher, K. J., MacCallum, R. C., Atkinson, C., Malarkey, W. B., and Glaser, R. (2003). Chronic stress and age-related increases in the proinflammatory cytokine IL-6. *The Proceedings of the National Academy of Sciences of the United States of America*, 100, 9090–5.

Kissane, D. (2012). Presentation at the American Psychiatric Association Annual meeting, Philadelphia, PA.

Lett, H. S. et al. (2009). Dimensions of social support and depression in patients at increased psychosocial risk recovering from myocardial infarction. *International Journal of Behavioral Medicine*, 16(3), 248–58.

Levy, R. L. (2010). Exploring the intergenerational transmission of illness behavior: from observations to experimental intervention. Annals of Behavioral Medicine, 41(2), 174–82.

Levy, R. L. et al. (2010). Cognitive-behavioral therapy for children with functional abdominal pain and their parents decreases pain and other symptoms. *American Journal of Gastroenterology*, 105(4), 946–56.

López, S. R., Ramírez García J. I., Ullman, J. B., Kopelowicz, A., Jenkins, J., Breitborde, N. J., and Placencia, P. (2009). Cultural variability in the manifestation of expressed emotion. *Family Process*, 48(2), 179–94.

Luttik, M. L., Jaarsma, T., Moser, D., Sanderman, R., and van Veldhuisen D. J. (2005). The importance and impact of social support on outcomes in patients with heart failure: an overview of the literature. Journal of Cardiovascular Nurs*ing*, 20(3), 162–9.

Mahler, H. I., and Kulik, J. A. (2002). Effects of a videotape information intervention for spouses on spouse distress and patient recovery from surgery. *Health Psychology*, 21, 427–37.

Martire, L. M., Lustig, A. P., Schulz, R., Miller, G. E., and Helgeson, V. S. (2004). Is it beneficial to involve a family member? A meta-analysis of psychosocial interventions for chronic illness. *Health Psychology*, 23(6), 599–611.

Martire, L. M., Schulz, R., Helgeson, V. S., Small, B. J., and Saghafi, E. M. (2010). Review and meta-analysis of couple-oriented interventions for chronic illness. *Annals of Behavioral Medicine*, 40(3), 325–42.

McCubbin, M., Balling, K., Possin, P., Frierdich, S., and Bryne, B. (2002). Family resiliency in childhood cancer. *Family Relations*, 51, 103–11.

Mittelman, M. (2005). Taking care of the caregivers. *Current Opinion in Psychiatry*, 18, 633–9.

Moos, R. H. (1986). *Family Environment Scale*, Edition 2. Palo Alto, CA: Consulting Psychologists Press.

Moos, R. H., and Moos, B. S. (1981). *Family Environment Scale Manual*. Palo Alto, CA: Consulting Psychologists Press.

Neacsiu, A. D., Rizvi, S. L., Vitaliano, P. P., Lynch, T. R., and Linehan, M. M. (2010). The dialectical behavior therapy ways of coping checklist: development and psychometric properties. *Journal of Clinical Psychology*, 66(6), 563–82.

Politi, M. C., Enright, T. M., and Weihs, K. L. (2006). The effects of age and emotional acceptance on distress among breast cancer patients. *Support Care Cancer*, 15, 73–9.

Reblin, M., and Uchino, B. N. (2008). Social and emotional support and its implication for health. *Current Opinion in Psychiatry*, 21, 201–5.

Revenson, T. A., and Majerovitz, D. S. (1990). Spouses' support provision to chronically ill patients. *Journal of Social and Personal Relationships*, 7, 575–86.

Reynolds, P., Hurley, S., Torres, M., Jackson, J., Boyd, P., and Chen, V. W. (2000). Use of coping strategies and breast cancer survival: results from the black/white cancer survival study. *American Journal of Epidemiology*, 152, 940–9.

Rodroguez-Artalejo, F. et al. (2006). Social network as a predictor of hospital readmission and mortality among older patients with heart failure. *Journal of Cardiac Failure*, 12, 621–7.

Rohrbaugh, M. J., Shoham, V., and Coyne, J. C. (2006). Effect of marital quality on eight-year survival of patients with heart failure. *American Journal of Cardiology*, 98, 1069–72.

Rohrbaugh, M. J., Shoham, V., and Dempsey, C. L. (2009). Gender Differences in Quit Support by Partners of Health-Compromised Smokers. *Journal of Drug Issues*, 39(2), 329–46.

Ryan, C. E., Epstein, N. B., Keitner, G. I. Miller, I. W., and Bishop, D. S. (2005). *Evaluating and Treating Families: The McMaster Approach*. Routledge: New York.

Saarijärvi, S. (1991). A controlled study of couple therapy in chronic low back pain patients. Effects on marital satisfaction, psychological distress and health attitudes. *Journal of Psychosomatic Research*, 35, 265–72.

Saarijärvi, S., Alanen, E., Rytökoski, U., and Hyyppä, M. T. (1992). Couple therapy improves mental well-being in chronic low back pain patients. A controlled, five year follow-up study. *Journal of Psychosomatic Research*, 36 (7), 651–6.

Sayers, S. L., Riegel, B., Pawlowski, S., Coyne, J. C., and Samaha, F. F. (2008). Social support and self-care of patients with heart failure. *Annals of Behavioral Medicine*, 35, 70–9.

Sharpley, C. F., and Rogers, H. J. (1984). Preliminary validation of the Abbreviated Spanier Dyadic Adjustment Scale: Some psychometric data regarding a screening test of marital adjustment. *Educational Psychological Measures*, 44, 1045–50.

Shoham, V., Rohrbaugh, M. J., Trost, S. E., and Muramoto, M. (2006). A family consultation intervention for health-compromised smokers. *Journal of Substance Abuse Treatment*, 31(4), 395–402.

Spanier, G. B. (1976). Measuring dyadic adjustment: New scales for assessing the quality of marriage and similar dyads. *Journal of Marriage and the Family*, 38, 15–28.

Sterba, K. R., DeVellis, R. F., Lewis, M. A., DeVellis, B. M., Jordan, J. M., and Baucom, D. H. (2008). Effect of couple illness perception congruence on psychological adjustment in women with rheumatoid arthritis. *Health Psychology*, 27(2), 221–9.

Tomaka, J., Thompson, S., and Palacios, R. (2006). The relation of social isolation, loneliness, and social support to disease outcomes among the elderly. *Journal of Aging Health*, 18(3), 359–84.

Vaughn, C. E., and Leff, J. P., (1976). The influence of family life and social factors on the course of psychiatric illness: A comparison of schizophrenic and depressed neurotic patients. *British Journal of Psychiatry*, 129, 125–37.

Wamboldt, F. S., Bender, B. G., and Rankin, A. E. (2011). Adolescent decision-making about use of inhaled asthma controller medication: results from focus groups with participants from a prior longitudinal study. *The Journal of Asthma*, 48(7), 741–50.

Wamboldt, F., Bender, B., Wamboldt, M., Bihun, J., Milgrom, H., and Szefler, S. (2000). Psychosocial correlates of pediatric MDI adherence. *American Journal of Respiratory & Critical Care Medicine*, 161(3), A711.

Wearden, A. J., Tarrier, N., Barrowclough, C., Zastowny, T. R., and Rahill, A. A. (2000). A review of expressed emotion research in health care. *Clinical Psychological Review*, 20(5), 633–66.

Weihs, K., Fisher, L., and Baird, M. A. (2002). Families, health, and behavior: A section of the commissioned report by the committee on Health and Behavior: Research, Practice and Policy, Division of Neurosciences and Behavioral Health and Division of Health Promotion and Disease Prevention, Institute of Medicine. National Academy of Sciences. *Families, Systems, & Health*, 20, 1, 7–47.

Wyman, P. A., Moynihan, J., Eberly, S., Cox, C., Cross, W., Jin, X., and Caserta, M. T. (2007). Association of family stress with natural killer-cell activity and the frequency of illnesses in children. *Archives of Pediatric Adolescent Medicine*, 161, 228–34.

Zhang, X., Norris, S. L., Gregg, E. W., and Beckles, G. (2007). Social support and mortality among older persons with diabetes. *Diabetes Education*, 33, 273–81.

2 Family Factors in Promoting Health

The Case of Childhood Asthma

Frederick S. Wamboldt and Marianne Z. Wamboldt

- Families have a major influence in promoting health and good treatment outcomes in chronic illnesses such as asthma.
- Family factors influence asthma outcomes by influencing self-management behaviors.
- Different family factors influence different self-management behaviors.
- Pay special attention to families whose illness narratives and stories suggest they are not confident in their plan to manage the chronic illness.
- The community and broader sociocultural context of any given family can be an equally important factor in influencing asthma outcomes.

Asthma is the most common chronic illness of childhood, and the prevalence in children continues to increase over time. Currently asthma affects 9.6% of children in the US, although there are strong health disparities with black and Puerto Rican children having a rate at least double that of the general population, and death rates being even more skewed (Centers for Disease Control and Prevention, 2011a; Gold and Wright, 2005). Although asthma affects people of all ages, it is estimated that 80–90% of all cases of asthma start during infancy and early childhood (Yunginger et al.,1992). A cornerstone of asthma therapeutics is "self-management"—helping persons with asthma recognize and manage their asthma symptoms when they arise, as well as reduce their exposure and reactivity to asthma "triggers" in the environment (National Heart, Lung and Blood Institute, 2003, 2007). Given that asthma usually starts in early childhood, "self-management" is a family affair. In this chapter, childhood asthma is used as an illustrative case in showing ways in which families can promote health in the context of a common, chronic illness, drawing from the literature as well as from research our teams have conducted in this area over several decades.

What is Asthma?

Asthma is a chronic breathing disorder characterized by episodic and reversible attacks of difficulty breathing due to the airways in the lungs closing (National Heart, Blood and Lung Institute, 2003). Common symptoms of an asthma attack include wheezing, shortness of breath, chest tightness, and coughing. These asthma symptoms, and the obstruction of the airways leading to them, are believed to arise from two major underlying biological factors that are related but distinct, namely, inflammation and hyperreactivity (i.e. "twitchiness") in the airways. These biological processes arise both from genetic propensity, as well as key environmental exposures, most importantly, certain respiratory viruses, irritants (esp., tobacco smoke), and aero-allergens (e.g. molds, vermin). Families of children at high genetic risk for developing asthma appear to be able to delay by several years, but not totally prevent, their children developing asthma, most importantly by limiting their children's exposure to these environmental factors (Kurukulaaratchy, Matthews, and Arshad, 2004; Sly, 2011).

Once asthma begins, no cure exists; however, asthma is usually relatively easily controlled by: (1) partnering with health-care professionals regarding staging of asthma severity and control and appropriate use of certain medications most importantly, "quick-relievers," i.e., bronchodilators, to reverse airway obstruction during an attack, and "long-term controllers," usually inhaled corticosteroids, to decrease airway inflammation and hyperreactivity; (2) having and following an "action plan" to both prevent and treat asthma attacks; and (3) avoiding asthma "triggers" in the environment (National Heart, Blood and Lung Institute, 2003). In terms of medications, use of a long-term controller is recommended when asthma is "persistent" rather than "intermittent:" which is defined as asthma symptoms occurring at least twice a week. In pediatric asthma, there is an age-appropriate, developmental progression to asthma management between children and their parents, starting, of course, with parents having primary responsibility, and handing over more responsibility as children mature (Wamboldt and Wamboldt, 2001).

Despite the fact that asthma, at least on paper, should usually be quite easy to manage, children and their families far too often have significant problems managing asthma (Centers for Disease Control and Prevention, 2011a). Nearly 60% of US children with asthma have at least one asthma attack a year. Children having asthma attacks miss on average 4.5 days of school per year. Each year, about one quarter of children with asthma need treatment in an emergency room, and 7% are hospitalized for an asthma attack. About a quarter of children and families have never been trained how to recognize and deal with asthma attacks. It is estimated that 40% of the uninsured cannot afford asthma medications. Taken as a whole, these data have led the Centers for Disease Control and Prevention to make it a priority to help people get information about how to better manage asthma. This data was key in our examination of how families can best promote health in childhood asthma.

A Model of How Families Influence the Course of Pediatric Asthma

Figure 2.1 illustrates the simple model with which our group began examining how families can best promote health in the context of childhood asthma. Several points about this model are worth emphasizing. First is the assumption that families influence outcomes in childhood asthma by influencing key asthma management behaviors. This is not to say that families may not influence asthma outcomes directly, perhaps through physiological mechanisms, but it does underscore our assumption that the vast majority of family effects on asthma outcomes pass through these behavioral links. This being said, there is some evidence for direct physiological effects. Best established are emotional triggers for asthma (Lehrer, Isenberg, and Hochron, 1993; Liangas, Yates, Wu, Henry, and Thomas, 2004). However, the emotions that most frequently trigger asthma are strong, forceful emotions—such as angry rants, temper tantrums, raucous laughter, and weeping tearfulness—and it appears that these function as "exercise" triggers that cool and dry the airways and promote asthma attacks in the same way that physical exercise can trigger asthma (Liangas et al., 2004). Second, the model posits that there may be different family behaviors involved in influencing various aspects of treatment adherence and outcomes, but does not explicitly specify which factors are involved with which behaviors or outcomes. Finally, outcome is construed as multidimensional and incorporates not only the child with asthma, but also how much other family members are affected by asthma. In the ensuing text, we will see how this model and the underlying assumptions have held up in our research.

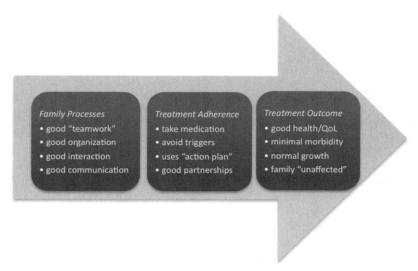

Figure 2.1 Hypothesized model: family factors influence childhood asthma outcomes through behavioral adherence

Family Influences on Treatment Adherence Behaviors

Much of what we have learned about how families influence asthma treatment adherence behaviors and outcomes arose through our longitudinal Family and Asthma Study (FAAS). We recruited two distinct samples of children with persistent asthma, and their families. One sample came from children attending Denver Public Schools (DPS), with oversampling of schools serving poorer families more at risk to experience health disparities. With such a recruitment strategy, these children broadly represented the average level of health care available to such children across metro-Denver as their asthma care providers came from a variety of clinics throughout the community. The second sample was recruited from children who received care in a large Health Maintenance Organization (HMO) in Denver that has a strong commitment to and reputation for providing innovative, cost-efficient, evidence-based treatment for asthma. All children and their families were assessed in our Behavior Research Center at frequent intervals across at least twelve months using procedures that have been previously reported (Bender et al., 2000; Hoet et al., 2003; O'Connor et al., 2004; Wamboldt, Ho et al., 2002). Table 2.1 summarizes relevant demographic and asthma-related characteristics of the children in these two samples.

Table 2.1.   Demographic and Asthma Characteristics of FAAS Participants

DPS Sample – 57 of 66 children completed study

83% = Inhaled corticosteroid; 17% = cromolyn or nedocromil
Age: mean = 10.9 ± 2.3 yrs; range = 7.1 to 17.2 yrs
29 boys, 28 girls
29 white, 28 non-white
70% Hollingshead SES class II & III

HMO Sample – 70 of 79 children completed (pool = 88)

All but one child on inhaled corticosteroid
Age: mean = 11.3 ± 2.0 yrs; range = 7.4 to 15.9 yrs
42 boys, 28 girls
62 white, 8 non-white
69% Hollingshead SES class II & III

Adherence with Asthma Controller Medications

As stated above, existing guidelines state that children classified as having persistent asthma should take a daily asthma controller medication, typically an inhaled corticosteroid (ICS), whether they have symptoms or not, to prevent asthma attacks (National Heart, Blood and Lung Institute, 2003). We tracked children's adherence to this recommended therapy using small electronic monitors that were attached to their inhaler and which tracked the number of "puffs" taken each day for up to 45 days (Bender et al., 2000; O'Connor et al., 2004). The display on these devices was turned off so that the devices would not serve as an intervention reminding children or their parents to take the controller medication. In addition, all children were given their controller medication free of charge so that cost was not a factor in their adherence behavior. Figures 2.2 and 2.3 show examples of "good" and "poor" adherence using data from these devices, as well as some of the common sources of error. The child showing good adherence was prescribed three puffs of medication, twice a day. The record shows that at least one set of doses was taken every day, and both sets on most days, so that over 93% of the prescribed doses were in fact taken. One can see that an additional puff was recorded with some doses, perhaps representing a "test puff" in which the inhaler is sprayed in the air to see if the canister still contains medication; a common practice, albeit one that is not recommended. Similarly, on some doses it appears that one puff might be missing. These devices have a pressure-sensitive disk on top of the device that records the triggering of the inhaler. However, it is possible, especially for children with smaller hands, to press the side of this disk, discharging medication but not activating the recording mechanism. We dealt with these sources of error by accepting what the device recorded except that we truncated the number of puffs per day to the maximum puffs prescribed daily if the recorded number of puffs exceeded the maximal daily dose—one never got "extra credit" for taking more medication than was prescribed. The child showing poor adherence took very few sets of doses, and often showed gaps of no use where the biological benefit of the controller medication would have disappeared, potentially increasing inflammation and hyperresponsivity in the airways. However, these gaps do not guarantee an asthma attack, any more than missing birth control pills for several days guarantee a pregnancy—in both cases one needs an exposure to something "risky" in the environment for these adverse outcomes to occur. This fact can create significant psychological barriers to controller medication use, as missed doses are not tightly linked to asthma symptoms, allowing one to believe that one does not need to use as much medication as is prescribed.

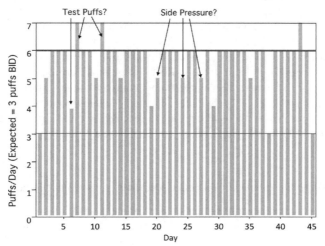

Figure 2.2   Example of a "Good" inhaled controller medication adherence record

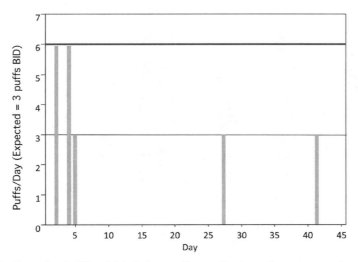

Figure 2.3   Example of a "Poor" inhaled controller medication adherence record

Across the twelve months of adherence measurement, each child's adherence was summarized as the mean of all daily adherence estimates (#prescribed/#taken) truncated at 100% maximum per day. Median 12 month adherence with inhaled asthma controller medication was 50.4% of prescribed doses taken in the DPS sample (range = 4.6-100%) and 51.2% in the HMO sample (range = 9.8-100%). As can be seen in Figure 2.4, less than 25% of children in both samples took > 75% of the inhaled controller medication prescribed to them across one year, with essentially equal numbers of children in each quartile. The major difference in the distributions of adherence across the samples was that the HMO sample contained approximately half the number of subjects with ultra-poor adherence (i.e., <25%) as compared to the DPS sample. The major effect that was seen from all the efforts spent to promote better asthma management in the HMO group was a halving of the subgroup of children taking 25% or less of their controller medication. This may not be a trivial effect, given that adverse asthma outcomes do cluster in those who take very little to no controller medication (Suissa, Ernst, Benayoun, Baltzan, and Cai, 2000; Williams et al., 2004). However, these data do underscore that much more work needs to be done to discover ways to help families promote better use of controller medication in their children with asthma (Bender, Milgrom, and Apter, 2003).

What Family Factors Influenced Controller Medication Adherence Behavior?

We examined a variety of family structural and process factors to see which influence controller medication adherence (Wamboldt, Bender et al., 2000; Wamboldt, Bender et al., 2002). Structural factors included the child's age (7–17 years); child's gender

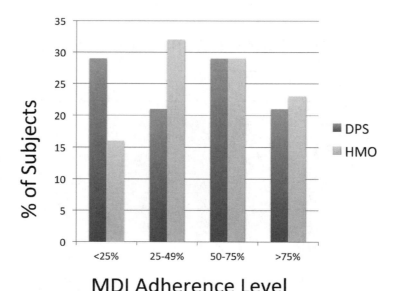

Figure 2.4   Distributions of 12 months inhaled controller medication adherence scores by study sample

(girls are certain to have better behavior than boys, right?); household socio-economic status (SES); and mother aloneness (i.e., single parent versus multiple adult household). The family processes selected were "parent-child relationship inflammation" operationalized as the "high criticism" code using Magana-Amato's Five Minute Speech Sample for Expressed Emotion (FMSS) (Magana et al., 1985; Wamboldt, O'Connor, Wamboldt, Gavin, and Klinnert, 2000), and "parental advice quality" using an adaption of McDowell and Parke's techniques using vignettes to assess how parental advice influences children's responses to interpersonal dilemmas (McDowell and Parke, 2009; McDowell, Parke, and Spitzer, 2002). Briefly, the FMSS asks the parent to talk about their thoughts and feelings of their child with asthma for five minutes with little feedback from the interviewer, with the resulting speech sample coded for the presence of a "critical" profile based on the valence of the initial statement, the overall appraisal of the parent-child relationship, and the presence of actual critical comments. As we have previously reported (Wamboldt et al., 2000), we prefer to view the "high criticism" profile as a measure of "relationship inflammation" as a speech sample does not need to show overt criticism to yield a "high criticism" rating. The Dual Goal Vignette requires the parent to give advice to their child about a situation where good asthma management conflicts with other aspects of family life. We specifically developed a story stem that described a child who is very excited because s/he will soon be going to a local amusement park to celebrate a friend's birthday. However, the child's asthma flares, and does not respond quickly to quick-reliever medication. The parent and child make the decision that the child will need to miss the birthday party. Just then the friend calls on the telephone saying how excited s/he is to be going to the party soon. The child tells his/ her friend that because of an asthma attack, s/he will not be able to go. The friend hangs up the phone saying, "If you don't come to my party, you aren't my friend anymore." The parent is asked to advise their child how to deal with this dilemma. The resulting advice is coded for clarity, specificity, and directness using 1–5 point scales.

Table 2.2 shows the results of regression models examining how these factors collected during the baseline visit predict controller medication adherence recorded over the next 12 months. In the DPS sample using stepwise forward selection regression techniques, we were able to explain about 40% of the variance in adherence behavior, with poorer adherence in those with non-white race/ethnicity, older children

Table 2.2. Regression Models Predicting 12-Month Controller Medication Adherence Behavior.

	Incremental Variance (R2) Explained by Model		
Predictor Variable	DPS - Free	HMO - Forced	HMO - Free
Total R2 Explained	39.9% ***	33.3% ***	33.8% ***
Child Race/Ethnicity	15.9% **	7.1% *	7.1% *
Child Age	12.0% **	21.3% ***	21.3% ***
FMSS "Criticism"	6.9% *	2.7% †	2.7% †
Advice Quality	5.0% *	1.9%	N.S.
Single Parent	N.S.	N.S.	2.7% †
Child Gender	N.S.	N.S.	N.S.
Family SES	N.S.	N.S.	N.S.

*** = p < .001; ** = p <.01; * = p < .05; † = p < .15

(adolescents), presence of "relationship inflammation," and poorer advice quality (Wamboldt et al., 2000). Forcing the DPS model on the HMO data, we explained 33% of the variance; while using forward selection methods with the HMO sample, we explained 34% of the model, with child age, race/ethnicity, relationship inflammation, and mother aloneness entering (Wamboldt et al., 2002). In these samples we were not able to find any other variable that explained the influence of race/ethnicity on controller adherence, although we will offer some speculations later in this chapter.

Family Influences on Adherence with Home Environmental Recommendations

As stated above, in addition to taking daily controller medication, families are encouraged to reduce household asthma triggers, including not exposing the child with asthma to secondhand tobacco smoke—estimated as causing 20% of all asthma attacks in children (DiFranza and Lew, 1996)—or to pets with fur or feathers. In the combined DPS and HMO samples, 38% of the children lived in households with at least one smoker, despite the fact that tobacco smoke was reported as an asthma trigger for over 80% of these children. Similarly 67% of children had a household pet with fur or feathers, despite 65% reporting their family pet as an asthma trigger (Wamboldt et al., 2002).

Another important finding was that the three forms of adherence—inhaled controller medication, avoidance of tobacco smoke exposure, and avoidance of pet allergen exposure—were not correlated, and each is associated with distinct family factors. Tobacco smoke exposure was associated with lower SES, poorer asthma knowledge, and greater asthma-related and general family stress. Pet allergen exposure was associated with white race, and greater asthma knowledge. Taken together these results imply that there are not "good families" who do all that they are advised to do, and "bad families" who do not adhere, a disappointment to many physicians who would like an easier world to work within. Rather each distinct type of asthma adherence has different associated family factors. Efforts to improve family asthma management need to deal differently with each of these different health promotion behaviors.

Stories about the Impact of Asthma on Families

At the start of the baseline FAAS visit, families were invited to tell us the story of how their child's asthma has affected their family life (Fiese and Wamboldt, 2003). They were further asked to not tell us the "medical" story, but rather what they would "tell a friend over a cup of coffee." Stories were coded to reflect three different orientations of how families were dealing with asthma: "partnership" in which families told us that they all shared in asthma management activities using a clear and flexible strategy, as well as a solid partnership with their child's health-care provider; "coordinated-care" in which the family used a clear, but often relatively rigid strategy, sometimes not well in sync with their provider's recommendation; and "reactive" in which families reported no clear strategy managing asthma, rather reported being buffeted by recurrent symptoms and associated anxiety. Compared to the other two narrative types, those families coded as "reactive" showed poorer controller adherence and more emergency room (ER) visits for asthma attacks over the subsequent year. This suggests that by listening to families' story about the impact of asthma on their lives, one can assess whether or not the family feels able to competently deal with their child's asthma, with no apparent significant difference between either type of the more successful strategies, despite our original predictions.

Wisdom from FAAS Participants Ten Years Later

We had the opportunity to conduct focus groups with FAAS participants ten years after their initial participation when the children with asthma were now teenagers and young adults (Wamboldt, Bender, and Rankin, 2011). We constructed focus groups to gather diverse perspectives, including across prior controller medication adherence, from older versus younger participants, and across racial/ethnic minority groups. One major prompt for discussion was showing various "patterns" of controller medication adherence, including the "good" adherence profile shown in Figure 2.2, a.k.a., "Stacey Steady"; the "poor" adherence profile from Figure 2.3, a.k.a., "Lee Low"; and two intermediate patterns, each taking about 50% of prescribed puffs per day, "Haley Halfway," who took one of two sets of doses almost every day; and "Carrie Clump," who took all daily doses for several weeks in a row, then showed little to no use.

A consistent finding from the focus groups was that children and their families varied greatly on how routinized their life was. More consistent routines tended to facilitate better controller medication adherence, although we were frequently reminded that much of teen life conspires against routines. Second, parents were identified as being much more important than health-care providers, due to their greater availability as well as greater difficulty deceiving them. However, parents were often reported as having a very difficult road to walk, as too much attention and oversight was attributed to "over-anxious" parents, whereas focus group participants consistently linked poorer adherence to "bad parents who don't care." In addition, a variety of problems were connected to parental disagreement, conflict or divorce. These included fathers who attributed their child's asthma to "weakness" or "physical deconditioning" and pushed exercise rather than medication, in opposition to their spouses, sometimes with serious, adverse consequences. Advice from parents appeared to be especially important, although correspondingly difficult, during the pre-teen and young teen years, when children reported distress about their asthma making them different from their peers. Pragmatically, children growing up in two households often face different rules and routines concerning asthma management in each household, and given the relative stinginess of health insurance plans to dispense multiple controller inhalers, often have difficulty ensuring that they have a controller inhaler in each home.

Other Findings Potentially Suggesting Family Influences Worthy of Further Study

How and Why Might Race/Ethnicity Influence Controller Medication Adherence

We have found that families from racial/ethnic groups experiencing increased levels of health disparities are more likely to have beliefs about asthma controller medications that are associated with poorer adherence (Bender, Rand, Rankin, Tran, and Wamboldt, 2005; Le et al., 2008). These include beliefs such as:

I don't have the kind of asthma that requires me to take my controller medication every day;

I only take my controller medication when I am sick;

I have not needed to take as much ICS as the doctor prescribed;

If I use my ICS every day, it won't work as well when I really need it.

Additionally, it is possible that the increased rates of morbidity and/or mortality experienced by members of racial/ethnic minorities affect family asthma management. Across the US, blacks and Puerto Ricans have at least twice the prevalence of asthma than whites and other Hispanics, and an even more skewed rate of death from asthma (Centers for Disease Control and Prevention, 2011a; Gold and Wright, 2005). Additionally, blacks and all Hispanic groups have three to five times the hospitalization rate for asthma attacks compared to whites, and double the rate of missed days from school from asthma. As we discussed above, families who describe asthma as having more impact on their lives, especially those having more "reactive" narratives, had poorer adherence as well as more frequent ER visits. Experiencing more adverse effects from your child's asthma may well be a potent factor in feeling less "in charge" and more emotionally challenged by asthma, as well as having more difficulty forming a successful strategy for managing asthma (Kaptein, Klok, Moss-Morris, and Brand, 2010).

We have also had the chance to study families who have had a child who had an episode of asthma that threatened their life by requiring intubation or mechanical ventilation, or who experienced a hypoxic seizure during an asthma attack (Kean, Kelsay, Wamboldt, and Wamboldt, 2006). Compared to age, gender and race/ethnicity matched children with asthma who never had a life-threatening asthma attack, those children with a history of a life-threatening attack (LTA) were more likely to rate their asthma attack as being a traumatic event (90% *vs.* 69%), as did their parents (100% *vs.* 67%). Additionally, children with history of a life-threatening attack had higher rates of Post-Traumatic Stress Disorder (PTSD) symptoms (20% vs. 11%), as did their parents (29% *vs.* 14 %). When a person has posttraumatic stress, they often avoid objects or places that remind them of the trauma, as those triggers lead to increased anxiety. One hypothesis is that children and their parents who were traumatized by a severe asthma attack may avoid inhalers or other medications, doctors' offices, etc., as these may function as "triggers" for their PTSD. This can explain some types of reduced adherence. Given the excess asthma-related mortality and morbidity experienced by blacks and Hispanics, it seems plausible that rates of trauma and frank PTSD may be higher in these ethnic groups, with the expected ensuing difficulties for asthma management (Wamboldt, Weintraub, Krafchick, Berce, and Wamboldt, 1995).

Summary and Implications for Clinical Work and Future Research

In Figure 2.5, we present a revision of our original model, incorporating the lessons learned from our research. Three revisions are especially important: 1) personal and family asthma management behaviors are more often than not performed less well than current guidelines recommend, almost certainly a major preventable reason for the excess morbidity and mortality currently seen for asthma; 2) these behaviors necessary to successfully manage asthma all appear to be separate and distinct behaviors with different personal and family factors being called in to play to achieve success with each specific adherence behavior; 3) the overall confidence or efficacy of a family to successfully deal with asthma is measurable, in our case using family narratives, and likely reflects the cognitive and emotional schema used by the family in dealing with asthma; and 4) a variety of broader sociocultural factors, (e.g. social disadvantage, poverty, and minority race/ethnicity status) are related to disparities in asthma outcomes, and may exert their influence through the family's schema or worldview, which then influences their observed asthma management behaviors. We will discuss each of these in turn.

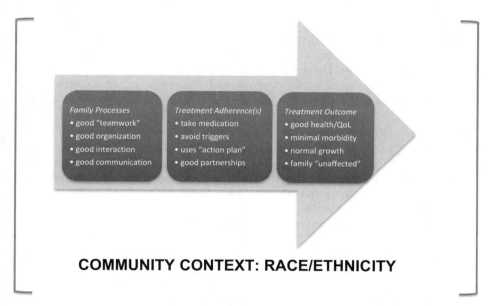

Figure 2.5   Revised model: Family factors influence childhood asthma outcomes through behavioral adherence

Lots of Room Exists to Improve Families' Asthma Management Behaviors

Perhaps the most striking and sobering aspect of our work has come from seeing the extent to which most families have difficulty with some aspect of asthma management, be it regularly taking controller medication or avoiding environmental asthma triggers. In its landmark 2003 report, the World Health Organization stated that across chronic diseases (World Health Organization, 2003):

Poor adherence to treatment of chronic diseases is a worldwide problem of striking magnitude;

The consequences of poor adherence to long-term therapies are poor health outcomes and increased health-care costs;

Increasing the effectiveness of adherence interventions may have a far greater impact on the health of the population than any improvement in specific medical treatments; and

Health systems must evolve to meet new challenges.

Although this call was sounded almost a decade ago, too few have heard and taken these messages to heart. Here are some suggestions for action.

Ask regularly about difficulties following treatment recommendations, and make understanding and change be key goals in therapeutic efforts. The Centers for Disease Control and Prevention recommend that in every health contact, whether in a primary medical or mental health setting, a health-care provider should ask the brief "5 As" intervention for tobacco use and secondhand smoke exposure: *Ask* about tobacco use/second-hand smoke (SHS) exposure, *Advise* to quit/change, *Assess* willingness to change, *Assist* in change attempt, and *Arrange* follow-up (Fiore et al., 2000; Schroeder, 2005; Williams, Williams, and Korn, 2005). Similarly, inquiries into difficulties being experienced in following the other recommended treatments for asthma, grounded in the assumption that difficulty is the norm, are very fruitful and welcome as long as they are done in a non-judgmental, optimistic, supportive, and family-centered fashion. Even if the patient or family is not ready to change now, they will almost invariably appreciate that your willingness to help is ultimately on target and fosters their alliance with you as an ally for health. When you are asked, "Doctor, how come you ask me every time I see you if I want to quit smoking?" it is very hard to argue with, "I am sure that you want and deserve a doctor who is not going to ignore the single most important thing you could do for you and your family's health, right?"

Work collaboratively and proactively with the families' other health-care providers and community supports. Sometimes problems following treatment recommendations arise from rather simple and straightforward causes, most importantly, lack of knowledge about what to do. Helping the family learn what to do through visits with their primary provider or community support groups is very beneficial, although quite often involves helping them navigate increasingly complex systems. This being said, many if not most problems following treatment recommendations are much more multi-faceted and complex, such as the family with three persons with asthma, who all share the controller inhaler of the one person in the family who has health insurance, or the parent whose own traumatic history of having asthma as a child is causing them to avoid and under-estimate the asthma symptoms their young child is now experiencing. Fortunately, such complexity is well within the therapeutic acumen and talents of most family systems-oriented providers to help with over the long-term.

Different Adherence Behaviors are Associated with Different Family Factors

A simple belief held by many health-care providers is that there are "good" patients and families who do everything you ask them to do, and "bad" ones who do little to nothing. Our work finds no support for this belief. Each of the family adherence behaviors that we have studied has a different set of associated family factors, and knowing how a family performs on one of these behavioral recommendations does not tell you much about how they are performing on another. If we think about what each asthma management behavior demands of a family, this situation makes much more sense.

Controller medication adherence is a learned habit. There are many challenges inherent in taking an asthma controller (Virchow et al., 2008), a few of which we describe below. Up front, much more physical coordination is required to successfully use an asthma inhaler than take a pill. Typically one must shake the canister, position it properly near the mouth so that the spray goes down the throat, and time the dispensing of the medication properly with breathing in, a set of behaviors tricky even for an adult to learn, let alone asking a parent to master with the moving target of a very young child. Not surprisingly, lack of parent-child teamwork and/or overt conflict has been found by us and others to be related to poorer controller medication adherence and worse asthma outcomes (Chen, Bloomberg, Fisher, and Strunk, 2003; Wamboldt, Wamboldt, Gavin, Roesler, and Brugman, 1995).

Second, as opposed to the rescue medications, inhaled controller medications are to be taken multiple times every day whether asthma symptoms are present or not. Furthermore, there are no immediate benefits noticed after taking these medications— benefits often take weeks of regular use to achieve—and indeed, minor throat or voice irritation is not uncommon. Finally, these medications are somewhat "forgiving" when not taken, as adverse consequences do not usually rapidly or automatically ensue, and as stated above, if no environmental risk factors or triggers are present, non-use may not have any consequences for an extended period of time. This combination of low immediate benefits, higher side effects, and minimal mid-term consequences of non-use allow patients and families ample opportunity to develop beliefs and emotions that do not reinforce regular use, and indeed, foster "forgetting" or neglect (Bender, Rand, and Wamboldt, 2006; Munro, Lewin, Swart, and Volmink, 2007). Accordingly, pairing medication taking with an existing behavior routine, e.g. before twice-a-day tooth-brushing, or if none exists, developing one, e.g. as part of a game when dressing the child in the morning and while reading a bedtime story at night, can help embed medication taking within a routinized habit (Cramer, 1995; Fiese and Wamboldt, 2000; Fiese, Wamboldt, and Anbar, 2005). Some evidence exists that children from more disadvantaged backgrounds experience significantly fewer routines within their families (Flores, Tomany-Korman, and Olson, 2005).

Smoking as a coping strategy and addiction. We and others have found that smoking occurs most often in families with more disadvantage and stress (Gilman, Abrams, and Buka, 2003; Wamboldt et al., 2008; Wamboldt et al., 2002). Although many people report that at least early in their career, smoking helps them both relax and focus for a short time, evidence suggests that over time smoking increases stress, and quitting smoking reduces stress (Parrott, 1999). From a family perspective, having that person change their smoking behavior by either quitting, smoking less, or only smoking outside, requires an alteration in family process that supports the person who smokes in changing what they may view, correctly or incorrectly, as one of their existing coping strategies. Given that increased irritability is a very common consequence early after cessation, families often are very challenged in providing this support during this phase, and support from a trusted clinician may be crucial.

Pets as a family luxury. In the homes of many disadvantaged families, the resident animals that trigger asthma are most typically vermin. It is usually in the context of greater resources and/or luxury that families voluntarily invite pet animals with fur and feathers into their homes. A number of beliefs that accompany more resources may help with this, e.g. "Our house is big enough that we can keep the pet away from our child so the allergens will not matter." However, in houses with forced air HVAC systems, these allergens, which are respirable particles, are blown throughout the home, and indeed, because they tend to be somewhat sticky, adhere to surfaces that collect dust, such as curtains, stuffed animals, and carpets. Furthermore, current "green" efforts to improve home energy efficiency may not always be "healthy." For example, "tightening a house's envelope" and thereby reduce air exchange, has the potential to actually increase indoor asthma triggers (Manuel, 2011). Finally, since pets very often are considered "members of the family," the recommendation by the health-care provider that the family find another home for the pet that triggers their child's asthma, is very often discarded out-of-hand. Hence, alternate containment strategies, having the pet always outside, or keeping the child's bedroom as a "pet-free zone," often are the best solutions to seek (National Heart, Blood and Lung Institute, 2007), yet families often require help from an experienced clinician to succeed in doing so.

Family Narratives as a Window into the Family's Sense of Confidence and Efficacy in Managing Asthma

Listening to family narratives and stories can help inform the observer about the beliefs, affect, interactional processes, and relational rules operating within that family (Fiese et al., 1999, 2001; Fiese and Wamboldt, 2003). Our work has found that a rather simple approach to having families talk about their experience of their child's asthma yields information that relates their success at asthma management. Specifically, the stories of some families make it clear that they have a plan, in which they experience a sense of confidence or efficacy, for dealing with asthma; others tell stories suggesting that they experience themselves as more rudderless, being buffeted by and reacting to asthma. Telling stories describing a plan imbued with confidence and efficacy, whether or not the story was consistent with existing asthma management guidelines, both concurrently and prospectively over the subsequent year, was associated with better controller medication adherence as well as less urgent health-care utilization for asthma. This finding seems highly congruent with reports that parental depression appears to be strongly associated with adherence problems as well as adverse outcomes in pediatric asthma, even when confounds such as parental smoking are controlled for (Lange et al., 2011).

In our opinion, family stories are an easily obtained and highly naturalistic, yet an under-used window for gaining understanding into how families understand the illness, which can then lead to promoting better management of chronic illness. We will give two examples of how this may play out. First, they serve a very useful triage function. Presence of a story showing some existing plan may indicate a family, whose asthma management while perhaps not perfect, is not at the highest risk. Given that risk for morbidity and mortality increases exponentially in those having the most difficulty performing recommended asthma management behaviors, one can rather quickly discover where one's time and effort, whether as a clinician or researcher, might be most profitably focused. Second, and perhaps more important, the language used in the stories, especially those families who appear more disorganized and/or traumatized provides extremely helpful clues as to how to best ally with and help support that particular family in therapy.

Paying Attention to the Broader Sociocultural Context in which Families Reside

Asthma is an illness characterized by stark, and under-explained, health disparities. Throughout the United States, black and Puerto Rican children have at least double the rate of having asthma, and an even greater chance of dying from asthma, compared to whites and Hispanics of non-Puerto-Rican ancestry. Additionally, black and all Hispanic children with asthma have much higher rates of missing school and being hospitalized as a result of an asthma attack (Centers for Disease Control and Prevention, 2011a; Gold and Wright, 2005).

From a family systems perspective, Robinson's Community Development Model shows promise for guiding future efforts aimed at eliminating health disparities (Robinson, 2005). A fundamental assumption of this model is that race/ethnicity is not a characteristic of a person or a family, it is rather a contextual variable that refers back to a specific community (Jones, 2001). Furthermore, communities, like families, have a shared consciousness that is formed primarily out of relevant history, culture, context, and geography, with secondary inputs from language, literacy, salient positive and cross-generational imagery, and the diversity within the community (Robinson, 2005). Ultimately, to eliminate health disparities, clinical, research and public health efforts must focus upon and interact with communities in a competent fashion and thereby help the community develop in terms of health-related material capacity and infrastructure as well as social capital. Useful guides for working alongside communities to improve health are available from various U.S. government funding agencies (Agency for Healthcare Research and Quality, 2003; Centers for Disease Control and Prevention and National Institutes of Health, 2011b).

We hope that by presenting highlights from our family research in the area of childhood asthma, and attempting to contextualize our work within the broader literature and other noteworthy efforts, readers of this chapter will continue to move forward this important mission—to promote health within children, adults, families, and communities.

Acknowledgements

Funding for the research presented herein and/or the writing of this chapter has come from NIH grants R03-MH48683, R01-HL53391, R01-HL8828, R01-HL45157, R01-HL70267, R01-HL64938, M01-RR00051, U54-RR025217, the Environmental Protection Agency Region 8, and the MacArthur Foundation Early Childhood Transition Research Network. GlaxoWellcome, Rhône-Poulenc Rorer, and Schering-Plough helped us provide free inhaled controller medications to the children in the Family and Asthma Study.

References

Agency for Healthcare Research and Quality. (2003). The Role of Community-Based Participatory Research: Creating Partnerships, Improving Health. Retrieved from: <www.ahrq.gov>.

Bender, B., Milgrom, H., and Apter, A. (2003). Adherence intervention research: what have we learned and what do we do next? *Journal of Allergy and Clinical Immunology*, 112(3), 489–94.

Bender, B., Wamboldt, F. S., O'Connor, S. L., Rand, C., Szefler, S., Milgrom, H., and Wamboldt, M. Z. (2000). Measurement of children's asthma medication adherence by self report, mother report, canister weight, and Doser CT. *Annals of Allergy Asthma & Immunology*, 85(5), 416–21.

Bender, B. G., Rand, C., Rankin, A., Tran, Z. V., and Wamboldt, F. S. (2005). Self-reported adherence in the Childhood Asthma Management Program – Continuation Study. *Proceedings of the American Thoracic Society*, 2 (Abstract Issue), A587.

Bender, B. G., Rand, C., and Wamboldt, F. (2006). Improving Asthma Medication Adherence. In S. J. Szefler and S. Pederson (Eds), *Childhood asthma* (2009 Edition, pp. 581–604). New York: Marcel Dekker.

Centers for Disease Control and Prevention (2011a). Vital signs: asthma prevalence, disease characteristics, and self-management education: United States, 2001–2009 MMWR. Morbidity and mortality weekly report. (2011/05/06 Edition, Vol. 60, pp. 547–52).

Centers for Disease Control and Prevention and National Institutes of Health. (2011b). Principles of Community Engagement, Second Edition. (NIH Publication No. 11-7782). Retrieved from <http://www.atsdr.cdc.gov/communityengagement/>.

Chen, E., Bloomberg, G. R., Fisher, E. B., Jr., and Strunk, R. C. (2003). Predictors of repeat hospitalizations in children with asthma: the role of psychosocial and socioenvironmental factors. *Health Psychology*, 22(1), 12–18.

Cramer, J. A. (1995). Optimizing long-term patient compliance. Neurology, 45(2 Suppl. 1), S25–8.

DiFranza, J. R., and Lew, R. A. (1996). Morbidity and mortality in children associated with the use of tobacco products by other people. *Pediatrics*, 97(4), 560–8.

Fiese, B., Sameroff, A., Grotevant, H., Wamboldt, F., Dickstein, S., and Fravel, D. (1999). The stories that families tell: Narrative coherence, narrative interaction, and relationship beliefs. *Monographs of the Society of Research in Child Development*, 64(2).

Fiese, B., Sameroff, A., Grotevant, H., Wamboldt, F., Dickstein, S., and Fravel, D. (2001). Observing families through the stories that they tell: A multidimensional approach. In P. Kerig and K. Lindahl (Eds), *Family Observational Coding Systems: Resources for Systemic Research* (pp. 259–71). Mahwah, NJ: Lawrence Erlbaum.

Fiese, B. H., and Wamboldt, F. S. (2000). Family routines, rituals, and asthma management: A proposal for family-based strategies to increase treatment adherence. *Families, Systems & Health*, 18(4), 405–18.

Fiese, B. H., and Wamboldt, F. S. (2003). Tales of pediatric asthma management: Family-based strategies related to medical adherence and health-care utilization. *Journal of Pediatrics*, 143(4), 457–62.

Fiese, B. H., Wamboldt, F. S., and Anbar, R. D. (2005). Family asthma management routines: connections to medical adherence and quality of life. *Journal of Pediatrics*, 146(2), 171–6.

Fiore, M. C., Bailey, W., Cohen, S., Dorfman, S., Goldstein, M. G., Gritz, E. R. et al. (2000). Treating tobacco use and dependence: clinical practice guideline: Rockville, MD: U.S. Department of Health and Human Services, Public Health Service.

Flores, G., Tomany-Korman, S. C., and Olson, L. (2005). Does disadvantage start at home? Racial and ethnic disparities in health-related early childhood home routines and safety practices. *Archives of Pediatrics & Adolescent Medicine*, 159(2), 158–65.

Gilman, S. E., Abrams, D. B., and Buka, S. L. (2003). Socioeconomic status over the life course and stages of cigarette use: initiation, regular use, and cessation. *Journal of Epidemiology & Community Health*, 57(10), 802–8.

Gold, D. R., and Wright, R. (2005). Population disparities in asthma. *Annual Review of Public Health*, 26, 89–113. doi: 10.1146/annurev.publhealth.26.021304.144528.

Ho, J., Bender, B. G., Gavin, L. A., O'Connor S. L., Wamboldt, M. Z., and Wamboldt, F. S. (2003). Relations among asthma knowledge, treatment adherence, and outcome. *Journal of Allergy and Clinical Immunology*, 111(3), 498–502.

Jones, C. P. (2001). Invited commentary: "race," racism, and the practice of epidemiology. [Comment]. *American Journal of Epidemiology*, 154(4), 299–304; discussion 305–96.

Kaptein, A. A., Klok, T., Moss-Morris, R., and Brand, P. L. (2010). Illness perceptions: impact on self-management and control in asthma. [Review]. *Current Opinion in Journal of Allergy and Clinical Immunology*, 10(3), 194–9. doi: 10.1097/ACI.0b013e32833950c1.

Kean, E. M., Kelsay, K., Wamboldt, F., and Wamboldt, M. Z. (2006). Posttraumatic stress in adolescents with asthma and their parents. *Journal of the American Academy of Child & Adolescent Psychiatry*, 45(1), 78–86.

Kurukulaaratchy, R. J., Matthews, S., and Arshad, S. H. (2004). Does environment mediate earlier onset of the persistent childhood asthma phenotype? *Pediatrics*, 113(2), 345–50.

Lange, N. E., Bunyavanich, S., Silberg, J. L., Canino, G., Rosner, B. A., and Celedon, J. C. (2011). Parental psychosocial stress and asthma morbidity in Puerto Rican twins. *The Journal of Allergy and Clinical Immunology*, 127(3), 734–40 e731–7. doi: 10.1016/j.jaci.2010.11.010.

Le, T. T., Bilderback, A., Bender, B., Wamboldt, F. S., Turner, C. F., Rand, C. S., and Bartlett, S. J. (2008). Do asthma medication beliefs mediate the relationship between minority status and adherence to therapy? *Journal of Asthma*, 45(1), 33–7.

Lehrer, P. M., Isenberg, S., and Hochron, S. (1993). Asthma and emotion: A review. *The Journal of Asthma*, 30 (1), 5–21.

Liangas, G., Yates, D. H., Wu, D., Henry, R. L., and Thomas, P. S. (2004). Laughter-associated asthma. *The Journal of Asthma*, 41(2), 217–21.

Magana, A. B., Goldstein, M. J., Karno, M., Miklowitz, D. J., Jenkins, J., and Falloon, I. R. H. (1985). A brief method for assessing expressed emotion in relatives of psychiatric patients. *Psychiatry Research*, 17, 203–12.

Manuel, J. (2011). Avoiding health pitfalls of home energy-efficiency retrofits. *Environmental Health Perspectives*, 119(2), A76-79. doi: 10.1289/ehp.119-a76.

McDowell, D. J., and Parke, R. D. (2009). Parental correlates of children's peer relations: an empirical test of a tripartite model. *Developmental Psychology*, 45(1), 224–35. doi: 10.1037/a0014305.

McDowell, D. J., Parke, R. D., and Spitzer, S. (2002). Parent and child cognitive representations of social situations and children's social competence. *Social Development*, 11(4), 469–86.

Munro, S., Lewin, S., Swart, T., and Volmink, J. (2007). A review of health behaviour theories: how useful are these for developing interventions to promote long-term medication adherence for TB and HIV/AIDS? BMC Public Health, 7, 104. doi: 10.1186/1471-2458-7-104.

National Heart, Lung and Blood Institute (2003). Expert panel report: guidelines for the diagnosis and management of asthma. [Bethesda, Md.]: U.S. Dept. of Health and Human Services, Public Health Service, National Institutes of Health, National Heart, Lung, and Blood Institute, National Asthma Education and Prevention Program.

National Heart, Lung and Blood Institute. (2007). So you have asthma. (NIH Publication No. 07-5248). U.S. Department of Health and Human Services, National Institutes of Health, Retrieved from <http://www.nhlbi.nih.gov/health/public/lung/asthma/have_asthma.htm>.

O'Connor, S. L. et al. (2004). Measuring adherence with the Doser CT in children with asthma. *The Journal of Asthma*, 41(6), 663–70.

Parrott, A. C. (1999). Does cigarette smoking cause stress? *The American Psychologist*, 54(10), 817–20.

Robinson, R. G. (2005). Community development model for public health applications: overview of a model to eliminate population disparities. *Health Promotion Practice*, 6(3), 338–46.

Schroeder, S. A. (2005). What to do with a patient who smokes. *Journal of American medical Association*, 294(4), 482–7.

Sly, P. D. (2011). The early origins of asthma: who is really at risk? Current Opinion in *Journal of Allergy and Clinical Immunology*, 11(1), 24–8. doi: 10.1097/ACI.0b013e328342309d.

Suissa, S., Ernst, P., Benayoun, S., Baltzan, M., and Cai, B. (2000). Low-dose inhaled corticosteroids and the prevention of death from asthma. *New England Journal of Medicine*, 343(5), 332–6.

Virchow, J. C., Crompton, G. K., Dal Negro, R., Pedersen, S., Magnan, A., Seidenberg, J., and Barnes, P. J. (2008). Importance of inhaler devices in the management of airway disease. *Respiratory Medicine*, 102(1), 10-19. doi: 10.1016/j.rmed.2007.07.031.

Wamboldt, F., Bender, B., Wamboldt, M., Bihun, J., Milgrom, H., and Szefler, S. (2000). Psychosocial correlates of pediatric MDI adherence. *American Journal of Respiratory & Critical Care Medicine*, 161(3), A711.

Wamboldt, F. S., Balkissoon, R. C., Rankin, A. E., Szefler, S. J., Hammond, S. K., Glasgow, R. E., and Dickinson, W. P. (2008). Correlates of household smoking bans in low-income families of children with and without asthma. *Family Process*, 47(1), 81–94.

Wamboldt, F. S., Bender, B., Ho, J., Milgrom, H., Rojas, S., Szefler, S., and Wamboldt, M. Z. (2002). Correlates of MDI adherence: A replication study. *American Journal of Respiratory & Critical Care Medicine*, 165(8), A197.

Wamboldt, F. S., Bender, B. G., and Rankin, A. E. (2011). Adolescent Decision-Making about Use of Inhaled Asthma Controller Medication: Results from Focus Groups with Participants from a Prior Longitudinal Study. *The Journal of Asthma*, 48(7), 741–50. doi: 10.3109/02770903.2011.598204.

Wamboldt, F. S., Ho, J., Milgrom, H., Wamboldt, M. Z., Sanders, B., Szefler, S. J., and Bender, B. G. (2002). Prevalence and correlates of household exposures to tobacco smoke and pets in children with asthma. *Journal of Pediatrics*, 141(1), 109–115.

Wamboldt, F. S., O'Connor, S. L., Wamboldt, M. Z., Gavin, L. A., and Klinnert, M. D. (2000). The Five Minute Speech Sample in children with asthma: Deconstructing the construct of Expressed Emotion. *Journal of Child Psychology & Psychiatry & Allied Disciplines*, 41(7), 887–98.

Wamboldt, F. S., Wamboldt, M. Z., Gavin, L. A., Roesler, T. A., and Brugman, S. M. (1995). Parental criticism and treatment outcome in adolescents hospitalized for severe, chronic asthma. *Journal of Psychosomatic Research*, 39, 995–1005.

Wamboldt, M. Z., and Wamboldt, F. S. (2001). Psychosocial aspects of severe asthma in children. In S. J. Szefler and D. Y. M. Leung (Eds). *Severe Asthma: Pathogenesis and Clinical Management*, 2nd Edition (Vol. 159, pp. 471–503). New York: Marcel Dekker.

Wamboldt, M. Z., Weintraub, P., Krafchick, D., Berce, N., and Wamboldt, F. S. (1995). Links between past parental trauma and the medical and psychological outcome of asthmatic children: A theoretical model. *Families, Systems & Health*, 13(2), 129–49.

Williams, G. C., Williams, S. A., and Korn, R. J. (2005). Secondhand smoke (SHS) deserves more than secondhand attention: Modifying the 5As model to include counseling to eliminate exposure. *Families, Systems & Health*, 23(3), 266–77.

Williams, L. K., Pladevall, M., Xi, H., Peterson, E. L., Joseph, C., Lafata, J. E., and Johnson, C. C. (2004). Relationship between adherence to inhaled corticosteroids and poor outcomes among adults with asthma. *The Journal of Allergy and Clinical Immunology*, 114(6), 1288–93. doi: 10.1016/j.jaci.2004.09.028.

World Health Organization. (2003). Adherence to long-term therapies: Evidence for action. Retrieved from: <http://www.who.int/chp/knowledge/publications/adherence_report/en/>.

Yunginger, J. W., Reed, C. E., O'Connell, E. J., Melton, L. J. 3rd, O'Fallon, W. M., and Silverstein, M. D. (1992). A community-based study of the epidemiology of asthma. Incidence rates, 1964–1983. *The American Review of Respiratory Disease*, 146(4), 888–94.

3 Family Adaptation to Chronic Medical Illness and Disability
An Integrative Model

John S. Rolland

- A comprehensive family systems model for assessment and clinical intervention with families facing chronic illness and disability is outlined.
- The psychosocial demands of illness based on their pattern of onset, course, outcome, incapacitation, and level of uncertainty are described.
- The crisis, chronic, and terminal phases of illness, the transitions between phases, and the psychosocial developmental tasks associated with each phase are delineated.
- The interface of illness, individual, and family development; multigenerational legacies of illness and loss; and how these relate to coping and adaptation to chronic illness are described.
- How health belief systems affect a patient's or family's response to illness is described.

Introduction

Illness, disability, and death are universal experiences in families. The real question is not if we will face these issues, but when in our lives they will occur, under what conditions, how serious they will be, and for how long. With major advances in medical technology, people with formerly fatal conditions are living much longer. This means that ever-growing numbers of families are living with chronic disorders over an increasingly long time span and coping with multiple conditions simultaneously. This chapter provides a normative, preventive model for psychoeducation, assessment, and intervention with families facing chronic and life-threatening conditions. This model offers a systemic view of healthy family adaptation to serious illness as a developmental process over time in relation to the complexities and diversity of contemporary family life, modern medicine, and existing flawed models of health-care delivery and access to care.

Overview of the Family Systems Illness Model

Over the past thirty years, family-centered, collaborative, biopsychosocial models of health care have grown and evolved (Blount, 1998; Doherty and Baird, 1983; Engel, 1977; McDaniel, Campbell, Hepworth, and Lorenz, 2005; McDaniel, Hepworth, and Doherty, 2012; Miller, McDaniel, Rolland, and Feetham, 2006; Rolland, 1994; Seaburn, Gunn, Mauksch, Gawinski, and Lorenz, 1996; Wood et al., 2008). There is substantial evidence for the mutual influence of family functioning, health, and physical illness (Carr and Kristen, 2010; D'Onofrio and Lahey, 2010; Weihs, Fisher, and Baird, 2001) and the usefulness of family-centered interventions with chronic health conditions (Campbell, 2003; Hartmann et al, 2010; Kazak, 2002; Law and Crane, 2007; Matire et al., 2004, 2010; Shields et al., 2012). Weihs et al. (2001) summarized the increasing body of research regarding the impact of serious illness on families across the lifespan and the relationship of family dynamics to illness behavior, adherence, and disease course. In this report, a broad definition of family was used. Family was defined as a "group of intimates with strong emotional bonds ... and with a history and a future as a group" (p. 8). Most illness management takes place within the context of the family environment. Interventions in health settings aim to help families adjust to and live with the demands of an illness or disability, assist families in navigating the health-care system, and enhance quality of life for the entire family.

There is a clear need for a conceptual model that provides a guide useful to both clinical practice and research, one that allows a dynamic, open communication between these disciplines. What is most needed is a comprehensive way to organize our thinking about all the complex interactions between biological illness, family, individual family members, and professionals involved in providing care. We need a model that can accommodate the changing landscape of interactions between these "parts of the system" over the course of the illness and the changing seasons over the life course.

Families enter the world of illness and disability without a psychosocial map. To master the challenges presented by an illness or disability, families must understand the impact of the condition on the entire family network. The Family Systems Illness Model that was developed by Rolland (1984, 1987, 1990, 1994a, 1998) is based on a strength-oriented perspective, viewing family relationships as a resource and empha-sizing possibilities for resilience and growth, not just liabilities and risks (Walsh, 2006). This model provides a framework for assessing the impact of an illness or disability on family life and for structuring interventions to meet the needs of family members.

Defined in system's terms, an effective psychosocial model for assessing the impact of illness on family life needs to encompass all persons affected by the condition. First, we need to broaden the unit of care from the medical model's narrow focus on the ill individual to the family or caregiving system. By using a broad definition of family as the cornerstone of the caregiving system, as suggested by the Institute of Medicine report (2001), we can describe a model of successful coping and adaptation based on family system strengths. The family-centered model described in this chapter views a broad range of family forms and processes as normative, and uses as its central reference point the idea of goodness of fit between the psychosocial demands of the illness in relation to family challenges and resources over time.

In situations of chronic disorders, a basic task for families is to create a meaning for the illness situation that preserves their sense of competency and mastery. At the extremes, competing ideologies can leave families with a choice between a biological explanation and one of personal responsibility (e.g. illness as retribution for wrong-doing). Families desper-ately need reassurance that they are handling illnesses appropriately (bad things do happen to good people). These needs often occur in the context of a vague or nonexistent psycho-social map. Many families, particularly those with untimely disorders, find themselves in unfamiliar territory and without guides. This highlights the need for a preventive, psychoe-ducational approach that helps families anticipate normative illness-related developmental tasks over time in a fashion that maximizes their sense of control and mastery.

To create a normative context for their illness experience, families need the following foundation. First, they need a psychosocial understanding of the condition in systems terms. This means learning the expected pattern of practical and affective demands of a disorder over the life course of the condition. This includes a timeframe for disease-related developmental tasks associated with different phases of the unfolding disorder. Second, families need to understand themselves as a systemic functional unit. Third, they need an appreciation of individual and family life-cycle patterns and transitions to facilitate their incorporation of changing developmental priorities for the family unit and individual members in relation to evolving challenges of a chronic disorder. Finally, families need to understand the cultural, ethnic, spiritual, and gender-based beliefs that guide the type of caregiving system they construct. This includes guiding principles that define roles, rules of communication, definitions of success or mastery, and fit with beliefs of the health-care providers. Family understanding in these areas facilitates a more holistic integration of the disorder and the family as a functional family health/illness system evolving over time.

The Family Systems Illness Model addresses three dimensions: (1) "psychosocial types" of health conditions, (2) major developmental phases in their natural history, and (3) key family system variables (Figure 3.1). It attends to the expected psychosocial demands of a disorder through its various phases, family systems dynamics that emphasize family and individual development, multigenerational patterns, and belief systems (including influences of culture, ethnicity, spirituality, and gender (Figure 3.2). The model emphasizes the match between the psychosocial demands of the disorder over time and the strengths and vulnerabilities of a family.

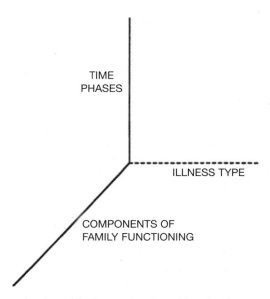

Figure 3.1   Three dimensional model: illness type, time phase, family.
Excerpted from: Rolland, J. S., "Chronic illness and the life cycle: A conceptual framework," *Family Process*, 26, 203–221, 1987.

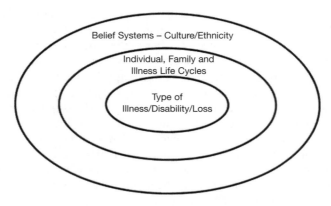

Figure 3.2   Family systems - illness model
From: Rolland, J. S. *Families, illness and disability: An integrative treatment model.*
New York: Basic Books, 1994

Psychosocial Types of Illness

The standard disease classification used in medical settings is based on purely biological criteria that are clustered in ways to establish a medical diagnosis and treatment plan rather than on the psychosocial demands on patients and their families. I have proposed a different classification scheme that provides a better link between the biological and psychosocial worlds, and thereby clarifies the relationship between chronic illness and the family (Rolland, 1984, 1994a). The goal of this typology is to define meaningful and useful categories with similar psychosocial demands for a wide array of chronic illnesses affecting individuals across the life span.

Onset

Illnesses can be divided into those that have either an acute onset, such as strokes, or a gradual onset, such as Alzheimer's disease. For acute-onset illnesses, emotional and practical changes are compressed into a short time, requiring more rapid family mobilization and crisis-management skills. Families able to tolerate highly charged emotional situations, exchange roles flexibly, problem solve efficiently, and utilize outside resources will have an advantage in managing acute-onset conditions. Gradual onset conditions, such as Parkinson's disease, allow a more gradual period of adjustment.

Course

The course of chronic diseases can take three general forms: progressive, constant, or relapsing/episodic. With a progressive disease, such as Parkinson's disease, the family is often faced with a perpetually symptomatic family member whose disability worsens in a stepwise or gradual way. The family must live with the prospect of continual role change and adaptation to continued losses as the disease progresses. Increasing strain on family caregiving is caused by exhaustion, with few periods of relief from the demands of the illness, and with more caregiving tasks over time. Diabetes is an example of a progressive disease with a long and unpredictable course.

With a constant-course illness, the occurrence of an initial event, such as a single heart attack, is followed by a stable biological course. Typically, after an initial period of recovery, the illness is characterized by some clear-cut deficit or limitation. The family is faced with a semipermanent change that is stable and predictable over a considerable time span. The potential for family exhaustion exists without the strain of new role demands over time.

Relapsing- or episodic-course illnesses, such as asthma, are distinguished by the alternation of stable low-symptom periods with periods of flare-up or exacerbation. Families are strained by both the frequency of transitions between periods of crisis and noncrisis, and ongoing uncertainty of when a recurrence will occur. This requires family flexibility to alternate between two forms of family organization. The wide psychological discrepancy between low-symptom periods versus flare-up is a particularly taxing feature unique to relapsing diseases.

Outcome

The extent to which a chronic illness leads to death or shortens one's life expectancy has profound psychosocial impact. The most crucial factor is the initial expectation of whether a disease will cause death. On one end of the continuum are illnesses that do not typically affect the life span, such as arthritis. At the other extreme are illnesses that are clearly progressive and fatal, such as metastatic cancer. An intermediate, more unpredictable category includes both illnesses that shorten the life span, such as heart disease, and those that may bring sudden death, such as hemophilia. A major difference between these kinds of outcome is the degree to which the family experiences anticipatory loss and its pervasive effects on family life (Rolland, 1990, 2004).

Incapacitation

Disability can involve impairment of cognition (e.g. Alzheimer's disease), sensation (e.g. blindness), movement (e.g. stroke with paralysis), stamina (e.g. heart disease), disfigurement (e.g. mastectomy), and conditions associated with social stigma (e.g. AIDS; Olkin, 1999). The extent, kind, and timing of disability imply sharp differences in the degree of family stress. For instance, the combined cognitive and motor deficits caused by a stroke necessitate greater family reorganization than those caused by a spinal-cord injury, in which cognitive abilities are unaffected. For some illnesses, like stroke, disability is often worst at the beginning. For progressive diseases, like Alzheimer's disease, disability looms as an increasing problem in later phases of the illness, allowing a family more time to prepare for anticipated changes and an opportunity for the ill member to participate in disease-related family planning while still cognitively able (Boss, 1999).

The predictability of an illness, and the degree of uncertainty about the specific way in which it unfolds, overlays all other variables. For illnesses with highly unpredictable courses, such as multiple sclerosis, family coping and adaptation, especially future planning, are hindered by anticipatory anxiety and ambiguity about what family members will actually encounter. Families able to put long-term uncertainty into perspective are best prepared to avoid the risks of exhaustion and dysfunction.

By combining the types of onset, course, outcome, and incapacitation into a grid, we generate a typology that clusters illnesses according to similarities and differences in patterns that pose differing psychosocial demands.

Time Phase of Illness

Too often, discussions of "coping with cancer," "managing disability," or "dealing with life-threatening disease" approach illness as a static state and fail to appreciate the evolution of illness processes over time. The concept of time phases provides a way for clinicians and families to think longitudinally and to understand chronic illness as an ongoing process with normative landmarks, transitions, and changing demands. Each phase of an illness poses its own psychosocial challenges and developmental tasks that may require significantly different strengths, attitudes, or changes for family adaptation. Core psychosocial themes in the natural history of chronic disease can be described as three major phases: crisis, chronic, and terminal.

Time Line and Phases of Illness

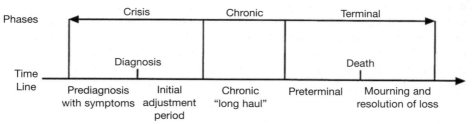

Figure 3.3   From: Rolland, J. S. *Families, illness and disability: An integrative treatment model.* New York: Basic Books, 1994

Crisis Phase

The crisis phase includes any symptomatic period before diagnosis through the initial readjustment period, after a diagnosis, and initial treatment planning. This phase presents a number of key tasks for the ill member and family. Moos (1984) describes certain universal, practical, illness-related tasks, including (a) learning to cope with any symptoms or disability, (b) adapting to health-care settings and treatment procedures, and (c) establishing and maintaining workable relationships with the health-care team. Also, there are critical tasks of a more general, existential nature. Families optimize well-being when they can (a) create a meaning for the illness that maximizes a sense of mastery and competency, (b) grieve for the loss of health, (c) gradually accept the illness as long-term while maintaining a sense of continuity between their past and future, (d) pull together to cope with the immediate crisis, and (e) in the face of uncertainty, develop flexibility toward future goals.

During this initial adjustment period, health professionals have enormous influence over a family's approach to, and sense of competence and their strategies to accomplish these developmental tasks. Initial meetings and advice given at the time of diagnosis can be thought of as a "framing event." Since families are so vulnerable at this point, clinicians need to be extremely sensitive in their interactions with family members and aware of messages conveyed by their behavior. Who is included or excluded (e.g. patient) from a discussion, can be interpreted by the family as a message of how they should plan their communication for the duration of the illness. For instance, if a clinician meets with parents separately from adolescents to give them information about a cancer diagnosis and prognosis, they may assume they were being instructed implicitly to protect their adolescent from any discussion of the illness. Clinicians can ask patients who they would like to include in important discussions, or can help reframe these experiences for families by asking them about their preferences.

With life-threatening conditions that can cause sudden death (e.g. heart attack), there is a higher premium on early frank conversation. Knowing an ill member's wishes concerning heroic medical efforts and life support can benefit everyone. For example, in one family, the father had serious heart disease. Everyone, including the father, became emotionally paralyzed by fear because end-of-life decision-making had been avoided. Family consultations facilitated the father making his wishes known regarding the limits on life-saving efforts. This relieved his family members because they knew his feelings if they had to make life-and-death decisions. For the father, making his wishes known not only gave him a sense of personal control over the end of his life, but also freed his energy to focus on living well and maximizing his physical well-being. Despite the short-run challenge of having end-of-life discussions, it is important to keep in mind that many of the most wrenching end-of-life experiences for families occur when the wishes of a dying member are unknown or have been disregarded. With conditions involving progressive dementia, such as Alzheimer's disease, there is added incentive for conversations before the affected person's cognitive impairment makes meaningful discussion impossible (Boss, 1999).

Chronic Phase

The chronic phase, whether long or short, is the time span between the initial diagnosis and readjustment. This era can be marked by constancy, recurrence (e.g. cancer), progression, or episodic flare-ups. It has been referred to as "the long haul," or "day-to-day living with chronic illness" phase. Often, the patient and family have come to grips psychologically and organizationally with permanent changes and have devised an ongoing coping strategy. The ability of the family to maintain the semblance of a normal life, attending as equitably as possible to both the illness and to normative developmental tasks, is key during this period. If the illness is fatal, this is a time of living in limbo. For certain highly debilitating but not clearly fatal illnesses, such as a massive stroke or dementia, the family can feel saddled by an exhausting problem "without end." Paradoxically, the family may feel its hope to resume a "normal" life can only be realized after the death of the ill member. The maintenance of maximum autonomy for all family members in the face of prolonged adversity helps to offset trapped, helpless feelings.

For long-term disorders, customary patterns of intimacy for couples become skewed by discrepancies between the ill member and the well spouse/caregiver (Rolland, 1994b). As one young husband lamented in a clinical meeting regarding his wife's cancer, "It was hard enough two years ago to absorb that, even if Mary was cured, her radiation treatment would make pregnancy impossible. Now, I find it unbearable that her continued slow, losing battle with cancer makes it impossible to go for our dreams like other couples our age." Normative ambivalence and escape fantasies often remain underground and contribute to survivor guilt. Psychoeducational family interventions that normalize such emotions related to threatened loss can help prevent destructive cycles of blame, shame, and guilt.

Terminal Phase

In the terminal phase of an illness, the inevitability of death becomes apparent and dominates family life. At this point, the family must cope with issues of separation, death, mourning, and beginning the reorganization process needed for the resumption of family life beyond the loss (Walsh and McGoldrick, 2004). Families adapt best to this phase when able to shift their views of hope and mastery from controlling the illness to a successful process of "letting go." Optimal coping involves emotional openness as well as dealing with the myriad practical tasks at hand. This includes seeing this phase as an opportunity to share precious time together, to acknowledge the impending loss, to deal with unfinished business, and to say good-byes. If they have not determined beforehand, the patient and key family members need to decide about such things as a living will, the extent of medical heroics desired, preferences about dying at home, in the hospital, or at hospice, and wishes about a funeral or memorial service and burial or cremation.

Transition Between Phases

Critical transition periods link the three time phases. Transitions in the illness course are times when families reevaluate the appropriateness of their previous life structure in the face of new illness-related developmental demands. Helping families resolve unfinished business from the previous phase can facilitate movement through the transitions. Families can become permanently frozen in an adaptive structure that has outlived its utility (Penn, 1983). For example, the usefulness of pulling together in the crisis phase can become maladaptive and stifling for all family members through the chronic phase.

The following table outlines the developmental tasks associated with each illness phase.

Phases of Illness Developmental Tasks

Crisis Phase

1. Family understand themselves in systems terms
2. Psychosocial understanding of illness
   a. In practical and emotional terms
   b. In longitudinal and developmental terms
3. Family appreciation of developmental perspective (individual, family, and illness life cycles)
4. Crisis reorganization
5. Create meaning that promotes family mastery and competence
6. Define challenge as shared one in "WE" terms
7. Accept permanence of illness/ disability
8. Grieve loss of family identity before chronic disorder
9. Acknowledge possibilities of further loss while sustaining hope
10. Develop flexibility to ongoing psychosocial demands of illness
11. Learn to live with symptoms
12. Adapt to treatments and health-care settings
13. Establish functional collaborative relationship with health-care providers

Chronic Phase

1. Maximize autonomy for all family members given constraints of illness
2. Balance connectedness and separateness
3. Minimize relationship skews
4. Mindfulness to possible impact on current and future phases of family and individual life cycles

Terminal Phase

1. Completing process of anticipatory grief and unresolved family issues
2. Support the terminally ill member
3. Help survivors and dying members live as fully as possible with time remaining
4. Begin the family reorganization process

The New Genetics and An Extended Illness Timeline

New genetic technologies are enabling physicians to test for increased risk of developing a serious and life-threatening illness before it actually occurs. This means that individuals and families now can be living with illness risk information long before loved ones have developed symptoms of those illnesses (Miller et al., 2006). This significantly increases the amount of time and energy that families spend considering an illness and lengthens the illness timeline to include nonsymptomatic phases (Rolland and Williams, 2005). The nonsymptomatic phases are awareness, pretesting, test/post-testing, and long-term adaptation. These nonsymptomatic phases are distinguished by questions of uncertainty. Fundamental issues include the potential amount of genetic knowledge medically available, decisions about how much of that information various family members choose to access, and living with the psychosocial impact of those choices.

For some, the nonsymptomatic crisis phase begins when predictive testing becomes available, continuing through the decision to pursue testing and initial posttesting adaptation. For others, this phase begins as individuals reach significant developmental milestones and begin to consider testing. Sometimes, plans for having children raise fears of passing on a mutation and thus spark an interest in testing. Some women decide to be tested for hereditary breast and ovarian cancer genes when they reach an age that coincides with the age when another blood relative—a mother, aunt, or older sister—was diagnosed. During the posttesting phases, families need to accept the permanence of the genetic information and develop meanings that preserve their sense of competency in the face of future uncertainty or loss (Rolland, 2006a; Werner-Lin, 2008).

The involvement of the health-care system is very different with predictive testing than with a diagnosed illness. Despite the enormous psychosocial impact of positive testing results, families usually have limited contact with health professionals after initial testing. This highlights the need for ongoing, family-centered, collaborative approaches to prevent isolation, anxiety, and depression.

We can orient families to the value of prevention-oriented consultations at key future life-cycle transitions, when the experience of genetic risk will likely be heightened. Concerns about loss may surface that family members had postponed or thought were "worked through." It is vital to prepare family members that concerns about genetic risk and decisions about whether to pursue genetic testing will be more activated with upcoming transitions, such as launching young adults, marriage or partner commitments, or starting a family. Also, such feelings can be reactivated by critical events, such as genetic testing of another family member, diagnosis of a serious illness in immediate or extended families or friends, or death of a loved one. Clinicians can help family members decide about circumstances when further family discussion would be helpful, who would be appropriate to include, and how to discuss genetic risk with children or adolescents.

Clinical and Research Implications

This model provides a framework for clinical practice by facilitating an understanding of chronic illness and disability in psychosocial terms. Attention to features of onset, course, outcome, and incapacitation provides markers that focus clinical assessment and intervention with a family. For instance, acute-onset illnesses demand high levels of adaptability, problem solving, role reallocation, and balanced cohesion. In such circumstances, helping families to maximize flexibility enables them to adapt more successfully.

An illness time line delineates psychosocial developmental phases of an illness, each phase with its own salient developmental challenges. In particular, mastering initial crisis phase related tasks provides a foundation to successful adaptation over the long haul. Attention to time allows the clinician to assess family strengths and vulnerabilities in relation to the present and future phases of the illness.

The model clarifies treatment planning. Goal setting is guided by awareness of the aspects of family functioning most relevant to the particular type or phase of an illness. Sharing this information with the family and deciding on specific goals offers a better sense of control and realistic hope. This process empowers families in their journey of living with a chronic disorder. Also, it educates family members about warning signs to alert them to seek help at appropriate times for brief, goal-oriented treatment. The framework is useful for timing family psychosocial checkups to coincide with key transition points in the illness.

This framework can help in research design. The typology and time-phase framework can facilitate research aimed to sort out the relative importance of different psychosocial variables across a spectrum of chronic disorders. Particular "psychosocial types" of disorders can be considered crudely matched as to onset, course, outcome, incapacitation, and level of uncertainty. Specific typology variables can be utilized to analyze and compare individual and family dynamics related to different conditions over time. Time phases can facilitate a methodology for longitudinal studies. Multiple observations can be spaced at intervals that correspond to different time phases.

Multifamily psychoeducational or support groups and workshops for patients and their families (Gonzalez and Steinglass, 2002; McFarlane, 2002; Steinglass, 2011) provide cost-effective preventive services that decreases family isolation, increases networking, and can identify high-risk families. Multifamily groups can be designed to deal with different types of conditions (e.g. progressive, life-threatening, relapsing). Brief psychoeducational "modules," timed for critical phases of particular "types" of diseases, enable families to digest manageable portions of a long-term coping process. In time-limited (e.g. four session) or one-day formats, couples and families can increase coping skills and discuss common disease-related relationship challenges with others in similar situations. For instance, through the Chicago Center for Family Health, we have developed programs in partnership with local medical centers to help families dealing with diabetes and cystic fibrosis and, in collaboration with the MS Society, the Resilient Partners Program for couples living with multiple sclerosis.

Family Assessment

As chronic illnesses become incorporated into the family system and all its processes, coping is influenced by illness-oriented family dynamics that concern the dimension of time and belief systems.

Multigenerational Legacies of Illness, Loss, and Crisis

A family's current behavior, and therefore its response to illness, cannot be adequately understood apart from its history (Bowen, 1993; Byng-Hall, 1995; McGoldrick, Garcia-Preto, and Carter, 2010; Framo, 1992; Walsh, and McGoldrick, 2004). Clinicians can use historical questioning and construct a basic genogram and timeline (McGoldrick, Gerson, and Petry, 2007) to track nodal events and transitions to gain an understanding of a family's organizational shifts and coping strategies as a system in response to past stressors, and, more specifically, to past illnesses. Such inquiry helps explain and predict the family's current style of coping, adaptation, and meaning-making. A multigenerational assessment helps to clarify areas of strength and vulnerability. It also identifies high-risk families burdened by past unresolved issues and dysfunctional patterns that cannot absorb the challenges presented by a serious condition.

A chronic illness-oriented genogram focuses on how a family organized itself and adapted as an evolving system around previous illnesses and unexpected crises. A central goal is to bring to light areas of consensus and "learned differences" (Penn, 1983) that are sources of cohesion, resilience, and potential conflict. Patterns of coping, replications, shifts in relationships (e.g. alliances, triangles, cutoff), and sense of competence are noted. These patterns can be transmitted across generations as family pride, myths, taboos, catastrophic expectations, and belief systems (Seaburn, Lorenz, and Kaplan, 1992; Walsh and McGoldrick, 2004). In one case involving a couple where the husband was diagnosed with basal cell carcinoma, the oncologist discussed a favorable prognosis. In spite of this reassurance, the wife believed her husband would die from this skin cancer. This resulted in increased marital discord and ultimately a couple's consultation. In the consultation interview, when asked about prior experiences with illness and loss, the wife revealed that her own father had died tragically of a misdiagnosed malignant melanoma. This woman had a catastrophic fear based on both sensitization to cancer (particularly related to the skin) and the possibility of human error by health professionals. Had the oncologist inquired about prior experiences at the time of diagnosis, earlier intervention could have been facilitated.

Also, it is useful to inquire about other forms of loss (e.g. divorce, migration), crisis (e.g. job loss, traumatic event), and protracted adversity (e.g. poverty, racism, war, political oppression). These experiences can provide transferable sources of resilience and effective coping skills in the face of a serious health problem (Walsh, 2006). Clinicians need to ask specifically about positive family-of-origin experiences with illness and loss that can serve as models to adapt to the current situation.

Illness Type and Time-Phase Issues

A family may have certain standard ways of coping with any illness, but there may be critical differences in their styles and success in adaptation to different "types" of diseases. It is important to track prior family illnesses for areas of perceived competence, failures, or inexperience. Inquiry about different illness types may find, for instance, that a family dealt successfully with non-life-threatening illnesses, but reeled under the weight of metastatic cancer. Such families might be well equipped to deal with less severe conditions but be particularly vulnerable if another life-threatening illness were to occur. Some families may lack familiarity with chronic illness. The following case consultation highlights the importance of family history in uncovering areas of inexperience.

Case Example

Joe, his wife Ann, and their three teenage children presented for a family evaluation ten months after Joe's diagnosis with severe asthma. Joe, 44 years old, had been successfully employed for many years as a spray painter. Apparently, exposure to a new chemical triggered the onset of asthmatic attacks that necessitated hospitalization and occupational disability. Although somewhat improved, he continued to have persistent, moderately severe respiratory symptoms. Initially, his physicians had predicted that improvement would occur, but remained noncommittal as to the level of chronicity to be expected. Continued breathing difficulties contributed to increased symptoms of depression, uncharacteristic temperamental outbursts, alcohol abuse, family discord, and finally admission to an alcohol detoxification unit. In the initial assessment, after his discharge to outpatient psychiatric treatment, the psychiatrist inquired as to the family's prior illness experience. This was the nuclear family's first encounter with chronic illness, and their families of origin had limited experience. Ann's father had died seven years earlier of a sudden and unexpected heart attack. Joe's brother had died in an accidental drowning. Neither had experience with disease as an ongoing process. Joe had assumed that improvement, meant "cure." In addition, Joe had a history of alcoholism that had been in remission for twenty years. Illness for both Joe and his wife had meant either death or recovery. The physician/family system was not attuned to the hidden risks for this family coping with the transition from the crisis to the chronic phase of his asthma, the juncture where the permanency of the disease needed to be addressed.

Tracking a family's coping capabilities in the crisis, chronic, and terminal phases of previous chronic illnesses highlights legacies of strength as well as complications in adaptation related to different points over the course of the illness. One man grew up with a partially disabled father with heart disease and witnessed his parents' successful renegotiation of traditional gender-defined roles when his mother went to work while his father assumed household responsibilities. This man, now with heart disease himself, has a positive legacy about gender roles from his family of origin that facilitated a flexible response to his own illness.

Another family with a member suffering from chronic kidney failure functioned very well in handling the practicalities of home dialysis. However, in the terminal phase, their limitations with emotional expression left a legacy of unresolved grief. Tracking prior illness experiences in terms of time phases helps clinicians see both the strengths and vulnerabilities of a family, which counterbalances the assignment of dysfunctional labels that emphasize only the difficult periods.

Although many families have healthy multigenerational family patterns of adaptation, any family may falter in the face of multiple disease and other major stressors that impact in a relatively short time. With progressive, disabling diseases or the concurrence of illnesses in several family members, a pragmatic approach that focuses on expanded or creative use of supports and resources outside the family is most productive.

Interweaving of the Illness, Individual and Family Development

A developmental lens provides a powerful way to construct a normative framework for serious illness. To place the unfolding of chronic disease into a developmental context, it is vital to understand the intertwining of three evolutionary threads: illness, individual, and family development.

Individual and Family Development

Concepts of human and family development have evolved from models that centered on a sequence and unfolding of phases to ones that are more varied, fluid, and multidimensional, consistent with contemporary individual and family life course trajectories (McGoldrick, Garcia-Preto, and Carter, 2010). Serious health conditions are one example of major, often unexpected, life challenges that can significantly alter the sequence and character of a family's and members' life course. For purposes of this discussion, life structure is a useful central concept for both family and individual development. "Life structure" refers to core elements (e.g. work, child-rearing, caregiving) of an individual's or family's life at any phase of the life cycle. Individual and family development have in common the notion of phases (each with its own developmental priorities) and are marked by the alternation of life structure–building/maintaining (stable) and life structure–changing (transitional) phases (Levinson, 1986). The primary goal of a building/maintaining phase is to form a life structure and enrich life within it based on the key choices an individual/family made during the preceding transition. Transition phases are more fluid, because previous individual, family, and illness life structures are reappraised in the face of new developmental challenges that may involve major changes rather than minor alterations.

At a macro level, the family life cycle can be viewed as oscillating between phases where family developmental tasks require intense bonding or relatively higher cohesion, as in early child-rearing, and phases such as families with adolescents, when the external family boundary is loosened, with increasing personal identity and autonomy (Combrinck-Graham, 1985). Ethnic and racial differences influence the specific cultural expression of these phases.

These unifying concepts provide a foundation for understanding the experience of chronic disorders. The life cycle contains alternating transition and life structure–building/maintaining phases and particular phases can be characterized as requiring greater or lesser degrees of family cohesion. Illness, individual, and family development each pose priorities and challenges that move through phases of being more or less in sync with each other.

Generally, serious disorders exert an inward cohesive pull on the family system. Analogous to the addition of a new family member, illness onset sets in motion an inside-the-family focused process of socialization to illness. Symptoms, loss of function, the demands of shifting or acquiring new illness-related roles, and the fears of further disability and/or death all push a family to focus inward.

The need for family cohesion varies enormously with different illness types and phases. The tendency for a disease to pull a family inward increases with the level of disability or risk of progression and death. Progressive diseases over time inherently require greater cohesion than constant-course illnesses. The ongoing new demands with illness progression keeps a family's energy focused inward, often impeding the development of other members. After an initial period of adaptation, a constant-course disease (without severe disability) permits a family to get back on track developmentally. Relapsing illnesses alternate between periods of drawing a family inward and times of release from immediate demands of disease. But, the on-call nature of many such illnesses keeps part of the family focus inward despite asymptomatic periods, hindering the natural flow between phases of development.

Diagnosis of a serious illness can precipitate a family transition in which one of the family's main tasks is to accommodate the anticipation of further loss and possibly untimely death. If illness onset coincides with launching or post-launching phases in family development, it can derail a family's natural momentum. For an affected young adult, it may require a heightened dependency and return to the family of origin for disease-related caregiving. The autonomy and individuation of parents and child can be jeopardized. Separate interests and priorities may be relinquished or put on hold. Family processes, as well as disease severity, will influence whether the family's reversion to a child-rearing-like structure is a temporary detour or a long-term reversal.

When disease onset coincides with a phase in family development requiring higher cohesion (e.g. early child-rearing), it can prolong this period. At worst, the family can become enmeshed and developmentally stuck. Alternatively, with chronic disorders, there is a risk of labeling enmeshment when the normative lengthening of developmental phases for child and family is disregarded. Often, families coping with a chronically ill child are tentative about giving more autonomy, not because of inherent family dysfunction, but, rather, because of anticipation of further loss coupled with a lack of preventive psychoeducation from professionals.

With major health conditions, previous norms concerning family organization may need greater flexibility. Enmeshment with blurred generational boundaries is overdiagnosed as family dysfunction. Yet the very real demands on older children and adolescents to assume more adult functions, in the interest of family well-being, need to be distinguished from rigid pathological descriptions of "parentified" children. For instance, when a parent develops a serious disorder during a child-rearing phase of development, a family's ability to stay on course is severely taxed. The impact is twofold: a new family burden is added to loss of parental functioning. To meet simultaneous child-rearing and caregiving needs, an older child or grandparent may need to assume parental responsibilities. These forms of family adaptation are appropriate if structural realignments are flexible, shared, and sensitive to competing age-related developmental needs. Strong extended kin networks facilitate family adaptation.

In clinical assessment, a basic question is: What is the fit between the psychosocial demands of a condition and family and individual life structures and developmental tasks at a particular point in the life cycle? How will this fit change as the course of the illness unfolds in relation to the family's and each member's development?

Systemically, at the time of diagnosis it is important to know the phase of the family life cycle and the stage of individual development of all family members. Chronic disease in one family member can profoundly affect developmental goals of another member. For instance, an infant disability can be a serious roadblock to parents' preconceived ideas about competent child-rearing, or a life-threatening illness in a young married adult can interfere with the well spouse's readiness to become a parent. Also, family members frequently adapt in varied ways. Each member's ability to adapt, and the rate at which he or she does so, is related to his or her own developmental phase and role in the family. When family members are in tune with each other's developmental processes, while promoting flexibility and alternative means to satisfy developmental needs, successful long-term adaptation is maximized.

When illness onset coincides with a transition in the individual or family life cycle, issues related to existing and anticipated loss are magnified. Transition periods are often characterized by upheaval, rethinking of prior commitments, and openness to change. Such times often hold a greater risk for the illness to become either embedded or ignored in planning for the next life phase. During a transition period, the process of thinking through future commitments can bring to the forefront family norms regarding loyalty through sacrifice and caregiving. The following example highlights this point.

Case Example

In one Latino family, the father, a factory worker and primary financial provider, had a heart attack. Dad's rehabilitation was uneventful, with appropriate lifestyle modifications, and a return to work. The family, including the oldest son, age 15, seemed relatively unaffected. Two years later, his father experienced a second more life-threatening heart attack and became totally disabled. His son, now 17, had dreams of going away to college. The specter of financial hardship and the perceived need for a "man in the family" created a serious dilemma for the son and the family, which surfaces with declining academic performance and alcohol abuse. There is a clash between developmental issues of individuation and the ongoing demands of a progressive, life-threatening type of heart disease on the family. Further, there is a resurgence of fears of loss fueled not only by the recurrence, but also its timing with a major developmental transition for the oldest son. The son may fear that if he were to move away, he might never see his father alive again. There was a clash between simultaneous transition periods: (1) the illness transition to a more disabling, progressive, and life-threatening course; (2) the son's individual transition to early adulthood with individuation, leaving home, and educational pursuits; and (3) the family developmental transition from the "living with teenagers" to "launching young adults" phase. It also illustrates the significance of the type of illness: one that was less incapacitating and life-threatening might have interfered less with individual and family developmental priorities. At the time of initial diagnosis, inquiry about anticipated major transitions over the next three to five years and discussing them in relation to the specific kind of heart disease and its related uncertainties would help avert a future crisis.

It is essential to situate these developmental issues in the context of cultural values, socioeconomic considerations, availability of family or community resources, and access to health-care. In many cultures, as in this Latino family, a strong emphasis on loyalty to family needs would normatively take priority over individual goals, especially with a major illness or disability.

Illness onset that coincides with a life structure–building/maintaining developmental phase presents a different challenge. These phases are characterized by living out choices made during the preceding transition. Relative to transition phases, family members try to protect their own and the family unit's current life structure. Milder conditions may require revision, but not a radical restructuring. A severe condition (e.g. traumatic brain injury) can force families into a more complete transition at a time when individual/family inertia is to preserve the momentum of a stable phase. To navigate this kind of crisis successfully, family adaptability often requires the ability to transform the entire life structure to a prolonged transitional state.

The timing of chronic illness in the life cycle can be normative (e.g. expectable in relation to chronological and social time) or non-normative (e.g. "off-time"). Chronic illness is considered a normally anticipated challenge in later adulthood, whereas its occurrence earlier is "out of phase" and developmentally more disruptive (Neugarten, 1976). For instance, chronic diseases that occur in the child-rearing phase can be more challenging because of their potential impact on family child-rearing responsibilities. The actual impact will depend on the "type" of illness and pre-illness family roles. Families with flexible gender-influenced rules about financial provision and child-rearing will tend to adjust better.

The concept of "out of phase" illnesses can be refined to highlight patterns of strain over time. Because diseases have an inward pull on most families, they are more disruptive to families in a launching children phase of development. If the particular illness is progressive, relapsing, increasingly incapacitating, and/or life-threatening, then the unfolding phases of the disease will be punctuated by numerous transitions. Under these conditions, a family will need to alter its life structure more frequently to accommodate shifting and increasing demands of the disease. This level of demand and uncertainty keeps the illness in the forefront of a family's consciousness, constantly impinging on its attempts to get back "in phase" developmentally.

Finally, the transition from the crisis to the chronic phase is the key juncture at which the intensity of the family's socialization to living with chronic disease is lessened. In this sense, it offers a window of opportunity for the family to reestablish or sometimes chart a "new normal" developmental course.

An overarching goal is to deal with the developmental demands of the illness without family members sacrificing their own or the family's development as a system over time. It is important to determine whose life plans were or might be canceled, postponed, or altered, and when plans put on hold and future developmental issues will be addressed. In this way, clinicians can anticipate developmental nodal points related to "autonomy within" versus "subjugation to" the condition. Family members can be helped to strike a healthier balance, with life plans that resolve feelings of guilt, over-responsibility, and hopelessness, and find family and external resources to enhance freedom both to pursue personal goals and to provide needed care for the ill member.

Health/Illness Belief System

When illness strikes, a primary developmental challenge for families is to create meaning for the illness experience that promotes a sense of mastery and competency (Kleinman, 1988; Rolland, 1994a, 1998; Wright, and Bell, 2009). Because serious illness is often experienced as a betrayal of our fundamental trust in our bodies and belief in our invulnerability (Kleinman, 1988), creating an empowering narrative can be a formidable task. Family health beliefs help us grapple with the existential dilemmas of our fear of death, our tendency to want to sustain our denial of death, and our attempts to reassert control when suffering and loss occur. They serve as a cognitive and interpersonal map guiding decisions and action, and provide a way to approach new and ambiguous situations for coherence in family life, facilitating continuity between past, present, and future (Antonovsky and Sourani, 1988; Reiss, 1981). Inquiry into and curiosity about family beliefs is perhaps the most powerful foundation for collaboration between families and health professionals (Rolland, 1998; Wright, and Bell, 2009). There is growing research evidence that family members' distress about a disease, such as cancer, can be more closely associated to perceived risk or appraisals of seriousness than objective characteristics of the disease (Franks and Roesch, 2006; Hurley et al, 2006; Thompson and Kyle, 2000).

In the initial crisis phase, it is valuable for clinicians to inquire about key family beliefs that shape the family's illness narrative and coping strategies. This inquiry includes tracking beliefs about (1) normality; (2) mind-body relationship, control, and mastery; (3) assumptions about what caused an illness and what will influence its course and outcome; (4) meanings attached by a family, ethnic group, religion, or the wider culture to symptoms (e.g. chronic pain; Griffith and Griffith, 1994, McGoldrick, Pearce, and Garcia-Preto, 2005), types of illnesses (e.g. life-threatening), or specific diseases (e.g. HIV/AIDS; Sontag, 2001); (5) multigenerational factors that have shaped a family's health beliefs; and (6) anticipated nodal points in illness, individual, and family development when health beliefs will likely be strained or need to shift. Clinicians should also assess the fit of health beliefs among family members as well as between the family and health-care system and the wider culture.

Beliefs about Normality

Family beliefs about what is normal or abnormal, and the importance members place on conformity and excellence in relation to the average family, have far-reaching implications for adaptation to chronic disorders. When family values allow having a "problem" without self-denigration it enables family members to seek outside help and yet maintain a positive identity. When families define help-seeking as weak and shameful, it undercuts this kind of resilience. With chronic disorders, in which problems are to be expected and the use of professionals and outside resources are necessary, a belief that pathologizes this normative process adds insult to injury.

Two excellent questions that can elicit these beliefs are, "How do you think other average families would deal with a similar situation to yours?" and, "How would families ideally cope with your situation?" Families with strong beliefs in high achievement and perfectionism may apply standards that are impossible to achieve. Particularly with untimely conditions that occur early in the life cycle, there are additional pressures to keep up with socially expectable developmental milestones of peers. The fact that life goals may take longer or need revision requires a flexible belief about what is normal and healthy. To effectively sustain hope, particularly with long-term adversity, families need to embrace a flexible definition of normality.

Mind-Body Relationships

Varied conceptualizations of the mind-body relationship have been the subject of discourse and debate for millennia. Traditional mental health theories and research endeavors have been pathology-based, emphasizing character traits or emotional states that affect body chemistry adversely. More recently, the public has been increasingly drawn to popular literature citing the importance of positive attitudes in healing, emphasizing the unity of mind and body. Clinicians must be mindful that families may be familiar with and open to positive attitudes as a powerful source of healing.

As clinicians assess family beliefs about illness, it is useful to distinguish beliefs about the mind as a logical, thinking process that can determine actions that may help in healing the body (e.g. seeking medical care, changing diet or activity patterns) from those of the mind as a source of thought or energy that can directly impact body physiology. These beliefs about mind and spirit often extend beyond the individual to include family, community, or a higher spiritual power. Anthropologists have found tremendous diversity in the role of family, community, God, or nature as a source of healing. Such beliefs are typically expressed in the form of rituals (Imber-Black, Roberts, and Whiting, 2003). In our society, for example, a family's religious community will often organize a prayer service to promote healing for an ill member. Clinicians can inquire about the role of spirituality in family life (Walsh, 2009), and family beliefs regarding healing rituals that are important expressions of these beliefs. Sometimes important family healing rituals conflict with hospital rules, leading to power struggles that alienate families and erode a functional collaborative relationship with the health-care team.

The Family's Sense of Mastery Facing Illness

It is vital to determine how a family defines mastery or control in general and in situations of illness (Taylor et al., 2000; Thompson and Kyle, 2000). Mastery is similar to the concept of health locus of control, which can be defined as the belief about influence over the course/outcome of an illness (Lefcourt, 1982). It is useful to distinguish whether a family's beliefs are based on the premise of internal control, external control by chance, or external control by powerful others.

Families with an internal locus of control believe they can affect the outcome of a situation. In illness, such families believe they have direct control of their health and have the power to recover from illness (Wallston, 2004). An external orientation entails a belief that outcomes are not contingent on the individual's or family's behavior. Families that view illness in terms of chance believe that illness occurs as a matter of luck and that fate determines recovery. Those who see health control as in the hands of powerful others view health professionals, God, or sometimes powerful family members, as exerting control over their bodies and illness course.

A family's beliefs about mastery strongly affect its relationship to an illness and to the health care system. Beliefs about control affect treatment adherence and a family's preferences about participation in their member's treatment. When families view disease course/outcome as a matter of chance, they tend to establish marginal relationships with health professionals and they may not adhere to treatment recommendations, largely because their belief system minimizes the importance of their own or the professional's impact on a disease process. Also, poor minority families too often receive inadequate care or lack access, leading to a fatalistic attitude and lack of engagement with health-care providers, who may not be trusted to help. Because any therapeutic relationship depends on a shared belief system about what is therapeutic, a workable accommodation among the patient, family, and health-care team in terms of these fundamental beliefs is essential. Families that feel misunderstood by health-care professionals are often reacting to a lack of joining at this basic value level.

A family may adhere to a different belief about control when dealing with biological issues as distinct from typical day-to-day issues. Therefore, it is important to inquire about: (1) a family's core values, (2) beliefs about control for serious illness, and (3) the specific disease. For instance, regardless of the actual severity or prognosis in a particular case, cancer may be equated with "death" or "no control" because of medical statistics, cultural myth, or prior family history. Alternatively, families may have enabling stories about a relative or friend, who in spite of cancer and a shortened lifespan, lived a "full" life centered on effectively prioritizing the quality of relationships and goals. Clinicians can highlight these positive narratives to help families counteract cultural beliefs that focus exclusively on control of biology as defining success.

The goodness of fit between family beliefs about mastery can vary depending on the illness phase. For some disorders, the crisis phase involves protracted care outside the family's direct control. This may be stressful for a family that prefers to tackle its own problems without outside control and "interference." The patient's return home may increase the workload but allow members to reassert more fully their competence and leadership. In contrast, a family guided more by a preference for external control by experts can expect greater difficulty when their family member returns home. Recognition of such normative differences in belief about control can guide an effective psychosocial treatment plan that affirms rather than disrespects core values.

In the terminal phase, a family may feel least in control of the biological course of the disease and the decision-making regarding the overall care of the dying member. Families with a strong belief about being involved in a member's health care may assert themselves more vigorously with health providers. Effective decision-making about the extent of heroic medical efforts requires a family–provider relationship that respects the family's basic beliefs (Lynn, Schuster, Wilkinson, and Simon, 2007).

Clinicians must be cautious about judging the relative usefulness of minimization versus direct confrontation with and acceptance of painful realities. Often both are needed. The healthy use of minimization, or selective focus on the positive, and timely uses of humor should be distinguished from denial. The skilled clinician can support both the usefulness of hope and the need for treatment to control the illness or a new complication. Families can be helped to confront denial and illness severity when there is hope that preventive action or medical treatment can affect the outcome, or when an illness is entering its terminal phase. Yet, to cope with an arduous, uncertain course, families often need simultaneously to acknowledge the condition while minimizing treatment risks or the likelihood of a poor outcome.

Family Beliefs about the Cause of an Illness

When a significant health problem arises, it is natural to wonder, "Why me (or us)?" and "Why now?" (Roesch and Weiner, 2001). We attempt to construct an explanation or story that helps organize our experience. With the limits of current medical knowledge, tremendous uncertainties persist about the relative importance of myriad factors, leaving individuals and families to make idiosyncratic attributions about what caused an illness. A family's causal beliefs need to be assessed separately from its beliefs about what can influence the outcome. Responses will generally reflect a combination of medical information and family mythology. Beliefs might include punishment for prior misdeeds (e.g. an affair), blame of a particular family member ("Your drinking made me sick!"), a sense of injustice ("Why am I being punished?"), genetics (e.g. cancer runs on one side of the family), negligence of the patient (e.g. careless driving) or of parents (e.g. sudden infant death syndrome), religious beliefs (punishment for sin), or simply bad luck.

Optimal family narratives respect the limits of scientific knowledge, affirm basic competency, and promote the flexible use of multiple biological and psychosocial, and spiritual healing strategies. In contrast, causal attributions that invoke blame, shame, or guilt are particularly important to uncover, as they can derail family coping and adaptation. With a life-threatening illness, a blamed family member may be held accountable if the patient dies. A husband who believes his drinking caused his wife's coronary and subsequent death may increase self-destructive drinking in his profound guilt. The following case vignette illustrates how self-blame may remain hidden and the importance of early inquiry.

Case Example

Lucy and Tom G., a young couple, have a child Susan, aged five, who is terminally ill with leukemia. The pediatric oncologist offered the parents the choice between an experimental treatment with a low probability of success or halting treatment. Tom's position was "Let's stop; enough is enough." Lucy, on the other hand, felt, "We must continue; we can't let her die." The couple could not reach an agreement and the physician was immobilized. He requested a consultation for the couple.

When the consultant asked, "What is your explanation of how your daughter got leukemia?" the critical story emerged. Tom basically saw it as bad luck. Lucy, however, had a very different belief. During her pregnancy with Susan, Lucy's father had a heart attack and died several months later from a second episode. Lucy experienced this as a time of great stress and grief, which she felt adversely affected Susan's intrauterine life. After Susan's birth by normal delivery, Lucy was still mourning the loss of her father and felt that this affected the quality of her bonding with Susan and led to a hidden depression in her infant. Further, Lucy had read research linking depression with a lowering of the effectiveness of the immune system, which could, in turn, decrease normal surveillance and clearing of cancer cells from the body. She believed this combination of factors caused her child's cancer and that if she had been a more competent mother, this never would have happened. Lucy said she had never told this story to anyone (including her husband), because no one had ever asked, and she was very ashamed. She had hoped for a cure, so that the whole issue could be resolved. She could not accept stopping treatment because, to her, it meant that Susan's death would then be her fault.

Belief System Adaptability

Because illnesses vary enormously in their responsiveness to psychosocial factors, both families and providers need to distinguish beliefs about their overall participation in a long-term disease process, beliefs about their ability to control the biological progression of an illness, and flexibility in applying these beliefs. Families' experience of competence or mastery depends on their grasp of these distinctions. Optimal family and provider narratives respect the limits of scientific knowledge, affirm basic competency, and promote the flexible use of multiple biological and psychosocial healing strategies.

A family's belief in their participation in the total illness process can be thought of as independent of whether a disease is stable, improving, or in a terminal phase. Sometimes, mastery and the attempt to control biological process coincide, as when a family tailors its behavior to help maintain the health of a member with cancer in remission. This might include changes in family roles, communication, diet, exercise, and balance between work and recreation. Optimally, when an ill family member loses remission and the family enters the terminal phase of the illness, participation as an expression of mastery is transformed to a successful process of letting go that eases suffering and allows palliative care to be provided (Lynn et al., 2007).

Families with flexible belief systems are more likely to experience death with a sense of equanimity rather than failure. The death of a patient whose long, debilitating illness has heavily burdened others can bring relief as well as sadness to family members. Relief over death, even when it ends patient suffering and family caregiving and financial burdens, can trigger guilt reactions that may be expressed as depression and family conflict. Clinicians need to help family members accept ambivalent feelings they may have about the death as natural, as well as often ending the suffering of a loved one.

Thus, flexibility within both the family and the health-care team is a key variable in optimal family functioning. Rather than linking mastery in a rigid way with biological outcome (survival or recovery) as the sole determinant of success, families can define control in a more "holistic" sense, with involvement and participation in the overall process as the main criteria defining success. This is analogous to the distinction between curing "the disease" and "healing the system." Psycho-social-spiritual healing may influence the course and outcome, but a positive disease outcome is not necessary for a family to feel successful. This flexible view of mastery permits the quality of relations within the family, or between the family and health-care professional, to become more central to criteria of success. The health-care provider's competence becomes valued from both a technical and caregiving perspective not solely linked to the biological course.

Ethnic, Spiritual, and Cultural Beliefs

Ethnic, racial, and spiritual beliefs and dominant cultural norms can strongly influence family values concerning health and illness (McGoldrick, Giordano, and Garcia-Preto, 2005; Rolland, 2006b; Walsh, 2009). Significant ethnic differences regarding health beliefs often emerge at the time of a major health crisis. Although American families are a continuum that frequently represents a blend of different ethnic, racial, and spiritual beliefs, health professionals need to be mindful of the diversity of belief systems of various subpopulations in their community, particularly as these are expressed in different health behavior patterns. Cultural norms vary in the definition of the appropriate "sick role" for the patient, the kind and degree of open communication about the disease, who should be included in the illness caregiving system (e.g. extended family, friends, professionals), who is the primary caretaker (most often wife/mother/daughter/daughter-in-law), and the kind of rituals viewed as normative at different illness phases (e.g. hospital bedside vigils, healing, and funeral rituals). This is especially true for racial minority groups (e.g. African-American, Asian, Hispanic) that experience discrimination or marginalization from Euro-American culture. Illness provides an opportunity to encourage role flexibility and shift from defining one female member as the caregiver to a collaborative caregiving team that includes male and female siblings/adult children.

Clinicians need to be mindful of these cultural differences among themselves, the patient, and the family in order to forge a workable alliance that can endure a long-term illness (Seaburn, Gunn, Mauksch, Gawinski, and Lorenz, 1996). Effective collaboration occurs when professionals explore and understand families' cultural and spiritual beliefs about illness and healing. Disregarding these issues can lead families to distance themselves from health-care providers and community resources—a major source of adherence issues and treatment failure. Sometimes, professionals may need flexibility to suspend their need to be "in charge." This requires an acceptance that patients, not physicians, retain final responsibility for decisions about their bodies.

Fit Among Health-Care Provider, Health System, and Family Beliefs

It is a common error to regard "the family" as a monolithic unit that feels, thinks, believes, and behaves as an undifferentiated whole. Clinicians should inquire both about the level of agreement and tolerance for differences among family members' beliefs and between the family and health-care system. Family beliefs that balance the need for consensus with diversity and innovation are optimal and maximize permissible options. If consensus is the rule, then individual differentiation implies disloyalty and deviance. If the guiding principle is "We can hold different viewpoints," then diversity is allowed. This is adaptive because it facilitates the use of novel and creative forms of problem solving that may be needed in a situation of protracted adversity, such as serious illness. Families need open communication and effective conflict resolution when members differ on major health-care/treatment decisions.

The same questions concerning beliefs asked of families are relevant to the health-care team:

1. What are health professionals' attitudes about theirs and the family's ability to influence the course/outcome of the disease?
2. How do they see the balance between their own and the family's participation in the treatment process?
3. If basic differences in beliefs about control exist, how can these differences be bridged?

Utmost sensitivity to family values is needed to forge a therapeutic alliance. Many breakdowns in relationships between "noncompliant" or marginal patients and their providers can be traced to natural disagreements at this basic level that were not addressed. Normative differences among family members' health beliefs may emerge into destructive conflicts during a health crisis, as in the following case.

Case Example

The consultation-liaison psychiatrist was called by the ICU (intensive care unit) head nurse to intervene with a patient and his mother, who were disrupting the unit because the mother insisted on staying at her son's bedside, despite customary rules limiting family visits to ten minutes. When Stavros, a first-generation Greek American, had been admitted for intractable angina, his mother wanted to keep a 24-hour bedside vigil in his hospital room, so she could tend to her son at any hour. His wife, Dana, from a Scandinavian family, greatly resented the "intrusive behavior" of her mother-in-law, who in turn criticized Dana's emotional "coldness" and relative lack of concern. Stavros felt caught between his mother and wife, and complained of increased symptoms.

In such situations, clinicians need to sort out normative cultural differences from pathological enmeshment. In this case, all concerned behaved according to their own cultural norms. In Greek culture, it is normal to maintain close ties to one's family of origin after marriage and expected that a mother would tend to her son in a health crisis. A son would be disloyal not to allow his mother that role. This sharply differs from the wife's northern European traditions. Each side pathologized the other, creating a conflictual triangle, with the patient caught in the middle. In this case, the psychiatrist needed to affirm multicultural differences, thereby promoting a transformation of process from blaming or demonizing to respectfully accommodating varied cultures. This facilitated a successful compromise between the rules of the ICU and culturally influenced health behaviors of the family.

It is common for differences in beliefs or attitude to erupt at any major life cycle or illness transition. For instance, in situations of severe disability or terminal illness, one member may want the patient to return home, whereas another prefers long-term hospitalization or transfer to an extended care facility. Because the primary caregiver role is typically assigned to the wife/mother, she is the one apt to bear most burdens in this regard. Anticipating the collision of gender-based beliefs about caregiving with the potentially overwhelming demands of home-based care for a dying family member can help families flexibly modify its rules and avert the risk of family caretaker overload, resentment, and deteriorating family relationships.

The murky boundary between the chronic and terminal phase highlights the potential for professionals' beliefs to collide with those of the family. Physicians can feel bound to a technological imperative that requires them to exhaust all possibilities at their disposal, regardless of the odds of success. Families may not know how to interpret continued life-saving efforts, assuming real hope where virtually none exists. Health-care professionals and institutions can collude in a pervasive societal wish to deny death as a natural process beyond technological control (Becker, 1973). Endless treatment can represent the medical team's inability to separate a general value placed on controlling diseases from their beliefs about participation in a patient's total care, which includes bio-psycho-social-spiritual well-being.

Conclusion

Facing the risks and burdens of chronic illness or disability, the most resilient families are able to harness their experience to improve the quality of life. Families can achieve a balance between accepting limits and promoting autonomy and connectedness. For conditions with long-range risks, including genomic disorders, families can maintain mastery in the face of uncertainty by enhancing the following capacities: acknowledge the possibility of loss, sustain hope, and build flexibility into both the family's and each member's life-cycle planning that conserves and adjusts major goals and helps circumvent the forces of uncertainty.

A serious illness provides an opportunity to confront catastrophic fears about loss. This can lead family members to develop a better appreciation and perspective on life that results in clearer priorities and closer relationships (Walsh, 2006). Seizing opportunities can replace procrastination for the "right moment" or passive waiting for the dreaded moment. Serious illness, by emphasizing life's fragility and preciousness, provides families with an opportunity to heal unresolved issues and develop more immediate, caring relationships. For illnesses in a more advanced stage, clinicians should help families emphasize quality of life by defining goals that are attainable more immediately and that enrich their everyday lives.

Finally, clinicians need to consider their own experiences and feelings about illness and loss (McDaniel, Hepworth, and Doherty, 1997). Awareness and ease with our own multigenerational and family history with illness and loss, our health beliefs, and our current developmental phase will enhance our ability to work effectively with families facing serious illness.

Living well with the strains and uncertainties of illness can be a monumental challenge. The Family Systems Illness Model offers a way to address this challenge and make the inevitable strains more manageable. Attending to the psychosocial demands of different kinds of conditions over time within a multigenerational, developmental, and belief system context can provide a strength-based framework—a common language that facilitates collaborative, creative problem solving and quality of life for families facing illness, disability, and loss.

References

Antonovsky, A., and Sourani, T. (1988). Family sense of coherence and family adaptation. *Journal of Marriage and the Family*, 50, 79–92.

Becker, E. (1973). *The denial of death*. New York: Free Press.

Blount, A. (1998). *Integrated primary care: The future of medical and mental health collaboration*. New York: Norton.

Boss, P. (1999). *Ambiguous loss: Learning to live with unresolved grief*. Boston: Harvard University Press.

Bowen, M. (1993). *Family therapy in clinical practice*. New York: Jason Aronson.

Byng-Hall, J. (1995). *Rewriting family scripts*. New York: Guilford Press.

Campbell, T. (2003). The effectiveness of family interventions for physical disorders. *Journal of Marital and Family Therapy*, 29(2), 263–81.

Carr, D., and Sringer, K. W. (2010). Advances in families and health research in the 21st century. *Journal of Marriage and the Family*, 72 (3), 743–61.

Combrinck-Graham, L. (1985). A developmental model for family systems. *Family Process*, 24, 139–50.

Doherty, W., and Baird, M. (1983). *Family therapy and family medicine: Towards the primary care of families*. New York: Guilford Press.

D'Onofrio, B. M., and Lahey, B. B. (2010). Biosocial influences on the family: A decade review. *Journal of Marriage and the Family*, 72 (3), 762–82.

Engel, G. L. (1977). The need for a new medical model: A challenge for biomedicine. *Science*, 196, 129–136.

Framo, J. (1992). *Family-of origin therapy: An intergenerational approach.* New York: Brunner/ Mazel.

Franks, H. M., and Roesch, S. C. (2006). Appraisals and coping in people living with cancer: A meta-analysis. *Psychooncology,* 15 (12), 1027–37.

Gonzalez, S., and Steinglass, P. (2002). Application of multifamily discussion groups in chronic medical disorders. In W. R. McFarlane (Ed.). *Multifamily groups in the treatment of severe psychiatric disorders* (pp. 315–40). New York: Guilford Press.

Griffith, J., and Griffith, M. (1994). *The body speaks.* New York: Basic Books.

Hartmann, M., Bazner, E, Wild, B, Eisler, I., and Herzog, W. (2010). Effects of interventions involving the family in the treatment of adult patients with chronic physical diseases: A meta-analysis. *Psychotherapeutics and Psychosomatics,* 79, 136–48.

Hurley K., Miller S. M., Rubin L., and Weinberg D. S. (2006). The individual facing genetic issues: Information processing, decision making, perception, and health-protective behaviors. In Miller S. M., McDaniel S. H., Rolland J. S., and Feetham S. L. (Eds). *Individuals, families, and the new era of genetics: Biopsychosocial perspectives.* New York: W. W. Norton.

Imber-Black, E., Roberts, J., and Whiting, R. (Eds) (2003). *Rituals in families and family therapy* (2nd Edition). New York: Norton.

Kleinman, A. (1988). *The illness narratives: Suffering, healing, and the human condition.* New York: Basic Books.

Law, D., and Crane, R. (2007). The influence of individual, marital, and family treatment on high utilizers of health care. *Journal of Marital and Family Therapy,* 29 (3), 353–63.

Lefcourt, H. M. (1982). *Locus of control* (2nd Edition). Hillsdale, NJ: Erlbaum.

Levinson, D. J. (1986). A conception of adult development. *American Psychologist,* 41, 3–13.

Lynn, J., Schuster, J. L., Wilkinson, A., and Simon, L. N. (2007). *Improving care for the end of life: A sourcebook for health-care managers and clinicians* (2nd Edition). New York, NY: Oxford University Press.

Martire, L., Lustig, A., Schulz, R., Miller, G., and Helgeson, V. (2004). Is it beneficial to involve a family member? A meta-analysis of psychosocial interventions in chronic illness. *Health Psychology,* 23, 599–611.

Matire, L., Schulz, R., Helgeson, V., Small, B., and Saghafi, E. (2010). Review and meta-analysis of couple-oriented interventions for chronic disease. *Annals of Behavioral Medicine,* 40(3), 325–42.

McDaniel, S., Campbell, T., Hepworth, J., and Lorenz, A. (2005). *Family-oriented primary care* (2nd Edition). New York: Springer.

McDaniel, S., Hepworth, J., and Doherty, W. (Eds) (2012, in press). *Medical family therapy: A biopsychosocial approach to families with health problems* (2nd Edition). New York: Basic Books.

—(Eds). (1997). *The shared experience of illness: Stories of patients, families, and their therapists.* New York: Basic Books.

McFarlane, W. F. (Ed.). (2002). *Multifamily groups in the treatment of severe psychiatric disorders.* New York: Guilford Press.

McGoldrick, M., Garcia-Preto, N., and Carter, B. (2010). *The expanded family life cycle: Individual, family and social perspectives* (4th Edition). New York: Allyn & Bacon.

McGoldrick, M., Gerson, R., and Petry, S. (2007). *Genograms in family assessment* (3rd Edition). New York: Norton.

McGoldrick, M., Pearce, J. K., and Garcia-Preto, N. (2005). *Ethnicity and family therapy* (3rd Edition). New York: Guilford Press.

Miller, S., McDaniel, S., Rolland, J., and Feetham, S. (Eds). (2006). *Individuals, families, and the new era of genetics: Biopsychosocial perspectives.* New York: Norton.

Moos, R. (ed.). (1984). *Coping with physical illness: Two new perspectives.* New York: Plenum Press.

Neugarten, B. (1976). Adaptation and the life cycle. *Counseling Psychologist*, 6(1), 16–20.

Olkin, R. (1999). *What psychotherapists should know about disability*. New York: Guilford Press.

Penn, P. (1983). Coalitions and binding interactions in families with chronic illness. *Family Systems Medicine*, 1(2), 16–25.

Reiss, D. (1981). *The family's construction of reality*. Cambridge, MA: Harvard University Press.

Roesch, S., and Weiner, B. (2001). A meta-analytic review of coping with illness: Do causal attributions matter. *Journal of Psychosomatic Research*, 50 (4), 205–19.

Rolland, J. S. (1984). Toward a psychosocial typology of chronic and life-threatening illness. *Family Systems Medicine*, 2, 245–63.

—(1987). Chronic illness and the life cycle: A conceptual framework. *Family Process*, 26(2), 203–21.

—(1990). Anticipatory loss: A family systems developmental framework. *Family Process*, 29(3), 229–44.

—(1994a). *Families, illness, and disability: An integrative treatment model*. New York: Basic Books.

—(1994b). In sickness and in health: The impact of illness on couples' relationships. *Journal of Marital and Family Therapy*, 20(4), 327–49.

—(1998). Beliefs and collaboration in illness: Evolution over time. *Families, Systems and Health*, 16(1/2), 7–27.

—(2002). Managing chronic illness. In M. Mengel, W. Holleman, and S. Fields (Eds), *Fundamentals of clinical practice: A textbook on the patient, doctor and society* (2nd Edition). New York: Plenum Press.

—(2004). Helping families with anticipatory loss and terminal illness. In F. Walsh, and M. McGoldrick (Eds), *Living beyond loss: Death in the family* (2nd Edition). New York: Norton.

—(2006a). Living with anticipatory loss in the new era of genetics: A life cycle perspective. In Miller, S., McDaniel, S., Rolland, J., and Feetham, S. (Eds). *Individuals, families, and the new era of genetics: Biopsychosocial perspectives*. New York: Norton.

—(2006b). Genetics, family systems, and multicultural influences. Families, Systems, and Health, 24 (4), 425–42.

Rolland, J. S., and Williams, J. K. (2005). Toward a biopsychosocial model for 21st century genetics. *Family Process*, 44 (1), 3–24.

Seaburn, D., Gunn, W., Mauksch, L., Gawinski, A., and Lorenz, A. (Eds). (1996). *Models of collaboration: A guide for mental health professionals working with physicians and health-care providers*. New York: Basic Books.

Seaburn, D., Lorenz, A., and Kaplan, D. (1992). The transgenerational development of chronic illness meanings. *Family Systems Medicine*, 10, 385–95.

Shields, C., Finley, M., Chawla, N., and Meadors, P. (2012). Couple and family interventions in health problems. *Journal of Marital & Family Therapy*, 38 (1), 265–81.

Sontag, S. (2001). *Illness as Metaphor and AIDS and its Metaphors*. Picador USA: Farrar, Straus, & Giroux.

Steinglass, P. (2011). Multiple family groups for adult cancer survivors and their families. *Family Process*, 50(3), 393–410.

Taylor, S., Kemeny, M., Reed, G., Bowers, J., and Gruenwald, T. (2000). Psychological resources, positive illusions, and health. *American Psychologist*, 55(1), 99–109.

Thompson, S., and Kyle, D. (2000). The role of perceived control in coping with the losses associated with chronic illness. In J. Harvey, and E. Miller (Eds), *Loss and trauma: General and close relationship perspectives*. Philadelphia: Brunner-Routledge.

Wallston, K. A. (2004). *Control and Health. In Norman Anderson (Ed.) Encyclopedia of Health & Behavior, Volume One*. Thousand Oaks, CA: Sage Publications. 217–20.

Walsh, F. (2006). *Strengthening family resilience* (2nd Edition). New York: Guilford Press.

—(Ed.). (2009). *Spiritual resources in family therapy* (2nd Edition). New York: Guilford Press.

Walsh, F., and McGoldrick, M. (Eds). (2004). *Living beyond loss: Death in the family*. New York: Norton.

Weihs, K. Fisher, L., and Baird, M. (2001). Families, health, and behavior. Commissioned report: Institute of Medicine, National Academy of Sciences. Washington, DC: National Academy Press.

Werner-Lin, A. (2008). Beating the biological clock: The compressed family life cycle of young women with BRCA gene alterations. *Social Work in Health Care*, 47 (4), 416–37.

Wood, B. L., Lim, J., Miller, B., Cheah, P., Zwetsch, T., Ramesh, S., Simmens, S. (2008). Testing the biobehavioral model in pediatric asthma: Pathways of effect. *Family Process*, 47 (1), 21–40.

Wright, L. M., and Bell, J. (2009). *Beliefs and Illness: A model for healing*. Calgary, AB: 4th Floor Press.

Part II

Involvement of the Family in the Health-Care System

Overview of Part II

Chapter 4: Family-Centered Care

This chapter describes family-centered care and introduces the work of the Institute of Patient Family Centered Care (PFCC) (www.ipfcc.org). The PFCC provides on-site consultation, training, and technical assistance to hospitals, health systems, and other organizations and agencies for all phases of implementing a patient- and family-centered approach to care. A key element in family-centered care is the recognition of the health care needs of family caregivers. The American College of Physicians has established guidelines for collaboration between physicians and family caregivers. The American Psychological Association has developed a "Caregiver Briefcase" with sections on practice, research, and advocacy. Barriers to PFCC are reviewed under the headings of attitude, education, and organization. A case example concludes this chapter.

Chapter 5: Behavioral Interventions for Disruptive Family Situations in the Medical Setting

This chapter is written by Nora Cavelli, a psychiatric nurse on the psychosomatic medicine service at the University of Colorado Hospital. She refines behavioral interventions that have traditionally been used in psychiatric settings and applies them to the medical setting. She encourages staff to seek solutions by turning "concerns about disruptive behaviors" into "behavioral expectations." She provides the multidisciplinary team with a constructive way to think about disruptive behavior, a method of managing disruptive behavior that results in continued best practice and the containment of challenging family situations in the medical setting. This chapter is illustrated with case examples and descriptions of behavior care plans.

Chapter 6: The Caregiver's Perspective

Families experience caregiving in ways that are specific to their culture and ethnicity. African-American, Mexican-American, Asian-American caregiving perspectives are described in this chapter. Evidence-based caregiver interventions across the life cycle are reviewed: caregiving for children, adolescents, spouses, elderly, and caregiving at the end of life. A discussion of palliative care practice is included, with a special section on working with children of a dying family member. A brief discussion of screening tools is included at the end of the chapter.

Chapter 7: Parenting with Chronic and Life-Threatening Illness: A Parent Guidance Model

This chapter is authored by Drs Ellen O'Donnell, Kamryn Eddy and Paula Rauch and highlights The Marjorie E. Korff PACT (Parenting at a Challenging Time) Program. This program was founded and developed by Dr Paula Rauch, at Massachusetts General Hospital (www.mghpact.org) in 1997. This unique parenting program addresses common challenges and needs of parents with cancer. In this chapter, typical child developmental stages are reviewed and the authors provide clinicians with age-appropriate strategies for communicating with children about illness. Ways that clinicians can support patients and families with children are outlined. This chapter concludes by pointing out the need for clinician self-care.

4   Family-Centered Care

- Family-centered care means an organizational shift in the delivery of health care.
- Safety is enhanced by involving the family in patient care.
- Family-centered care acknowledges the needs of family caregivers.
- Physician ethical guidelines exist for involving the family caregiver.
- Attitudinal, organization, and educational barriers to the implementation of family-centered care exist.

Introduction

The Institute of Medicine's report, Crossing the Quality Chasm: A New Health Care System for the 21st Century (2001), advocates for family involvement. "The health care system should make information available to patients and their families that allows them to make informed decisions when selecting a health plan, hospital, or clinical practice, or choosing among alternative treatments" (2001, page 62). Decision-making and choice regarding the treatment plan must be clearly explained to the patient and family and communication framed as "a collaborative conversation."

This chapter focuses on the benefits of family-centered care and provides examples of how to make systemic organizational changes within the health-care system. A patient and family-centered approach to health care represents an organizational shift in health care from a paternalistic model of health care to an egalitarian model that shares decision-making with patients and families. This chapter reviews the core principles of family-centered care, discusses improving patient safety by working with the family, and how to communicate with the family within Health Information Portability Privacy Act (HIPPA) regulations. Caregiver needs must be acknowledged and the American College of Physicians has created ethical guidelines for working with patients and their families. Lastly, a case example illustrates the difficulties of a caregiver's experience in the current health care environment.

Patient and Family-Centered Care

PFCC is an approach to health care that shapes policies, programs, facility design, and staff day-to-day interactions. PFCC is an approach to the planning, delivery, and evaluation of health care that is based on partnerships among health-care providers, patients, and families. The Institute for PFCC, a non-profit organization founded in 1992 is a valuable resource for policy makers, administrators, program planners, direct service providers, educators, design professionals, and patient and family leaders (http://www. ipfcc.org). The Institute offers a wide variety of free downloadable PDFs that can help with the implementation of change, such as "Advancing the Practice of Patient and Family-Centered Care: How to Get Started."

What does Patient and Family-Centered Care look like in Hospital Practice?

Family-centered care (FCC) began in the 1980s, first in children's hospitals and pediatric units and then cancer units, maternity departments, mental health facilities and lastly in general hospitals. The presence and participation of family members and friends as care partners saves money, enhances the patient and family experience of care, improves management of illnesses, enhances continuity of care, and prevents hospital readmissions (Boudreaux, Francis, and Loyacono, 2002; Brumbaugh and Sodomka, 2009; Chow, 1999; Davidson et al., 2007; Edgman-Levitan, 2003; Fumagalli et al., 2006; Garrouste-Orgeas, 2008; Halm, 2005; Lewandowski, 1994; Sodomka et al., 2006).

Hospitals can be designed to accommodate families. Waiting rooms can be adapted to seat family members of different sizes and ages, be equipped with tablet armchairs to facilitate laptop computers and be kid friendly. Patient rooms can include family-friendly amenities and give family members privacy by providing a partial partition or alcove. A sleep center can be set up. Family members need access to spaces away from patients such as lounges and family rooms. As the nation's population continues to diversify, hospitals need to make accommodations for cultural and religious differences, for example, creating prayer space and meditation rooms. Resource libraries accessible to visiting family members can help them learn more about the patient's disease and how to care for them at home.

PFCC has been implemented in several health care systems. The following abbreviated descriptions are taken from the PFCC website (www.ipfcc.org).

The Medical College of Georgia (MCG) Health System in Augusta, Georgia.

Patient and family-centered values are defined in the organization's strategic plan. The human resources department ensures that new staff possesses attitudes and skills consistent with patient and family-centered care. Behaviors for customer service and for patient and family-centered care are defined, and included in position descriptions and performance reviews. Over 125 patient and family advisors serve on the patient and family advisory council for all adult clinical programs, including the Patient Safety and Medicine Reconciliation Committee. The quality improvement data for The Medical College of Georgia (MCG)'s Neuroscience Center of Excellence adult inpatient unit improved after the implementation of PFCC (Sodomka et al., 2006).

QI from MCG's Neuroscience Center in Augusta Georgia

- Patient satisfaction scores rose from the 10th to the 95th percentile
- Length of stay in the neurosurgical unit decreased by 50%
- Medical error rate fell by 62%

- Discharges (volume) increased by 15.5%
- The nursing staff vacancy rate fell from 7.5% to 0%, with a waiting list of five registered nurses (RNs)
- Positive change in perceptions of the unit by faculty, staff, house staff

Cincinnati Children's Hospital Medical Center

Patient and family members are present on the Family Advisory Committee, on quality improvement teams, on hospital-wide teams and unit-based committees and task forces. Families are no longer viewed as visitors, and units are open 24/7. On many units, families are encouraged to be present for rounds and given choices about how they would like to participate. These patient and family-centered rounds are linked with the patient's discharge goals. The charge nurse and bedside nurse participate in rounds and ensure that discharge goals are printed out daily and available for the patient and family. Physician orders are written on a laptop in the patient's room during rounds. Residents review orders out loud so that everyone, including the patient and family, can hear them and verify accuracy.

QI data at Cincinnati's Children's Hospital Medical Center

- Patients discharged sooner
- Medical order entry error rates have been reduced from 7–9% to 1%
- Faculty report that PFCC rounds are a more effective way to teach
- Families are involved in decision-making

Dana-Farber Cancer Institute (DFCI), Brigham and Women's Hospital, and Massachusetts General Hospital

At Dana-Farber/Partners CancerCare Program, patients and families were asked to envision the ideal experience for cancer care. They participated in the development of tools to measure patient perceptions of and satisfaction with care and in efforts to improve patient safety. DFCI has an Adult and a Pediatric Patient and Family Advisory Council and at least one Council member participates on almost every management and operating committee at the Institute. As a result, Council members have the opportunity to gain first-hand familiarity with DFCI's broad scope of operations. These changes were implemented after a fatal chemotherapy overdose.

The DFCI Family Councils' Accomplishments

- Revamped the process by which patients are admitted to and move through the Emergency Department
- Established a central office and support staff to support the Council, and a phone line for patients and families to access the Council
- Worked on passage of the Massachusetts Pediatric Palliative Care Bill
- Worked to reduce waiting times in clinics and infusion centers

- Developed an end-of-treatment transition program in pediatric oncology which has been widely implemented and expanded to adult care
- Participated in the planning of renovations for all inpatient, ambulatory, radiology, and radiation therapy areas
- Published articles in the hospital bi-weekly newsletter, and the quarterly newsletters by patients and families for patients and families and the hospital community
- Rounding on inpatient and outpatient care units
- Participated in the implementation of a family participation in rescue events policy

The University of Washington Medical Center, Seattle

A Patient and Family-Centered Steering Committee was developed. The Committee reported to the Chief Nursing Officer. Following initial training and technical support on how to create partnerships with patients and families, the Medical Center created Patient and Family Advisory Councils for three clinical areas—Rehabilitation, Oncology, and Perinatal Care.

Maine Medical Center, Portland

A Strategic Initiative Alignment Team was developed and included a family advisor. The Volunteer Services Department collaborated with clinical and administrative leaders to recruit, train, and support patient and family advisors to serve on teams for specific clinical areas. Progress and the tracking of outcomes are built into the strategic planning process and monitored by hospital senior leadership.

Initial success then failure

Concord Hospital, New Hampshire

Patient and family members were included on an interdisciplinary team to implement initiatives in its adult cardiac surgery program. Family-centered rounds featured a struc-tured way for reviewing the patient's care over the previous 24 hours, for planning care for the next 24 hours, and for openly discussing and tracking "glitches" in care. Data from the program during this time period showed improvements in clinical outcomes, patient satisfaction, and staff satisfaction (Uhlig, Brown, Nason, Camelio, and Kendall, 2002). Despite positive outcomes, the changes were not sustained. Creating ongoing, sustainable partnerships with patients and families requires profound changes in organi-zational culture and leadership behaviors. Creating such partnerships produce benefits but also causes tension within the organization. Individual practitioners struggle to adopt the new practices, which may be accepted in varying degrees. Senior leaders must be able and willing to promote and maintain interdisciplinary collaboration, combined with partnerships with patients and families in order to sustain change.

Boston Medical Center

A Parents as Partners Program was created to advance the practice of family-centered care and to support the involvement of families in quality improvement efforts. A staff liaison position was created at the departmental level, and a member of the community whose children received care in the hospital was appointed to it. Parents became involved in advisory roles and helped develop and staff a variety of innovative programs. Parent advisors tackled issues such as reducing the number of unkept appointments, developing programs to encourage father involvement in their children's health care and development, and enhancing family-centered, culturally competent communication skills for medical students and residents. Despite initial success, the central department-wide coordination was eliminated in 2002 because of fiscal pressures. Since that time there has been no central coordinator and no unified means for recruiting, training, and supporting family advisors. Since the disbanding of the central program, patient satisfaction scores, which increased dramatically following the introduction of the centralized program, have fallen. Experiences at other similar institutions indicate that the presence of the central coordinator is key factor in maintaining change. Having a designated staff liaison for collaborative endeavors facilitates the ongoing, effective participation of patient and family advisors.

Specific Examples of Family Participation in Patient Care

Bedside Rounds

Family-centered rounds is a model of communicating and learning between the patient, family, medical professionals, and students that occurs at the bedside, on an inpatient ward. Family-centered rounding helps to develop a unified care plan (Sisterhen, Blaszak, Wood, and Smith, 2007). Families want to participate in ward rounds, especially family members of special populations such as neonates and infants, those with cognitive impairment, and patients whose severity of illness or disability limits their understanding and participation. Teams must be sensitive and flexible to each family's unique situation and needs, and ask for permission to round at bedside. Family-centered rounds are a planned, purposeful interaction that requires the permission of patients and families as well as the cooperation of physicians, nurses, and ancillary staff.

Families in the Neonatal intensive care unit (NICU)

Parental involvement in neonatal care is a key part of a family-centered care model. Helen Harrison (1993), who introduced the principles of FCC to the NICU, outlined family-centered principles that include the maximum involvement of families, allowing parents to stay with their infant, the promotion of parenting skills and encouraging contact with support groups after discharge. Several studies support parental involvement in the care of the hospitalized infant (Gooding et al., 2011). Mothers who participate in the Creating Opportunities for Family Empowerment program (an educational-behavioral program about how to engage with and care for their hospitalized infant), are less stressed than mothers who did not participate in the program. In addition, infant length of stay is reduced with family involvement, by 5.3 days, according to Örtenstrand, Westrup, and Broström (2010) and by 4 days, according to Melnyk et al., 2006, Melnyk and Feinstein, 2009.

Respect in neonatal care means respect for the presence of non-traditional families, such as blended families, unmarried couples, and gay and lesbian families. When parents see themselves as a unit, and are seen by others as one unit, then their view of their parenting is as a joint project (Ellberg, Högberg, and Lindh 2010). Nurses have a very important role in helping parents assess infant behavior and respond in a developmentally supportive manner (Griffin, 2006).

New parents feel more at ease helping to care for their infant in the NICU when a Family Support Specialist is present (Cooper et al., 2007). New parents report less stress and higher parenting confidence when aided by a family support specialist. New mothers of very preterm infants who received peer support through a "buddy" program experienced less anxiety, less depression, and greater social support than mothers who did not participate in the peer support program (Preyde and Ardal, 2003).

This benefit is extended when siblings are allowed to visit. A higher number of sibling visits is associated with fewer behavior problems and decreased aggressive and regressive behavior in the siblings (Ballard, Maloney, and Shank 1984). A greater sense of family unity also occurs (Montgomery, Kleiber, Nicholson, and Craft-Rosenberg, 1997.)

Skin-to-skin contact between parent and child is an FCC-related practice with strong evidence of impact on infant health. Increased skin-to-skin contact is associated with fewer apneic episodes (Cleary, Spinner, Gibson, and Greenspan, 1997), increased sleep time (Graven and Graven, 2008), increased maturation rate of the circadian system (Feldman and Eidelman, 2002), production of more regular heart rate (Aucott, Donohue, Atkins, and Allen, 2002), and reduced infection frequency (Ludington-Hoe 2003). There are also reports of a lower prevalence of moderate-to-severe bronchopulmonary dysplasia in the infants whose parents had unlimited access, compared to controls, supporting the role of parental involvement in reducing infant morbidity (Örtenstrand et al., 2010).

FCC programs also result in families who are more satisfied with overall care, including positive communication between physician and parents, regardless of the severity of a neonatal adverse outcome, making parents feel that their opinions are being respected and providing them with more opportunities to become involved in their child's care (Gooding et al., 2011). Hospital administrators where NICUs have a designated March of Dimes NICU Family Support staff person report greater ability to recruit and retain NICU staff (Gooding et al., 2011).

Family Presence During Resuscitation

Family presence during resuscitation began in 1982, in Foote Hospital in Jackson, Michigan. Allowing family members to be present during certain periods of resuscitation efforts helps families cope with unsuccessful resuscitation (York, 2004). When there was a positive outcome, family members felt their presence benefited the patient and they all gained a better understanding of the situation. Conversely, family members who were not present commented that they would have preferred to have been present during resuscitation (Pasquale, Pasquale, Baga, Eid, and Leske, 2010).

Allowing family members to be present during resuscitation must be preceded by staff education and follow an established protocol. A pilot study can identify issues that need to be addressed early in the implementation phase. An allocated area designed specifically for family members of patients being resuscitated needs to be within close proximity of unfolding events. A private, comfortable room with a phone line and seating for large families should be close to where the resuscitation is occurring.

A recommended protocol is as follows: Families should be involved as early as possible during the resuscitation process. Consent of the attending physician should be obtained. Next, the family facilitator should communicate with the family and assess for the patient's and/or family's wishes concerning family presence. If the family wishes to be present, the responsibilities of the family facilitator include preparing them for what they may see and hear in the resuscitation room, describing any procedures that may be performed, and explaining that they may be asked to leave the room during certain procedures. Families should be encouraged by the family facilitator to ask questions, stand close to the bed, and touch, and speak to their loved one. The family facilitator should remain in close proximity to family members, providing support and encouragement, and answering questions during resuscitation efforts. If resuscitation is successful, family members should be allowed time with the patient. If resuscitation is unsuccessful, family members may still want time with their loved one. Inform families that a meeting with the family facilitator or pastoral care is available. When meeting with families, allow time for family members to ask questions and to express feelings.

Families in the Intensive Care Unit (ICU)

Shared decision-making is the FCC model of medical decision-making in the ICU. In shared decision-making, a partnership is formed with the ICU team, patient, and family. Through this partnership, patients' preferences are identified, the anxiety of families lessened, and physicians have appropriate input into decisions. In traditional settings, family members with a relative in ICU experience symptoms of depression (29.5%) and symptoms of anxiety (49%) (Garrouste-Orgeas et al., 2008). Families favor a 24-hour visitation policy, but this can be unsettling for staff. In a study in an ICU with a 24-hour visitation policy, where 115 ICU patients and their families were recruited, nurses perceived more disorganization of care than physicians ($p = .008$). The physicians reported greater family trust ($p = .0023$) but experienced greater unease when examining the patient ($p = .02$) (Garrouste-Orgeas et al., 2008).

Literature Review on the Impact of Inpatient FCC

A multidisciplinary task force of experts in critical care practice was convened to assess the impact of FCC. The task force members reviewed more than 300 articles from the literature between 1980 and 2003. The topics was divided into subheadings: decision-making, family coping, staff stress related to family interactions, cultural support, spiritual/religious support, family visitation, family presence on rounds, family presence at resuscitation, family environment of care, and palliative care. The level of evidence in most cases (Cochrane level 4 or 5), indicating the need for further research. Nevertheless, the task force recommended the use of a shared decision-making model, early and repeated care conferencing to reduce family stress and improve consistency in communication, honoring culturally appropriate requests for truth-telling and informed refusal, spiritual support, staff education and debriefing to minimize the impact of family interactions on staff health, family presence at both rounds and resuscitation, open flexible visitation, way-finding and family-friendly signage, and family support before, during, and after a death (Davidson et al., 2007).

The Outpatient Setting

The medical home is promoted throughout the US as a way to improve patient care in the outpatient setting. The American Academy of Family Physicians defines the medical home as: "a patient-centered medical home integrates patients as active participants in their own health and well-being." (http://www.aafp.org/online/en/home/policy/policies/p/patientcenteredmedhome.html). Families contribute to the medical home especially when care involves children, adolescents and the elderly. Many family members come to outpatient appointments and want to participate in patient care. Families come with strong opinions about health care and have usually looked online for health information (Fox and Jones, 2009). Often this information is conflicting and confusing for patients and their family members. Sites, including "Patients Like Me" (http://www.patientslikeme.com), help individuals or families connect to others in search of support or information. The Internet can also be used to help families provide input into a treatment plan. Members of the care team can help families sort through this information.

Using the Internet to help integrate families into health-care decision-making has been tried with asthma. "TLC-Asthma," is a telephone-linked communications system used at Boston University Medical Center (Adams et al., 2003). The system uses automated telephone calls to monitor, educate, and counsel families. The system communicates with children or their parents using digitized human speech and they respond using the telephone keypad or by speaking into the receiver. Clinicians or family members can initiate calls into the system. The system was designed to maintain weekly contact with families and was found to be useful and worthwhile (Luo, Adams, Fuhlbrigge, and Friedman, 2005).

Families want information, dialogue with others, and some control over the medical decision-making process. In a study by Jackson, Cheater, & Reid (2008), information alone was inadequate to meet the needs of families who also needed emotional support and help with taking a role in the decision-making process. These needs transcended specific health conditions and are usually poorly met by clinicians.

Safety, the Patient and the Family in PFCC

Susan Sheridan, a health-care leader, described her vision of patient safety (Henriksen et al., 2008, page 26): "In 2025, patient-centered care will be viewed as a comprehensive continuum and will not cease when a medical error occurs or because of the perceived threat of liability; it will honor and respect the needs of the patients and their families who have been harmed. Disclosure, no longer optional in 2025, will be understood as simply the 'right thing to do' and as the cornerstone of patient-centeredness, not just a strategic maneuver. Disclosure and apology will be validated by compensation when appropriate and/or the implementation of sincere changes in policy and practice to prevent similar events in the future. Patients and families will be considered a valued source of input to policy and practice changes by being integrated into root cause analyses, accrediting surveys, and other investigations. Also, in the event of medical error, patients and family members will be able to report errors to a responsive, authoritative entity via a national consumer reporting system that assures accountability and systemic learning and improvement."

Leape, another advocate of patient and family involvement in the promotion of patient safety comments: "The family is respected as part of the care team—never visitors—in every area of the hospital, including the emergency department and the intensive care unit. Whether pursuing healthy living, as patients receiving care, or as future patients, individuals and their families must play a central role. The guiding principle is 'If health is on the table, then the patient and family must be at the table, every table, now' " (Leape et al., 2009, page 426).

Confidentiality, the Patient and the Family in PFCC

The government health-care policies, commonly referred to as HIPAA, are frequently misunderstood as restricting what information can be given to families. HIPAA stands for the Health Insurance Portability Accountability Act and is intended to protect patient information by setting rules for the use of health information. HIPAA is concerned with balancing the patient's right to privacy with public responsibility. To protect the public interest, HIPAA permits the release of certain types of patient information to the police department, state public health officials, or public agencies such as the Centers for Disease Control and Prevention (CDC). The important point for families is that HIPAA focuses on giving consumers more control over their care and supports patient and family involvement in the planning and delivery of care.

Patients and their families have the right to decide who will be involved in their care. They have the right to define "family." Problems occur when staff decides not to talk to family members "because of HIPAA." The following is extracted from the website of the US Department of Health and Human Services (http://www.hhs.gov/hipaafaq/notice/488.html) and provides guidance for health-care providers in family involvement in patient care.

> The HIPAA Privacy Rule at 45 CFR 164.510(b) specifically permits covered entities to share information that is directly relevant to the involvement of a spouse, family members, friends, or other persons identified by a patient, in the patient's care or payment for health care. If the patient is present, or is otherwise available prior to the disclosure, and has the capacity to make health-care decisions, the covered entity may discuss this information with the family and these other persons if the patient agrees or, when given the opportunity, does not object. The covered entity may also share relevant information with the family and these other persons if it can reasonably infer, based on professional judgment that the patient does not object. Under these circumstances, for example:

- A doctor may give information about a patient's mobility limitations to a friend driving the patient home from the hospital
- A hospital may discuss a patient's payment options with her adult daughter

- A doctor may instruct a patient's roommate about proper medicine dosage when she comes to pick up her friend from the hospital
- A physician may discuss a patient's treatment with the patient in the presence of a friend when the patient brings the friend to a medical appointment and asks if the friend can come into the treatment room

Even when the patient is not present or it is impracticable because of emergency circumstances or the patient's incapacity, a covered entity may share information with the person when, in exercising professional judgment, it determines that doing so would be in the best interest of the patient. See 45 CFR 164.510(b). Thus, for example:

- A surgeon may, if consistent with such professional judgment, inform a patient's spouse, who accompanied her husband to the emergency room, that the patient has suffered a heart attack and provide periodic updates on the patient's progress and prognosis
- A doctor may, if consistent with such professional judgment, discuss an incapacitated patient's condition with a family member over the phone

In addition, the Privacy Rule expressly permits a covered entity to use professional judgment and experience with common practice to make reasonable inferences about the patient's best interests in allowing another person to act on behalf of the patient to pick up a filled prescription, medical supplies, X-rays, or other similar forms of protected health information. For example, when a person comes to a pharmacy requesting to pick up a prescription on behalf of an individual he identifies by name, a pharmacist, based on professional judgment and experience with common practice, may allow the person to do so.

Acknowledging the Needs of Family Caregivers

In 2008, according to Suzanne Mintz, a cofounder of the National Family Caregiver's Association (NFCA), the estimated market value of the family caregivers' services was $375 billion annually with close to one third of the U.S. population providing care for a chronically ill, disabled or aged family member or friend during any given year and spending an average of 20 hours per week providing care for their loved one. Two thirds of caregivers are women and 13% of family caregivers are providing 40 hours of care a week or more. (http://www.thefamilycaregiver.org/who_are_family_caregivers/ care_giving_statstics.cfm, retrieved July 2011.)

Of special note, there are 1.3 to 1.4 million child caregivers nationwide (National Alliance of Caregiving, retrieved May 2012, http://www.caregiving.org/). In 2003, the first national survey of child caregivers in the United States revealed that 72% are caring for their mother or grandparent. The most common care recipient conditions are Alzheimer's disease or dementia, disease of the heart, lung, or kidneys, arthritis and diabetes. The child caregivers tend to live in households with lower incomes than non-caregivers.

In a study of child caregivers, 213 child caregivers and 250 non-caregiving children, aged 8 to 18 years' old, were interviewed by telephone, for approximately 12 minutes.

They were asked about the way they spend time, their self-perceptions and moods, and their school work and the experiences that differentiated them from their peers. Over half of the child caregivers help their care recipient with activities of daily living (ADLs), such as bathing, dressing, toileting, and feeding. Nearly all help with instrumental ADLs, such as shopping, household tasks and meal preparation. The most common activities reported are keeping the care recipient company (96%), helping with chores (85%), grocery shopping (65%) and meal preparation (63%). At least 75% of the child caregivers who help with any given task say that someone else helps also.

Child caregivers show more anxious or depressed behavior than non-caregivers, according to parents' reports, and to feel that no one loves them. Younger caregivers are more likely to complain that they feel worthless or inferior. Caregivers aged 12 to 18 are more likely to behave antisocially than non-caregivers of the same age especially getting along with teachers, bullying or acting mean towards others and associating with kids who get in trouble. Child caregivers are similar to their peers in terms of their views on relationships with others, their overall level of responsibility compared with non-caregivers and school problems. Nevertheless, some children report that their caregiving responsibilities affect their schoolwork or school activities. Boy caregivers are twice as likely to feel that it is "no use showing their feelings" and more likely to feel sad than are boys who are not caregivers. Positive effects of caregiving include caregivers' tendency to feel appreciated for help they give, they are less likely to feel people expect too much from them or to feel angry about all they have to do. Overall, child caregivers' feelings of self-esteem, sadness, loneliness, and fun are similar to those of non-caregivers.

Family caregivers face many physical, emotional and financial demands that make them vulnerable to stress-related conditions, both physical and psychological (see Chapter 5). Caregiving impacts caregivers' health, which, in turn, affects their ability to provide care. The Caregiver Health Effects Study demonstrated a strong link between caregiving and mortality risk, finding that elderly caregivers supporting disabled spouses at home were 63% more likely to die within four years than non-caregiving elderly spouses (Schultz and Beach, 1999). In addition, family caregivers often lack the time and energy to prepare their own meals, exercise, or engage in their own preventive medical care. Physicians must stress the importance of caregiver self-care for the benefit of both the caregiver and the patient and identify appropriate sources of community support services, such as home health aides, respite or adult day care. When a family caregiver is also a patient of the treating physician, the physician should focus on the needs of the caregiver as well as the needs of the patient.

The American Psychological Association (APA) has a "Caregiver Briefcase" that is available online (http://www.apa.org/pi/about/publications/caregivers/index.aspx). The briefcase contains caregiving facts, a practice section with common caregiver problems and interventions, and sections on research, education, and advocacy. The website and its contents are useful for family members as well as professionals. Services for adult caregivers are not appropriate for children, nor do agencies that typically deal with adult caregivers have experience working with children. Other countries such as the United Kingdom (http://www.nice.org.uk) have sophisticated services for children e.g. support groups, Internet chat groups, retreats, and summer camps.

The APA offers ways for family members to integrate into health-care teams. For example, electronic medical records can allow family members access to portions such as the patient's problem and medication lists and most recent laboratory findings. Family caregivers can provide ongoing, real-time observations about the patient through the portal, as well as share information about what it is like to be a family caregiver. Those secure messages become part of the patient's permanent medical record (Blueprint for Change: Achieving Integrated Health Care for an Aging Population, accessed May 2012, from   http://www.apa.org/pi/aging/programs/integrated/integrated-healthcare-report. pdf).

Ethics, Patient, Family and Physician Boundaries

Shifting patient decision-making to family members is a delicate negotiation between the patient's ability to make independent decisions and the family's desire to protect the patient from potentially poor decisions. At critical times, such as in the intensive care unit (ICU), or when a patient is dying, the family has to step up and assume decision-making responsibility for the patient. The family is more involved if the patient suffers from a comorbid psychiatric illness, delirium, dementia, or developmental disability.

To help physicians understand the ethics of this process, the American College of Physicians offers guidelines to help the physician know how best to collaborate with the patient and caregiver (Mitnick, Leffler and Hood, 2010). These guidelines are endorsed by ten medical professional societies: Society of General Internal Medicine, American Academy of Neurology, American Academy of Hospice and Palliative Medicine, American College of Chest Physicians, American College of Osteopathic Internists, the American Geriatrics Society, American Medical Directors Association, American Thoracic Society, Society of Critical Care Medicine and the Endocrine Society (see list below).

Ethical Guidelines for Collaboration with Family Caregivers

- Respect for the patient's dignity, rights and values should guide all patient-physician-caregiver interactions
- Physician accessibility and excellent communication are fundamental to supporting the patient and family caregiver
- Recognize the value of family caregivers as a source of continuity regarding the patient's medical and psychosocial history
- Facilitate end of life adjustments for the family
- Ensure appropriate boundaries when the caregiver is a health-care professional
- Do not expect the caregiver to function in a professional capacity
- Ensure the caregiver receives appropriate support, referrals and services

Family caregivers say that clear direct communication is their most pressing need (Auerbach et al., 2005). A physician's use of medical jargon and technical terminology can be confusing to family members (Rabow, Hauser, and Adams, 2004). The Alzheimer's Association conducted telephone interviews with 376 caregivers and 500 primary care physicians (PCPs) and found that physicians believed they provided far more information to caregivers than caregivers believed they received (http://www.alz.org/national/documents/report_communicationgap.pdf). In these interviews, caregivers underestimated their own information needs about the disease and its treatment and while PCPs were aware of what the caregivers should know, this information was not effectively communicated to the caregivers. This information gap included medication treatments and what to expect from them, how the disease affects the patient, how the disease progresses, how to manage abnormal behavior and how long the disease will last.

When patients and their caregivers disagree about treatment needs and preferences, the physician may find that they are expected to take sides, or at least help resolve the disagreement. The physician's first responsibility is to ensure that patient and caregiver have adequate information and a common shared understanding of the illness and expected outcome. If a patient wants care at home, the physician needs to make sure that the caregiver fully understands and agrees to what this care entails and be able and willing to provide such care. If the caregiver is unable to provide the care that the patient asks for, then the physician needs to help the family develop alternatives. These issues are more prominent at the end of life (Kaldjian, Curtis, Shinkunas, and Cannon, 2009).

Case example: Ms Stout and her Son, Paul

Ms Stout is a 58-year-old divorced mother of two. Her eldest son, Paul, aged 35, has cystic fibrosis and is the recipient of a lung transplant. He has several developmental delays and his comprehension of medico-legal documents becomes quite limited when he is medically ill and on narcotics. In the inpatient hospital setting, he does not retain information presented to him. His outpatient medical team is aware of this and includes his mother in all treatment decisions. However, in the hospital, the medical teams do not appreciate his limitations. They question the mother's continual presence and see her as "over involved and enmeshed with her adult son." Ms Stout says that she has to fight with each new physician team to get them to understand that they need to involve her in all her son's health-care decisions. The younger male physicians especially, identify with Paul.

Paul presents as a normal young man. He is handsome, agreeable, open, and friendly with the staff. Paul has limited social contacts outside of the hospital and because of his lengthy involvement in the hospital care system; he is comfortable in the hospital and especially enjoys his interaction with the female nurses. He understands basic procedures because they have been repeated so many times. However, he does not understand his complex health-care needs. Unless you specifically test his comprehension, his deficits are not recognized.

His mother knows all details of his history and is a better resource than the chart. She insists on being present at all times, despite the strain of her other commitments. Each time her son is admitted, she faces scrutiny and repeatedly has to explain herself and her son's limitations to each new physician. She finds this situation to be exhausting and humiliating. She does not understand why her presence cannot be accepted as helpful.

Conclusion

In developing countries, families are involved in the care of the patient out of necessity (Renshaw, 2009). Family members take care of patients, feed them, change them, and assist the nurses. Families stay in waiting rooms and sleep by the bedside. They provide reassurance, comfort to their sick relatives, and act as their advocates. In developed countries, families have been encouraged to give over the care of their sick relative to the doctors and nurses who are better educated and trained in medical diagnosis and treatment. In the nineteenth century, fear of infections prompted hospitals to discourage visitors. As the health of the general population has improved and the general public is more educated about basic hygiene, families can be invited back into health-care settings as health-care partners.

As more people develop chronic illnesses and have experiences as patients and caregivers, the pressure to involve family members increases. Where does the resistance to involve family members in patient care come from? There is an unfounded unspoken fear on the part of health professionals that families want something that the health-care provider cannot guarantee: that their relative "will get well and everything will be fine." Health-care providers may limit what they say to family members in order "not to upset them." The family members perceive that they are being brushed off and dismissed and as a result, they develop feelings of apprehension. A small upset or misunderstanding can then unleash the repressed feelings resulting in family members lashing out, most often at the nurses. When health-care teams include the family and develop collaborative relationships with families, the likelihood of this kind of conflict is reduced.

Resistance also comes from the perception that family involvement is not necessary for patient care. Many of the consequences of isolating the patient from their family are invisible in the hospital. For example, the consequences to the care of the neonate only become apparent after discharge, in the home setting. Education of all staff needs to include the invisible consequence to the patient when family caregivers are excluded.

Family caregivers also need preparation to join the medical team. If there is a single family spokesperson, it is easier to integrate the family into the treatment team. The list below summarizes the barriers to FCC.

Barriers to PFCC

Attitudinal Barriers

- Families will be unreasonable
- Families will compromise confidentiality
- Unaware of the research on the benefits of PFCC
- The belief that PFCC is time-consuming and costs too much

Educational Barriers

- Lack of skills for collaboration for professionals, administrators, patients and families
- Lack of knowledge of the benefits of patient and family-centered care

Organizational Barriers

- Lack of guiding vision
- Top-down approach with insufficient effort to build staff commitment
- Grass-roots effort that lacks leadership, commitment and support
- Scarce fiscal resources and competing priorities
- No funded coordinator

Future goals for FCC include setting up health information systems that allow families access to reliable health information, contact with their physician and ongoing family monitoring of chronic illnesses. All health-care providers must be better educated on the benefits of family-focused care. Health-care institutions need to continue to work on integrating families into the delivery of patient care. The intellectual support for PFCC is compelling. However, the change that has to occur in the hospital setting is extensive, sweeping, and challenging to implement.

References

Adams, W. G. et al. (2003). TLC-Asthma: an integrated information system for patient-centered monitoring, case management, and point-of-care decision support. *American Medical Informatics Association Annual Symposium Proceedings*, 1–5.

Alzheimer's Association. Alzheimer's Disease Study: Communication gaps between primary care physicians and caregivers. May 2001. Available at: http://www.alz.org/national/documents/alzheimerreport.pdf. Accessed 11 November 2009.

Aucott, S., Donohue, P. K., Atkins, E., and Allen, M. C. (2002). Neurodevelopmental care in the NICU. Mental Retardation and Developmental Disabilities, 8, 298–308.

Auerbach, S. M., Kiesler, D. J., Wartella, J., Rausch, S., Ward, K. R., and Ivatury, R. (2005). Optimism, satisfaction with needs met, interpersonal perceptions of the health-care team, and emotional distress in patients' family members during critical care hospitalization. *American Journal of Critical Care*,14, 202–10.

Ballard, J., Maloney, M., Shank, M. et al. (1984). Sibling visits to a newborn intensive care unit: implications for siblings, parents and infants. *Child Psychiatry and Human Development*, 14, 203–14.

Boudreaux, E. D., Francis, J. L., and Loyacono, T. (2002). Family presence during invasive procedures and resuscitations in the emergency department: A critical review and suggestions for future research. *Annals of Emergency Medicine*, 40(2), 193–205.

Brumbaugh, B., and Sodomka, P. (2009). Patient and family-centered care – The impact on patient safety and satisfaction: A comparison study of intensive care units at an academic medical center. Presented at the 4th International Conference on Patient and Family-Centered Care: Partnerships for Quality and Safety, Philadelphia, PA.

Chow, S. M. (1999). Challenging restricted visiting policies in critical care. *Canadian Association of Critical Care Nurses*, 10 (2), 24–7.

Cleary, G. M., Spinner, S. S., Gibson, E., and Greenspan, J. S. (1997). Skin-to-skin parental contact with fragile preterm infants. *Journal of American Osteopathic Association*, 97, 457–60.

Committee on Quality of Health Care in America 2001. *Crossing the quality chasm: a new health care system for the 21st century*. Washington DC: National Academy Press, 2001.

Cooper, L., Gooding, J., Gallagher, J. Sternesky, L., Ledsky, R., and Berns S.D. (2007). Impact of a family-centered care initiative on NICU care, staff and families. *Journal of Perinatology*, 27, S32–S37.

Curtis, J. R., White, D. B. (2008). Practical guidance for evidence-based ICU family conferences. Chest, 134(4), 835–43.

Davidson, J. *et al.* American College of Critical Care Medicine Task Force 2004–2005, Society of Critical Care Medicine. (2007). Clinical practice guidelines for support of the family in the patient-centered intensive care unit: American College of Critical Care Medicine Task Force 2004–2005. *Critical Care Medicine*, 35 (2), 605–22.

Edgman-Levitan, S. (2003). Healing partnerships: The importance of including family and friends. In S. B. Frampton, L. Gilpin, and P. A. Charmel (Eds). *Putting patients first: Designing and practicing patient-centered care*. San Francisco, CA: Wiley & Sons, Inc.

Ellberg, L., Högberg, U., and Lindh V. (2010). 'We feel like one, they see us as two': new parents' discontent with postnatal care. *Midwifery*, 26(4),463–8.

Feldman, R., and Eidelman, A. I. (2002). Skin-to skin contact accelerates autonomic and neurobehavioral maturation in preterm infants. *Developmental Medicine and Child Neurology*, 45, 274–81.

Fox, S., Jones, S. (2010). The social life of health information. The Pew Internet and Amerian Life Project 2009 from: http://pewinternet.org/Reports/2009/8-The-Social-Life-of-Health-Information.aspx.).

Fumagalli, S., Boncinelli, L., Lo Nostro, A., Valoti, P., Baldereschi, G., Di Bari, M. et al. (2006). Reduced cardiocirculatory complications with unrestrictive visiting policy in an intensive care unit: Results from a pilot, randomized trial. *Circulation*, 113, 946–52.

Garrouste-Orgeas, M. et al. (2008). Perceptions of a 24-hour visiting policy in the intensive care unit. *Critical Care Medicine*, 36(1), 30–5.

Gooding, J. S., Cooper, L. G., Blaine, A. I., Franck, L. S., Howse, J. L., and Berns, S. D. (2011). Family support and family-centered care in the neonatal intensive care unit: origins, advances, impact. Seminars in Perinatology, 35(1), 20–8.

Graven, S., and Graven, M. (2008). The full-term & premature newborn: Sound & the developing infant in the NICU: conclusions & recommendations for care. *Journal of Perinatology*, 20, S88-S93.

Griffin, T. (2006). Family-centered care in the NICU. *Journal of Perinatal Neonatal Nursing*, 20 (1), 98–102.

Halm, M. A. (2005). Family presence during resuscitation: A critical review of the literature. *American Journal of Critical Care*, 14(6), 494–511.

Harrison, H. (1993). The principles for family-centered neonatal care. *Pediatrics*, 92, 643–50.

Henriksen, K., Oppenheimer, C., Leape, L. L., Hamilton, K., Bates, D. W., Sheridan, S. et al. (2008). Envisioning Patient Safety in the Year 2025: Eight Perspectives. In: Henriksen K., Battles J. B., Keyes M. A., Grady M. L. (Eds). *Advances in Patient Safety: New Directions and Alternative Approaches (Vol. 1: Assessment)*. Rockville, MD: Agency for Healthcare Research and Quality.

Jackson, C., Cheater, F. M., and Reid, I. (2008). A systematic review of decision support needs of parents making child health decisions. Health Expectations: An International Journal of Public Participation. *Health Care and Health Policy*, 11, 232–51.

Kaldjian, L. C., Curtis, A. E., Shinkunas, L.A., and Cannon, K. T. (2009). Goals of care toward the end of life: a structured literature review. *American Journal of Hospice and Palliative Care*, 25(6), 501–11.

Leape, L., Berwick, D., Clancy, C., Conway, J., Gluck, P., Guest, J. et al. (2009). Transforming healthcare: A safety imperative. *Quality and safety in health care*, 18, 424–8.

Lee, M. D., Friedenberg A. S., Mukpo, D. H., Conray, K., Palmisciano, A., and Levy, M. M. (2007). Visiting hours policies in New England intensive care units: Strategies for improvement. *Critical Care Medicine*, 35(2), 497–501.

Lewandowski, L. A. (1994). Nursing grand rounds: The power to shape memories: Critical care nurses and family visiting. *Journal of Cardiovascular Nursing*, 9(1), 54–60.

Ludington-Hoe, S. M. (2003). Physiological responses to skin-to-skin contact. *Heart Lung*, 19, 445–51.

Luo, R. Q., Adams, W. G., Fuhlbrigge, A. L., and Friedman, R. H. (2005). Usage patterns and clinical impact of an automated asthma management system for children and their parents. *American Medical Informatics Association Annual Symposium Proceedings*, 1038.

Melnyk, B., and Feinstein, N. (2009). Reducing hospital expenditures with the COPE (creating opportunities for parent empowerment) program for parents and premature infants. *Nursing Administration Quarterly*, 33, 32–7.

Melnyk, B. M. et al. Reducing premature infants' length of stay and improving parents' mental health outcomes with the Creating Opportunities for Parent Empowerment (COPE) neonatal intensive care unit program: A randomized controlled trial. *Pediatrics*, 118, e1414–37.

Mitnick, S., Leffler, C., and Hood, V. L. for the American College of Physicians Ethics, Professionalism and Human Rights Committee. (2010). Family caregivers, patients and physicians: ethical guidance to optimize relationships. *Journal of General Internal Medicine*, 25(3), 255–60.

Montgomery, L., Kleiber, C., Nicholson, A., Craft-Rosenberg, M. (1997). A research-based sibling visitation program for the neonatal ICU. *Critical Care Nurse*, 17, 29–40.

O'Connor, A. M. et al. (2009). Decision aids for people facing health treatment or screening decisions. *Cochrane Database Systematic Review*, 8, (3), CD001431.

Örtenstrand, A., Westrup, B., Broström, E. et al. (2010). The Stockholm neonatal family centered care study: effects on length of stay and infant morbidity. *Pediatrics*, 125, e278–85.

Pasquale, M. A., Pasquale, M. D., Baga, L., Eid, S., and Leske, J. (2010). Family presence during trauma resuscitation: ready for primetime? *Journal of Trauma*, 69 (5),1092–9.

Preyde, M., Ardal, F. (2003). Effectiveness of a parent "buddy" program for mothers of very preterm infants in a neonatal intensive care unit. *Canadian Medical Association Journal*, 168, 969–73.

Rabow, M. W., Hauser, J. W., and Adams, J. (2004). Supporting family caregivers at the end of life. "They don't know what they don't know." *Journal of American Medical Association*, 291, 483–91.

Renshaw, M. (2009). 'Family-centered care' in American hospitals in late-Qing China. *Clio Medica*, 86, 55–79.

Schulz, R., and Beach, S. R. (1999). Caregiving as a risk factor for mortality: the caregiver health effects study. *Journal of American Medical Association*, 282, 2215–19.

Sisterhen, L. L., Blaszak, R. T., Wood, M. B., and Smith, C. E. (2007). Defining family-centered rounds. Teaching and Learning in Medicine, 19 (3), 319–22.

Sodomka, P. (2006). Engaging patients and families: A high leverage tool for health care leaders. *Hospitals and Health Networks*, 28–9. Retrieved 10 Aug 2010, from http://www.hhnmag.com/hhnmag_app/jsp/articledisplay.jsp?dcrpath=HHNMAG/PubsNewsArticle/data/2006August/0608HHN_FEA_QualityUpdate&domain=HHNMG.

Sodomka, P., Scott, H., Lambert, A., Meeks, B., and Moretz, J. (2006). A case study: building a patient and family model of care in an academic medical center; the role of informatics in supporting patient partnerships; a 12-year history and future vision. In: Weaver C., Delaney C., Weber P., Carr R. (Eds). *Nursing & informatics for the 21st century: cases, practice, & the future.* Chicago, IL: HIMSS Publishing.

Sodomka, P., Spake, M. A., and Rush, J. J. (2010). Enterprise-wide effort brings patient perspective into mix. *Journal of Healthcare Risk Management*, 29, 4, 28–32.

Uhlig, P. N., Brown, J., Nason, A. K., Camelio, A., and Kendall, E. (2002). System innovation: Concord Hospital. *Joint Commission Journal of Quality Improvement*, 28(12), 666–72.

York, N. L. (2004). Implementing a family presence protocol option. *Dimensions of critical care nursing*, 23 (2), 84–8.

5 Behavioral Interventions for Disruptive Family Situations in the General Medical Setting

Nora Cavelli

- Behavioral interventions from inpatient psychiatry are applied in the medical setting.
- Seeking solutions turns staff concerns about disruptive behaviors into behavioral expectations.
- Behavior care plans support cooperative relationships between families and staff.
- Involving leadership is appropriate in difficult family situations.

Introduction

Clinical skills that are effective for managing behaviors in inpatient psychiatry can be transferred to the medical setting with the goal of managing disruptive situations with the families of medically ill patients. Four clinical theories contribute to the behavioral approaches described in this chapter: Solution-Focused Brief Therapy drawn from the work of Steve DeShazer and Insoo Kim Berg (De Jong and Berg, 2002), Dialectical Behavior Therapy pioneered by Marsha Linehan (Linehan, 1993), family assessment from Margaret Roath (Roath, 1996), and behavior modification (Skinner, 1974). Four case studies are composites of family situations that are commonly encountered.

The starting point for many disruptive behaviors is a pattern of difficult interactions with family members of medically ill patients. The purpose of behavioral interventions is to diminish the intensity and frequency of disruptive behaviors, not to conduct therapy with families. This chapter presents new ways of thinking about disruptive family situations and provides new clinical tools for managing them.

Family member's emotions intensify in face of a loved one's critical illness and the demands of treatment. For example, a boyfriend is anguished when he sees how much pain his girlfriend experiences during dressing changes for her severe burns. He blames himself that he was not home at the time to prevent her injuries and constantly thinks "if only I had been there … ". His usual capacity to adapt is overwhelmed and his usual ways of coping becomes ineffective. He lashes out at staff when he feels helpless to prevent his girlfriend's pain. His ability to cooperate with staff becomes impaired and patient care suffers.

Under stress, family members may become less able to comprehend what is taking place and more likely to misinterpret staff's intentions and changes in care. A mother knows that nurses must change her son's position every two hours. Her understanding conflicts with a new physician order not to move him when he is hypotensive. In anger, the mother accuses staff of being negligent and demands to talk to the doctor. Her ignorance is understandable, but her desperate efforts to be helpful make it hard for her to cooperate. She argues with nursing staff about the conflict and by so doing, interferes with her son's plan of care.

Under stress, family members may be more apt to misinterpret medical information. Professionals talk about what they are doing, while families silently wonder what they mean. The blood test result is reported; does that mean things are getting worse? Do the doctors really know what is wrong? They hear a multi-syllable cognate of Greek or Latin; does that mean the doctors think the patient is going to die? What is frequently omitted from discussions with families is what they can expect. If families understand what the blood test will tell them and how long it will take to receive the results, families gain confidence in the process of care. Similarly, when families' behaviors are difficult, it reduces their stress to tell them what behavior is expected. This communication increases the likelihood of improved cooperation.

Under stress, family members may distort staff's intentions: are they conducting experiments on my loved one? Has this treatment ever been tried before? The family member may begin to resist the staff's requests to leave the room, suspecting that the staff has ulterior motives. Once faltering cooperation becomes a pattern, it tends to worsen, and if it is not addressed, it can spiral into resentful and punitive interactions between families and clinicians. When families are not responding to the staff's customary and well-intended approaches, when a family's cooperation with treatment falters and patient care becomes disrupted, psychiatric consultation is frequently requested. Behavior care plans help establish cooperative relationships between staff and family members.

Behavior Care Plans

Behavior care plans provide new ways of thinking about disruptive family situations and provide interventions that fall outside the skill sets of non-psychiatric professionals. The behavior care plans may at first seem counterintuitive. For example, when family members are too demanding, the typical response is to try to accommodate them. However, the problem is that they are competing with patient care. The counterintuitive approach is to communicate what is expected of them behaviorally and to explain how the expected behaviors benefit them.

Behavior care plans employ elements that are common in clinical practice: assess and identify goals, define expectations, plan and implement interventions, and evaluate outcomes. First, staff's concerns and then the family member's concerns are identified. The staff's concerns are translated into behavioral expectations for families. Second, the family member is informed how staff will intervene when the family member does not meet those expectations. The psychiatric consultant helps the staff implement the behavior care plans by coaching staff to evaluate and assess outcomes. The table below provides the structure of a generic behavioral care plan.

It is important to emphasize that behavior care plans are not coercive and are not contracts, since there is no *quid pro quo*. When the question arises, "What are the consequences?" the consultant explains that consequences imply coercion and that behavior care plans outline expectations and provide staff with interventions when behaviors deviate from these expectations.

Structure of a Generic Behavior Care Plan

Goal. This is the desired behavioral goal for the family to support consistent treatment. The goal can also describe behaviors that lead to a desired outcome.

Expectations of Behavior. How the family is to act (instead of behaviors you want them to stop).

Warning Signs of Escalating Behavior. Identifies what to look for and how to assess if the behavior progresses from mild to moderate to severe; use objective descriptions, for example, instead of "agitated" write, "talks louder."

Interventions by Staff. These interventions are scripts of what staff is to do or say, not only when behavior is meeting expectations, but also when behavior escalates.

Signatures by Staff and Family. This acknowledges review of the behavior care plan. Families are not required to sign, and if they refuse, write "reviewed but declines to sign."

Check boxes indicate which copy goes to the family. The copy with original signatures becomes part of the medical record.

Assess and Identify Goals

Behavior care plans focus only on significantly disruptive patterns of behavior and are not intended to eradicate all annoyances. The first step is to identify the most troublesome behaviors with the goal of diminishing their intensity and frequency. Warning signs that lead up to the disruptive behavior are also identified and described.

The second step is to describe each expected behavior in concrete, objective phrases. This primes positive behavior and avoids provoking anger by staff saying what not to do. Most family members do not respond well to being criticized. Similarly, avoid warning family members about adverse medical outcomes related to their behavior, because it will likely be understood as a threat or retaliation.

The language used to describe behavior is important. What did the person do to show aggression? How did the person show agitation? A familiar parallel is subjective, objective, assessment, and plan (SOAP) charting. Observable data are both subjective (S) and objective (O). Subjective symptoms are a person's self-disclosure, such as quotations of what they say: "I am in pain," or "I do not want a salad." Objective signs are what anyone can see and hear, such as, yelling, standing too close, waving their arms, or throwing a meal tray. The subjective and objective data together are distinguished from assessment (A), which is the interpretation of what the objective data mean. The phrase, "aggressive" is an assessment phrase. The behavior, throwing a meal tray (objective), may variously be interpreted (assessment) as aggressive or impulsive.

Define Expectations and Plan Interventions

Behavioral expectations are the opposite of the negative behavior. The opposite of talking louder or yelling, is the expectation to discuss things calmly. So, when the family member yells his demands, you say, "I will come back when things are calm," and walk away. When you remain during negative behavior, your presence reinforces the negative behavior. After you have left, if the family member continues to escalate, hospital security can be involved, if you think this is needed.

Using the person's own words strengthen behavioral interventions. As described in Case One below, when Jim began to slip into old ways by making urgent demands for non-urgent matters, it is enough for staff simply to ask, "Do you need to surrender protection?" This approach shows an artful pairing of Jim's self-identified role as "protector" with staff's role to provide patient care without interference. This phrasing also compliments Jim by acknowledging his self-understanding that he needs to surrender his protective role to others in the hospital setting. Staff's attitude and non-verbal communication must match the positive verbal content.

Implement and Evaluate Outcomes

Once goals and expectations are identified, the psychiatric consultant coaches the staff how to implement the behavior care plan. The consultant models the specific scripted phases. Coaching concentrates on seeking solutions for problem behaviors, defining expectations, and describing how staff intervenes when expectations are not met. Once staff understand the rationale for the interventions, they can improvise when new problematic situations arise.

Behavior care plans encourage basic expectations to (1) speak calmly even when something upsets you, (2) show respect even when you disagree with or dislike something, (3) follow staff's instructions, and (4) participate in the plan of care reviewed with you. Behavior care plans are reviewed with the family member with staff present. A behavior care plan does not require the family member's agreement. A space for signatures acknowledges that the plan was reviewed. If the family member does not want to sign it, then the plan reads "Reviewed but did not sign."

Follow-up by the consultant reinforces the behavior care plan and helps staff practice and assess their interventions. Repeated coaching and practice are required to master new skills, and amendments are made to behavior care plans. It is important for staff to understand that behavior care plans neither explore psychiatric diagnoses nor discuss clinical reasons for the negative behaviors.

Clinical Theories and Principles

Four clinical theories are used to develop behavior care plans. These are Solution-Focused Brief Therapy, Dialectical Behavior Therapy, Family Therapy, and Behavior Modification. These are evidence-based theories and their abridged use in focal applications is effective only to the extent that their application is consistent with the original clinical theory. The selection of a particular clinical theory is the one that best manages the targeted behavior. For the sake of brevity, they are presented below in a simplified form.

Solution-Focused Brief Therapy—Doing More of What Works

Seeking solutions requires a change from a medical perspective of exploring symptoms, reaching a diagnosis (identifying the problem), and prescribing treatments. The perspective for SFBT comes from the belief that solutions are not found in the problem but in exceptions when the problem is absent. This is called "what works."

Instead of professionals prescribing treatment, family members describe situations when the problem is absent or only minimally bothersome, and the family member prescribes what to do more of (what they are doing when the problem is absent) and what not to do more of (what they are doing when there are problems).

Dialectical Behavior Therapy (DBT) is useful when family members make demands that fall outside of treatment goals. The DBT concepts of validation and change inform the phrasing for behavioral interventions. When announcing discharge, for example, you might say, "While I see you are still in some distress (validation), you have made encouraging progress (change)." If you acknowledge only how well things are going, they will demonstrate how much distress they still experience. If you acknowledge only how distressing things are, they may demonstrate how angry they are at being devalued.

Solution-Focused Brief Therapy (SFBT) identifies what works, either by doing more of what works or changing what does not work. Shifting from problem-focus to solution-focus allows families to see how something can be different in the future and brings hope. An SFBT intervention used in behavior care plans is: Acknowledge, Compliment, Bridge, and Assign (Bari Platter, 2000, personal communication). Interventions from SFBT look beyond problems by seeking solutions. This means that family's goals are paired as much as possible with the behaviors that are expected from family members, and includes the interventions that family members may expect from staff when expectations are not met.

Family therapy treats relationships rather than individuals. A three-continuum assessment (Roath, 1996) is useful in consultations. The focus on relationships moves the consultant away from diagnosing and treating individuals toward aligning behavioral expectations for interacting with others. The following table describes the continuum to evaluate relationships. Think of solutions, rather than problems, responsibility rather than blame, and clear rather than mixed messages.

Continuum for Evaluating Relationships in Families		
Solutions	versus	problems
Responsibility	versus	blame
Clear	versus	mixed messages

Behavior modification uses positive priming to reinforce a behavior (Alvin Stein, 1998, personal communication). Positive priming means that the last meaningful phrase leaves the strongest impression. Instead of saying, "Don't slam the door," for example, say, "Close the door, quietly." Saying, "Close the door, quietly'" primes the behavior of quiet closure of the door. Interventions are more effective when the family member is primed to do what is expected.

Common Family Situations

Patient Family-Centered Care is successful to the extent that patients, family members, and professionals understand and share the goals of treatment. Families can generally be relied upon to embrace medical care and to cooperate with staff. When this is so, there are few, if any, disruptions. Disruptions typically arise when family members have demands that fall outside the patient plan of care or expectations that run contrary to the standards of practice. Note that the phrase "patient plan of care" includes all aspects of patient care, and the phrase "behavior care plan" distinguishes behavioral interventions from all the other interdisciplinary contributions. The starting point for behavior care plans is the understanding that families' difficulties are real, and that families are doing the best they can.

Case studies are composites of four common situations (1) family's verbally aggressive statements, (2) frequent, unreasonable demands made by family members on their own behalf, (3) family's accusation towards staff and (4) family's joining with patients to demand medically contraindicated treatment.

Case One Situation: Family's Verbally Aggressive Statements

Family members who initially embrace the goals of treatment may experience increasing difficulty as they recognize how severe the illness is, and as they become fatigued as days lengthen into weeks at the bedside. Interpersonal and intrapersonal conflicts come to the fore and further intensify their emotions. In some cases, family members may want to protect the patient from painful procedures.

Case One: "I feel Like Killing Someone!"

The patient is an otherwise healthy, middle-aged female, who presents with significant total body surface burns from a house fire. This is her second week in critical care. Her boyfriend, Jim, is the contact person for the patient's family, as agreed in an earlier family meeting. He stays at her bedside for days and often overnight. Jim is present during painful dressing changes for her burns, until one day he expresses his distress as he watches her "suffering that way" and says, "I feel like killing someone." Although he apologizes after the attending physician speaks with him about it, staff is concerned about their safety when he is nearby. The charge nurse requests a consultation for behavioral management.

Case One: Staff's Concerns

Consultations begin by asking the requesting staff to describe the problem behaviors and how these behaviors adversely affect patient care. The staff's point of view, their complaints, attitudes, and what they need, guide the assessment. The consultant works to identify the particular problems, to find clues about how receptive staff will be to accept behavioral approaches unfamiliar to them, and to clarify what staff expects from Jim. The behavior care plan gives a model for communicating expectations to Jim, instead of telling him to stop a negative behavior. The behavior care plan focuses on changing staff's complaints into expectations, and changes expectations into assignments. Identifying behaviorally phrased expectations for Jim and scripting interventions for staff lay a foundation for cooperation by increasing expected behaviors and decreasing disruptive behaviors.

Staff sees Jim as a quiet man who grows increasingly tense whenever staff encourages him to rest at home. He is unwilling to leave the patient's side, and when he does go home, he calls the nursing station frequently. When he is at her bedside, he silences beepers on the ventilator against staff's instructions, makes urgent demands for discontinued orders, and insists repeatedly, that non-urgent care be given immediately. He views changes in the patient care plan as inconsistencies or mistakes, which intensifies his anxiety.

Staff interprets his vigilance, in part, as regret over his girlfriend's injuries. He tells them, "the one time I'm not there, something like this happens," referring to his being away from home when the fire occurred. Staff has already intervened successfully to stop his frequent calls from home by instructing him to call no more than twice per shift and to call only after 9 o'clock am and pm. He meets this expectation without difficulty.

Case One: Family's Needs

The next step in the assessment is to ask Jim privately about what happened. Taking time to identify his point of view, his needs, and his worries, provides clues about how to encourage him toward expected behaviors. What drives him and what he desires from staff, will then be paired with staff expectations to decrease his interference with patient care. The behavior care plan will show Jim how to succeed by giving him assignments of what he is to do (expectations).

Jim agrees to meet with the consultant but keeps a downcast gaze with only furtive eye contact. Initially he speaks softly, measuring his words. He voices no complaints but instead says he regrets his behavior. He recognizes that he upset others and admits that what he said was wrong, even asking the doctor to relay his apology to the nurses because he feels inadequate to do so himself. He is frustrated with himself and embarrassed about what he said.

He spontaneously discloses that he is already taking what he calls "corrective measures." By this he means that when he recognizes he is getting anxious, he leaves and walks around outside the hospital until he is calm. He leaves the patient's room during treatments, when the staff asks him to do so. He seeks to fulfill his role as the patient's protector by "being visible to her whenever she opens her eyes." He admits it is hard to take time away to rest at home and he does what he calls "surrendering protection" to the staff.

Case One: Discussion

Jim's response shows his desire to support his girlfriend's treatment by taking the initi-ative to discover his own "corrective measures" and to exercise self-control to "surrender protection." Jim's conflict with staff relates to his need to assuage his guilt about being absent during the fire, and being visible whenever she opens her eyes in order for him to make things right. In these ways he is fulfilling his duty to her. However, he finds it unbearable to see her in pain, and he attempts to protect his girlfriend from staff during painful dressing changes.

His acceptance of feedback about his behavior shows self-control, and his self-reflection shows initiative to make changes on his own. He demonstrates no significant risk of harm to others but instead reflects an emotionally charged sense of responsibility for the pain and for the recovery of his girlfriend.

Case One: Planning Interventions

In this case, when staff observes warning signs in Jim's behavior, such as his phoning frequently from home, staff reminds him, "Do you need to surrender protection?" When he gets too anxious about the patient's level of pain during a procedure, staff reminds him, "Do you need to take corrective measures?" This changes the dynamic from criticism, to a solution-focused expectation, where staff reminds Jim of his solutions and their expectations. The behavior care plan fosters cooperation. Once the behavior care plan is complete, staff is responsible for its implementation.

Conflicts can be diminished by saying what is expected. A good example is a nurse intuitively telling Jim, "Let the ventilator beep, because we need to know why it is beeping." The nurse tells Jim what to do, "Let the ventilator beep," and then gives the reason: "Because we need to know why it is beeping." This approach lets the nurse guide Jim toward what is expected, rather than correcting him by telling him to "Stop silencing the beeper."

Case One: Outcomes

Ideally, behavior care plans match each warning sign (Jim's anxiety at dressing changes) with expectations (going for a walk), so that staff's expectations (unimpeded care) are matched by Jim's behavior (self-identified corrective measures). Promoting patient care occurs by pairing staff's expectations with Jim's needs, so that he recog-nizes how being the protector (visible whenever she opens her eyes) can push him to say inappropriate things unless he surrenders protection. When his many calls from home distract staff from patient care, they remind him to surrender protection. Using Jim's words gives recognition to, and indirectly compliments, him by using his solutions.

Case One: Behavior Care Plan

Expectations of Jim's behavior:

1. Continue to take "corrective measures"
    Leave to walk around until you are calm
    Let alarms ring so staff know why they are going off
2. Continue to "surrender protection"
    Leave during dressing changes and when staff ask you to
    Call only twice per shift, and only after 9 o'clock.

Warning signs of Jim's escalating behaviors:

*   Repeating himself frequently after he informs staff and staff acknowledges him
*   Questioning what staff is doing or grimacing when his girlfriend is in pain

Interventions by staff:

*   When Jim gets anxious, ask "Do you need to take corrective measures"?
*   If Jim calls from home too often or turns off alarms, ask "Do you need to surrender protection?'
*   Tell him what you want him to do, for example, "Let the ventilator alarm ring," instead of telling him to stop what you do not want him to do, "Do not silence the ventilator."
*   Tell him what is expected, "Let the ventilator ring," with a rationale, "So we know why it is ringing," thus avoiding conflict and giving him an assignment of what to do.
*   Enter in each shift report how well Jim meets expectations of his behavior and what worked well.

Family's Signature Acknowledges Review   Date
Staff's Signature Acknowledges Review   Date
Copy to family   Original to medical record

Case Two Situation: Frequent, Unreasonable Demands made by Family Members, on their Own Behalf

Health-care professionals usually assume that patients and their families seek treatment for the purpose of getting better and going home. However, medically necessary treatment can be used, instead, as an opportunity for family members to seek extra-therapeutic goals, as you will see in the next case example. Family demands outside the patient plan of care become disruptive and stressful for staff.

Case Two: "Change the Channel!"

The patient, a 75-year-old married male executive, presents after a massive stroke, is unconscious, and is not expected to recover. His wife, Eustace, calls nurses into his room to massage her husband's shoulders or feet, or to change the channel on the television that she constantly watches. When their adult children visit, they are unobtrusive and cajole their mother Eustace with mild disapproval about the way she seeks attention from staff for things she can do for herself. The children apologize to staff and privately tell them that Eustace has always been this way, expecting her husband and others to see to her every comfort.

Case Two: Staff Concerns

The consult question is for recommendations to manage Eustace's demands. First the consultant interviews staff about the specifics of the problematic behaviors and the extent of their adverse effects. Staff expresses concern that Eustace's self-focus diverts their attention from the patient and that it is difficult for them to restrain their annoyance at her attitude toward them. The staff wishes that the consultant make her behaviors disappear.

Case Two: Families' Needs

The adult children's perceptions about their mother matches what staff observes. They talk about how their mother has always used her husband's status to gain favors and how Eustace is oblivious to other people except as agents to provide for her.

Case Two: Discussion

The positions are well entrenched: the patient's self-absorbed wife, the apologetic but minimally involved adult children, and nursing staff's annoyance. There is little common ground to allow pairing Eustace's needs with staff's expectations of her behavior. Despite staff's sustained sympathy and care for the patient, their attitude is dismissive and impatient toward Eustace. Her requests are outside the patient plan of care and exceed appropriate levels of assistance from staff. The openly apologetic comments of her adult children confirm staff's realization that Eustace cannot cooperate.

Given Eustace's habit to take advantage of her husband's influence, it would seem that customer recovery would be an ideal way to respond to her. Hospitals promote customer recovery as a successful strategy to improve patient and family satisfaction. However, customer recovery has reverse effects for families who are not focused on recovery. To illustrate, customer recovery offers a blameless apology, for example, "I am so sorry you are not comfortable in the patient's room." Such an apology would be misinterpreted by Eustace as an admission of unacceptable service and would validate her dissatisfaction. In short, it would make things worse. Another customer recovery approach is to offer parking or cafeteria coupons to compensate for minor inconveniences, but this rewards Eustace's inappropriate behavior.

Behavior care plans offer alternative strategies that allow staff to maintain the patient care plan, as well as to provide a scripted way for staff to decline requests that fall outside of the patient care plan. This is not anticipated to improve Eustace's behavior, but it prevents worsening of the situation by helping staff redirect inappropriate requests. By providing an alternative approach, a behavior care plan lessens the negativity that can exert adverse effects on patient care and staff morale.

This case also illustrates how behavior care plans support ethical practice. Eustace brings staff face-to-face with potential ethical compromise resulting from their interminable frustrations. How does frustration become an issue for ethical practice? Ethical practice is based on one's professional obligation and personal desire to serve the best interests of patients and their families. Once Eustace's demeaning attitude and constant demands begin to affect staff personally, their resentment and avoidance can become overt hostility. Behavior care plans support ethical practice by providing an independent psychiatric consultation to help staff develop appropriate behavioral interventions.

Behavior care plans also support hospital accountability by alerting hospital managers when families behave in disruptive ways, despite staff's interventions. In anticipation that Eustace will take her discontents to the highest level, hospital leadership is involved as soon as possible, so that they are aware of, rather than surprised by the situation. It is good to hear "never worry alone" (Anne Playter, 1990, personal communication). Hospital management has a dual obligation to promote patient care and protect staff from abuse.

Case Two: Planning Interventions

The consultant considers possible options. For unreasonable requests, one option is to tell her no and assign what is expected. Solution-Focused Brief Therapy gives scripts to redirect others. These scripts are a series of intentionally crafted phrases known as "acknowledge, compliment, bridge, and assign" (Bari Platter, 2000, personal communication). The first step is to acknowledge her request, by using her words. The second step is to compliment a specific behavior, appropriate in the moment, if any. The third step is a transition with a brief rationale, and the fourth step is to say what you want from her, instead of what she wants from you.

By saying what you want, you prime that expectation. It is a way to say "no" in a "yes" tone of voice. The "yes" part is accomplished by acknowledging Eustace's request by showing her you hear and understand what she said. Saying "no" is accomplished by replacing her unreasonable request with an assignment of what she is to do. A sample script is provided below.

If Eustace persists in continuing to make demands after repeated redirection, then the next intervention is to call upon immediate supervisors and managers, first to explore further solutions, second to review and support staff's efforts, and third to make administration aware of the situation should Eustace complain to administration. Staff gains confidence when leadership is readily available and attentive to their concerns. When Eustace realizes there is upper-level approval for the behavioral expectations and for staff's interventions, then two responses are possible. She may acquiesce to the behavior care plan or she may appeal to yet higher levels. In the latter case, restricted visitation may be necessary as a last resort to contain the disruption to patient care.

Case Two: Outcome

The best outcome in this case is significantly limited by Eustace's intransigence. There is one potentially positive outcome, however, and that is to use staff's documentation of her demands for personal service, if necessary, to justify restricting her visitation. However,

Case Two: Behavior Care Plan

Acknowledge, compliment, bridge and assign:

Acknowledge: "You want me to change the channel."
- Say this in a casual, matter-of-fact tone.
- Lilt your voice downward, as you do to make a statement.
- Guard against lilting your voice upward, as you do to ask a question.

Compliment: compliments are used, for this purpose, not as a courtesy and not as encouragement, but as a way to reinforce a specific behavior that staff wants the person to repeat.
- Omit the compliment phrase because at this moment she is not demonstrating a behavior that staff wants her to repeat.
- Eustace's behavior in the moment lacks something positive because it is simply asking staff to do what she can do for herself.

Bridge: "Since my focus is patient care."
- This gives a rationale or a reason, in a brief phrase.
- Transition to an assignment of what behavior is expected of her (instead of what she is doing).

Assign: "Please use the channel changer to get the channels you want."
- You might point to the channel changer as you say this.
- Say this in the same way you say, "Please pass the salt" to tell her what is expected.
- Resist a compelling inclination is to say what you will do.
- The purpose is to redirect her request, by assigning an appropriate behavior.

staff should not interpret restricted visitation as a consequence against Eustace. The benefit of behavior care plans is to draw negative behaviors toward expected behaviors and to create certainty for families by describing expectations and the interventions staff will use when expectations are not met. The intention is to diminish further conflict by redirecting her disruptive behavior.

Case Three Situation: Family's Accusations Towards Staff

In their role as caregivers, family members may advocate too aggressively for loved ones. In the stress of acute care, the family pushes for the best treatment prompts them to challenge a patient's plan of care. When family caregivers assume a directive role, they tend to create conflicts with hospital staff that pushes them away and disrupts patient care.

Case Three: "What are you Doing to my Son!"

The patient is a 15 year-old male in the second month of his admission, who remains in critical condition from organ rejection and sepsis after a transplant eight months before. His mother, Molly, brings him from a rural hospital to a major urban hospital for treatment of his life-threatening complications. She has left her other children and an ill husband at home. For the duration of her son's hospitalization, Molly rarely leaves his bedside, and her constant vigilance ignites like fireworks whenever staff approaches his bed. As she rushes to stand near staff, she fires her questions in the rapid staccato of an automatic weapon. As the mother of a minor child, Molly must be involved to exercise informed consent on her son's behalf, and she is on duty and on guard, while her teenage son lies pale and motionless.

Case Three: Staff's Concerns

Staff observes from their ongoing attempts to work with Molly that her most common emotional response is anger. Her accusations and aggressive manner intimidate staff. Molly routinely stalls patient care by demanding confirmation of physician's orders before permitting treatment to continue. Although physicians brief her during their rounds, she challenges treatment, for example, demanding that her son be turned every two hours, despite physician orders that her son's position not be changed because of a hypotensive episode. Molly's anger escalates to physical aggression when she throws a needleless syringe at a nurse.

A planning meeting is arranged for members of the inpatient and outpatient teams to discuss how to work effectively with Molly. Staff is frequently brought to tears and several nurses experience lasting negative effects from their interactions with her. Her mistrust of staff and her outbursts deeply distress staff across all disciplines, and her ongoing challenges delay patient care.

Case Three: Family's Needs

Consultants usually meet with the staff first and then with family. In this situation, the consultant does not meet with Molly, because the treatment team prefers not to add to the number of staff already involved, since any attempts to address issues with Molly results in renewed attacks. Staff's overall observation is that Molly's main goal is to advocate for her son. This role provides her with a strong sense of self and self-worth. Molly mentions in passing that she has fought many battles in her life and has success-fully overcome many traumas. In her role as her son's advocate, she wants to fight with the same furor that otherwise served her well. Molly believes staff looks down on her, and she tells a nurse one day, "You just think I am white trash." Staff describes her being chronically "in attack mode," adding that, "when her son dies, she will have nothing left." Molly does not yet know that her son's physicians anticipate that his condition will not improve and that he will die soon.

Case Three: Discussion

At the planning meeting, a team member suggests ways to "enhance Molly's sense of control" by letting her post a list of her expectations on the door of her son's room. These are, in essence, a list of grievances against staff, namely to wash your hands, to wear a mask, not to leave syringes in the mattress, and to say what you are doing before you start. Unfortunately, this intervention would only perpetuate Molly's demand to direct her son's medical care and is therefore counterproductive.

A second suggestion is to encourage Molly to talk with the patient representative, so that she has "a neutral person to help her feel heard and to investigate both sides of the issue." This is customarily helpful, but it is unlikely to help when cooperation is already failing, because it expands the pool of people involved. Although no one would suggest restricting Molly's access to available resources, it is helpful in these situations to contain rather that expand the situation.

A behavior care plan seeks to link Molly's advocating for her son with staff's expectations of her behavior. The behavior care plan seeks to translate Molly's disruptive behavior into expectations for cooperative behaviors. From the staff's perspective, the first goal is to identify what behaviors are expected of Molly to support her son's treatment, versus disrupt her son's treatment. The second goal is to encourage her to meet her own needs through supportive behaviors.

The intensity of Molly's behavior captivates staff, and it is not unusual for staff to ask consultants in difficult situations, "What do you think is wrong with her? Do you think she has a personality disorder?" Allowing conjecture about Molly's possible psychopathology is beyond the scope of consultation, because family members are not our patients, so conjecture about diagnosis in the absence of a formal evaluation is speculation and inadvertently objectifying and demeaning. Consultation, in this case, is intended to address staff's concerns and family's needs, in order to enhance the working relationship.

Case Three: Planning Interventions

The conclusions from the interdisciplinary meeting, described above, are twofold. On the one hand, Molly has to be fully involved with medical decision-making for her son, but on the other hand, she can better support his care by keeping tensions away from the patient's room and by waiting until she can talk calmly before she addresses things that upset her. The resident physician and the charge nurse volunteer to meet daily with Molly after morning rounds, in order to update her about the patient plan of care for that day and to support staff by preventing her challenging patient care.

The behavior care plan is intended to identify only the most disruptive behaviors. There are three behavioral expectations for Molly: (1) to speak quietly (instead of yelling), (2) to express disagreement respectfully (instead of cursing, accusing), and (3) to stand quietly by the door and out of the way (instead of rushing at staff) until staff completes what they need to do.

There are four interventions for staff; (1) to acknowledge, compliment, bridge, and assign, (2) to remind Molly of the supportive behavior described above, (3) to agree with her complaints or use contrasting for her accusations and (4) to leave when Molly persists in challenging them. Each of these interventions is scripted so that all staff intervenes in a similar way. Examples of how staff manages Molly's disruptive behavior follow.

Molly greets the nurse who is arriving for the day shift by waving a used, capped syringe and saying, "Look what I found in the mattress!" The natural response is to offer some explanation, even though the nurse has no idea of what happened. Although it seems counterintuitive to do so, agree with Molly and join her implied complaint.

Agreeing, means the nurse says "You are right, that should not happen." For Molly, this is like putting her money into a vending machine and not getting the product. Molly shakes the machine by repeating herself in a louder voice, again waving the syringe and telling the nurse, "I found this used syringe in the mattress!" The nurse may simply rephrase the same response as before, "Wow, that should not happen," and to move beyond what will become a stalemate, by suggesting, "Please place that syringe in the sharps container."

Molly continues, "No! I am keeping it for my poster as evidence!" It seems that the choice is between insisting that the syringe go into the sharps container or letting Molly violate the sharps policy by keeping the syringe. Does the nurse want to wrestle Molly for the syringe or call security to secure it? Is there any efficacy to talking about a poster of evidence? Resoundingly, no! Tell her, "Okay, I will make a note that you are keeping the syringe." This documents what happened, since Molly refuses to dispose of it. At that time, if there is no reason to remain in the patient's room, leave. It is automatic for health care professionals to offer education, but in this case, providing information when a question is actually an accusation, automatically defaults to an argument.

Another example of how Molly provokes conflict is illustrated when she demands, "What are you doing to my son!" It is important to recognize when a question is not an inquiry for information, rather an accusation. The natural response is to explain rather than to assess if this is an inquiry for information, an accusation, or a complaint. The phrasing, what are you doing to my son, is the clue that this is an accusation, since an inquiry would be phrased differently: what are you doing for my son or with my son? Here, the task is to clarify Molly's concern, and the nurse might say, "You sound alarmed; please tell me what is concerning to you."

Molly then clarifies this first accusation, "What are you doing to my son!" by another accusation. Whatever Molly says is wrong, the nurse might say, "I would not want you to think [whatever Molly accuses] because [whatever is actually intended]." This skill is called contrasting (Patterson, Grenny, Miller, and Switzler, 2002). "Are you still trying to hurt my son?" is not something anyone would ask in quite that way, and the contrasting response would be, "I would not want you to think I am trying to hurt your son, because I am giving him something for pain." It is simply contrasting what you are accused of doing with what you are intending to do. Another example of contrasting is to say, "I would not want you to think that I am neglecting your son so he will have pressure ulcers, because it is not safe to move him is until his blood pressure gets better." What makes this phrasing work is to keep from saying, "I am not doing that," which are fighting words. Instead, "I would not want you to think such-and-such" acknowledges Molly's accusation and simply contrasts that with what you are actually intending to do.

Contrasting

When a question is actually an accusation, use contrasting.

When you are asked, "Why are you neglecting my son? You did not change his position every two hours the way you are supposed to!"

Respond by saying, "I would not want you to think I am neglecting your son, because he should not be moved until his blood pressure is stable."

By leading with the phrase, "I would not want you to think" you acknowledge what the person says instead of opposing an incorrect perception.

By following with the phrase, "because ..." affirms your concern is to do what is safe or beneficial.

Recognizing when a question is actually not a question but a complaint, an accusation, or a lament, is necessary for responding appropriately. For example, if a family member asks, "Why does this have to happen?" what do you say? Is an answer obligatory? Instead of taking educational leave to resolve this philosophical matter, respond by saying, "I wish things could be different" (Brent Van Dorsten, personal communication, 2011). The brilliance of this intervention is that there is neither an impossible explanation nor an unwarranted apology, just an artful blend of acknowledgement and empathy that allows silence in face of an unanswerable circumstance.

Case Three: Behavior Care Plan

Goal
- Molly is fully involved and informed about medical decisions, and fully to support care without tension or distraction at bedside.
- Benefits for Molly: to be fully supportive of your son's care by having a calm, respectful manner with staff and by waiting to address issues, until you can express yourself calmly.

Supportive behaviors expected of Molly:

- Speak no louder than normal conversation, even when something is upsetting
- Express yourself respectfully, even when you disagree
- Stand out of the way or near the door until staff finishes what they need to do.

Warning signs of Molly's escalating behavior:

- Talking louder and creating tension by arguing with staff's explanations
- Insisting that something be done immediately the way you understand it, even against doctor's orders.

Interventions by staff:

- Document in each shift note what is helping to lessen the intensity of staff-family interactions and support patient care:
- For initial warning signs of escalating behavior, remind Molly of a matching Supportive Behavior.
  a) For example, ask her, "Please stay calm" rather than, "Don't yell at me."
  b) Lessen conflict by asking for what you DO want rather than telling her to STOP what you don't want.
  c) Use few words, with pauses, to allow processing; keep a neutral tone and calm manner.
- When Molly brings up a concern or an objection, then respond:
  a) Acknowledge: (repeat) what she wants: "You want me to turn you son's position, because of skin breakdown."
  b) Bridge: Give a rationale, a brief transition phrase: "Since the doctor has changed that order,"
  c) Assign: What you want Molly to do and say it as you would say 'please pass the salt'; "please wait until I finish before we talk about this."
- If warning signs continue after an initial effort (1 or 2 above), then stop the interaction.
  a) At that point, to continue is to engage in an argument that only intensifies the situation, making things worse.
  b) For example, when you ask for a Supportive Behavior, and she answers by talking louder, talking over you, or interrupting you,
  c) Stop the conversation by saying, "We can pick this up when things are calm" and
  d) Leave even if she continues talking.
- If her behavior continues to escalate, and she is creating tension, ask her to leave, involving other staff as needed.
- Later, review the incident with her, if possible, by asking which Supportive Behavior would make a difference.
  a) What Supportive Behavior would she use for things to go differently in that situation?
  b) Which of her Warning Signs keeps her from supporting staff in her son's treatment?

Family's signature acknowledges review   Date
Staff signature indicates review with family   Date

Case Three: Outcome

The nurse manager decides not to implement a behavior care plan immediately but to hold it in reserve. The nurse manager chooses graceful phrases to talk with Molly "about being supportive of her son's care" as a way to reframe Molly's urgency for control, giving Molly an opportunity to affirm that her son is getting good care and to agree that, "It is not good to have tension in the room." The nurse manager has helped Molly save face and Molly, in response, for the first time admits that her son is not doing well.

These approaches with family members teach staff to introduce solutions that avoid opposition and power struggles, which in turn reduce staff's exposure to stressful encounters. Staff sometimes complains, after an effort to implement a behavior care plan that, "She has not changed a bit!" This invites coaching by the consultant to review the rationale for the behavior care plan: for staff to change by using behavioral interventions that reduce the intensity and frequency of hostile exchanges.

Case Four Situation: Families join with Patients to Demand Medically Contraindicated Treatment

Professionals offer medical services from the perception that patients want to recover and resume living their lives, so that physicians may not discern right away when someone is motivated by extra-therapeutic goals. This case study addresses behavioral management in a situation of iatrogenic opioid dependence when greater doses of narcotics are required for adequate pain relief. There are confounding issues, on the one hand, to provide adequate pain relief based on the patient's subjective report of pain, while on the other hand, to be vigilant about opioid misuse in excess of what is adequate for pain management. Dialectical Behavior Therapy provides helpful behavioral interventions for responding to requests from patients who want to extend their stay so they can continue to receive IV narcotics.

Case Four: I Cannot Stand this Pain!

Emma is a 30-year-old, married white female who presents with chronic abdominal pain that requires frequent hospitalization for nausea, vomiting, pain, and diarrhea. Recently there is an escalation of her complaints and the severity of her symptoms, and she is admitted for inpatient pain management. She has had ten admissions in the last three and a half months. When IV pain medications are tapered in preparation for discharge on oral narcotics, she becomes angry, making back-to-back requests, cries, yells, writhes in pain, and talks over physicians to demand pain medications even to the point of sedation.

Case Four: Staff's Concerns

The attending physician requests a consultation for a behavior care plan. The goal is to expedite discharge of the patient that afternoon. The physician is confident that her demand for higher doses far exceeds what is adequate for managing her pain and is causing harmful side effects. Nurses report being overextended because of the patient's demands. They report she wants narcotics to the point of sedation but that she seems to move, eat, and converse comfortably, without pain, unless she notices that staff is observing her.

Case Four: Family's Needs

The patient's mother and husband reportedly accept Emma's complaints as medically legitimate. They join Emma in asserting that the physical cause of her pain remains unidentified and believe her pain is not properly managed. Emma telephones them frequently complaining about how much pain she is experiencing, and that she is not receiving adequate relief for her pain. The family complains to the patient representative about her "poor care."

Case Four: Discussion

The goal of the consultation is to help the team expedite the patient's discharge that afternoon, and to develop a plan in anticipation of vigorous objections and opposition from the patient and her family. It is important in consultation to review the medical record for a complete and independent assessment. The medical record gives a lengthy, ample history from a variety of sources, about the patient's pain. Iatrogenic opiate dependence is well documented by several physicians. Consultations by the service covering acute pain management together with negative findings from earlier medical work-ups for complaints with unclear etiology are consistent with the conclusions of the inpatient medical team.

Dialectical Behavior Therapy is a good approach for intervention where there are diametrically opposed points of view and when there is no common ground on which to build cooperation. DBT is a form of cognitive-behavioral therapy that includes crisis management and emotional regulation in cases where dysregulated emotions create repeated catastrophic emotional states. The notion of 'dialectic' comes from the economic theory of Karl Marx and describes the historical process by which a thesis and an opposing antithesis create a synthesis.

The thesis in DBT is called "the emotional mind" which refers to dysregulation of hyperactive emotions, and the antithesis in DBT is called "the rational mind" which refers to a hypofunctioning process of reasoning. DBT identifies "wise mind," as the synthesis of the emotional mind and the rational mind. DBT provides an effective script to approach a volatile conversation.

Case Four: Planning Intervention

DBT skills are used to facilitate Emma's discharge and to manage the irresolvable, opposite positions. The thesis is that the physician wants Emma to leave the hospital, and he will no longer administer IV narcotics. The antithesis is that Emma and her family wants her to remain in the hospital and receive IV narcotics. These opposing positions are conceptualized to all concerned as "putting us in a bind." Emma and her family are asked to decide how they want to handle it. Instead of a power struggle over opposing wishes, the decision and "the bind" are put into the patient and the family member's hands. The phrasing of the dilemma is important.

Understanding how DBT views the etiology of emotional dysregulation is necessary to understand why phrasing is so significant. The etiology has two components, a nurture component which is characterized as an invalidating environment and the nature component which is characterized by an inherent vulnerability. Together, they account for the chronic pattern of emotional dysregulation. Interventions must use phrasing that combines both validation and change.

The validation phrase acknowledges Emma's experience in the moment, by saying, "It makes sense that you experience relief only from IV opiates." The change phrase recognizes the patient's efforts, strengths and resourcefulness, and presents the opposing view, by saying, "I will not in good conscience prescribe IV pain medications because they are doing medical harm and provide no medical benefit." The synthesis puts the dialectic into the patient's hands, by saying, "We are really in a bind here, because the only thing that helps your pain is IV hydromorphone, and I will not cause medical harm by prescribing IV pain medications; how do you want to handle this?" The synthesis phrase is successful by drawing on the patient's emotional effectiveness (wise mind) and minimizing a struggle over a conflict about discharge, by asking how she wants to handle the dilemma.

Always pair validation, which is the acknowledgement of how difficult the patient's situation is, with the recognition of her strength and resourcefulness. If you emphasize only how difficult it is for her, without recognizing how hard she is trying, then the patient will show you how angry that makes her. If you emphasize only how hard she is trying without recognizing how difficult her pain is for her, she will show you how miserable she really is. An example of validation and change phrasing is given in the table.

Validation and Change

"Even though your pain has been terribly difficult (validation), taking more IV hydromorphone is making things worse (change). We are in a bind because what you want is what I am unwilling to prescribe; so how do you want to proceed?"

This phrasing combines the opposites of validation and change. Validation phrases recognize the patient's experience in the moment, and prevents invalidation. Change phrases recognize how hard the patient is trying to make improvements, and prevents feelings of vulnerability.

Instead of letting opposing positions create power struggles, define "the bind we are in." Handing it to the patient decreases the potency of the stalemate since the patient cannot change the physician's decision but can decide how she wants to proceed.

Case Four: Outcomes

The patient reluctantly chooses to leave but without overt anger, and the physician is pleased to have averted a dramatic scene. He appreciates the way DBT allows a respectful way to present irresolvable opposite views.

Conclusion

At the earliest signs of faltering cooperation with families, requests for consultation can introduce new clinical tools to non-psychiatric professionals. Consultation serves multidisciplinary practice by addressing how to recognize and support families who are overwhelmed by medical crises and confused by a hospital culture that is foreign to them. Healthcare is founded on a tacit understanding that people who seek hospital care do so from a desire to get better and go home, but when that is not the case, then behavioral approaches can manage disruptive behaviors of families during hospital care.

Behavior care plans are based on four evidence-based, clinical theories, primarily behavior modification and adaptations of cognitive-behavioral therapy, namely Solution-Focused Brief Therapy and Dialectical Behavior Therapy, and lastly family therapy. Behavior care plans begin by assessing the concerns of staff and the needs of families, as a way to identify behavioral expectations that are the opposite of the most disruptive behaviors. The purpose is not to conduct therapy but to diminish the frequency and intensity of disruptive behaviors and to foster cooperation by describing, in objective, behavioral terms, what is expected from the family and how staff will intervene when expectations are not met.

Ongoing, informal conversations among consultants, staff, physicians, and managers are beneficial for professional development. Coaching by consultants helps staff develop behavioral skills to mediate disruptive behaviors and diminish their adverse effects on patient care and staff morale. When staff is encouraged to seek solutions, they broaden their range of understanding and their ways of responding to difficult situations. Should initial behavioral interventions at the bedside require further support, staff can continue to explore solutions by seeking input from leaders whose involvement supports staff's efforts and shows concern for their well-being.

Excellence in health-care is identified, in part, by patient family centered care and patient satisfaction, and the engagement of the family in patient care is a legitimate focus for clinical attention. Gaining behavioral skills allows staff to promote cooperative relationships with families when their usually effective efforts at customer recovery have not been helpful. Families benefit from and are thankful for professionals who respectfully help them understand their hospital experience, so that families leave with a sense of having been respected and acknowledged.

References

De Jong, P., and Berg, I. K. (2002). *Interviewing for Solutions*, 2nd Edition, Pacific Grove, CA: Wadsworth Group.

Linehan, M. M. (1993). *Skills Training Manual for Treating Borderline Personality Disorder*. New York: Guilford Press.

Patterson, K., Grenny, J. McMillan, R., and Switzler, A. (2002). *Crucial Conversations: Tools for talking when the stakes are high*. Hightstown, NJ: McGraw-Hill.

Roath, M. (1996). *Marital and Family Therapy in Psychiatric Secrets*. James. L. Jacobson and Alan M. Jacobsen (Eds)., Philadelphia, PA: Hanley and Belfus, p. 244–8.

Skinner, B. F. (1974). *About Behaviorism*. New York: Vintage/Random House.

6   The Caregiver's Perspective

- Cultural differences exist in the experience of caregiving.
- Caregivers experience both reward and burden in caregiving.
- Caregiver interventions range from family inclusion, to psychoeducation to family therapy.
- Physician ethical guidelines exist for working with caregivers.
- Palliative care is a specialty that routinely practices family inclusion.

Introduction

Rosalyn Carter states: "There are only four kinds of people in the world—those who have been caregivers, those who are currently caregivers, those who will be caregivers and those who will need caregivers" (http://www.thefamilycaregiver.org/who_are_family_caregivers/). The primary caregiver is the main person in the family who takes on the active role of caregiving, while other family members more passively adjust to the changing family dynamics. Caregiver research and caregiver interventions are usually directed at the primary caregiver. However, the whole family is affected by the presence of illness.

Families experience caregiving in ways that are specific to their culture and ethnicity. This chapter reviews the caregiving experiences of African-Americans, Mexican-Americans and Asian-Americans and then reviews evidence-based caregiver interventions through the stages of the family life cycle. The family life cycle is a major determinant of how an illness is studied the family. For example, when a child is ill, the mother-child dyad is the most commonly studied family relationship, although the benefit of involving fathers and siblings in caregiver interventions has been shown (Kazak et al., 1999). For patients in their middle years of life, caregiver research targets the marital relationship. At the end of life, caregiver research focuses on caregiver burden. Where possible in this chapter, the emphasis is on interventions that can be implemented in the clinician's office.

Caregivers ask for "help coping" with their ill relative. The caregiver has to manage both the practical aspects of caring, such as assistance with daily activities, as well as being able to give emotional support to their relative. Caregivers tend not to ask for help for themselves, citing the greater need of the other person. It is therefore important to encourage caregivers to develop good self-care skills.

Family caregivers do not like the term "caregiver burden," and it is better to ask caregivers about specific times when there has been suffering, hurts, or sadness.

Caregivers with limited financial or family resources report that the negatives of caregiving exceed the positives (Wells, Cagle, Bradley, and Barnes, 2008), although many caregivers do derive reward from caregiving, acknowledging that they "have a chance to give back" or "I can show how much I care" (Heru, Ryan and Iqbal, 2004). Caregiving is an honor and an important family role in many cultures. Acknowledging the rewards as well as the difficulties is crucial for working with caregivers. The American College of Physicians offers ethical guidance to physicians to help develop mutually supportive patient, physician, caregiver relationships (Mitnick, Leffler and Hood, 2010).

Ethical Guidelines for Collaborating with Caregivers

- Recognize the caregivers as a source of continuity for the patient's history and care
- Facilitate transition for serious chronic illness to palliative care services
- Recognize and treat caregiver distress
- Ensure appropriate boundaries with caregiver in delivering patient care
- Continue to monitor caregivers for distress after the death of the patient.

(Abbreviated from Mitnick, Leffler and Hood, 2010)

Cultural Differences in the Caregiving Experience

Families experience caregiving in ways that are specific to their culture and ethnicity. General descriptions of the caregiving experience are easily accessible; however the nuances of caregiving in different cultures have received scant attention. A systematic review of the literature, from 1980 to 2009, identifies differences between the caregiving experiences of African-American (AA), Latino, and Chinese-American caregivers (Napoles, Chadiha, Eversley, and Moreno-John, 2010). Ethnic differences in caregiving occur at multiple levels such as intrapersonal, interpersonal, and environmental, and in multiple domains such as psychosocial health, life satisfaction, caregiving appraisals, spirituality, coping, self-efficacy, physical functioning, social support, filial responsibility, familism, views toward elders, use of formal services and health care. Only eleven of 47 intervention studies in this review tailored caregiver intervention to specific cultures and eight of these eleven studies were from one Alzheimer caregiver's initiative.

Appraisals of caregiving burden and the experience of depression in caregivers vary by ethnicity. AA caregivers report lower levels of caregiver burden and depression than white caregivers, and Latino and Asian-American caregivers report higher levels of depression than white caregivers (Pinquart and Sorensen, 2005).

Reliance on family, religion and prayer are coping strategies that differ between cultures. Most minority cultures have a strong family orientation and a mistrust of "white culture" institutions.

Health-care disparities exist in the availability of culturally appropriate interventions and also in the utilization of interventions. For example, Hispanic older adults use home health-care services (HHCS) less frequently than other groups (Centers for Medicare and Medicaid Services, 2003). HHCS ease hospital-to-home transition, teach caregivers how to give quality care, and enrich caregivers' relationships with older adults (Onder et al., 2007). The process of deciding to use HHCS was analyzed in MA elders (n = 11) and their family caregivers (n = 12). The elders and their caregivers identified three stages in coming to the decision to use HHCS: Taking Care of our Own, Acknowledging Options, and Becoming Empowered. These MA families found a way to accept HHCS while maintaining their cultural norm of taking care of their elders. When an understanding of cultural differences is made part of the process, MA traditional family values, such as elders' staying at home as long as possible, can be honored.

African-American Caregivers

The AA reliance on family for caregiving is greater than among whites, especially regarding the provision of care in the home (Cagney and Agree, 1999). Specific caregiver themes were identified by AA family caregivers who were caregiving for a relative at the end of life, through in-depth interviews and focus groups (Turner, Wallace, Anderson, and Bird, 2004). These caregivers (n = 88) were mostly women (88%) who came from various regions of the United States and included all socioeconomic groups. The main theme of the AA caregivers was that home care preserves dignity in old age compared with nursing home care, which was perceived as demeaning and embarrassing. Sharing caregiving responsibilities among family members and working as a team was emphasized. The AA community also identified the following themes as important at the end of life: faith, family communication, support groups, trust and learning to work with the system. In most of the focus groups, caregivers reluctantly realized that they might have to turn over care of their relative to a nursing home at some point. Culturally sensitive family interventions can help AA families by facilitating decision-making and improving trust at the end of life.

Mexican-American Caregivers

In MA families, female family members usually provide care in the home. In a study of caregivers recruited from an oncology clinic, MA (n = 34) caregivers were compared to non-Hispanic whites (Wells, Cagle, Bradley, and Barnes, 2008). The MA caregivers were less educated, had lower incomes, limited English language skills, greater competing life roles, and greater change of informal networks of family. They were caring for relatives in poorer health than their white counterparts and had more role-related emotional distress and more negative physical health consequences. The MA caregivers provided care from two hours per week to 24 hours per day. The women were low-to-moderately acculturated, aged 13–74 years of age, most were born in Mexico, and several had traveled to the United States to become caregivers. Spanish was the primary language for both speaking and writing for 29.4%. The themes that emerged from the study were: becoming stronger; life restructuring; strategizing; struggling; and getting support.

Themes of Female Mexican Caregivers

- Becoming stronger
- Life restructuring
- Strategizing
- Struggling
- Getting support.

(Wells et al., 2008)

Becoming Stronger

MA families value the caregiving role. MA women experienced emotional, cognitive, and spiritual growth through their role as a caregiver. The role of caregiver is supported by the culture and feelings of importance and appreciation by others are common. The MA caregivers acknowledged the rewards for caregiving, and felt "satisfied with her role." Becoming stronger meant helping the patient get quality care, helping the family become closer, and learning more about health care and advocacy. Caregiving also strengthened their faith in God.

Life Restructuring

Caregiving necessitates changes in family roles and frequently women move their residence to become caregivers. A caregiver first meets the patient's needs, then her family members' needs, and lastly, her own needs. The women believed that caregiving is the "right thing to do" and "nothing is more important than caring for a sick loved one." Caregivers provided encouragement to the patient, scheduled appointments, provided transportation, did house-keeping and helped with medications.

MA caregivers frequently give up jobs to provide full-time care with resulting financial consequences. Caregivers also face difficulties in balancing work, caregiving and family demands and family conflicts can arise as the family negotiates these changes.

Strategizing

Caregivers believed that they could provide better care than nonfamily members, and that with quality care, the patient becomes stronger and "keeps going." By being there, caregivers worried less and felt emotionally closer to the patient and other family members who assisted with care. Advocating meant learning to navigate the health-care system. Caregivers emphasized patience and "dealing with one day at a time." In order to appear strong, they did not share their frustrations with the patient. This was felt to be very important in holding the family together. Keeping a positive attitude, believing in the doctor and the treatment, facing situations with strength, and encouraging the patient to overcome illness through the treatment were important caregiver strategies.

Caregivers experienced sadness away from the patient. They expressed their feelings with their husbands, and in prayer. Many caregivers asked God to give them strength and patience and believed that God was the "ultimate decision-maker." They believed that health-care providers worked "under God's guidance." They did not attend church regularly but reported feeling supported by their faith. Caregivers shared information and talked frequently with other women in their communities. Caregivers wanted help with providing emotional support to the patient, medication administration, and meal preparation.

Struggling

Caregivers struggled with several issues; being uncertain about what was best to do for their loved one, having no money, getting sick, and needing an interpreter. Being uncertain also included "the family getting depressed" when the doctor did not provide direction on managing illness, when promises to deliver health-care services were not kept, and when there is no cure. Caregiver uncertainty contributed to a delay in accessing palliative care services for terminally patients. Having little money and/or insurance to pay for patient care or meet other caregiver needs was a frequently expressed challenge.

Caregivers had their own symptoms such as stomachaches, headaches, lack of sleep, inability to get out of bed to provide care, and chest pain. The caregivers did not associate these symptoms with caregiving. Motivation to take care of themselves was based on staying well to continue caregiving.

Caregivers noted that the doctor's inability to speak Spanish, lack of an interpreter, and the lack of educational materials in Spanish blocked their ability to provide care.

Getting Support

The caregiver's family helped with money, childcare, housing, and transportation as well as helping with emotional support, such as listening to frustrations or accompanying the caregiver to the clinic. Caregivers appreciated phone calls to confirm appointments and being included in the assessment process. Caregivers identified nurses who encouraged them to improve self-care.

Caregivers did not generally choose to accept outside services, even though this would help families with limited budgets. Barriers to care included long waits in the clinic for appointment times, the lack of Spanish print material, and the lack of available interpreters. Caregivers who felt supported were best able to effectively strategize to provide quality care. These caregivers most successfully experienced "becoming stronger."

Working with Hispanic Caregivers

- Preserve the caregiver's need to be strong in front of her family
- Have private conversations with the caregiver to assess emotional and learning needs during health-care encounters
- Offer confidential supportive assistance
- Teach about self-care
- Organize caregiver education
- Provide access to pastoral care during clinic waits

Asian-American Caregivers

Asian-American cultures emphasize interdependence and the importance of family over the individual. Asian-Americans place high emphasis on respect for older persons, obedience to parents, and filial obligations to aging parents (Olson, 2001). Caring for the elderly at home is considered a moral and social responsibility and placement in an institution is considered a failure of filial duty. When Asian-American caregivers are studied, cultural barriers to accepting care services are found. Hong (2004) extracted data about Asian-American caregivers (n = 157), from the Family Caregiving in the U.S. Survey that was conducted in 1997. The Asian-American caregivers had a mean age of 38.8 years, 58.6% were spouses or children, 52.2% were female and 77.1% were working either full-time or part-time. The barriers were categorized as service provider barriers (47.8%) and personal barriers (52.2%). Service barriers included the "service is not available," "bureaucracy too complex," or "can't find qualified providers." The most frequently unmet service needs were in adult day care, meal services, and personal care. Asian-Americans have dietary preferences that are unlikely to be met by the traditional American diet served in day care or senior centers. Service centers are also unlikely to cater to clients who speak Mandarin or other Asian languages. Personal barriers included caregivers feeling "too proud to accept it" or "didn't want outsiders coming in." These personal barriers are consistent with Asian-American cultures and traditions that emphasize self-sufficiency, family obligation, and privacy. These cultural barriers play a role in older Asian-Americans postponing personal care services until their need is overwhelming. Building mutual understanding and trust through outreach and educational programs, collaboration with community leaders, use of Asian-American staff, and use of client's native language can be helpful.

Evidence-Based Caregiver Interventions

Each caregiver has unique needs and challenges. A family intervention can focus on the patient, the caregiver, or the whole family. Initially a family educational intervention can be tried. However, if there is significant family conflict, a family systemic intervention may be needed. Despite the many possible variables, there are general goals for caregiving interventions.

Goals of Caregiver Family Interventions

- Help families cope with and manage the stresses as a team rather than as individuals
- Mobilize the patient's natural support system
- Prevent the disease from dominating family life and sacrificing normal developmental and personal goals
- Enhance family closeness
- Reduce social isolation and resulting anxiety and depression
- Increase mutually supportive interactions among family members
- Build additional extra-familial support, with the goal of improving disease management and the health and well-being of patients and all family members
- Help reorganize the family, with adjustments of roles and expectations as needed, to ensure optimal patient self-care
- To minimize intra-familial hostility and criticism and to reduce the adverse effects of external stress and disease-related trauma on family life.

(Adapted from Weihs, Fisher and Baird, 2002)

General caregiver interventions focus on the family's adjustment to illness, patient adherence to treatment and reorganization of family roles. Specific caregiver interventions can focus on tasks such as helping with pain management, but regardless of the situation, the principles of caregiver intervention are similar. Teaching families the steps of problem solving has lasting value as they can apply these principles to each new problem that arises.

Problem-Solving Steps

- Identification of the problem
- Communication of the problem with all family members
- Development of different options to solve the problem
- Choosing the solution
- Putting the solution into practice
- Returning together to discuss the success or difficulties implementing the solution.

Caregiving for Children

The developmental stage of the child affects their understanding of illness. Parents need guidance when explaining illness and treatment to their children. Children also need help in understanding illness in their family members, especially if the illness is terminal and the child faces loss of a parent. The cognitive and emotional development of children is described in this chapter (p. 109) and in Chapter 7.

Parental caregivers may use different individual coping strategies and family conflict can arise if each parent has non-compatible coping strategies. If one parent thinks it is best to "keep the child a child and don't tell them anything about their illness" and the other parent thinks that the child should "know everything," then the child will feel they have to choose between their parents, or will direct certain questions to the caregiver they think will be most receptive.

Parents' confidence in managing their child's chronic illness is enhanced by reinforcing strategies such as building relationships with the child's care providers (Kratz, Uding, Trahms,Villareale, and Kieckhef, 2009). A study of caregivers (n = 199) identified helpful strategies (see below). These caregivers were mostly married white women with health insurance and only 38% characterized their child's condition as severe. While this is a select sample, the strategies can be helpful for all parental caregivers. This information is easily shared with parents in an office setting.

Helpful Strategies for Parents Coping with their Child's Illness

- Be prepared. Carry your own medical record, learn the language, learn the law, build relationships with your child's care providers and teach people what works best for you.
- Connect with peers.
- Become an advocate. Providers cannot read your mind. Speak up, be specific, become part of the team. Educate, share information and raise awareness with your child's classmates and friends.
- Care for your own personal needs.
- Recognize rewards. These children bring a depth of understanding to people around them. Be appreciative of the little things.

(Adapted from Kratz et al., 2009)

The physician can reinforce these strategies, acknowledge the personal impact of the child's illness on the family, and express an understanding of common challenges that all parents face. Helpful questions and comments that the physician can ask to support parental caregivers are outlined below.

Strategies to Support Parental Caregivers

- "How are you doing?"
- "What are you finding works best?"
- "I know it doesn't change things, but I can tell you I have heard other parents express similar thoughts and feelings." "Have you been in touch with other parents?"
- "Many parents find it helpful to connect with others in a similar situation. This can happen in a variety of ways, like one-to-one conversations, participating in groups, or via the web.
- "What do you think would work best for you right now?"
- "This can feel quite overwhelming and frightening. However, I've learned that over time parents find their stride and their confidence grows. One step in that direction is for us to focus on what's most important to you right now."

Ask for the parent's observations and include their suggestions into your thinking and planning. Work at problem solving together. "What do you think is going on here?" "What suggestions do you have?" "Here's what I'm thinking, what about you?" "Let's think about next steps together."

Mere participation in a parenting support program is not enough however, to ensure a good family outcome. Parents who receive help that is empowering and supportive are more likely to report greater well-being, satisfaction with parenting, and family unity (Dunst, Trivette, and Hamby, 2007). Good professional support is associated with better family quality of life (Davis and Gavidia-Payne, 2009). The following studies show the benefit of family inclusion and family psychoeducation for parents of children with chronic illnesses.

Parents can be taught how to manage their children's symptoms effectively. Children's complaints of abdominal pain can be reduced with a three-session intervention that targets parents' responses to their children's complaints (Levy et al., 2010). Children (n = 200), with three or more episodes of recurrent unexplained abdominal pain during a three-month period were subjected to a parental intervention that taught parents how to manage their complaints of pain. The intervention was highly effective in teaching parents how to reduce their solicitous responses to their child's symptoms (p < 0.0001), when compared with control group parents. Many of these differences were maintained six months after the intervention.

The first session teaches relaxation training as a stress and symptom management tool and introduces concepts of social learning, modeling, and reinforcement. Relaxation training includes training in paced diaphragmatic breathing, progressive muscle relaxation, and training in imagery. Parents are taught how to redirect attention to wellness behaviors, coping and skill building rather than focusing on the child's illness behavior. The second session examines cognitions regarding symptoms. Parents and children are helped to identify and modify dysfunctional cognitions. The third session focuses on the consolidation of skills and helps the families develop a plan for maintaining their newly learned skills. Components of this brief social learning/cognitive-behavioral therapy intervention can be applied in a variety of health-care settings. In the office, for example, clinicians can discuss parental responses to children's symptoms, encourage a focus on wellness behaviors, and discourage a focus on illness behaviors.

Caregiving for Adolescents

One of the greatest challenges for families is balancing the adolescent's need for self-determination with the parental need to protect. In the case of chronic illness, this balance becomes crucial when poor control and poor compliance have life-threatening consequences. The management of chronic childhood illnesses, such as diabetes, often becomes a battleground for adolescents and their families, fighting for autonomy and control. At the Joslin Clinic in Boston, children and adolescents with diabetes were randomly assigned to a family-focused intervention intended to reduce family conflict, or to standard care (Laffel et al., 2003). Both groups met three to four times a year. The family-focused intervention emphasized teamwork, particularly in the area of insulin injections and measurement of blood glucose. An RN, who had received basic family skills training, ran the family-focused intervention. The intervention reduced family conflict, improved the management of the diabetes, prevented complications, and improved family relationships, at little added expense to the clinic.

A version of this intervention called "The WE CAN intervention" has been expanded successfully to four different sites with 122 families participating (Nansel et al., 2009). The WE CAN intervention is individualized to each family but the traditional steps of problem solving are followed. The RN or family therapist works with the family guiding them through the problem-solving steps.

The WE CAN Problem-Solving Acronym

- Work together to set goals
- Explore possible barriers and solutions
- Choose the best solution
- Act on your plan
- Note the results.

Caregiving for Spouses

A collaborative problem solving approach has been tested with couples managing diabetes (Trief et al., 2011). Couples (n = 44), in which one partner had poor glucose control, were randomly assigned to a couple's intervention, an individual intervention, or individual diabetes education. All intervention contacts were by telephone and all interventions resulted in clinical improvements. This study deserves replication, as the numbers in each group were small.

Female spouses tend to assume more care for their spouse, taking a "we" or dyadic coping approach, compared to male spouses. In a study of diabetes and caregiving, the men avoided experiencing or expressing vulnerability and did less for their spouses than the female spouses did for the male patients (Knudson-Martin and Mahoney, 2009).

Pain management is a frequent focus of family conflict. Spouses frequently ask "Should I do things for her because of the pain, even when I think she can do things for herself?" or "How do I know how much pain he is in, and how much he just wants sympathy?" Families frequently are unsure how best to respond to the person with chronic pain. A three-session couple's psychoeducational intervention for pain management resulted in 25% improvement in caregivers feeling that they could help the patient control pain better (Keefe et al., 2005). These results are significant because the caregivers in the control group rated themselves as having deteriorating self-efficacy. An RN provided the intervention in the family's home over several weeks. Written materials, videotape and audiotapes were used to help educate the patient and partner about cancer pain and its management and to teach pain coping strategies.

In Session 1, the nurse provides an overview of the program, distributes materials and answers questions. In Session 2, relaxation training and the use of pleasant imagery as an aid to pain control are introduced. In Session 3, patients are taught to pace their activity level. Patients identify activities that they have trouble tolerating, and learn to break them up into periods of activity and rest (e.g. ten minutes of activity followed by five minutes of rest). A three-step behavioral rehearsal procedure is used: (1) the therapist guides the patient and partner through the use of a particular coping skill (e.g. relaxation training) and review their reactions, (2) the patient's partner is asked to serve as a coach, guiding and encouraging the patient in use of the coping skill, and (3) the therapist provides feedback to the patient and partner about the partner's performance as a coach and the patient's response. At the end of Session 3, coping skills are reviewed. A plan for coping with problems that might arise in the near future is developed. This is an example of a short-term, focused, easily implemented family psychoeducational intervention for management of chronic illness symptoms. The basic principles can be introduced in an outpatient clinic setting.

Caregiving for the Elderly

Most dementia programs include a caregiving component. A five-session caregiver intervention study has been shown to be of benefit in three continents: New York City, U.S., Manchester, U.K. and Sydney, Australia (Mittelman, Brodaty, Wallen and Burns, 2008). Caregivers showed benefit with reduction in depressive symptoms, not accounted for solely by antidepressant use. The benefit increased over the next two years, even though the individual and family counseling sessions occurred in the first three months of the study. The intervention consisted of one individual caregiver session, followed by three sessions that included family members who were invited by the caregiver to participate, and one additional individual caregiver session. *Ad hoc* counseling was available to the caregivers and their family members throughout the study. The content of the intervention was dependent on the needs of each caregiving family but all interventions included education about Alzheimer's disease, information about community resources, and help in managing difficult patient behavior. Emotional support and assistance for the caregiving spouse was the main focus of the intervention. Common topics of discussion were how and where to provide care, who should provide care, how to ask for and offer help, what kind of help was needed, and who was willing and able to provide help. It is impressive that in the New York City arm of the study, improvement in depression for the caregivers was apparent five years after enrollment.

In a study of Alzheimer's caregivers (n = 254) who had experienced the death of their spouse, caregivers who received an enhanced caregiver support intervention versus usual care, had lower depressive symptoms compared with controls (Haley et al., 2008). It is important to provide spousal caregivers with community resources. There are many national caregiving groups, often specific to the disease. There is a website for spousal caregivers (http://www.wellspouse.org/) which provides local information for each state.

Caregiving for Patients with Terminal Illness

Palliative care practices a multidisciplinary team approach that includes families. Palliative care practitioners usually have some training in basic family skills. When a family member is gravely ill, palliative care provides guidance and care to both the patient and their family. Telephone interviews with family members (n = 190) of patients who had recently died, found that the family's satisfaction with the quality of medical care at the end of life was improved by receiving palliative care services. Family members who had received palliative care services reported that their emotional or spiritual needs were met (65%), as compared with usual care (35%) and greater self-efficacy (67%), as compared usual care (44%) (Gelfman, Meier and Morrison, 2008). Palliative care is an example of a medical specialty where family inclusion is part of their mandate.

Many palliative care services offer support to the bereaved, for example, condolence letters, memorial cards, grief brochures, memorial services, telephone calls, personal meetings, self-help groups, social group meetings, and individual, family, or group therapy. A supportive telephone call four weeks after the death, was received well by 72% of bereaved family members (Kaunonen, Tarkka, Laippala, and Paunonen-Ilmonen, 2000). However, there is a lack of agreement on what bereavement support should be offered and to whom. What do families say they need? In a study in Sweden, 46% of family members (n = 248) who were assessed 3 to 5 months after a family member's death, expressed a need for bereavement follow-up (Milberg, Olsson, Jakobsson, Olsson, and Friedrichsen, 2008). Most family members wanted a personal meeting with the staff member who had had the most contact with the patient and the family. According to the families in this study, the best time for support was 2–6 weeks into bereavement. The family members wanted to talk about what had happened during the palliative phase (e.g. if the patient had suffered or not), about their present situation, their feelings of loneliness, and about the future.

Recovery from bereavement has traditionally been thought to occur by helping the bereaved person express feelings of loss and other negative emotions. However, an alternative view has been suggested where positive emotions are enhanced and negative grief-related emotions are minimized. Self-transcendence is an example of a positive emotion. This can occur, for example, when a family member is able to fulfill the patient's last wish to die at home. This Dual Process Model of Coping with Bereavement promotes adaptive coping and suggests that grief be experienced in small doses (Stroebe, and Schut, 1999). A focus on the past (feelings of loss and grief) is balanced with a focus on the present and a focus on the future, such as finding a new identity and taking on new roles. The bereaved person is encouraged to take a break from the stress, and to feel joy or other positive emotions after the patient's death.

The Palliative Care Family Meeting

Family meetings between the patient, their family, and health care professionals have multiple purposes, including the sharing of information and concerns, clarifying the goals of care, discussing diagnosis, treatment, prognosis and developing a plan of care. Recently developed guidelines help clinicians conduct family meetings in the palliative care setting (Hudson, Quinn, O'Hanlon, and Aranda, 2008). These clinical guidelines advocate that family meetings be conducted routinely on admission to a palliative care service. This preventative approach is recommended rather than waiting until a crisis develops and then calling a meeting.

Clinical Practice Guidelines for Conducting Family Meetings in Palliative Care

1. Preparing for a family meeting
    a) A family meeting is offered to all lucid patients. This invitation should explain the role that palliative care has in supporting families as well as the patient.
    b) The patient identifies key family caregivers and/or friends to be involved in medical and care planning discussions.
    c) A family genogram can be done to determine key relationships within the patient's family. It could be introduced thus: "Can I spend a few minutes just working out who is in your family?"
    d) Ask the patient if they have any particular issues/concerns or questions they would like discussed at the meeting.
    e) Identify the most appropriately skilled person from the multidisciplinary team to convene the family meeting.
    f) Establish the issues that the patient and family carer would like discussed.
    g) Invite only the relevant health professionals.

2. Conducting a family meeting
    a) Introduction with ground rules e.g. "We would like to hear from all of you, however could one person please speak at a time, each person will have a chance to ask questions and express views."
    b) Briefly outline the purpose of the family meeting and then confirm with the family and patient that they agree. Identify any additional key concerns.
    c) Determine what the patient and family already know. Ask each family member in turn if they have any questions about current status, plan, and prognosis.
    d) Address each objective of the meeting.
    e) Offer relevant resources. Examples include guidebooks, brochures, power of attorney documents, advance care directive information, etc.
    h) Conclude the discussion by summarizing areas of consensus, disagreements, decisions, and the ongoing plan.
                      (Adapted from Hudson, Quinn, O'Hanlon, and Aranda, 2008)

Palliative care family meetings help family caregivers have their needs met (Hudson, Thomas, Quinn and Aranda, 2009). Family interviewing techniques in palliative care are becoming more sophisticated, borrowing from the rich family therapy literature (Dumont and Kissane, 2009). Generally, at the beginning of therapy, most questions are linear i.e. direct questioning, but as the interview progresses, questions can become more circular. This means that the family members participate in asking and answering open-ended questions. This allows a more complete picture of what the family, as a whole, is experiencing. The use of strategic questions, such as "What would the family reaction be if mother decided she wanted hospice at home?" can help the family develop new perspectives.

The Family COPE model (McMillan et al., 2006) uses a problem solving approach to help families assess and manage symptoms of persons with cancer at home. This approach is taught in three sessions and is effective in improving caregiver quality of life (p = 0.03), reducing burden related to patients' symptoms (p < 0.001), and caregiving tasks burden (p = 0.038), compared with hospice care alone or hospice plus emotional support. This intervention is manualized and easily replicated. The list below outlines the essential components of this model.

McMillan's COPE Model

Creativity: View problems from different perspectives.
   Develop new strategies for solving caregiving problems.
   "What could I do to distract Dad from his pain?"

Optimism: Have a positive, but realistic, attitude toward the problem-solving
   process.
   "I believe I can help Dad with his pain."
   Communicating realistic optimism to the patient by showing understanding and
   hope.

Planning: Set reasonable caregiving goals.
   Think out, in advance, the steps necessary to reach those goals.
   "How can I get Dad ready for our family holiday party?"

Expert information: When to get professional help.
   What non-professionals need to know about the nature of the problem.
   What family caregivers can do on their own to deal with the problem.
   "Where can I go to get help with Dad's pain?"
   Symptom assessment.

Several meta-analyses show that family interventions are of limited benefit for caregivers with family members who are dying. Interventions that buffer against psychological distress in the short-term have most benefit (Candy, Jones, Drake, Leurent and King, 2011). In a Cochrane Review of RCTs, eleven RCTs (n = 1,836 caregivers) met inclusion criteria, with nine interventions delivered directly to the caregiver. Seven interventions aimed to improve coping skills, and two interventions aimed to enhance caregiver well-being. Most interventions were given by an RN, SW, or family therapist and ranged from two to nine sessions. In two studies, up to 50% of caregivers declined to participate (Hudson, Aranda, and Hayman-White, 2005, Kissane et al., 2006).

A second meta-analysis of 29 trials, found that psychological well-being of family caregivers of cancer patients could be improved in the short-term (Northouse, Katapodi, Song, Zhang, and Mood, 2010). Many studies were underpowered, making any conclusions fairly tentative. Providing help for caregivers at this difficult time is not straightforward as their needs are complicated by grief.

A third systematic review (Hudson, Remedios and Thomas, 2010) identified 14 studies of psychosocial interventions for family caregivers of palliative care patients. Five studies were RTCs, two were prospective studies, five pre-test/post-test projects and two were qualitative studies. The studies aimed to improve psychosocial support, caregiver coping, symptom management and sleep promotion, and provide psychoeducation. Studies were excluded if they were patient-focused, were designed for caregivers during the bereavement process, if they involved "complementary therapies" such as massage, or were interventions involving caregivers of patients with non-life-threatening disease.

Two studies that had the highest evidence were able to improve caregiver well-being. The first effective study was a psychoeducational program that had a positive effect on caregivers' perceptions of their role (Hudson et al. 2005). This intervention consisted of three sessions that focused on the role of a caregiver in the palliative care context, strategies for self-care and for caring for their relative, strategies for caring for a person when death is approaching, and an overview of bereavement supports. Caregivers receive a copy of a Carer Guidebook designed specifically for preparing family caregivers (http://www.centreforpallcare.org). Hudson et al. (2012) have gone on to refine this intervention into a single session hospital-based psychoeducation group program for caregivers. Those who participated reported benefit in their level of preparedness (p < .05), although almost 50% of eligible caregivers declined to participate.

The second study is McMillan et al. (2006) COPE study where three groups are compared: a coping skill training intervention, a hospice plus emotional support, and usual hospice care. At 30 days, the coping skills intervention had improved caregiver quality of life (p = 0.03), burden of patient symptoms (p < 0.001), and caregiving task burden (p = 0.038), compared to the other interventions. None of the groups showed change in caregiving mastery, problem-focused or emotion-focused coping.

A third psychosocial support intervention had no benefit to caregivers (Walsh et al., 2007). Support was provided over six weeks, for 271 distressed caregivers of patients receiving palliative care. A comprehensive assessment of domains of need was made: past, present and future issues were discussed and advice, information, and emotional support provided. Sometimes a telephone call took the place of a visit. The advisors met weekly with the research team for debriefing, for advice on any issues that arose, and to ensure that all domains of carer need were covered in the intervention. These domains were: (a) patient care; physical health needs; need for time away from the patient in the short-term and longer term; need to plan for the future; psychological health, relationships and social networks; relationships with health and social service providers; finances.

Reducing grief among families at risk of poor psychosocial outcome was tried with family-focused grief therapy (Kissane et al., 2006). Two hundred and fifty-seven families of patients dying from cancer were screened with the twelve-item Family Relationships Index. One hundred and eighty-three were considered to be at risk and were randomly assigned to family-focused grief therapy (53 families, 233 individuals) or a control condition (28 families, 130 individuals). Family-focused grief therapy consisted of four to eight sessions of 90 minutes' duration, over nine to eighteen months. The intervention aimed to enhance the functioning of the family, through exploration of its cohesion, communication of thoughts and feelings, and handling of conflict. There were three phases: (1) assessment concentrates on identifying issues and concerns relevant to the specific family and on devising a plan to deal with them, (2) intervention focuses on the agreed concerns, and (3) termination consolidates gains and confronts the end of therapy. The overall impact of family-focused grief therapy was modest, with a reduction in distress at 13 months. Individuals with high levels of distress and depression at baseline improved in these areas but global family functioning did not change. Sullen families and those with intermediate functioning tended to improve overall, whereas depression was unchanged in hostile families. Of note, over 50% of caregivers approached declined to participate.

In summary, it is unclear how best to meet the needs of caregivers caring for patients at the end of life. McMillan's COPE model is brief and easy to implement and deserves replication and refinements. In the office setting, families can be provided with basic information about accessing services and coping well.

Helping Families Help their Children in the Palliative Care Setting

Parents often want to know what, when and how to tell their children that a parent is dying. The guidelines presented here are based on a qualitative study of 87 children from different age groups (Christ and Christ, 2006). In brief, children need age-appropriate information, and involvement with their dying parent. Children process information based upon their cognitive and emotional stage of development (see Chapter 7 for details). Generally, in the hospital setting, children visiting a sick parent should have visits that are planned, structured, and focused on positive active interaction with their parent. The length of visit should be limited according to the developmental age of the child and the physical and mental state of the parent. The treatment their parent is receiving and the purpose of equipment such as IVs, oxygen, etc., that is in their parent's hospital room must be explained. Communicate about the parent's condition in small increments and in an ongoing way, with greater detail, as appropriate, for older children. Helping and caring for the ill parent can be discussed, and the child assured that they will continue to be cared for and loved by other family members. Children generally experience emotional reactions intermittently and for brief periods of time interspersed with rapid return to normative functioning. If the child has prolonged feelings of sadness or grief, a formal evaluation should be sought. The following guidelines are summarized from this study and presented here to emphasize the need to include children in the care of patients.

Guidelines Relating to 3- to 5-Year-Olds

- Gradually and consistently explain changes with their parent, without being overly optimistic/pessimistic.
- Children can learn "script" of events without fully comprehending meaning and importance; at this age, death is not understood as permanent.

- Separation from primary caregiver is a major concern at this age.
- Establish consistent time when child can ask questions and share feelings, using play and art to concretize what is happening in family.
- Having "a good cry together" is frightening for young children.
- Anticipate separation anxiety and reassure children that they will be cared for.
- Normalize intermittent, brief intense emotional expression—changing subject and going off to play are important.
- Encourage planned, time-limited visits during prolonged parental hospitalizations. Assure child has toys, activities to do and that parent's limited capacity is explained.
- Offer families consultation for additional concerns.

Guidelines Relating to 6- to 8-Year-Olds

- Provide timely information to children about parent's illness: explain what child is seeing and hearing e.g. explain patient's withdrawal is caused by illness, not lack of love. Once children believe their own view of events, it can be difficult to alter.
- Children can be overcome by parent's strong anger or sadness. Controlled emotions are effective for discussing events.
- Normalize high emotionality at this age.
- Normalize children's temporary reductions in school performance.
- Engage other family, friends, etc to listen to emotional concerns if parent has difficulty listening empathically due to own distress.
- Reassure child about parent's ability to provide care even when they express emotion.
- Acknowledge situation's uncertainty and difficulty for everyone. Anticipatory anxiety can occur at this age, and children need support that family will continue.
- Reassure children that this is not their fault.
- Communicate with the child's teachers and others about parent's illness.
- Arrange consistent substitute caregiving with people who communicate well with child.
- Prepare child for medical emergencies that may require parents to leave the house unexpectedly.
- Give permission to ask questions and express emotions, as they fear they may upset others.
- Normalize children's need to maintain developmentally appropriate activities.
- Remind parents of their central role in maintaining self-esteem by providing praise.
- Prepare children to visit with parent in the hospital, explain what they are seeing, and make time for clarification afterward.
- Consider professional consultation for children this age if severe anxiety, fear, school phobia, preoccupation with self-blame, or persistent depression occur.

Guidelines Relating to 9- to 11-Year-Olds

- Give detailed information when parent's diagnosis is verified: name of the disease, specifics, symptoms, known causes, treatments, possible side effects—optimistic, hopeful communication, not unrealistic. Account for child's observations.

- Assure children the illness is not their fault.
- Acknowledge the stress of uncertainty for everyone, as well as the strength of family unit.
- Children this age may have feelings of sadness and loss about possibility of parent's death.
- Have child visit during prolonged hospitalizations, explain parent's condition and treatment, meet medical and nursing staff, and explore the hospital environment.
- Help child remain involved in after-school activities, sports, and ongoing contact with friends.
- Support children's interest in helping with patient's care, but child should not be independently in charge of the parent's care.
- Remind parents that coalitions and special preferences within the family may cause distress.
- Encourage children's interest in reading or writing about the disease or treatment.

Screening Tools

Screening tools help connect caregivers and their families with the level of service that they need. Families with minimal need can receive support and education from staff. Families with moderate need can receive family treatments such as psychoeducational approaches that are tailored to their difficulties. Families with significant need can be referred for a family assessment and treatment. The goal of screening caregivers is to determine what level of support and intervention is needed, then to match their need with the appropriate intervention. There are several screening tools that can be used in the clinician's office.

The distress thermometer is a widely available screening tool for cancer patients (Holland and Bultz, 2007). It is brief and easy to incorporate into a system of distress management (Snowden et al., 2011). The distress thermometer assesses the patient's perception of practical problems e.g. child care, housing, insurance/financial and transportation; physical problems e.g. eating, fatigue, getting around; emotional problems e.g. memory/concentration, depression, fear, spiritual/religious concerns; and family problems e.g. dealing with children, dealing with partner, dealing with close friend/relative.

A screening tool for families, called the Psychological Assessment Tool (PAT2.0), is used in pediatric oncology clinics (Kazak et al., 2007). The PAT2.0 assesses family structure and resources, family social support, family problems, parent stress reactions, family beliefs, child problems, and sibling problems. It takes less than ten minutes to complete. It categorizes families as low, medium, or high-risk families. In the pediatric cancer clinic, most families are low risk, endorsing three or fewer items, medium-risk families endorse items such as family stressors, child adjustment difficulties, financial concerns, etc., and about 10% of families are high-risk, with severe psychopathology and/or significant social or financial difficulties (Pai et al., 2008). This stratification allows interventions to be tailored to the family's needs.

Another brief tool is the twelve-item Family Relationships Index (FRI) (Moos and Moos, 1981). The FRI measures family perceptions of cohesiveness, expressiveness, and capacity to deal with conflict. The FRI identified all at-risk families in a study of families of cancer patients (Edwards and Clarke, 2005). The high sensitivity of the FRI makes it suitable as a screening measure for families at risk.

The Family Assessment Device (FAD) is a self-report tool that can function as a screening tool (Epstein, Baldwin and Bishop, 1983). This is the self-report tool that is associated with the McMaster model. It has been extensively validated (Miller, Epstein, Bishop, and Keitner, 1985) and translated into over twenty languages. A brief twelve-item general functioning variation is available and suitable for screening (see Appendix, p. 230).

A one-item screening tool for marital satisfaction can provide the clinician with an indication of couples in need of intervention (Bailey, Kerley and Kibelstis, 2012; Bailey, 2007) (see Chapter 10, p. 189 for details). Good marital quality is associated with better patient outcome for many illnesses (Heru, 2010) and this brief tool was acceptable to patients, who expressed pleasure at being asked about their relationship.

Conclusion

Caregivers are a broad and diverse group that includes friends, extended family, as well as children. Understanding the cultural norms of caregiving is vital in order to provide interventions that will be received positively. Interventions vary with the stage of illness and the family developmental stage. Interventions for families with children and adolescents can create a greater sense of well-being, satisfaction with parenting, and reduce family conflict. Spousal caregiver interventions are effective for improving pain management and improving diabetic control. Brief interventions help dementia caregivers develop fewer depressive symptoms. In the terminal phase of illness, the evidence for effective caregiver interventions is poor, but suggests that teaching coping skills or problem-solving skills are most helpful. Families want and express benefit from a palliative care family meeting and from contact with the care team after death.

At a minimum in the clinician's office, clinicians should include the family in the patient meeting and provide the family with educational handouts. Clinicians can offer caregivers support by firstly acknowledging their role. Providing emotional support and practical information on managing the care of their loved one, are common features of the interventions that were found to be most helpful for caregivers. Screening caregivers is important as long as there are referral sources or interventions that can be offered.

After family inclusion, the next level of intervention is provide psychoeducational interventions such as a family program. Psychoeducational approaches require the clinician to have skill in managing emotionally charged situations. Other important skills include an understanding of how the family contributes to treatment adherence (see Chapter 2), the role of family life cycle (see Chapter 3), and the stage and impact of the illness on the family. Psychoeducational interventions focus on reducing the family's experience of stress and focus on improving the experience of chronic illness, without changing the underlying family dynamics. (Chapter 10 describes psychoeducational interventions in detail.) If it becomes apparent that significant family changes are needed, family assessment and family systems intervention are indicated. These steps are outlined in Part Three.

References

Bailey, J. (2007). Diet, exercise and marriage? Presented at the 2007 Uniformed Services Academy of Family Physicians Scientific Assembly, Portland, OR.

Bailey, J., Kerley, S., and Kibelstis, K. (2012) A brief marital satisfaction screening tool for use in primary care medicine. *Family Medicine*, 44(2), 105–9.

Cagney, K. A., and Agree, E. M. (1999). Racial differences in skilled nursing care and home health use: the mediating effects of family structure and social class. *The Journals of Gerontology, Series B: Psychological Sciences and Social Sciences*, 54(4), S223–36.

Candy, B., Jones, L., Drake, R., Leurent, B., and King, M. (2011). Interventions for supporting informal caregivers of patients in the terminal phase of a disease. *Cochrane Database of Systematic Reviews*, Issue 6. Art. No. CD007617.

Centers for Medicare and Medicaid Services. (2003). Medicare Home health agency utilization and expenditure data by race and age group calendar year 2001. Centers for Medicare and Medicaid Services unpublished data. The data were extracted from the Health Care Information System. Retrieved from <http://www.Medicarestats@cms.hhs.gov>.

Christ, G. H., and Christ, A. E. (2006). Current approaches to helping children cope with a parent's terminal illness. *Cancer Journal for Clinicians*, 56, 197–212.

Crist, J. D., García-Smith, D. and Phillips, L.R. (2006). Accommodating the stranger en casa: how Mexican-American elders and caregivers decide to use formal care. *Research and Theory for Nursing Practice*, 20(2), 109–26.

Davis, K., and Gavidia-Payne, S. (2009). The impact of child, family and professional support characteristics on the quality of life in families of young children with disabilities. *Journal of Intellectual Developmental Disabilities*, 34(2), 153–62.

Dumont, I., and Kissane, D. (2009). Techniques for framing questions in conducting family meetings in palliative care. *Palliative Supportive Care*, 7(2), 163–70.

Dunst, C. J., Trivette, C. M., and Hamby, D. W. (2007). Meta-analysis of family-centered helpgiving practices research. *Mental Retardation & Developmental Disabilities Research Review*, 13(4), 370–8.

Edwards, B., and Clarke, V. (2005). The validity of the family relationships index as a screening tool for psychological risk in families of cancer patients. *Psychooncology*, 14(7), 546–54.

Epstein, N. B., Baldwin, L. M., and Bishop, D. S. (1983). The McMaster Family Assessment Device. *Journal of Marital and Family Therapy*, 9, 171–180.

Gelfman, L. P., Meier, D. E., and Morrison, R. S. (2008). Does palliative care improve quality? A survey of bereaved family members. *Journal of Pain Symptom Management*, 36, 22–8.

Haley, W. E., Bergman, E. J., Roth, D. L., McVie. T., Gaugler, J. E., and Mittelman, M. S. (2008). Long-term effects of bereavement and caregiver intervention on dementia caregiver depressive symptoms. *Gerontologist*, 48(6), 732–40.

Heru, A. (2010). Improving marital quality in women with medical illness: integration of evidence-based programs into clinical practice. *Journal of Psychiatric Practice*, 16(5), 297–305.

Heru, A. M., Ryan, C. E., and Iqbal, A. (2004). Family functioning in the caregivers of patients with dementia. *International Journal of Geriatric Psychiatry*, 19(6), 533–7.

Holland, J. C., and Bultz, B. D. (2007). The NCCN Guideline for distress management: A case for making distress the sixth vital sign. *Journal of the National Comprehensive Cancer Network*, 5, 3–7.

Hong, L. (2004). Barriers to and unmet needs for supportive services: Experiences of Asian-American caregivers. *Journal of Cross-Cultural Gerontology*, 19, 241–60.

Hudson, P. L., Aranda, S., and Hayman-White, K. (2005). A psycho-educational intervention for family caregivers of patients receiving palliative care: a randomised controlled trial. *Journal of Pain and Symptom Management*, 30, 329–41.

Hudson, P. L., Quinn, K., O'Hanlon, B., and Aranda, S. (2008). Family meetings in palliative care: Multidisciplinary clinical practice guidelines. *BioMed Central Palliative Care*, 7, 12.

Hudson, P. L., Remedios, C., and Thomas K. (2010). A systematic review of psychosocial interventions for family carers of palliative-care patients. *BioMedCentral Palliative Care*, 9, 17.

Kaunonen, M., Tarkka, M. T., Laippala, P., and Paunonen-Ilmonen, M. (2000). The impact of supportive telephone call intervention on grief after the death of a family member. *Cancer Nursing*, 23(6), 483–91.

Kazak, A. E., Rourke, A. T., Alderfer, M. A., Pai, A., Reilly, A. F., and Meadows, A. T. (2007). Evidence-based assessment, intervention and psychosocial care in pediatric oncology: A blueprint for comprehensive services across treatment. *Journal of Pediatric Psychology*, 32, 1099–1110.

Kazak, A. E., Simms, S., Barakat, L., Hobbie, W., Foley, B., Golomb, V., and Best, M. (1999). Surviving cancer competently intervention program (SCCIP): a cognitive-behavioral and family therapy intervention for adolescent survivors of childhood cancer and their families. *Family Process*, 38(2), 175–91.

Kissane, D. W., McKenzie, M., Bloch, S., Moskowitz, C., McKenzie, D. P., and O'Neill, I. (2006). Family-focused grief therapy: a randomized controlled trial in palliative care and bereavement. *American Journal of Psychiatry*, 163, 1208–18.

Keefe, F. J. et al. (2005). Partner-guided cancer pain management at the end of life: A preliminary study. *Journal of Pain and Symptom Management*, 29, 263–72.

Knudson-Martin, C. (2009). An Unequal Burden: Gendered Power in Diabetic Care. In

Knudson-Martin, C., and Mahoney, A. R. (Es.). *Couples, Gender, and Power: Creating Change in Intimate Relationships*. New York: Springer.

Kratz, L., Uding, N., Trahms, C. M. Villareale, N., and Kieckhefer, G. M. (2009). Managing childhood chronic illness: parent perspectives and implications for parent-provider relationships. *Families, Systems and Health*, 27(4), 303–13.

Laffel, L. M., Vangsness, L., Connell, A., Goebel-Fabbri, A., Butler, D., and Anderson, B. J. (2003). Impact of ambulatory, family-focused teamwork intervention on glycemic control in youth with type 1 diabetes. *Journal of Pediatrics*, 142, 409–16.

Levy, R. L. et al. (2010). Cognitive-Behavioral Therapy for children with functional abdominal pain and their parents decreases pain and other symptoms. *American Journal of Gastroenterology*, 105(4), 946–56.

McMillan, S. C., Small, B. J., Weitzner, M., Schonwetter, R., Tittle, M., Moody, L., and Haley, W. E. (2006). Impact of coping skills intervention with family caregivers of hospice patients with cancer: A randomized clinical trial. *Cancer*, 106(1), 214–22.

Milberg, A., Olsson, E. C., Jakobsson, M., Olsson, M., and Friedrichsen, M. (2008). Family Members' Perceived needs for bereavement follow-up. *Journal of Pain Symptom Management*, 35(1), 58–69.

Miller, I. W., Epstein, N. B., Bishop, D. S., and Keitner, G. I. (1985).The McMaster Family Assessment Device: reliability and validity. *Journal of Marital Family Therapy*, 11, 345–56.

Mitnick, S., Leffler, C., and Hood, V. L. for the American College of Physicians Ethics, Professionalism and Human Rights Committee. (2010). Family caregivers, patients and physicians: ethical guidance to optimize relationships. *Journal of General Internal Medicine*, 25(3), 255–60.

Mittelman, M. S., Brodaty, H., Wallen, A. S., and Burns, A. (2008). A three-country randomized controlled trial of a psychosocial intervention for caregivers combined with pharmacological treatment for patients with Alzheimer disease: effects on caregiver depression. *American Journal of Geriatric Psychiatry*, 16(11), 93–904.

Moos, R. H. and Moos, B. S. (1981). *Family Environment Scale Manual*. Consulting Psychologists Press: Palo Alto, California.

Nansel, T. R. et al. (2009). A multisite trial of a clinic-integrated intervention for promoting family management of pediatric type 1 diabetes: feasibility and design. *Pediatric Diabetes*, 10 (2), 105–15.

Napoles, A. M., Chadiha, L., Eversley, R., and Moreno-John, G. (2010). Reviews: developing culturally sensitive dementia caregiver interventions: are we there yet? *American Journal of Alzheimers Disease & Other Dementias*, 25(5), 389–406.

Northouse, L. L., Katapodi, M.C., Song, L., Zhang, L., and Mood, D. W. (2010). Interventions with family caregivers of cancer patients: Meta-analysis of randomized trials. *A Cancer Journal for Clinicians*, 60, 317–39.

Olson, L. K. (2001). *Age through ethnic lenses: Caring for the elderly in a multicultural society.* Lanham, MD: Rowman & Littlefield.

Onder, G., Liperoti, R., Soldato, M., Carpenter, I., Steel, K., Bernabei, R., and Landi, F. (2007). Case management and risk of nursing home admission for older adults in home care: Results of the aged in home care study. *Journal of the American Geriatrics Society*, 55(3), 439–44.

Pai, A. L. et al. (2008). The Psychosocial Assessment Tool (PAT2.0): psychometric properties of a screener for psychosocial distress in families of children newly diagnosed with cancer. *Journal of Pediatric Psychology*, 33(1), 50–62.

Pinquart, M., and Sorensen, S. (2005). Ethnic differences in stressors, resources, and psychological outcomes of family caregiving: a meta-analysis. *Gerontologist*, 45(1), 90–106.

Snowden, A., White, C. A., Christie, Z., Murray, E., McGowan, C., and Scott, R. (2011). The clinical utility of the distress thermometer: a review. British Journal of Nursing, 9, 20(4), 220–7.

Stroebe, M., and Schut, H. (1999). The dual process model of coping with bereavement: rationale and description. *Death Studies*, 23 (3), 197–224.

Turner, W. L., Wallace, B. R., Anderson, J. R., and Bird C. (2004). The last mile of the way: understanding caregiving in African American families at the end-of-life. *Journal of Marital & Family Therapy*, 30(4), 427–38.

Trief, P., Sandberg, J. G., Ploutz-Snyder, R., Brittain, R., Cibula, D., Scales, K., and Weinstock, R. S. (2011). Promoting couples collaboration in type 2 diabetes: The diabetes support project pilot data. *Families, Systems and Health*, 29(3), 253–61.

Walsh, K., Jones, L., Tookman, A., Mason, C., McLoughlin, J., Blizard, R., and King M. (2007). Reducing emotional distress in people caring for patients receiving specialist palliative care. British Journal of Psychiatry, 190, 142–7.

Wells, J. N., Cagle, C. S., Bradley, P., and Barnes, D. M. (2008). Voices of Mexican American caregivers for family members with cancer on becoming stronger. *Journal of Transcultural Nursing*, 19 (3), 223–33.

Weihs, K., Fisher, L., and Baird, M. A. (2002). Families, health, and behavior: A section of the commissioned report by the committee on Health and Behavior: Research, Practice and Policy, Division of Neurosciences and Behavioral Health and Division of Health Promotion and Disease Prevention, Institute of Medicine. *National Academy of Sciences. Families, Systems, & Health.* 20, 1, 7–47.

7 Parenting with Chronic and Life-Threatening Illness

A Parent Guidance Model

Ellen H. O'Donnell, Kamryn T. Eddy, and Paula K. Rauch

- Many patients with chronic and life-threatening illnesses are parents, grandparents, or primary caregivers of children.
- The parent guidance model of the PACT program is built on the assumptions that parents are experts about their own children and that open communication about a parent's illness and prognosis is best.
- Clinicians can provide direct support and guidance to parents and model for them ways of communicating with children about illness.
- Understanding typical child development and learning about each child's temperament are fundamental to providing effective support.
- Communication style is unique in each family but key concepts that help clinicians guide parents, are identifying prior coping skills and understanding family climate and culture.
- Strategies to support patients and families with children include maintaining life structure, carving out family time, appointing family supports, structuring visits, and making referrals when needed.
- Clinicians play a role in helping parents' communicate an end of life prognosis to children and help families navigate end of life care and legacy leaving.
- The PACT program is a model of a team approach, which prevents clinician burn-out.

Introduction

Epidemiological studies estimate that over 1.6 million men and women will be newly diagnosed with cancer in 2012, and that approximately 41% of men and women will be diagnosed with cancer at some point in their lives (Howlader et al., 2012). A recent study that used a representative public health survey estimated that 1.58 million cancer survivors in the US had children under 18 years of age living with them between 2003 and 2004 (Weaver et al., 2010). This number represents only a fraction of those parents and other primary or secondary caregivers who are living with the broader spectrum of chronic and life-threatening illnesses. In addition to dealing with their own emotional reactions to the diagnosis and treatment of a chronic or life-threatening illness, parents must determine how best to support their children during this experience. The Marjorie E. Korff PACT (Parenting at a Challenging Time) Program at Massachusetts General Hospital was established by Paula Rauch,

M.D., in 1996 to address the unique concerns of parents living with cancer and other major medical illnesses.

The PACT program is a hospital-based consultation service that provides parent guidance to parents, spouses, co-parents, and other family members with caretaking responsibilities who are affected by chronic and life-threatening illnesses. The mission of our program is to support parents living with cancer. However, the principles that guide us and strategies we suggest are applicable for families that face a variety of chronic and life-threatening illnesses (e.g. ALS, multiple sclerosis, diabetes, stroke, and brain damage). Our team includes child psychiatrists, psychologists, and social workers with extensive training in child development. Our child-trained clinical team works closely with family members and parents, whom we recognize as experts in their own children, to provide individualized guidance during an emotionally and physically trying time. We appreciate that each medical diagnosis is associated with its own set of symptoms and natural course and that this varies by patient and family. We bring a base of knowledge about the illnesses and child development and aim to partner with families to understand the unique meaning of an illness for them.

Our program uses a consultative framework wherein clinicians are available to families at any point in their illness course—ranging from the time of initial diagnosis to end of life care. In our program, families are most often referred by members of the patient's oncology or surgical team. We have the flexibility to conduct inpatient, outpatient, and telephone consultations allowing us to maximize our availability to families.

We provide no hard and fast rules for parents and caregivers to follow. Instead, we offer lessons we have learned from the collection of our experiences with families in which a parent or other caregiver is ill, combined with what we know about child development and family systems. We view parents as experts in their children and families, and our job as consultants is to use this imparted expertise to provide individualized guidance to parents in supporting their children.

In this chapter, we provide a model for supporting families during a parent's illness within this parent-guidance framework. In addition to providing consultation directly to families, our team is also involved in education and outreach efforts to support the development of similar parent guidance programs nationally and internationally (Muriel and Rausch, 2009; Rausch and Muriel, 2006). While this chapter focuses on parents with cancer, the guidelines shared can be applied to all primary and secondary caregivers with the broad spectrum of chronic and life-threatening illnesses.

Child Development and Temperament

Child Development

How an individual child understands a parent's illness is influenced by a variety of factors including the child's age, previous family experiences with illness and death, and temperamental and developmental differences (see Table 7.1). Parents need to be respected in knowing their own children best and so we advise beginning any consultation by asking parents to "tell us about each of your children." As you are listening, it is helpful to have a framework for understanding how a child's coping does or does not map onto what we know about normative child development and how children understand a parent being sick. A basic understanding of typical cognitive development in children helps anticipate the challenges for individual families and children in communicating about and coping with a parent's illness.

Infants and Toddlers (0 to 2 years)

A key developmental milestone for infants and toddlers is to achieve a secure attachment to primary caregivers. This is the foundation for later self-regulation. It is accomplished through everyday interactions with primary caregivers. Babies and toddlers thrive on routine. Predictability and consistency allow them to feel secure that the people who care for them most can be counted upon during their age-appropriate exploration of the social and physical worlds. Primary caregivers play an essential role in the infant and toddler's emotional development, so the impact of illness on an affected parent, or co-parent's responsiveness and emotional availability are key to the effect on the infant or toddler. The parent's responsiveness to an infant or toddler's basic needs and attempts at play and social interaction will most affect a very young child.

Guidance for parents of young children focuses on a discussion of how they can maintain consistent routines and schedules. While it helps to have caregivers be fewer and familiar to young children, it is also good to remind parents that children are capable of forming secure attachments to more than one person. The most frequent and familiar caregivers can be tasked with writing down routines and schedules and communicating them to others who care for the child. It is important, too, to remind parents that it is fine for there to be slight variations in routine with different caregivers (as there are for any child) but every effort should be made to keep key aspects (e.g. bedtimes, feeding times) the same. As much as possible, young children should be cared for at home or another familiar place.

Parents of very young children may need to be reminded that separation anxiety is normal in 18- to 24-month-olds. Crying around separations is a sign of a healthy attachment between the parent and child. Routine separations teach infants and toddlers to trust their environment and caregivers and help them develop self-regulation and self-soothing skills. Parents sometimes need to be reminded that their child's distress when they leave for treatment has nothing to do with their illness or prognosis. If separations for medical care are well planned for, they will not be any more distressing for a very young child than going to daycare or mom going on a business trip. An infant or toddler's temperament can have a significant impact on how stressful separations will be for a particular family. An easy-going child is less likely to react strongly to a separation than a more intense child. This is not necessarily a sign that a child is more or less affected by a parent's illness. It does, though, present a greater challenge for certain families. Parents of more intense infants may need extra support and guidance around how to maintain consistent routines. For example, an intense baby might do better with one consistent paid caregiver who cares for her when her parents cannot, rather than with several more informal caregivers, even if they are close family.

Preschoolers (3 to 6 years)

Egocentrism, associative logic, and magical thinking are key concepts for conceptualizing and predicting how a preschool age child is likely to understand and cope with a parent's illness. According to Piaget, egocentrism is the inability of a child in the preoperational stage of cognitive development to really consider any perspective other than her own. In young children, associative logic refers to their tendency to believe that any event that immediately precedes another must have caused the second event. Magical thinking is the belief that some object, event or action that is not logically related to a course of events can influence its outcome. An example of a young child's understanding of a parent's illness that illustrates these three concepts is the child who believes she is a bad girl because she jumped on daddy's tummy and gave him a tumor and that if she is good and gives him some of her grape medicine he will get better.

Because of their propensity for illogical thinking, preschoolers need to be asked early on and often about their understanding of a parent's illness. This allows misconceptions to be addressed before they become upsetting to the child. Preschoolers may need frequent reminders that they were not and are not the cause of the illness or of its symptoms (e.g. nothing they said or did caused mommy's hair to fall out or made her sick to her stomach or sad or tired on a given day). It is important to remember that very young children may not seem particular distressed by a parent's illness or even very serious symptoms. This does not reflect a lack of emotion or empathy on the part of the child, but reflects their developmental level of understanding and is somewhat adaptive. Their distress may show itself in other ways, such as regression around a previously achieved milestone (e.g. potty training or giving up a binky or lovey) or with a resurgence of separation anxiety. As with younger children, it is still important for preschoolers to maintain as many routines as possible and to allow for the fact that they may need more "babying" from either the sick parent or another important caregiver.

School-Age Children (7 to 12 years)

The focus of the school-age child is increasingly on life outside the home and family. A child in the elementary years of school is focused on friends, sports, activities, and school. He is working on understanding cause and effect logic and on mastering the subtleties of social interactions. Children at this developmental stage are often invested in fairness and may be particularly sensitive to the ways in which having a sick parent sets them apart from their peers. For example, a nine-year-old boy may be most upset when he is told he cannot play on the travel soccer team because of the logistics of transporting him to games when mom is in the midst of chemotherapy. School-age children are learning to tell and understand time but may still have an unrealistic sense of time passing. For this reason, they may feel as though the impact of a parent's illness on their daily life will never end. Similarly, extended hospitalizations can be difficult for the school-aged child. Marking the days of treatment or until a parent's anticipated return home on a calendar may be helpful.

It is important to remember that the school-age child still thinks in concrete terms. He may be very focused on the factual details of a parent's illness and treatment. It is sometimes a good idea to allow the school-age child to ask his own questions of a parent's doctor. Beginning in the elementary years and beyond, it is important to remind parents that their children may be seeking information out on their own—from friends or from the Internet. This information may not always be accurate or pertinent to their particular situation so needs to be monitored. We have had some parents direct their children to a particular website or resource that they find appropriate and relevant. Communication with a child's school is also critical to ensure that school personnel know to direct questions about a parent's illness back to the family rather than risk giving a child misinformation. Again, routines are important, but flexibility for a child whose parent is sick (e.g. reduced homework around a parent's surgery) may need to occur. Routines and responsibilities teach children that life goes on even when there is a challenge to be faced. Giving a child manageable responsibilities (e.g. taking the trash out for dad on Tuesdays, or regularly changing the water in grandma's bedside flowers) also gives him a sense of control that can help him to manage his worries.

Adolescents (13 years and older)

Teenagers are not only spending more time away from family and in the world of peers and school, they are in the process of forming an identity connected to but also separate from their parents and family. They are better able to contemplate existential and spiritual issues and to think long-term than the school-aged child. Yet their ability to reason abstractly and project forward into the future will not be fully mature until they are in their twenties. Teenagers may be capable of more mature thinking about a parent's illness but still lack the coping skills needed to manage their fears and worries. Teenagers especially may worry that a parent will die early because of their illness or have worries about their own genetic risk for illness. Adolescent girls, especially, seem to be significantly impacted when mothers have cancer (Grabiak et al., 2007). Teenagers may vacillate between wanting to escape a parent's illness by immersing themselves in their own lives or wanting to be at home assuming a caretaking role for parents or siblings.

One 15-year-old boy we knew attempted to do both of these things. He began spending more time at friends' homes rather than bringing his friends over to hang out and play video games as usual because he worried the noise would disturb his mother who needed rest during her treatment. His mother, though, was upset that he and his friends were not around as much and missed the distraction they provided. She thought he was upset about the change in her appearance and was running away because he was embarrassed to have his friends over. Only by pointing out to him that she missed having him and his friends around the house did she learn the real reason he had changed his routine.

Perhaps more than with any other age group, open communication with adolescents is key. Caregivers may need help understanding that a teenager's rapid shifts from apparent self-centeredness to concern and distress over a parent's illness are typical. Families should be concerned about teenagers who take on too many adult responsibilities, or who are spending less time at home and more time with different peer groups. They may be getting into trouble and engaging in risky behaviors (e.g. abusing drugs or alcohol or becoming involved in an unhealthy romantic relationship). Parents may be reluctant to give an adolescent information that they think might affect her decisions (e.g. of where to go to school), but young adults need and are entitled to accurate and complete information. This allows them to make the decisions that are right for them and minimizes the chances that they will regret being either too close or too far away during a time when a parent is sick.

Infants and Toddlers (0–2 years)

Developmental context: establishing attachment
- May be distressed by disruption in routines
- May show increased signs of separation anxiety
- Infant/ toddler temperament will impact stress level

Preschoolers (3–6 years)

Developmental context: driven by egocentrism, magical thinking, associative logic
- May attribute parent's illness/distress to own actions or attributes
- Distress may manifest in behavioral changes and/or regression or not at all
- Routines are still important and disruptions may fuel distress

School-Age children (7–12 years)

Developmental context: mastering skills, fairness, cause and effect logic, peer relationships
- May struggle with issues around fairness
- May have factual questions about illness that can be upsetting to adults
- All right to make allowances while also maintaining routines/ responsibilities

Adolescents (13 and older)

Developmental context: working on separation-individuation, identity formation
- Better able to think long-term and contemplate existential/spiritual issues
- Will still vacillate between separation/ independence and caretaking/dependence
- Open communication key to allowing them to make own informed decisions

Table 7.1   How Children Understand a Parent's Illness at Different Ages

The Role of Temperament

Temperament influences a child reaction to a parent's illness well beyond the infant and toddler years. Temperament is a description of personality traits that are innate and that affect how an individual reacts to situations and copes with challenges across the life span. In the 1960s and 1970s, Thomas and Chess published a series of papers outlining temperament along nine dimensions. Since then, Jerome Kagan has researched the effects of infant temperament in adolescence and adulthood. He condensed the understanding of temperament to two dimensions, inhibition, and reactivity. Inhibited/ uninhibited refers to a child's approach to unfamiliar people and situations. High reactive/low reactive refers to motor activity and distress in response to the unfamiliar. The biological foundation for temperament is in the concentration and density of receptors for neurotransmitters associated with mood, anxiety, and reactions to stress and temperament predicts risk for anxiety in adolescence (Kagan, 2005). However, it is important to remember that temperament is a rubric and does not determine how a child will cope with stress, including parental illness. There are advantages and disadvantages to different temperamental styles. Just as having a basic understanding of typical child development provides a guide for listening to families and children's stories of coping, so does a basic understanding of temperament.

It often helps to ask parents how a child has handled challenges in the past to understand how she is likely to understand and cope with the disruption of parental illness. For example, all children are likely to be upset and overwhelmed by a parent's strong emotion. A child who tends to be anxious and to worry (inhibited and high reactive) will be more tuned to a parent's change in affect and may assume a negative turn of events any time a parent becomes tearful. A more easy-going child, but one who is uncomfortable with outward displays of emotion in general (inhibited and low reactive), may also be upset by a parent's tearfulness, but for a different reason. She may need a different approach. Knowing something about a child's temperament also helps in listening for whether or not there is cause for concern about a change in a child's behavior. The teenager who tends to be more quiet and withdrawn with just a close group of friends and who is staying home often when a grandparent is sick may not be acting out of the ordinary. However, the usually outgoing socialite who suddenly drops sports and activities and spends every day after school at grandma's house may be showing signs of real distress.

The "Out of Sync" Child

While the developmental stages outlined above will be useful for most children, it is important not to assume a child fits neatly into one stage based only on his age. A child may have delays in development that make aspects of an earlier developmental stage important for understanding her reaction to and coping with a caregiver's illness. A school-aged child with language delays may express distress as increased separation anxiety or behavioral outbursts more typical of a preschooler. A teenager with Attention Deficit Disorder and its associated weaknesses in planning and organization may be affected by a change in family routines as much as a school-aged child would be. Children on the autism spectrum rely on routines even more so than a typical developing child, and disruptions to their schedule may be particularly stressful for them and for their families. Less often, but still sometimes the case, is the child with precocious skills who may understand a parent's illness at a more nuanced and detailed level than expected based on her age. It is important to remember, that a child with advanced verbal abilities may be able to understand and talk about a parent's illness at an adult level but still lack mature emotional and coping skills to manage distress.

Key Concepts about Communication

It is important to begin a conversation about communication with parents by asking what the children have been told and what parents believe that children know and understand. This will vary widely depending on the nature and course of a parent's illness, their symptoms and treatment, and the family culture around talking about difficult things. Beginning a consultation in this way also models for parents a useful way of beginning a conversation with their children: by asking what children have heard, observed, and understand already. Many parents will have shared only limited information with their children, telling them "just what they need to know." Other families may have shared every detail of discussion with the medical team with their children in a way that may actually have been overwhelming or confusing. Often, parents use confusing euphemisms in talking with their child (e.g. explaining that mom has a "lump" in her breast and never mentioning cancer). Many families will have seamlessly shared the information in a way appropriate for their children and their family, but still want to know how best to handle the questions and conversations that inevitably (and should) continue to come up.

Each family will have its own style of communication about both small and big matters. One way of assessing how a family talks about serious issues is by asking them to tell you about how they have discussed previous changes and challenges with their children—a move, a change in jobs or financial circumstances, or in some cases the illness or death of a family member or friend. Asking caregivers how children handled the delivery of previous news can help them think through what they might want to do the same, or differently when talking about their illness. This also serves to remind parents that, like any important issue affecting a family, children need to be included in the discussion early and in an age-appropriate way. Children should not be left to worry alone. Even in families where tradition or cultural norms dictate limited communication with children, it is important to share enough specific and factual information that children have some understanding of changes they see in their parent and experience in their lives. For all children, less information will lead to worries that are based on a child's fears and imagination rather than on the facts. It should be noted, though, that some of our most challenging consults have been with families where there are strict cultural boundaries between parents and children that limit communication. If a parent or family insists that it would be inappropriate to share detailed information with children about an illness, it is often helpful to have a conversation about how they might respond if the child later becomes upset when he learns that he was excluded from knowing details that were available to the adults in the family.

It is, of course, a caregiver's job to protect their children and parents may worry that sharing difficult information with children will be overwhelming or traumatizing. However, research shows that children given specific information about a parent's illness, and opportunities to discuss it, experience less anxiety than children who are not so informed (Visser et al., 2004). In our experience, children often know more than their parents think they do. They may have overheard a telephone conversation about a diagnosis or researched breast cancer online after a friend tells them about an aunt who also had a "lump" in her breast. Overhearing information is the situation most likely to lead children to worry, especially school-aged children and teenagers. They are likely to worry that the situation is more serious than they have been told and to feel excluded and mistrustful of parents. When a family has chosen to withhold what you think is important information from children, it helps to ask how they came to that decision. From there, you can begin a discussion that recognizes it is never easy to tell a child upsetting news, but that there are ways of making it easier.

Parents of young children often worry about how to tell a child about their illness while parents of older children often worry about how much to tell their children. The clinician's role is to provide guidelines and strategies that fit within a family culture while also encouraging a climate where children are informed and trust that they can express their worries and questions. With regard to when parents' should share information with children, the general rule of thumb is "the sooner the better." Adolescents report wanting detailed and specific information about a parent's cancer soon after the diagnosis with regular updates about treatment and prognosis (Grabiak, 2006). However, there may be times when parents delay relaying news for a few days or weeks until they have all of the facts or when they choose to put off telling a child about a diagnosis or change of prognosis or plan until after an upcoming important event in a family or child's life (e.g. a graduation). Again, it may be helpful to suggest to parents that they check in with the child after the fact to ask if the child is comfortable with his parents' decision or would have preferred to have been told immediately. Parents can then use that information to repair any damage that might have been done to open communication and to inform how they handle talking about things that arise in the future.

It is important to ask about the specific words that have been used in conversation with children. Often, parents will tell you they have told their children about their "cancer" or their "multiple sclerosis" but when you press further, they have not actually used those terms. On the other hand, a father may have told his 8-year-old daughter he is going to the hospital for chemotherapy without any explanation of what that means. We advise parents to use the appropriate medical terms for their illness and treatment and then to provide an age-appropriate explanation of those terms. It helps to point out to parents that euphemisms are by their very nature confusing. Talking about a "boo boo" or "having too much sugar" to a 6-year-old needs further explanation when referring to a tumor or diabetes. Young children especially, because of their developmentally appropriate self-centeredness, often worry that a parent's illness might be contagious. Using the correct terms for a chronic illness is especially important to differentiate it from more common illnesses of childhood. While euphemisms are not helpful, metaphors can be. For example, explaining chemotherapy as a strong medicine that is like a weed killer in a garden, is one that many parents find helpful in explaining its side effects. You need the chemotherapy to kill the weeds (cancer cells) but it is not possible to miss all the flowers (other fast growing cells like hair cells). There are many excellent children's books and resources that are available to help parents with these kinds of specific conversations with their young children (see Appendix, p. 230 for details).

We are often asked if we will talk to children with or for parents. While there are times when it may be appropriate to be in involved in a family meeting with the medical team and children, this is relatively rare. In our experience, the news of a diagnosis or change in course of an illness is best delivered by a parent, co-parent, or close caregiver in the same way that other important matters are discussed in that family. A more private and comfortable setting also will make children more likely to express their concerns and ask questions. If "family meetings" are a part of a family's culture and if children are relatively close in age this may be an appropriate way to share a diagnosis or change in plan. However, in a family where that is not the norm, being told there is going to be such a meeting can be frightening for children. For example, we have heard more than once that children expect to be told their parents are divorcing when such a meeting is called out of the blue and then are relieved to hear that it is "only" cancer. For most families, individual conversations in a place and at a time that are typical for that family (e.g. at dinner or bedtime or before night-time reading) are the most natural. It is important to remind parents and to model for them that flooding someone with information is not the most effective way of making sure they understand the most important points. For example, asking parents what they understand about what they have heard before from you and other providers shows them that slowing a conversation down to check in, to see what the child is hearing, makes it more meaningful. Some families plan regular check-ins to address ongoing questions and concerns but, for most, these conversations are easiest and most effective if they happen when and where most conversations occur.

Many children like to talk in the car or while helping to fix dinner because they are not forced to look a parent in the eye while talking about difficult topics.

One of the clinician's main tasks is to help parents identify the sometimes hidden meanings behind the questions children have: the music behind the words. It is often easier for an objective listener to hear the hidden fears and worries behind a child's concerns. For example, a child who wonders if an infection will prolong his mother's recovery from surgery may be wondering if a planned vacation will have to be canceled. Vice versa, questions about whether or not a planned vacation will have to be canceled may reflect a child's fears that a parent will die before then. Suggesting that parents ask open-ended questions (e.g. "What got you thinking about that?" or "How do you think mom got sick?") can help them better understand the meaning behind a child's concerns. It is important for parents to know that it is almost inevitable that they will be faced with a question they do not know how to answer. It is wise to help them identify other adults they trust who they feel comfortable having their children talk to (e.g. a favorite aunt, family friend, or school guidance counselor). They should keep that person up to date regarding what the children know and are struggling with and the terms they are using to talk about the situation. Parents are sometimes surprised and relieved when we suggest that a support person attend a meeting with them or speak with one of us to address their questions and concerns about the children. Parents might also identify key people to help should discussions arise around topics they know less about or feel less comfortable talking about (e.g. a minister they can consult with around issues of faith, death, and dying).

Key Concepts about Communication: Summary

- All children deserve to have information about what is going on
- Information is almost always best given by a parent, caregiver or other trusted adult rather than by clinicians and never by clinicians alone
- Conversations should happen at a time and place that fits with a family's culture
- Not necessarily all together—may be individual conversations
- Typically at home or in a more private place is better than a public place
- Not all the information needs to be relayed in one conversation
- Conversation should be ongoing and children should feel comfortable expressing concern and asking questions
- Euphemisms can be confusing but metaphors can be useful
- Seek support and consultation in talking with children about illness
- Clinicians can model effective communication for parents
- Asking how families have handled past challenges is a window into family culture and climate
- Help parents listen for the meaning behind children's questions and concerns
- Open-ended questions are best.

For Clinicians

- "Tell me what changes you think your children have noticed?"
- "How do you think your child understands what is happening?"

For Parents

- "What have you noticed that is different since mom started her new medication?"
- "What got you wondering about that?"

Ways to Support Patients and Families with Children

When a parent is ill, life as children know it is often disrupted. A parent's life becomes filled with clinical visits for treatment, or management of side effects, and may include acute or protracted hospital stays. Further, an ill parent may be compromised physically due to the illness or side effects of treatment, which can challenge how he or she interacts with the child. For a child, a parent's illness means that his or her own schedule changes. Perhaps someone other than mom or dad now picks him up from school. The number of activities she participates in outside of school may need to be reduced. His home may be filled with well-meaning visitors. It may also mean that mom or dad is not able to interact physically in the way the child is used to—roughhousing, sports, picking the child up, etc. In our experience, changes in the mental status of a parent that affect their mood and behavior are the most difficult for children.

Maintaining Life Structure

As much as feasible, maintaining a child's routine—consistent caregivers, schedule for school and after-school activities—gives the child a sense of stability that is comforting. For infants and toddlers, this might mean creating a transportable environment (e.g. moveable play mat, special blanket, or toys) and communicating the child's sleep, wake, eating, and changing schedule so that if the parent is not available, another loving adult can step in. For school-aged children, communicating about the weekday and weekend routines is important. Encourage parents to involve extended family or the parents of the children's friends to help to maintain the child's schedule. For children of all ages, putting the child's schedule on paper—naptimes or feeding times for the younger ones, and bus pick-ups, lunch preferences, and after-school activities for the older ones— lets the child know that you are aware of her needs and preferences, and that you are working to communicate these to whomever is involved in her care. By talking about the importance of stability and predictability, clinicians can help parents identify the things most important for a particular child and facilitate communication with other caregivers.

Carving out Family Time

Maintaining a routine at home helps children to feel that the world is safe and predictable. It is important for families to be able to set aside time to spend together when they can be uninterrupted. Whether it is at family dinners, time together to play a board game or watch television in the evening, ensure the children have time with their parents. We encourage parents to solicit feedback from their kids—what would they like to do together? Although some things may not be feasible when parents are recovering from surgery or undergoing treatment (e.g. roughhousing or playing sports), parents and kids can find new ways to connect. For example, a special bedtime story, an evening chat for older kids, or movie or game nights, can be new traditions for families. Ensuring the children understand that parents still want to spend time with them, even when illness or treatment makes it difficult, is important.

Sometimes children will want to spend time away from home—visiting friends, asking for sleepovers, increasing after-school activities or work. All children process things differently and as clinicians, we encourage parents to know their own children, to work to understand their perspectives. It is important for children to be connected and engaged outside of the home as well as to have meaningful time with family. Things tend to work best when parents clearly communicate their expectations to their children. For example, for the older teen who wishes to spend time with friends, communicating to her that Thursday and Sunday are family nights when she is expected to be home helps her to know what is expected of her and gives her gentle permission to spend time with friends without feeling guilty on the other nights.

Appointing a "Captain of Kindness" and a "Minister of Information"

Extended family and friends want to be helpful but are often unsure of what they can do. For some families, it is useful to appoint a "Captain of Kindness" and a "Minister of Information." The Captain can be a designated friend or family member who is responsible for letting well-wishers know what specific ways they can be helpful over time (e.g. bringing over a meal on a treatment day, driving Sammy to soccer practice on Tuesdays). The Minister is responsible for sharing sanctioned updates with interested family and friends, which can relieve parents from repeating their story and news. For some families, sharing information through a periodically updated website works well. One family we worked with described feeling that posting updates about mom's treatment combined with pictures of the kids made sharing information with extended family and friends easier than trying to communicate with each person individually. Including pictures of the children helped this family feel more comfortable as the site was not only about mom's cancer. For families with older children, we encourage parents to think together with their children about what information does and does not get communicated over the web. This discussion can help to keep children included and prevent them from ever feeling that they are the "last to know" any important piece of news. While every family is different, our job as clinicians is to help them think through what approach works best for their family.

Designating a point person is helpful at school, such as a teacher, counselor, or administrator with whom the family can communicate and to whom the child feels connected. As home life changes for a child when a parent is ill, so may their ability to focus on or prioritize schoolwork. Keeping teachers in the loop about a parent's illness allows them to make adjustments in assignment deadlines. Perhaps most importantly, keeping teachers aware enables them to be mindful of any changes in the child's emotional reactivity, behavior, relationships, or schoolwork that may be of concern, and to communicate this to parents. Some children appreciate having school be a "cancer-free" zone in which they can put their parent's illness out of their minds. For other kids, it can be difficult to concentrate at school, as their worry about their parents is preoccupying. Helping parents to use teachers better to understand how their own children are coping enables them to better support their children.

Structuring Visits

When a parent is in the hospital, it is important to think about whether and how to include children. In general, if a child expresses interest in visiting, parents should honor this request. Parents can ask questions to learn why the child wishes to visit—is she missing mom, curious about what happens at the hospital, hoping to share a piece of news, or simply wishing to spend time together? Gentle questions can help parents to understand what the child expects his parent will look like and how she imagines the visit would go. Other children may express worry about or disinterest in visiting mom or dad in the hospital; asking questions can help the parent understand and reassure the child when appropriate.

Clinicians can help families prepare for these visits. Prior to the visit, parents can prepare children for what to expect. What will mom or dad look like? Will she or he be connected to machines, and if so, what will those machines look like and be doing? Will there be a roommate? How will the child be able to interact with mom or dad? How long will the visit last? Parents can work with the clinical staff to determine the best time of day for a visit, e.g. when mom or dad is most likely to be awake and comfortable. Some families have found it helpful to take a photograph of mom or dad in the hospital to share with the kids prior to the visit as this can help them visualize what to expect and may make the meeting less scary or surprising.

During the visit, parents should be ready to ask children what they notice and to answer questions they have. It is important to help caregivers communicate to children that changes in a parent's appearance or behavior are due to illness or treatment and have nothing to do with the child visiting. For example, a parent may be sleepy or in pain related to treatment. Appreciating that a hospital visit with an ill parent may elicit a range of feelings can help parents to manage their own expectations. Some children may be comfortable and will relate to mom or dad similarly to how they would outside of the hospital, while other children may be less at ease, having a harder time engaging or indicating a readiness to leave quickly. For some children, having an activity available to him or her (e.g. a book, space to draw, games) can be helpful.

When visits are not possible or not permitted, parents can find other ways to help their children feel connected. For example, video calling allows parents to talk "face-to-face" with their children. We encourage the well co-parent to help younger children create a box for collecting recent school accomplishments, mementoes, letters, and drawings to share with mom or dad. Particularly for younger children, this gives them some structure and something to talk about during phone or video calls that otherwise might feel strained. It is good to remind everyone that even a very short call can be meaningful.

When a Referral is Necessary

Parents often ask us whether their children should be receiving mental health support when a parent is sick. To answer this question, we encourage parents to think about (1) whether their child's behavior has changed; and if so how; and (2) whether their child is having difficulty functioning at school, at home, or in relationships. Mental health support can take a variety of forms—a school counselor, a social worker, a psychologist or psychiatrist, support groups. Depending on the parent's specific observations and concerns, the clinician can give parents some tools to help understand their child's change in behavior, and then if necessary, think with them about what level of support may be a good starting point. Accessing mental health services outside of school can be challenging for families. Often speaking with the child's pediatrician or insurance company can help guide parents to local clinical resources.

End-Of-Life Care

Communicating the Prognosis

Talking with children about illness is especially challenging for parents whose prognosis is unclear and when a parent is nearing the end of life. Other families are challenged by having to talk with children following an acute event such as an accident or unexpected medical trauma that leads to a long hospitalization and risk of death. Clinicians can help parents to consider how best to deliver this information to children at different developmental levels. As with conveying news at any point in the illness course, we encourage parents to share information honestly. Asking a child what he has noticed lately can help to start this conversation, as can welcoming all questions. When the treatment plan and prognosis change, parents may choose to sit with the child and gently help put words to the story that the child has been watching play out around him.

For example, to communicate that the planned treatment is not working as expected: "The tumor in daddy's lung has gotten bigger and now the lung cancer has spread to other parts of his body too. The chemotherapy the doctors were using that we'd really hoped would shrink the tumors isn't working." If there are other treatment options, "Daddy's got the best doctors who are working really hard to figure out another treatment to try and we're really hoping that a different treatment will work, but daddy's body has gotten really really sick." If there are no other treatment options, parents can first help the child to make sense of what she is seeing, "Daddy's tried a lot of different kinds of treatments but the cancer keeps growing in his body. Have you noticed how tired he seems? Or how much he is been coughing lately? Because the tumors have gotten so big in his lungs, daddy's having a hard time breathing." Parents can then explain that there are no more treatments available and that instead, the goal is to help the parent be comfortable, "Right now, the doctors don't have any medicines that will make the cancer go away and giving him more chemotherapy or radiation could hurt his body. The doctors will give daddy some medicine so that he is more comfortable because he wants to spend as much time with us as possible."

From the initial diagnosis, parents may worry how they will respond if their child asks whether they are going to die. The fear of having to answer this question often keeps parents from beginning open communication about their illness with their children. It is important to address this, even when the prognosis is not terminal. Some parents will want to respond by being reassuring, "You don't need to worry about that;" others may be inclined to respond by normalizing death, "Everyone will die someday." Unfortunately, both responses can feel invalidating, leaving a child feeling unheard and worrying alone. Table 7.2 describes a child's understanding of death from a developmental perspective. Parents should try to understand what is motivating the child's question: what does the child really want to know? Gently asking the child whether there is anything they have noticed or heard that is making them wonder right now, or whether they have specific worries (e.g. not being able to stay in the same home) can start the conversation. As clinicians, we encourage parents to think about their own beliefs about death as this can also shape their responses.

Infants and Toddlers (0–2 years)

- Have no understanding of death
- Therefore, cannot be prepared in advance
- May continue to ask about, look for, and expect parent for many weeks

---

Preschoolers (3–6 years)

- Curious about death
- Imagine death is reversible
- May believe that they are responsible for their parent's illness or death (magical thinking)

School-Age children (7–12 years)

- Understand that death is permanent
- May imagine that they will find a cure for their parent's illness when they grow up

---

Adolescents (13 and older)

- Understand death in a way that is similar to adult understanding
- Can imagine a future without their loved parent and experience a range of emotions involved in picturing this future

---

Table 7.2   How Children Understand Death

When a parent's illness is terminal, parents may be able to give children "windows of safety" during which time the parent's death is unlikely. For example, when a child is aware that his mom will likely die from her cancer, he may be worried that if he leaves her even for a moment, she will die. If a parent can feel confident that he or she (or the co-parent) will not die in a given time-frame, conveying that can help to make a child feel safe and willing to engage in her regular activities. A parent may be able to say, "Mommy is really really sick, but the doctors aren't worried that she is going to die in the next week. She knows how important your school concert is and she would really like you to be able to go. Maybe we could record some of it to share with her?" Parents can let children know that they will not need to guess about how mom or dad is doing, or looking for clues. Instead, parents can reassure them that they will keep them informed and if things change, parents will let them know.

Setting for End-Of-Life Care

When a parent's death is anticipated, where to receive end-of-life care is a difficult and personal decision. For some families, an inpatient hospital or hospice setting may be best. This decision allows children more space to maintain their usual routine at home. However, the well parent must balance time at the hospital with time at home, and visits from the children should be facilitated whenever possible.

Other families may prefer to have the ill parent die at home, perhaps using home hospice services. Careful thought and planning can create an environment at home that allows children to control their time with the dying parent. For example, having the ill parent in a room with a door, rather than in the family room, enables the child to choose time with or away from the parent, medical equipment, and visiting relatives. Having the parent at home has the benefit of allowing the children to maintain home routines while having more access to the parent.

There is no single right way to manage these decisions and as clinicians, we can help families think through the options that will work best for them. Regardless of where a parent will die, the parents will want to provide opportunities for the child to say goodbye, and then to have an understanding from the child about how he or she wishes to learn that the parent has died. Children may wish to have private time with the dying parent to say goodbye before the parent dies, or they may want to share a letter or drawing either directly or by giving this to a well relative to give to mom or dad. Some children may wish to be called to the bedside during the parent's final hours, while other children may find this to be too upsetting and instead, would prefer to say goodbye earlier. Clinicians can help parents to understand and respect that there are many ways of saying goodbye, both directly, and after death through funeral and memorial services.

Legacy Leaving

One of the hardest things about losing a parent is the loss of the opportunity to continue to get to know the parent over time. Legacy gifts can be a way for parents to share a meaningful part of themselves—a memory, a memento, a piece of advice for the future—for their child to discover.

Funeral Planning

Funerals and memorial services are important in recognizing and honoring loved ones who have died. While the specifics of these services differ according to religious, cultural, or family traditions, the sentiments of celebrating a person's life and giving those who survive an opportunity to share and remember, are universal. As clinicians, we encourage parents to put their child's needs at the forefront of their planning. The most important part of this planning is anticipating what the funeral service will be like. This allows children to be prepared for what they will see and what will take place. Clinicians can help families to identify key people—a co-parent, or another trusted adult—who can have this discussion with the child after the parent has died.

While there is no hard and fast rule about when children are old enough to attend or participate in a funeral, typically children who are four years and older are included.

Consider whether the child will be present for parts or all of the services: there may be elements that can be frightening to young children, particularly when they do not yet have a sense of the finality of death. For example, a young child may believe a deceased parent is asleep and will wake back up: this can make an open casket, or the lowering of the casket at the cemetery quite frightening. Parents may also wish to think about how to involve the child in the funeral service if he or she is interested. Children may place a flower on the casket, or share a reading, for example.

The Importance of a Team Approach and Clinician Self-Care

It needs to be explicitly said that working with families affected by the untimely illness and sometimes death of a parent is incredibly difficult work. Many clinicians will be parents themselves and the issues raised in this work will touch on current concerns and bring up feelings around past experiences. It is important to be self-aware and to spend time in supervision, consultation, or therapy figuring out one's own trigger points. Self-care is critical to preventing burnout and also to being able to do the work well. Scheduling regular time to engage in activities outside of work is one aspect of self-care. Exercise, team sports, or individual activities such as running, yoga and swimming are especially helpful to many clinicians. Joining a book club focused on fiction can be a way of both distracting from and processing themes and issues raised in work in a healthy way with others from different fields. Obviously, individual clinicians will know what works best for them. Making the commitment to continue these activities in even the most stressful of weeks is again good modeling for families, particularly for the spouses, partners, and co-parents of sick parents but also for parents coping with illness. We often encourage parents to talk with their children about their commitment to their own health and well-being and the things that they are doing to stay as healthy as they can even as they face the challenges of a critical or chronic illness. It is important for clinicians to be mindful of doing this for themselves as well.

Self-care is especially difficult when working with patients in critical care where there may be an almost constant sense of time pressure to make decisions and to intervene as soon as an issue arises. Working with critically ill populations can take a hard toll on clinicians' family lives and intimate relationships if they fail to set boundaries around their work and on their time. For all of these reasons, taking a team approach to this work is critical. This is not work that can be done in a vacuum. Clinicians need to know that other colleagues are available to families when they are not available. Clinicians need to be able to refer to someone else when a case is beyond the scope of their expertise or brings up issues that are too personal or sensitive. We recognize that there are economic and institutional realities that may make it difficult or even impossible to formally establish a team like the PACT Program. However, clinicians need to lobby their administration, supervisors, and colleagues to come up with creative ways of ensuring that they are not working alone. For example, this may require seeking consultation from clinicians of a different specialty, or in a different department or even from a different institution. With the right support, parent guidance for families coping with a parent's chronic or critical illness can be incredibly rewarding and meaningful work.

References

Grabiak, B. R., Bender, C. M., and Puskar, K. R. (2007). The impact of parental cancer on the adolescent: An analysis of the literature. *Psycho-oncology*, 16, 127–37.

Howlader N. et al. (Eds). *SEER Cancer Statistics Review*, 1975–2009 (Vintage 2009 Populations), National Cancer Institute. Bethesda, MD, <http://seer.cancer.gov/csr/1975_2009_pops09/>, based on November 2011 SEER data submission, posted to the SEER web site, 2012

Kagan, J. Temperament. In Tremblay, R. E., Barr, R. G., and Peters, R. De V. (Eds). *Encyclopedia on Early Childhood Development* [online]. Montreal, Quebec: Centre of Excellence for Early Childhood Development; 2005: 1–4. Available at: <http://www.child-encyclopedia.com/documents/KaganANGxp.pdf>. Accessed 18 June 2012.

Muriel, A. C., and Rauch, P. K. (2009). Talking with families and children about the death of a parent. In G. Hanks, N. Cherny, N. Christakis, M. Fallon, S. Kaasa, and R. Portenoy (Eds). *Oxford Textbook of Palliative Medicine*, 4th Edition. Oxford, UK: Oxford University Press.

Rauch, P. K., and Muriel, A. C (2006). *Raising an Emotionally Healthy Child When a Parent is Sick*. New York, NY: McGraw-Hill.

Visser, A., Huizinga, G. A., van der Graaf, W., Hoekstra, H. J., and Hoekstra-Weebers, J. (2004). The impact of parental cancer on children and the family: a review of the literature. *Cancer Treatment Reviews*, 30, 683–94.

Weaver, K. E., Rowland, J. H., Alfano, C. M., and McNeel, T. S. (2010). Parental cancer and the family. *Cancer*, 116(18), 4391–401.

Part III

Family Systems Assessment and Interventions

Overview of Part III

Part Three provides an in-depth understanding of family systems assessment and family systems therapy for patients with medical illnesses. A systemic view of illness means "understanding the effect of illness on the family system and understanding the effect of the family system on the illness." Part Three focuses on the family as a unit, and describes the sophisticated techniques of family therapy that focus on changing family interactions.

Salvador Minuchin described "psychosomatic families" when he was working at the Philadelphia Child Guidance Clinic. He studied children with recurrent episodes of diabetic ketoacidosis that became easy to manage when the children were hospitalized. In these families, Minuchin and his colleagues (1975) studied the children and their families and identified dysfunctional family interactions that they thought contributed to the instability of their diabetes. He characterized these families as "enmeshed, overprotective, rigid, and avoiding conflict" and called these families "psychosomatic families."

Minuchin hypothesized that parental conflict was somehow transmitted to the child, which led to a worsening of the child's diabetes. In a stressful family interview, the children with diabetes had a rapid rise in free fatty acids (FFA), a precursor to diabetic ketoacidosis, which persisted even after the interview ended. The parents of these children had an initial rise in FFA levels, but their levels fell to normal when the diabetic child entered the room. Minuchin, Rosman, and Baker (1978) treated 15 children and their families with structural family therapy, with the goal of disengaging the diabetic child and establishing better family boundaries. The children in the successfully treated families had fewer subsequent admissions for ketoacidosis and their requirement for insulin was reduced.

Betsy Wood (2001) reformulated Minuchin's original theories and developed the biobehavioral family model (BBFM). The BBFM shows how the family emotional climate, the quality of parent-parent relations, the parent-child relational security, and the biobehavioral reactivity (emotion regulation/dysregulation) influence one another (Wood et al., 2008). She shows how family factors influence disease severity in stress-related illnesses such as diabetes and asthma. Other family researchers have validated the important role that families have in the outcome of children with asthma (Fiese, Winter, Wamboldt, Anbar, and Wamboldt, 2010) (also see Chapter 2).

We have learned a lot about families since Minuchin first described his psychosomatic families, but much work still needs to be done. Part Three focuses on the practicalities of assessing and improving family coping styles, and assessing and treating families using a family systems perspective. A case presentation illustrates how an assessment and several treatment sessions unfold. Lastly, multifamily group interventions are described, with the perspective that these effective interventions may become more common with future health-care system changes.

Chapter 8: Coping Well with Illness

This chapter reviews coping styles used by individuals, couples, and families. Coping has traditionally been considered an individual skill, with more recent interest in dyadic coping and family coping. Researchers have used different terms to describe coping, as well as different models of understanding and measuring coping, and this literature is especially complex. A case example brings these concepts alive and shows how to discuss coping styles in clinical practice.

Chapter 9: Family Systems Assessment

There are several models of family systems assessments that are used for patients with medical illness and their families. The theoretical background and the common factors for family systems assessment and treatment are outlined. A case example of a family systems assessment, using the McMaster model, is presented.

Chapter 10: Three Levels of Family Intervention

This chapter describes three levels of family intervention: family inclusion, family psychoeducation, and family systems therapy. A stepwise approach to involving families in the management of medical illness is presented. All clinicians can begin with family inclusion. Clinicians with some family skills training can provide psychoeducational interventions. Clinicians who have family systems training can provide family systems interventions. A case example shows how family inclusion progresses through family psychoeducation to a family systems assessment. While this progression is not much discussed, it may actually be how things work in the office as the clinician and family becomes more comfortable with participation in family-oriented care.

Chapter 11: Family Assessment and Treatment: The Case of Mr and Ms Dewey

This chapter describes one patient with serious medical illness and his spouse, as they progress through a family assessment and into family therapy. Each session is outlined in detail with commentary given as it occurs in real time. The model used is the Problem-centered Systems Therapy of the Family (Epstein and Bishop, 1981). This case shows how adaptation to illness is not just a matter of solving family problems but necessitates a real shift in family functioning. This case can be used for teaching, as there are ample areas for discussion and several areas where clinical difficulties could be managed differently. A set of teaching questions is included.

Chapter 12: Multifamily Group (MFG) Interventions

This chapter differentiates between three levels of multifamily groups: family support, family psychoeducational, and family systems therapy. The evidence base for MFGs is presented and several examples are given to show how to develop and run MFGs. With future changes in the health-care system, MFGs provide a cost-effective way to improve health care outcomes.

References

Epstein, N. B., Bishop, D. S. (1981). Problem Centered Systems Therapy of the Family. *Journal of Marital and Family Therapy*, 7 (1), 23–31.

Fiese, B. H., Winter, M. A., Wamboldt, F. S., Anbar, R. D., and Wamboldt, M. Z. (2010). Do family mealtime interactions mediate the association between asthma symptoms and separation anxiety? *Journal of Child Psychology & Psychiatry*, 51(2), 144–51.

Minuchin, S., Baker, L., Rosman, B. L., Liebman, R., Milman, L., and Todd, T. C. (1975). A conceptual model of psychosomatic illness in children. Family organization and family therapy. *Archives of General Psychiatry*, 32, 1031–8.

Minuchin, S., Rosman, B. L., and Baker, L. (1978). *Psychosomatic families; Anorexia nervosa in context*. Cambridge, MA: Harvard University Press.

Wood, B. L. (2001). Physically manifested illness in children and adolescents. A biobehavioral family approach. *Child and Adolescent Psychiatric Clinics of North America*, 10(3), 543–62.

Wood, B. L., Lim, J., Miller, B. D., Cheah, P., Zwetsch, T., Ramesh, S., and Simmens, S. (2008). Testing the Biobehavioral Family Model in Pediatric Asthma: Pathways of Effect. *Family Process*, 47, 21–40.

8 Coping Well with Illness

- Coping is a dynamic process and coping styles change over time.
- Coping well includes the use of individual, dyadic and family coping skills.
- Families benefit from having a therapeutic space to reflect on how they are coping with chronic illness.
- Families can learn new coping skills as part of a family systems therapy.
- Increasing the repertoire of coping skills improves family resilience.

Introduction

A family that copes well with illness identifies and solves the problems associated with the presence of illness. A family with good coping skills communicates about symptoms, negotiates role changes, develops new ways of emotionally being together, and develops new interests as a family. A family that copes well may change life goals or family health behaviors such as improving their diet, increasing exercise, and stopping smoking. Family changes can include a permanent change in roles if a family member gives up a job to stay home and become a full-time caregiver. Older children may give up some childhood activities to take on caregiving responsibilities.

Families do not usually think about what strategies or coping skills they use to manage the challenges of chronic illness; they just get along the best they can. Coping strategies tend to be automatic behaviors: "things I have always done to cope." Families may not think about their individual coping styles and probably do not think about or understand how each family member's individual coping style meshes with the coping styles of other family members. This chapter examines some of the research on coping styles and reviews the relationships between individual, couple, and family coping strategies.

Illness management is often punctuated by crises where change happens quickly, without the family having time to deliberate on what coping styles might work best. Family changes can become fixed therefore, not by choice, but by happenstance. Families often present in distress with no clear understanding of what their difficulties are. It can be hard for family members to differentiate between emotional difficulties such as "I am the primary caregiver and I feel overburdened," and more general practical problems such as "I am happy to be the primary caregiver but I need some extra help." Families can benefit from a therapeutic space to reflect on how they cope as individuals and how they cope together.

The concepts outlined in this chapter are brought together in a case example of the Ortiz Family. The family presents in distress, with no clear understanding of their difficulties, just knowing that "We can't go on like this!" During the assessment process the family members articulate their difficulties. A slow and detailed family assessment gives the family the opportunity to identify, discuss, and understand the difficulties they are facing as a family, and as individuals. The treatment plan uses a problem-solving approach, and focuses on current coping styles and future planning. The family is given a choice about how they want to handle the problems. The family therapist lays out options such as "continue with more of the same" or "making changes." The therapist is articulate about the risks and benefits of each option with the family.

What language is best to discuss coping? The language that professionals use is shaped by their discipline. Researchers talk about stress models and illness appraisals. Psychiatrists and psychologists ask about beliefs and feelings, acceptance of loss, and emphasize cognitive and behavioral changes. Family therapists think of systemic change, intergenerational legacies, and transactional patterns. Our colleagues in medical disciplines such as neurology, cardiology, and surgery use the term "coping with stress," and identify individuals that cope well and others that do not cope well. Patients also think in terms of "coping," and "coping well" is something individuals and families aspire to. Families are more likely to seek out programs that teach them "better coping skills," than they are to enter family therapy with its historic trappings of blaming the family.

Individual Coping Styles

Research has traditionally focused on measuring individual coping as a response to stress. In a stress process model, three mediators of the response to the stress of coping with illness are cognitive appraisal, what coping skills are used and coping resources that are available (Maes, Leventhal, and de Ridder, 1996). Cognitive appraisal describes the meaning that the caregiver ascribes to the illness. A negative appraisal of an illness can be improved with education, thus reaching a more accurate understanding of the illness. (How to assess and manage illness beliefs is discussed in Chapter 3, p. 51 and the influence of ethnicity on illness appraisal is discussed in Chapter 6, p. 109). If there is a positive illness appraisal but poor coping skills, the focus becomes improving coping skills. Thirdly, a lack of coping resources can be managed by increasing access to resources.

Individual coping is measured using instruments such as the Ways of Coping Checklist (Vitaliano, Russo, Carr, Maiuro, and Becker, 1985), the COPE (Carver, Scheier, and Weintraub, 1989), the Coping Self Efficacy Scale (Chesney, Neilands, Chambers, Taylor, and Folkman, 2006), and the Coping Inventory for Stressful Situations (CISS; Endler and Parker, 1990). The DBT-Ways of Coping Checklist (DBT-WCCL) is designed to assess the use of DBT coping skills (Neacsiu, Rizvi, Vitaliano, Lynch, and Linehan, 2010). Avoidance is generally seen as a negative coping skill, however in DBT, adaptive avoidance is considered a good skill. Adaptive avoidance means that the person temporarily pushes away thinking about a stressor and focuses on something else. There are also coping scales for specific illness, such as the Asthma-Specific Coping Scale (Aalto, Harkapaa, Aro, and Rissanen, 2002) (see below). The brief COPE can be downloaded free and can be easily used in the clinician's office (Carver, 1997). It is included in the Appendix, p. 230. The goal of these tools is mostly to identify deficits in coping.

Asthma-Specific Coping Scale

- Restricted lifestyle ("I avoid exertion")
- Hiding asthma ("I avoid talking about my asthma")
- Positive reappraisal ("I try to learn something positive from my falling ill and related experiences")
- Information-seeking ("I try to find out more about my asthma")
- Ignoring asthma ("I avoid thinking about my asthma")
- Worrying about asthma ("I am afraid that my asthma will get worse").

Gender and Cultural Influences

Gender matters. In a study of children with a parent with multiple sclerosis (MS) daughters coped better than sons, independent of the gender of the MS-affected parent (Steck, Amsler, Kappos, and Burgin, 2001). When asked, adolescents whose mothers had breast cancer, suggested that intervention programs teach coping skills in a gender-specific way (Davey, Gulish, Askew, Godette, and Childs, 2005).

A person's cultural and ethnic background influences their appraisal of the stress of caregiving and choice of coping styles (see Chapter 6, p. 109 for discussion of how ethnicity affects illness appraisal). Coping styles have been reported to be similar in African-American and white caregivers but different in Korean and Korean American caregivers (Knight and Sayegh, 2010). It is important to consider if language needs to be changed, or research constructs need to be tailored to allow accurate understanding for different cultural groups (Bernal and Domenech Rodriguez, 2009).

Changes Over Time

Coping is a dynamic process and coping styles change over time. Each person copes in their own way, depending on their experiences of illness, and their expectations of living with illness. In a family, the experiences and behaviors of all the individuals influence the way the family unit functions as a whole.

The initial stage of coping is called "assimilative," when the impact of the illness is being understood and absorbed by the patient and family. Emotional coping occurs when distress is highest, for example at the beginning of an illness when there is uncertainty about the diagnosis. Emotional coping is characterized by attempts to regulate negative emotions. For example, family members may blame themselves, blame others, engage in wishful thinking, or become avoidant.

At later stages of illness, coping becomes "accommodative," when attempts to change or cure the illness have been found to be ineffective. Emotional coping is replaced with a problem-based coping style. A problem-based coping style means that a stressor or problem is discussed and a solution is chosen from several alternatives. Reflective coping is the ability to generate and consider coping options, and to recognize the usefulness of a particular coping strategy in a given situation (Vriezekolk, 2011).

Individual Coping Skills

Less Adaptive Coping Skills

Emotional: There is nothing to be done, so I might as well stay in bed. I am afraid of getting sick.

Detachment: I try to forget the whole thing.

Wishful thinking: I am praying for a miracle. My family and neighbors are praying too.

Avoidance: I would rather watch TV than think about it.

Self-blame: I blame myself. No one else cares about me.

Worrying: What is the best hospital? Should I change doctors? What if the doctor is wrong?

Hiding Illness: I cannot let my friends know. They will not understand. They know me as a well person without any problems. I would rather just pretend. If I cannot hide it, I will stay home.

More Adaptive Coping Skills

Problem solving: I have books from the library and we are all going to read them. Then we can discuss it together. I am going to a support group.

Seeking information: I try to get information to understand the problem better.

Cognitive restructuring: I can still enjoy watching others do things I cannot do any more. I can still work part-time. I am no longer the boss, but I still have something to contribute.

Seeking social support: I talk to my good friend about how I am feeling.

Skill-based avoidance: When I get upset, I count to ten, take a breath, and sing a song.

Restricted lifestyle: I can walk a little with some help. You go for your long walk and then later we can go for my walk.

Personal growth: I have become more patient; I realize that I do not have to control every situation; I've become more tolerant; I'm changing as a person in a good way. I am praying for the strength to cope well.

Life priorities: I prioritize things more; I do not worry about material things so much.

Interpersonal benefit: I've gained new friends; I've become more involved in helping people; I appreciate the strength of people who face hardship.

Family benefit: This illness has brought us closer as a family.

Appreciation of life: I live each day to its fullest, life could be worse, I live for today. I thank God for the good things in my life.

Particular Coping Styles

Emotional coping becomes prominent when symptoms increase. In a study of 2,864 people coping with HIV, coping styles varied with the presence and intensity of symptoms. At the initial evaluation, passive copers had few symptoms, high levels of physical functioning, and high emotional well-being. At one-year follow-up, an increase in symptoms were associated with the increased use of an emotional coping style, whereas decreased symptoms were associated with the use of passive coping strategies. This suggests that distress induces emotional coping whereas when social support and emotional well-being are high, passive coping predominates and active coping efforts are less needed (Fleissman et al. 2003).

Emotional coping is also associated with the presence of psychological distress and psychiatric symptoms. In a study of people with multiple sclerosis, emotional coping was associated with more depression, distress, and poor social adjustment (Pakenham, 2005). About one third (n = 52) of mothers of children with cardiac disease met the criteria for poor adjustment based on an assessment of their coping skills (Davies, 1998). Poorer psychological functioning is associated with passive coping styles in spouses of patients after a stroke, at one year after the stroke (Wolters, Stapert, Brands, and van Heugten, 2011). In this study, higher initial passive coping predicted lower quality of life, more depressive symptoms and more strain. Also, younger and more educated people used more active coping. It is hard to determine which came first: poor coping or depression/anxiety. Regardless, symptoms such as acute pain, insomnia or the presence of anxiety or a depressive illness diminish the use of positive coping strategies.

Repression is a particular form of coping that is associated with low trait anxiety and high defensiveness (Myers, 2010). Higher rates of repressive coping have been found in chronic illness populations when compared with normal populations (Myers et al., 2007). Weinberger (1990, p. 338) described repressors as "people who fail to recognize their own affective responses ... who consider maintaining low levels of negative affect central to their self-concept [and] are likely to employ a variety of strategies to avoid conscious knowledge of their 'genuine reactions' ... repressors as a group, seem actively engaged in keeping themselves (rather than just other people) convinced that they are not prone to negative affect." A meta-analysis of 22 studies (n = 6,775) found that there was a higher risk for repressive copers to suffer from certain chronic diseases, with the most increased risk being for hypertension (Mund and Mitte, 2011). When families or couples present with difficulty adapting to illness, it is important to assess the individual style of each member. This helps the family understand and recognize that each person brings their own coping style to the family system.

Religion is often reported as a coping strategy. Religion can be a positive or a negative strategy, depending on how religion is used by the individual. Mixed results were found in studies looking at religion as a coping strategy for people with cancer. In this review, seven studies showed evidence of benefit, three studies found religious coping to be harmful and seven studies showed non-significant results. Many of these studies had methodological problems so no firm conclusions can be drawn (Thuné-Boyle, Stygall, Keshtgar, and Newman, 2006). However, religion can be considered a positive strategy if the person uses religion to seek strength to pursue positive adaptive coping but a negative strategy if the person is using religion for primarily avoidance or wishful thinking.

Coping Well Matters

Benefit-Finding

Many patients and family members find meaning in the face of adversity. Benefit-finding usually emerges later in the adjustment to chronic illness. Benefit-finding is associated with a positive illness appraisal and good coping strategies such as problem solving and seeking social support. Caregivers of patients with breast cancer, multiple sclerosis, and HIV/AIDS, report benefit such as wanting to give the best care and support (Packenham, 2009). Caregivers may decide to work fewer hours, in order to spend time with patients. Caregivers also report a greater appreciation of their own health and ability to enjoy physical pursuits and may change their diet and exercise program to align with their ill family member. Family connectedness is a frequent reported source of meaning and a critical aspect of well-being.

Benefit-finding can be measured using scales such as the Benefit-Finding Scale in Multiple Sclerosis (BFiMSS) (Pakenham and Cox, 2009). In a study of patients (n = 388) with MS and their caregivers (n = 232), Pakenham and Cox (2009) identified seven factors that measure benefit-finding: Compassion/Empathy, Spiritual Growth, Mindfulness, Family Relations Growth, Lifestyle Gains, Personal Growth, New Opportunities. In a study by Youngmee, Schultz, and Carver (2007), 779 caregivers of patients with cancer reported more benefit-finding if they used religious coping and perceived good social support. Specifically, coming to accept what happened and appreciating new relationships with others was associated with greater adaptation. Benefit-finding is also associated with higher marital adjustment, improved life satisfaction, and a more positive affect, especially at higher levels of appraised stress.

Coping skills can be taught. Clinicians can support benefit-finding by promoting a balance between acceptance and change, and encouraging the family to talk about their experience with others who are experiencing the same stressors. Discussing individual coping styles with the family helps each member understand what coping strategies they each use and how their thoughts, feelings, and behaviors affect other family members. Giving the family a handout that outlines different coping styles can help the discussion get started (see Appendix, p. 230). Providing a therapeutic space for family members to think together about how the family wants to cope and what coping well means to their family is an important intervention.

Coping skills can be taught through psychoeducational interventions. An eight-week psychoeducational intervention helped patients with multiple sclerosis (MS) develop new coping strategies for dealing with cognitive deficits and improved communication with caregivers. At two years, the coping skills group (n = 64) had better psychosocial role performance and coping behavior compared to the control group (n = 68) who were only given telephone support by peers (Schwartz 1999). Of importance, spouses were included in this intervention, attending at least three of the eight weekly meetings.

Dyadic Coping

Dyadic coping means that couples cope as a unit, viewing the illness as "our problem" and working together on solving illness-related problems. Dyadic coping includes decision-making about meals, exercise, and schedule. In order to do this, the couple usually shares an understanding of the illness. They usually have prior experience working together as a team on issues such as parenting, division of roles within the house etc. They are able to relax together, provide emotional support such as mutual calming and expressions of solidarity.

Shared illness beliefs underlie dyadic coping. Women with husbands who agree about the cyclic nature of their arthritis received practical and emotional support that matched their needs and had better psychological adjustment at follow-up (Yorgason et al., 2010; Sterba and DeVellis, 2009). In Sterba and DeVellis' (2009) study, 16 couples described their coping activities as either individual, shared, or a mix of both. Spouses with a shared illness appraisal helped their ill relative have less disability and better psychological adjustment at six-months' follow-up.

Dyadic coping is reflected in the amount of "we" talk that a couple engages in. The amount of "we-talk" used by caregiver spouses of patients with heart disease (n = 57) was associated with better health outcomes for patients, especially for female patients (Rohrbaugh, Mehl, Shoham, Reilly, and Ewy, 2008). In fact, the spouse's confidence in the patient's ability to manage the illness predicted four-year survival over and above what the patient's own self-efficacy ratings predicted (Rohrbaugh et al., 2004). In a sample of 191 patients with metastatic cancer and their partners, a prospective study showed that those who used positive dyadic coping had better marital adjustment at six-months' follow-up (Badr, Carmack, Kashy, Critofanilli, and Revenson, 2010).

Women are more likely to change their coping strategies to a communal style to help their male partner, than male partners are to change to a communal style to help their female partner (Lewis et al., 2006; Knudson-Martin and Mahoney, 2009). Of course, a couple may not want to work together to manage illness and it is worthwhile asking the following question: "Do either of you feel that the patient should do this alone?" If the answer is yes, it will be difficult if not impossible, to move the couple to a dyadic coping style. A second question, "Do your efforts to work together result in greater conflict?" followed up with, "How much do you want this to change?" can clarify their motivation to work together.

Dyadic Responses to Family Member's Complaints of Pain

Family members often ask how they should respond to their loved one's complaint of pain: "What is the best way to help my spouse manage pain? Should I give in and do things for them, or encourage them to do more themselves?" Patients who appraise pain as difficult to cope with, and who try to elicit support from others by a heightened display of pain, are known as "pain catastrophizers." Pain catastrophizing is associated with poorer outcomes such as intensified pain and disability, both in adults and children. Pain catastrophizing may result in short-term support but, over time, family members withdraw. This occurs because spouses perceive that "helping" does not reduce pain, and/or that the patient is becoming more helpless, dependent, and less functional. From a behavioral perspective, patients are reinforced for pain behaviors when the spouse is overly solicitous e.g. taking over the patient's chores. As a result, the patients become less active and more disabled. Patients may also interpret a family member's solicitousness as a sign of their inability to do things, and then see themselves as a burden to their families. Spouses may also decide not to respond if they believe that their partners have the ability to control their own pain. Spouses can become punitive with responses such as anger, irritation, and frustration occurring in response to complaints of pain. Negative spousal interactions correlate with increased pain, disability, and psychological distress in patients (Romano, Jensen, Turner, Good, and Hop, 2000).

Insecure attachment in both adults and children results in more negative appraisals of pain, more feelings of being unable to deal with pain, and excessive dependence upon others. In patients with insecure attachment, pain catastrophizing is likely to elicit negative rather than positive responses from others (Cano, Leong, Heller, and Lutz, 2009). In a study of schoolchildren (n = 1,332), less securely attached children had higher levels of catastrophizing and more negative parental responses. For securely attached children, higher levels of catastrophizing were associated with more positive parental responses (Vervoot, Goubert, and Cromberz, 2010).

Dyadic coping can be formally assessed using the Lyons, Michelson, Sullivan, and Coyne (1998) communal coping construct. This questionnaire asks "When you think about problems related to your heart condition, to what extent do you view those as 'our problem' (shared by you and your spouse equally) or mainly your own problem?" and "When a problem related to your heart condition arises, to what extent do you and your partner work together to solve it?" Shared coping includes mutual decision-making about meals, exercise, and schedule.

Assessing Dyadic Coping

- "When you both talk about the illness, how much do you use 'we-talk'"?
- "It is important that you both agree about what is causing the illness." "Can I answer any questions that might help you reach this understanding?"
- "Are there times in the past where you have successfully solved difficult problems?" "How did you do that?"
- "How do you respond when your spouse gets ill?
- "What can your spouse do that will help you get better?
- "Can you ask your spouse for help and support?
- "Can you work on your spouse's health problem together?"

Dyadic coping can be learned. In adaptation to stress, the "best coper" can be the model for the family coping style. In a study of 66 couples faced with the stress of forced relocation, nearly all the couples adapted to the stress "as a couple," rather than "as individuals" (Wamboldt, Steinglass, and Kaplan-De-Nour, 1991). This study took place in 1982, when Israel withdrew from the Sinai Peninsula. The couples were studied prior to the relocation and 18 couples were assessed 24 months after relocation. This study was prospective and the sample was stable prior to relocation, so the findings are not compromised the presence of other chronic stressors. At the two-year follow-up, 16 of the 18 couples were either "well-functioning" couples or "poorer functioning" couples. In all cases, the husband and wife became similar in terms of coping style. Only two couples showed a polarized pattern of adjustment and these couples had marital distress prior to the relocation. It appeared that one individual's coping ability drove the adjustment of their partner. Adjusting together as a couple made the stress of relocation easier to manage. Adaptation occurred through the development of shared meaning of the relocation that emerged from conversation within the couples. The couple then developed a shared worldview. The coping style of the "best coper" was the strongest predictor of adjustment for both members of the couple and for most couples, the best coper's style dominated.

A psychoeducational program can teach dyadic coping. The Resilient Partners discussion group developed in collaboration with the MS Society, focused on developing couples' strengths in coping with MS (Rolland, McPheters, and Carbonell 2008). The multifamily group program is based on the Family Systems Illness Model that integrates the demands of MS over time within a family developmental framework (see Chapter 3 for a discussion of this model and Chapter 12, p. 215 for specific details of this group).

Family Coping

Families that are resilient have good problem-solving skills, good communication, and a shared belief system (Walsh, 2003). Family factors that are associated with good illness outcomes have been known for the past decade (see the list below). However, there are many unanswered questions about the interaction between medical illness, coping styles, and family functioning. We can identify healthy family functioning at a single point in time, but what do we know about the process of coping over time? Is there a specific way that coping best evolves? What about the styles of children versus the styles of their grandparents? Do adolescents with chronic illness need to develop their own individual coping styles in order to individuate from their family? Can families with different individual coping styles still manage well? Does there need to be a specific overall family coping style? Is there a "best mix" of styles?

Protective Family Factors in Medical Illnesses

- Good communication
- Adaptability
- Clear roles
- Achieving family development tasks
- Supporting individual members
- Expressing appreciation
- Commitment to the family
- Religious/spiritual orientation
- Social connectedness
- Spending time together.

(Adapted from Weihs, 2002)

How do children learn to cope? Parents influence their children's coping styles through direct instruction and modeling. However, parents may not recognize all the coping strategies that children use. In a study of ten child–parent dyads where the child had suffered an injury, children and parents reported similarities in their perceptions of child coping, but parents did not recognize some specific distraction strategies (TV, music, texting friends) and specific types of social support (family, friends, spiritual) identified by the children. Parents and children had similar reports of relinquished coping, with the relinquishment sometimes being positive and sometimes representing feelings of helplessness. Additionally, parents did not identify their children's attempts at cognitive restructuring (Marsac, Mirman, Kohser, and Kassam-Adams, 2011). Parents are able to positively influence their child's coping with pain with cognitive-behavioral interventions (see Chapter 6, p. 109).

When adolescence is reached, family conflict over the adolescent's drive for autonomy often clashes with the parental role of monitoring their child so that their medical condition is kept under good control. The adolescent who is subjected to high levels of parental monitoring, frequently sees this activity as interference, feeling that they can take adequate care of themselves. Studies of family conflict in the management of diabetes illustrate this point well (Anderson et al., 2002). However in some situations, adolescents may cope by delaying independent behavior. In a study of youth with spina bifida (SB), there was no increase in family conflict in adolescence when compared with a control group (Jandasek, Holmbeck, DeLucia, Zebracki, and Friedman, 2009). This delay in the development of independent behavior may occur because of the continued complex challenges involved in managing SB (Friedman, Holmbeck, DeLucia, Jandasek, and Zebracki, 2009). Management of day-to-day tasks in families of youth with SB may necessitate a higher level of interdependence and close sharing of responsibilities between parent and child, thus precluding the large developmental shifts expected to occur during adolescence. Does this mean that individuation happens later, or not at all? Does family conflict occur later? Can these findings be extrapolated to other illnesses?

Generally, active coping is seen as healthier than passive coping, but that is not always true. In a study that compared family functioning and coping styles in families of children with cancer (n = 44) and HIV disease (n = 65), better family functioning was related to cognitive reframing, which is an active coping style, within the cancer group but better family functioning was associated with passive coping in the HIV group (Martin et al., 2012). In families (n = 61) with a relative with brain injury, passive family coping styles were related to poorer family functioning, a lower quality of life, and a higher caregiver strain. However, neither the coping styles nor the psychosocial outcomes of the caregivers were associated with patients' self-reported quality of life (Wolters, Stapert, Brands, and van Heugten, 2011).

In summary, changes in family functioning and family coping unfold over time. If a family coping with chronic illness has difficulties it may be for several reasons: the presence of additional stressors, the illness has entered a new phase or the family has entered a new life stage. Regardless, understanding family coping styles leads to more constructive problem solving. In the Ortiz case that follows, good individual coping skills do little to solve the presenting problem of an adolescent reaching maturity and the major caregiver deciding to pursue an alternative career. The key intervention in the Ortiz case is to provide a therapeutic space where the family can begin to identify their individual coping styles, and their lack of family coping. From this vantage point, the family could then develop new problem-solving strategies based on the family's shared perception of illness, shared coping, and a clarification of future family needs.

Case Example: The Ortiz Family Learns to Cope Together

Anna Ortiz was referred to the psychosomatic medicine service by the neurology team who asked for help with the following: How should we treat her psychotic symptoms in the context of her severe seizure disorder? The referring resident thinks that something is going on at home as the mother seems aggressive, "demanding that something be done."

Anna is a 29-year-old Hispanic female, with widespread cerebral cortical migration defects, admitted for assessment and management of difficult-to-control epileptic seizures and non-epileptic seizures (NES). She has multiple developmental delays. Two years prior to admission, there was a precipitous decline with an increase in epileptic seizures and NES as well as the onset of psychotic symptoms. An intermittently reinforcing pattern of benzodiazepine use in response to seizures began at that time. Increasing seizures and behavioral dysregulation are correlated with her mother's increasingly busy schedule. One specific decompensation was directly preceded by the mother's plan to travel for ten days.

Anna lives at home with her parents. She used to work as a clerk at the local grocery store but now she does not want to leave the house. Her older brother, Sam, left home eight years ago. Sam visits some weekends but he is generally not involved with Anna. Mr Ortiz works full time and is frequently traveling for business. Ms Ortiz works part-time and is going to school. The family used to socialize with other families who had children of Anna's age. They no longer do this as Anna's condition has worsened and Anna feels isolated because her peers have moved on with their lives.

Anna's psychiatric symptoms began at age 24. She has seen three psychiatrists in the recent past and according to her mother, "each tried different medicine, none seemed to help; some made her too sedated and others made her seizures worse, as well as caused her behavior to worsen." Anna has been hospitalized several times in recent months for behavioral difficulties and agitation. The patient and family agree that art therapy and learning self-soothing techniques help her. Currently, the family notes that she has been wearing gloves on her hands and she tells them that her hands smell of urine. Her father describes Anna's decreasing ability to complete ADLs and notes new behaviors such as coming downstairs half naked. There are no changes in sleep or appetite.

At interview, she is a plump, young woman with poor ADLs and a vacant stare. She is reluctant to voice her concerns. She denies depressed mood, but becomes tearful when asked if she has feelings of hopelessness. With encouragement, she explains that she does not wish to be in the hospital, and that there is frequent fighting with her family. She describes visual hallucinations of "images, usually places like the Paramount Theater and sometimes I see famous people." The visual hallucinations come on suddenly, and for a moment she will feel disoriented and worries about getting into trouble for being in the wrong place: "I'll get in trouble for being in LA." She endorses once sensing that the TV and radio waves telling her the epilepsy would go away, but doubts their veracity as it was immediately followed by a seizure and hospitalization.

At the family interview the following assessment was completed (see Chapter 9 for details of a family systems assessment).

> *Problem Solving*: Initially, the family only identifies problems with Anna; that her behavior has deteriorated and her personality changed and she can no longer be left

alone. With prompting, other problems are identified by the family. Anna identifies difficulty communicating with her family and feels that her parents do not understand her. The parents do not communicate to each other about Anna's problems. Ms Ortiz has been the main caregiver and she continues to try to resolve Anna's problems by consulting more doctors but is getting very frustrated and tired. Mr Ortiz defers to his wife on all issues related to Anna. Household practical problems get easily resolved. Emotional problems do not get identified or communicated and therefore do not get resolved.

Communication: Ms Ortiz is clear and direct. Mr Ortiz is quiet and does not communicate much, but when he does, he is direct but his communication can be masked. Masked communication means that he is vague and unclear in his statements. It can be difficult for his wife to know what he is trying to communicate at these times. There were several instances during the assessment when he made vague statements about their marriage, but his wife did not hear him or recognize what he was trying to communicate. Both parents say that Anna does not try to talk to them.

Behavior Control: Anna used to know the rules in the house but is no longer able to follow basic rules. Mother states that she thinks Anna knows the house rules and is being purposefully difficult. Mr Ortiz does not try to enforce rules, leaving this to his wife.

Affective Involvement: Ms Ortiz spends most of her time with her schoolwork and part-time job, and little time with her husband and daughter. She goes cycling when she feels frustrated and angry. Mr Ortiz plays golf with his friends. He alludes to having few interests in common with his wife.

Affective Responsiveness: Anna endorses all feelings but Ms Oritz states that she has not seen her happy for a while. Ms Ortiz feels strong emotions, mostly of frustration and anger. Mr Ortiz describes a full range of feelings but tends to keep all his feelings to himself, making it hard for others to know how he is feeling.

Roles: Anna does not do her chores, such as walking the dog, or cleaning the bathroom. Ms Ortiz used to leave a list of chores but for the past few years, Anna does not follow through. Anna used to love music, reading, walking the dog, but the family now must remind her to do basic ADLs such as brush her teeth and take a shower. She does go part-time to a day program, which she seems to enjoy. Anna used to stay several weeks with her grandmother but her grandmother is now unable to manage her worsening behaviors.

Ms Ortiz states very strongly and clearly that she does not want to be the primary caregiver any more. "I'm not available to cater to everybody, and they don't like it! I'm interested in what I do, I have been a stay at home mom for 20 years, I used to go to all her doctor appointments and respond to her seizures. I don't want to do this anymore." Mr Ortiz is the main provider, working full time and spending much time traveling for work. When he is at home, Mr Ortiz has started doing some domestic chores such as shopping, attending some doctor appointments, and responding to Anna's seizures.

When interviewed alone, the couple talks about being estranged. Mr Ortiz looks uncomfortable when asked about the future, and states he is not sure what the future holds (masked communication).

Case Formulation

After the family assessment, it is clear that the main problem is that the mother no longer wants to be the primary caregiver. Her husband is unable to step up because of his work responsibilities. In addition, the couple is now estranged. The mother had coped well with Anna's illness when this was her primary role. She discovered that when she was assertive/aggressive and demanding of the medical team, that she could get better care for Anna. This time, however, this strategy is not working and the mother is characterized as "the difficult parent." Mr Ortiz had coped all these years by being passive and absent. The couple never have had communal or dyadic coping styles. Anna's brother had left home and had been "exempted from the family problem."

Throughout Anna's childhood and adolescence, Ms Ortiz believed that her daughter would improve enough to live independently. Now she has to accept that this is not likely, that her daughter has had a significant worsening of her medical condition. However, Ms Ortiz cannot accept the role of primary caregiver anymore and wants her "own life."

Mr Ortiz does not want his daughter going into a group home. His values are based on his Hispanic background and the belief that family should care for Anna. Mr Ortiz states that he would be willing to stay home and care for his daughter. However after several weeks of trying to do this, he reluctantly agreed that this proved to be beyond his abilities and he agreed to work with his wife on securing long-term placement for Anna.

Treatment consisted of the couple coming together, working on a problem list they have generated together, and developing a plan together. They discussed spending more time as a couple, to try to reestablish their relationship. They talked about how they could cope as a team, as "we," rather than individuals. The brother was included in one assessment session and was willing to come home more often and take a more active role with his sister, helping her visit group homes and encouraging her to see this as the next developmental step in her life rather than as a rejection by her family, especially her mother. It is helpful for this family to understand their difficulties as a family life stage change with a change in family roles and a change in coping styles. They could feel positively about adding a communal coping style to their individual coping styles. They decided to try to make their marriage work and began to use the communal "we" style approach to solving problems together.

Conclusion

One of the major difficulties in trying to integrate research findings into clinical practice is that different concepts have been used, different outcomes measured and different results found. Most studies on coping are cross-sectional and do not take into account the type of illness or the life stage of the family. The study of relocation is important as it charts how couples' can develop a dyadic response to a defined stressor.

It is unclear whether families should be encouraged to use "active" coping styles as some studies found that "passive" coping skills were associated with a better patient and family outcome. At the very least, families should become aware of each other's coping styles and aim to develop a broad repertoire of coping skills. Many factors influence the development of coping styles and the choice of coping styles. Adolescents generally want to develop their own coping styles so that they can become independent autonomous adults.

Families can be encouraged to make an active choice in how they handle illness. Talking to families about coping skills is likely to be received positively. Providing handouts for individuals that refer to individual and family coping styles can be helpful. A family-focused approach to managing illness has been summarized by Weihs et al. (2002) and this outline is helpful for families (see below).

Family-Focused Interventions Help Families

- Manage stresses as a team
- Mobilize patient's natural support system
- Enhance family closeness
- Increase mutually supportive interactions
- Build extra-familial support
- Minimize intra-familial hostility and criticism
- Reduce adverse effects of external stress and disease-related trauma.

(Adapted from Weihs, 2002)

References

Aalto, A. M., Harkapaa, K., Aro, A. R., and Rissanen, P. (2002). Ways of coping with asthma in everyday life: validation of the Asthma Specific Coping Scale. *Journal of Psychosomatic Research*, 53,1061–9.

Anderson, B. J., Vangsness, L., Connell, A., Butler, D., Goebel-Fabbri, A., and Laffel, L. M. B. (2002). Family conflict, adherence, and glycemic control in youth with short duration Type 1 diabetes. *Diabetic Medicine*, 19, 635–42.

Badr, H., Carmack, C. L., Kashy, D. A., Critofanilli, M., and Revenson, T. A (2010). Dyadic coping in metastatic breast cancer. *Health Psychology*, 29(2), 169–80.

Bernal, G., and Domenech Rodriguez, M. M. (2009). Advances in Latino family research: cultural adaptations of evidence-based interventions. *Family Process*, 48, 169–78.

Carver, C. S., Scheier, M. F., and Weintraub, J. K. (1989). Assessing coping strategies: A theoretically based approach. *Journal of Personality and Social Psychology*, 56, 267–83.

Carver, C. S. (1997). You want to measure coping but your protocol's too long: Consider the Brief COPE. *International Journal of Behavioral Medicine*, 4, 92–100.

Cano, A., Leong, L., Heller, J. B., and Lutz J. R. (2009). Perceived entitlement to pain-related support and pain catastrophizing: Associations with perceived and observed support. *Pain*, 147, 249–54.

Chesney, M., Neilands, T., Chambers, D., Taylor, J., and Folkman, S. (2006). A validity and reliability study of the Coping Self-Efficacy scale. *British Journal of Health Psychology*, 11(3), 421–37.

Davies, C. C., Brown, R. T., Bakeman, R., and Campbell, R. (1998). Psychological adaptation and adjustment of mothers of children with congenital heart disease: stress, coping, and family functioning. *Journal of Pediatric Psychology*, 23, 219–28.

Davey, M., Gulish, L., Askew, J., Godette, K., and Childs, N. (2005). Adolescents coping with mom's breast cancer: developing family intervention programs. *Journal of Marital & Family Therapy*, 31(2), 247–58.

Endler, N. S., and Parker, J. D. A. (1990). *Coping Inventory for Stressful Situations (CISS): Manual.* Toronto: Multi-Health Systems.

Fleishman, J. A., Sherbourne, C. D., Cleary, P. D., Wu, A. W., Crystal, S., and Hays, R. D. (2003). Patterns of coping among persons with HIV infection: configurations, correlates, and change. *American Journal of Community Psychology*, 32(1–2), 187–204.

Friedman, D., Holmbeck, G. N., DeLucia, C., Jandasek, B., and Zebracki, K. (2009). Trajectories of autonomy development across the adolescent transition in children with spina bifida. *Rehabilitation Psychology*, 54 (1), 16–27.

Jandasek, B., Holmbeck, G. N., DeLucia, C., Zebracki, K., and Friedman, D. (2009). Trajectories of family processes across the adolescent transition in youth with spina bifida. *Journal of Family Psychology*, 23(5), 726–38.

Knight, B. G., and Sayegh, P. (2010). Cultural values and caregiving: the updated sociocultural stress and coping model. *Journal of Gerontology: Psychological Sciences*, 65B (1), 5–13).

Knudson-Martin, C., and Mahoney, A. R. (Ed.) (2009). *Couples, gender, and power: Creating change in intimate relationships.* New York: Springer.

Lewis, M. A., McBride, C. M., Pollak, K. I., Puleo, E., Fish, L., Butterifeld, R. M., and Emmons, K. M. (2006). Understanding health behavior change among couples: an interdependence & communal coping approach. *Social Science Medicine*, 62(6), 1369–80.

Lyons, R. F., Mickelson, K. D., Sullivan, M. J. L., and Coyne, J. C. (1998). Coping as a communal process. *Journal of Personal and Social Relationships*, 15, 579–605.

Maes, S., Leventhal, H., and de Ridder, D. T. D. (1996). Coping with chronic diseases. In M. Zeidner and N. S. Endler (Eds), *Handbook of Coping: Theory, research, applications* (pp. 221–51). Oxford: Wiley.

Marsac, M. L., Mirman J. H., Kohser, K. L., and Kassam-Adams, N. (2011). Child coping and parent coping assistance during the peritrauma period in injured children. *Families, Systems, & Health*, 29, (4), 279–90.

Martin, S., Calabrese, S. K., Wolters, P. A., Walker, K. A., Warren, K., and Hazra, R. (2012). Family functioning and coping styles in families of children with cancer and HIV disease. *Clinical Pediatrics*, 51(1), 58–64.

Mund, M., and Mitte, K. (2011). The costs of repression: a meta-analysis on the relation between repressive coping and somatic diseases. *Health Psychology*. Advance online publication. doi: 10.1037/a0026257.

Myers, L. B., Burns, J. W., Derakshan, N., Elfant, E., Eysenck, M. W., and Phipps, S. (2007). Current issues in repressive coping and health. In J. Denollet, I. Nyklicek, and A. Vingerhoets (Eds). *Emotion regulation: Conceptual and clinical issues* (pp. 69–86). New York: Springer.

Myers, L. B. (2010). The importance of the repressive coping style: findings from 30 years of research. *Anxiety Stress Coping*. 23 (1), 3–17.

Neacsiu, A. N., Rizvi, S. L., Vitaliano, P. P., Lynch, T. R., and Linehan, M. M. (2010). The dialectical behavior therapy ways of coping checklist: development and psychometric properties. *Journal of Clinical Psychology*, 66 (6), 563–82.

Pakenham, K., and Cox, S. (2009). The dimensional structure of benefit finding in multiple sclerosis and relations with positive and negative adjustment: A longitudinal study. *Psychology and Health*, 24 (4), 373–93.

Pakenham, K. I. (2005). The positive impact of multiple sclerosis (MS) on carers: Associations between carer benefit-finding and positive and negative adjustment domains. *Disability and Rehabilitation*, 27(17), 985–97.

Rohrbaugh, M. J., Mehl, M. R., Shoham, V., Reilly, E. S., and Ewy, G. (2008). Prognostic significance of spouse we-talk in couples coping with heart failure. *Journal of Consulting and Clinical Psychology*, 76(5), 781–89.

Rohrbaugh, M. J., Shoham, V., Coyne, J. C., Cranford, J. A., Sonnega, J. S., and Nicklas, J. M. (2004). Beyond the "self" in self-efficacy: Spouse confidence predicts patient survival following heart failure. *Journal of Family Psychology*, 18 (1), 184–93.

Rolland, J., McPheters J., and Carbonell E. (2008). "Resilient Partners: A Collaborative Project with the MS Society," Collaborative Family Healthcare Association's 10th Annual Conference.

Romano, J. M., Jensen, M. P., Turner, J. A., Good, A. B., and Hops, H. (2000). Chronic pain patient partner interactions: Further support for a behavioral model of chronic pain. *Behavior Therapy*, 31, 415–40.

Schwartz, C. E. (1999). Teaching coping skills enhances quality of life more than peer support: results of a randomized trial with multiple sclerosis patients. *Health Psychology*, 18, 211–20.

Steck, B., Amsler, F., Kappos, L., and Bürgin, D. (2001). Gender-specific differences in the process of coping in families with a parent affected by a chronic somatic disease (e.g. multiple sclerosis). Psychopathology, 34(5), 236–44.

Sterba, K. R., and DeVellis, R. F. (2009). Developing a spouse version of the Illness Perception Questionnaire-Revised (IPQ-R) for husbands of women with rheumatoid arthritis. *Psychology and Health*, 24(4), 473–87.

Thuné-Boyle, I. C., Stygall, J. A., Keshtgar, M. R., and Newman, S. P. (2006). Do religious/spiritual coping strategies affect illness adjustment in patients with cancer? A systematic review of the literature. Social Science & Medicine, 63(1), 151–64.

Vitaliano, P. P., Russo, J., Carr, J. E., Maiuro, R. D., and Becker, J. (1985). The ways of coping checklist: Revision and psychometric properties. *Multivariate Behavioral Research*, 20, 3–26.

Vervoort, T., Goubert, L., and Crombez, G. (2010). Parental responses to pain in high catastrophizing children: the moderating effect of child attachment. *Journal of Pain*, 11(8), 755–63.

Vriezekolk, J. E., van Lankveld, W. G., Eijsbouts, A. M. M., van Helmond, T., Geenen, R., and van den Ende, C. H. (2011). The Coping Flexibility questionnaire: development & initial validation in patients with chronic rheumatic diseases. *Rheumatology International*, June 10. DOI: 10.1007/s00296-011-1975-y

Walsh, F. (2003). Family resilience: A framework for clinical practice. *Family Process*, 42, 1–18.

Wamboldt, F. S., Steinglass, P., and Kaplan De-Nour, A. (1991). Coping Within couples: adjustment two years after forced geographic relocation. *Family Process*, 30, 347–61.

Weinberger, D. A. (1990). The construct validity of the repressive coping style. In J. L. Singer (ed.). *Repression and dissociation: Implications for personality theory, psychopathology, and health* (pp. 337–86). Chicago, IL: University of Chicago Press.

Weihs, K., Fisher, L., and Baird, M. A. (2002). Families, health, and behavior: A section of the commissioned report by the committee on Health and Behavior: Research, Practice and Policy, Division of Neurosciences and Behavioral Health and Division of Health Promotion and Disease Prevention, Institute of Medicine. *National Academy of Sciences. Families, Systems, & Health*, 20, 1, 7–47.

Wolters, G. G., Stapert, S., Brands, I., and van Heugten, C. (2011). Coping styles within the family system in the chronic phase following acquired brain injury: its relation to families' and patients' functioning. *Journal of Rehabilitation Medicine*, 43(3),190–6.

Yorgason, J. B. et al. (2010). Older couples' management of multiple-chronic illnesses: individual and shared perceptions and coping in type 2 diabetes and osteoarthritis. *Families, Systems, & Health*, 28(1), 30–47.

Youngmee, K., Schulz, R., and Carver, C. (2007). Benefit finding in the cancer caregiving experience. *Psychosomatic Medicine*, 69(3), 283–91.

9 Family Systems Assessment

- A family systems assessment seeks to understand the influence of symptoms and illness behaviors on the family and the influence of the family on symptoms and illness behaviors.
- A family systems assessment emphasizes circular causality, rather than linear causality, in the maintenance of a behavior.
- A family system has regulating feedback loops that maintain its stability.
- Family patterns can be transmitted through the generations.
- All family systems assessment evaluations and treatment models share common factors, in the same way that individual therapies share common factors.

Introduction

All families can benefit from a structured family systems assessment, in the same way that individuals can benefit from a general health check. A family is more able to cope with challenges if it knows its strengths and weaknesses. Weaknesses can be corrected, either by the family itself, or with the help of a therapist. Strengths help a family know how best to respond to a crisis.

This chapter reviews several family assessment models, but focuses on the McMaster model of family assessment. This assessment occurs across six dimensions of family functioning: problem solving, communication, roles, affective responsiveness, affective involvement, and behavior control. Each dimension is explained in detail, using case material.

Family Systems Theory

General systems theory offered the first family therapists a "scientific" way to look at families (Bertalanffy, 1968). "Systems theory" is a term derived from biology to identify self-regulating systems. The word "systems" is used to refer specifically to self-regulating systems, i.e. systems that are self-correcting through feedback. Self-regulating systems are found in the physiological systems of our body, in ecosystems, in climate and in our society and families.

The family is considered a self-regulating system because a change in one member results in change in other members. In order for families to run well, a division of tasks and roles occurs. In traditional families, one person, usually the male, assumes the role of wage earner and another family member, usually the female, devotes their time and energy to childcare. Maintaining the emotional balance in a family is traditionally the work of one family member, usually the female, who becomes the "emotional barometer" for the whole family. However, there are many family structures and styles and it is important to ask about different family roles, rather than make assumptions. When one family member develops a medical illness, the roles of the ill family member may be reallocated or modified. The family also has to figure out how to provide practical and emotional support to the ill member.

Gregory Bateson (1972) introduced cybernetic principles to the field of family therapy. Cybernetics is an approach to the exploration of systems and is relevant when the system being analyzed is a closed system, such as a family system. A closed system is where an action in the system causes a change in the system, and that change, in turn, feeds back into the system to stabilize the system. This "circular causal" feedback loop is a cybernetic principle. Family systems have regulating feedback loops that maintain their stability. Closed systems have specific characteristics such as homeostasis, and families develop particular relational patterns in order to maintain their homeostasis. One common pattern that stabilizes a family system is called triangulation which occurs when two members in the family system have conflict and a third member is "triangled in" to stabilize their relationship. Common family triangles include a child and his parents, two children and one parent, or a couple and an in-law. Second order cybernetics describes other influences on the family such as the influence of the school, neighbors, or extended family members.

Principles of a Family as a System

- The family is an organization.
- Each individual cannot be fully understood in isolation from the whole system.
- Families are organized emotional systems.
- Relational patterns are evident in how each person in the organization interacts in a predictable manner with the others.
- Circular causality and feedback loops keep the family stable.

The Family as an Organization.

The family is an organized system, rather than a group of individuals. A family systems assessment for families with medical illness looks for family strengths and weaknesses that influence the management of the illness AND identifies family trans-actions that either worsens or ameliorates illness symptoms. Family strengths are the basis for developing new family transactions. Assessing the health of the relationship before the illness, understanding the life stage of the person with the illness, the current family life stage, and the stage of the illness are important aspects of a good assessment.

Families are organized emotional systems. Certain family members, usually the women, become responsible for maintaining the emotional health and balance in a family. This role shifts when someone develops a medical illness and more emotional support is needed. If the person who has been providing the emotional support becomes ill, then a radical shift in how emotional stability is maintained in the family needs to occur if the family is going to continue functioning effectively.

Relational Patterns

A family systems interview emphasizes circular causality rather than linear causality. A family systems therapist seeks to understand what keeps a problem going i.e. problem maintenance, in addition to what has caused a problem. Asking circular questions forces family members to think about how they react to symptoms. Circular questions also identify relational transactional patterns that occur when family members try to manage symptoms. A relational transactional pattern is a set of repetitive behaviors between family members. It can include both verbal and non-verbal components. A good family systems assessment illustrates to the family how symptoms are maintained and reinforced by particular family transactions. Circular causality and feedback loops are ways of describing these relational patterns.

Conceptualizing the problem in relational terms means explaining a problem to the family in a systemic way: "Johnny's illness affects everyone in the family and everyone in the family affects Johnny's illness." Of course this must be explained in a sophisticated and detailed way, with specific examples. With a family systems approach, the family can understand how they influence Johnny's feelings, thoughts, and behavior and Johnny can understand how he influences other family members.

Relational patterns have cognitive, behavioral, and affective components, all of which can be targets of intervention. In the case of Johnny, his parents argue about how to manage his illness. Nina, his mother, takes Johnny's side against her husband, Zack, citing Zack's harsh tone and punitive stance. Zack then accuses her of babying Johnny and says that what Johnny needs is "to suck it up and keep going." Johnny and Nina then become allied together against Zack who becomes ostracized from the family. Zack stays away from the house more. Nina becomes angry, lonely, and begins to confide more in Johnny and spends time with Johnny playing videogames. Johnny enjoys this special attention. These relational patterns can be explained to the family and the specific components identified and explored. The cognitive beliefs are "Zack believes that Johnny needs more discipline. Nina believes that Johnny needs to be protected. The affective components are "Zack feels sad that Nina is angry with him. Nina feels afraid of Zack because he is punitive and harsh." The behavioral components are: " Zack leaves the house. Nina spends time with Johnny." These components are weaved together into relational patterns and transactions. Sometimes, these relational dynamics extend back through generations. Family assessment and therapy aim to understand and change these dysfunctional relational patterns.

Family Therapist and the Family Therapy System

In family therapy, the therapeutic alliance is with the relationship, rather than with the individual family members. The therapist needs to balance and manage the alliance so each family member feels understood and involved. The family systems therapist must be aware of how they enter the family system. The presence of the therapist affects the family system. Younger therapists often unconsciously align with younger family members, who are closer to their age. One psychiatric resident was asked why he continued to see an elderly couple, who were doing quite well. After a supervisory discussion, it became clear that he enjoyed being their "lost son" and enjoyed the unconditional positive regard of "his parents."

Common Factors in Family Systems Assessment and Treatment

All family system approaches share common factors, in the same way that individual therapies share common factors. The common factors in individual therapies are patient variables, therapist variables and variables related to the therapeutic relationship. Jerome Frank outlines additional common factors in individual therapies such as a rationale for treatment, the use of a model that the therapist believes in, and the instillation of hope for change (Frank and Frank, 1991). For couples and family therapies, additional common factors are: conceptualizing the problems in relational terms; therapy that aims to disrupt dysfunctional relational patterns; expanding treatment to include family members of the index patient; and an expanded therapeutic alliance (Sprenkle, Davis, and Lebow, 2009). These common factors are found in all family systems therapies.

Common Factors in Couples and Family Therapies

- Conceptualizing the problems in relational terms
- Therapy focused on disrupting the relational patterns and cognitive, behavioral, and affective elements can be a focus of treatment
- An expanded therapeutic alliance with the relationship, rather than with a series of individuals
- An expanded treatment model that includes all family members.

Family Systems Assessments for Medical Illnesses

Several family systems assessment models are used successfully with medically ill patients and their families. These models include Salvador Minuchin (1975)'s structural model, Susan McDaniel (1992)'s Medical Family Therapy which is used in a primary care setting, Betsy Wood (2001)'s biobehavioral model developed for children with asthma and their families, and Rohrbaugh (2011)'s FAMCON family consultation model for health behavior change e.g. smoking cessation. A brief overview is given of several assessment models that are relevant for working with families with medical illnesses, however the major focus in this chapter is the McMaster model assessment (Epstein, 1981) a general problem-solving model.

Developmental Family Systems Models

Developmental family systems models integrate an understanding of individual developmental theory with a family systems perspective (e.g. Gostecnik and Repic, 2009). These models pay attention to how childhood patterns are played out in adult relationships. The type of attachment that a person forms is based on their early childhood relationships (Bowlby, 1982), and when two people become a couple, each individual bring their past relational experiences into the new relationship. Early relational conflicts can become reactivated, without the couple having any understanding of their conflict. The importance of early relationships becomes evident in a family systems interview. "The why and the how of the past" often emerge effortlessly as the couple try to make sense of their difficulties.

Families pass their ways of handling illness and symptoms down through the generations. For example, if chronic illness has always been managed in previous generations by retreating to bed and being nursed by the youngest family member, then there may be an expectation that this will occur; that when the father becomes ill, the youngest daughter becomes his caregiver. By understanding how the family has traditionally managed illness and symptoms, the current family gains a valuable perspective (see p. 185, for an illustrative case).

Intergenerational patterns can be uncovered by creating a family genogram that outlines family illness and caregiving roles. Genograms can highlight intergenerational family alliances and conflicts, are immensely powerful for families and relatively simple to construct (McGoldrick, Gerson, and Shellenberger, 2008).

Object Relations Couples Therapy extends object relations theory to marital interactions. Object Relations Theory is an individual psychotherapy that focuses on the relationship between the child and primary caregiver. Object Relations Couples Therapy defines and disentangles the couple's mutual projections and introjective identifications. This model aims to help the couple support each other's needs for attachment, autonomy and development (Scharff and Scharff, 1997). Object relations models are based on individual dynamics and are less pertinent for families trying to cope with medical illness.

Family systems models focusing exclusively on managing medical illness have been developed. One model, called Medical Family Therapy, (MedFT), is based on a biopsychosocial approach to medical illness (McDaniel, Hepworth, and Doherty, 1992). It emphasizes the mind-body interaction and promotes attention to both mind and body at the intake interview. Patients are asked about psychological **and** physical symptoms, with the intention of linking them. The mutual influence of psychological **and** physical is captured in the phrase "Both-And." MedFT is practised alongside the physicians who are providing the medical care. MedFT is a treatment suited for the primary care setting and differs in important ways from traditional family systems therapy in that MedFT openly acknowledges the biological dimension of illness and accepts the focus on the patient. Improving the family's management of the patient's illness symptoms and behaviors is an important goal. To start this process in MedFT, the illness story is solicited, with special emphasis on the beliefs and appraisals of family members. Coping styles are respected, but with the goal of challenging unhealthy coping skills. The MedFT clinician works to increase the family's understanding of normal emotional responses to the presence of chronic illness in the family, to help them attend to normal family developmental issues and to increase their sense of agency. Ongoing communication is maintained with the family, with an open door policy for family consultation.

A second model, The Resilience Model of Family Stress, Adjustment and Adaptation provides a framework to determine if an illness has become a family crisis (Danielson, Hamel-Bissell B, and Winstead-Fry, 1993). Well-adapted families meet the demands of the illness, form a positive appraisal of the stress, are good problem solvers and have family structures described as "balanced" or "regenerative" (Olsen, Russell, and Sprenkle, 1983). Poorly adapted families have high vulnerability and a pile-up of stressors on top of other life-cycle stressors. Adjustment and adaptation are family processes that help the family develop resilience. Adjustment enlists family protective factors to maintain family integrity, functioning, and fulfil developmental tasks. Adaptation enlists recovery factors in the family's ability to "bounce back" and adapt in family crisis situations (McCubbin, Thompson, and McCubbin, 1996). Family types that reflect these skills are described by McCubbin and McCubbin (1989). Families "high in hardiness, coherence, flexibility, and bonding as well as those that value and participate in family time and routines, are considered stronger and more capable of enduring stress" (Danielson et al., 1993, p. 133). Family hardiness includes a family commitment to work together to solve the presenting problem. The hardy family reframes and redefines its hardships as challenges. The family views itself as having a sense of control and influence over the outcome. In this model, family typology is assessed using the Family Changes, Family Coherence, Family Flexibility, Family Bonding, and Family Social Support Scales. The scores from these scales are entered into a matrix that describes the families as having low, medium, and high resilience (Danielson et al., 1993, pages 406–11). Family vulnerability is assessed by using the Family Change Assessment Tool, which assesses the number of stresses and strains in the family. In the clinical situation, specific coping behaviors are assessed. These coping skills are ways the family reduces stressors, acquires additional resources, and manages family tensions and their accurate appraisal of the current situation. Acquiring additional resources means increasing both the quantity and the quality of social supports. Family interviews help families ascertain if they are doing well and positive healthy adaptations are reinforced by the family therapist.

Strategic models are models that interrupt problem maintaining behavior. Two models that are used for managing difficult illnesses behaviors are presented. First, is the FAMCON Model, which is shorthand for "family consultation" model. Rohrbaugh and Shoham (2011) have developed a family systems assessment for patients with poor health behaviors. Their assessment identifies persisting "problem maintaining behaviors," which are identified as "ironic processes." Ironic processes are well-intentioned solutions that maintain problem behaviors. For example, in patients who are having difficulty with smoking cessation, a common ironic process is the demand-withdraw interaction. What typically happens is that their spouse nags them to stop smoking, which leads, instead of quitting smoking, to the smoker withdrawing and feeling angry. This interaction is the opposite of what was intended, hence the name "ironic process." Their spouse has the best intentions but their intervention causes alienation and conflict, making the problem worse. Another common problem maintaining behavior is called the "symptom-system fit." This occurs when couples smoke together and experience closeness in the smoking ritual, which then reinforces the smoking behavior. The FAMCOM assessment occurs over two sessions where the complaint is defined in behavioral terms and problem maintaining behaviors such as ironic processes and symptom-system fit are identified. When families understand these relational transactions, they may initiate change on their own. The FAMCON treatment is described in detail in Chapter 10, p. 189.

Rohrbaugh and Shoham's Five Truths about Change-Resistant Health Problems

- How a problem persists is more important than how it began.
- Use the term consultation rather than family therapy.
- Investigate what people DO rather than what they HAVE i.e. illness.
- The path to clinical change may not be continuous and smooth.
- The more entrenched a problem, the more helpful are indirect, strategic interventions.

A second strategic approach uses Narrative Therapy, an approach which examines the ways in which illness "controls" the family (White and Epston 1990). In this approach, the illness is "externalized;" made to sit in its own chair in the therapy room and the family considers what ways the illness "controls" the family. This stimulates the family to use their strengths and resources to work together against the illness. A Narrative Therapy interview uses an interrogation technique; asking, "In what way has diabetes controlled this family? Has diabetes stopped you enjoying your time together? How has it been able to do that? How has diabetes made you forget about the good times? Are there times when you didn't let diabetes do this?" The goal is to help the family find ways that they have "resisted diabetes" and to help the family build on this experience.

The Narrative Therapy assessment and the FAMCON approach are helpful strategic approaches that are useful in situations when directly confronting a symptom or behavior makes the symptom or behavior worse. With direct confrontation, the therapist runs the danger of becoming yet one more person who nags the patient or family to change. A strategic approach helps mobilize the family's collective strengths against the problem symptom or behavior.

A Family Systems Interview

The following section describes a typical family interview using the McMaster model. Before starting a family systems interview it is worthwhile considering each of the following questions.

1. What is the family life-cycle stage?
2. What is the stage of illness?
3. What is the family's experience of health care?
4. What is it like to be in their shoes?
5. What do you know about the family's strengths?

Family Life-Cycle Stage

A family life-cycle has predictable stages with specific developmental tasks: marriage, birth of a child, parenting, launching of children, coping with illness, and death. In order for a family to function well, the challenges of each life stage need to be met successfully. Chronic illness has the capacity to derail the family's progression through the life stages.

Stage of Illness

In the acute phase of illness, perhaps lasting as long as two years, the family struggles with questions focused on finding a cure or a treatment that "will take the illness away." If the illness persists, then the family has to consider how best to adapt to the presence of illness. A progressive illness has a more consistent impact than an episodic illness. When illness comes to young family members, additional grief work and adjustment in the family needs to occur (see Chapter 3 for more discussion on life stage and illness interaction).

The Family's Experience of Health Care

A family that is receptive to health-care intervention is easier to work with. Families who have had negative experiences with health-care providers may be suspicious, doubtful, or dismissive. The clinician should know whether or not such experiences have occurred and make a determined effort to acknowledge and try to counter any such experiences. Asking the family, "What has been your experience with health care providers and the health-care system?" is usually adequate to elicit an honest response. It is important to consider racial and cultural barriers that may exist between health-care providers and recipients. When using interpreters, it is important to assess if there are communication barriers due to the interpreter's background, as ethnic tensions can be present even if the same language is spoken.

What is it Like to be in their Shoes?

Spending a few minutes reflecting on the family life stage, the type of illness, and the current situation can help the therapist develop a deeper empathic stance towards the family. What are the family's beliefs about illness and treatment? Do they expect a cure? How does their cultural background influence their experience of illness or the health-care system? What do you know about their coping skills or current life stressors?

What are the Family's Strengths?

Every family has strengths. For families with limited resources, getting everyone together and attending the family meeting together is a strength. Families are more receptive if we can acknowledge and reinforce what they do well.

The Family Systems Meeting

Orientation

A family meeting starts with an orientation and acknowledges the commitment that family members have made to help their relative. Family members will want to focus on the meaning of symptoms and what medications need to be taken in order to feel better. Family members may want to complain about the health-care system and difficulties accessing care. It is important to frame the first meeting and clarify the goals of the meeting. "Thank you all for coming in. I think it is important to meet with the families of all of my patients. Chronic illness takes its toll on everyone, the patient AND the family. This is an opportunity to look at how you all are doing together, as a family. It is important to acknowledge what you are doing well, so you can keep doing it, and also to identify areas that can be improved. Is that OK with everyone?"

The family has a natural tendency to revert to asking questions about the patient's current medical symptoms, with an emphasis on symptom resolution. For example "If only she could breathe better, then we could do the things we used to do" or "How come the medicine is not working? He is still in pain!" Re-focusing the family is essential in the beginning of the meeting. "Since all of your family is here, let us focus on understanding how your family functions and see what you are doing that is helpful and what you are doing that might be causing problems. I know it is difficult because your symptoms are hard to manage. How DO you all manage these symptoms, as a family?"

Assessing family functioning is best completed in a formal way across several dimensions to ensure a comprehensive evaluation. The model presented in this book is the McMaster model of Family Functioning (Epstein, Bishop, and Levin 1978), which assesses the following dimensions: problem solving, communication, roles, behavior control, affective involvement, and affective responsiveness. This assessment model is associated with the Problem-centered Systems Therapy of the Family (Epstein and Bishop, 1981) (see Chapters 10 and 11).

During the assessment, family members are asked for their level of agreement and satisfaction about how the family functions. For example: Is this a satisfactory division of labor? Does the family agree on how it communicates? Does everyone feel cared about and that their life and own development matters? Is the family satisfied with how it goes about solving problems? Does the family enjoy its time spent together? Is that time enough? Individual family members are often unaware of how other family members perceive family functioning.

As aspects of family functioning are brought to light and discussed, the family begins to see how it might make changes. Thus, the seeds of intervention are found in a good thorough assessment. It is not unusual for families to come back after the assessment, having made changes on their own.

McMaster Assessment Questions

Problem Solving: Problem solving refers to the ability to resolves problems to maintain effective family functioning. Instrumental problems are problems of everyday life, such as managing money, obtaining food, clothing, and housing and affective problems are those concerning emotions such as anger or depression. Families whose functioning is disrupted by instrumental problems rarely deal effectively with affective or emotional problems.

Communication: The verbal exchange of information within a family. Families can have marked difficulties with the emotional component of communication but can function very well in the instrumental area. Communication can be clear or masked (camouflaged). Communication can be direct or indirect (comments delivered to someone else rather than the intended person).

Roles: How the provision of resources, nurturance and support, sexual gratification, personal development, and maintenance and management of the family system are divided between members, including decision-making, boundaries, household finances and management.

Affective (Emotional) Involvement: How the family shows interest in and values the activities of other family members. Families who lack involvement with each other merely coexist in the same space without connection. Family members who are narcissistically involved are invested in others only in terms of what they can get, without real concern for others. Empathic involvement means that family members demonstrate true concern for others, even though these concerns are peripheral to their own interests. Over-involvement and symbiotic involvement are over-intrusive, over-protective, with blurred boundaries between family members.

Affective (Emotional) Responsiveness: Ability to respond with a full range of feelings, and whether or not the emotion experienced is consistent with the context. Welfare emotions consist of affection, warmth, tenderness, support, love, consolation, happiness, and joy. Emergency emotions are fear, anger, sadness, disappointment, and depression.

Behavioral Control: How a family establishes rules about behavior, such as parental discipline, and standards and expectations of behavior that adults set for each other. There are several styles of behavior control: rigid behavioral control, flexible behavior control, laissez-faire behavior control (where there are no standards or direction), and chaotic behavior control where standards shift in a random unpredictable fashion.

(Adapted from Keitner, Heru, and Glick, 2009, pp. 74–8)

Problem Solving

Problem solving is divided into instrumental or practical problem solving, and emotional problem solving. A family can usually manage to solve practical problems such as getting the ill member to appointments and managing crises. Being able to talk about how they feel about the emotional aspects of caregiving is more difficult. Family members may feel burdened, anxious, and overwhelmed by caregiving responsibilities. Can they identify this as a family, and if so, how do they work together on solving these emotional issues? It is important to ask the patient who they consider "family" as there may be other people, like neighbors, church members, or visiting health-care workers who are involved in identifying and solving problems. The emotional work of caregiving is difficult and emotional problem solving can be challenging. If one spouse becomes a caregiver, the marital relationship changes, perhaps become less equal, although many spouses find reward in caregiving (Heru and Ryan, 2006). For children with a shortened life span, anticipatory grieving occurs in other family members. For adolescents with chronic illnesses such as diabetes, teaching self-care skills and the parents' wish to protect often conflict with the adolescent's drive for independence. Siblings can get forgotten when the family focuses on the ill child. An ER visit changes the family's schedule, requiring siblings to spend extended periods of time away from home or family and a sibling can feel anxious, angry or guilty (Gold, Treadwell, Weissman, and Vichinsky, 2011). Women are more frequently the family health managers, and tend to be the emotional barometers in the family. It is important to help the family understand what the emotional difficulties are in the family and how well they are identifying and solving them.

A major goal of family assessment is to help families understand the steps of problem solving so that they can apply these steps to future problems. As therapy ends, the family is asked to solve their own problems with the therapist leading them through the steps of problem solving. When the family leaves therapy, they should have a thorough understanding of how to manage future problems.

The steps of problem solving are:

1. Identification of the problem
2. Communication about the problem
3. Development of strategies to manage the problem
4. Regrouping to discuss how the solution worked
5. If it did not work, trying other strategies.

Case Example: Assessing Emotional Problem Solving in the Jetson Family

Mr Jetson is on disability for several chronic medical illnesses and is now anticipating abdominal surgery to remove a tumor he believes is cancerous. He is a single parent of three teenagers, ages 19, 17, and 14. Their mother lives nearby but has significant difficulties maintaining a positive outlook and a stable home for their children. She undermines the children's efforts to care for their father, by telling them that he is too needy and they should not help him out when he asks. The father presents with feelings of helpless concerning his difficulties. He complains of fatigue and is unable to manage practical aspects of the household such as cleaning and cooking. The older teenagers, Zara and Scott, take turns to drive him to his appointments and to help him in practical ways, such as getting his medications from the pharmacy.

Mr Jetson brings his children to his psychiatrist to talk about what is going on because he states "they have issues with me" and he wants "a professional to talk to them." The psychiatrist enquires about Mr Jetson's expectations, but is told that there is nothing specific of concern. After introductions, the psychiatrist asks, "How have you, as a family, been coping emotionally with Dad's illness? Do each of you cope in your own way? Is there a special way you all cope as a family?" The children talk about how difficult it is because Scott, the middle child, aged 17, will not do his chores and is angry all the time. Zara, aged 19, tries to talk with Scott and support him, because she realizes that he is upset by what is going on with his father. Eva, aged 14 years, says she likes Zara to help her with her homework and voices no concerns about her father, that he seems fine to her, although she worries when he has to go to the doctors.

Zara and Scott are protective of Eva and say she needs to focus on her school work and it is OK that she does not have any chores. Zara and Scott say that they feel overwhelmed at times and that their mother undermines them when they try to talk with her about their father's illnesses. Zara and Scott fight with each other about chores, cooking and shopping responsibilities. Scott says he will do his chores when he wants and not when Zara tells him to. Mr Jetson is quiet during this discussion and says that he feels unable to manage the situation and that he is unsure how to respond to his children's feelings. On a positive note, he understands that emotional difficulties are getting in the way at home and that is why he has brought the family to a meeting.

This first session discusses aspects of affective (emotional) responsiveness. What are the most prominent feelings that each person in the family experiences? Does each person have a full range of feelings? Each teenager reports that they are able to enjoy school, interact with friends and experience pleasure, as well as being worried and concerned about their father. In addition, Scott says he is frustrated when his older sister tries to tell him what to do: "You are not my parent." Zara feels that, as the eldest girl, it is her responsibility to take care of things at home. They all care about their father's welfare but feel unsure about how to balance caring for him with the demands of their own lives. Mr Jetson states that he feels guilty that he is sick and placing this burden on his children but also has feelings of needing to be taken care of. All acknowledge that these feelings are causing tension and unease in the family. In summary, the Jetson family is having difficulty managing the emotional aspects of caregiving. Caregiving is affecting the developmental trajectory of the children, especially the older daughter who has become the family caregiver and substitute maternal parent.

Family intervention helps this family in many ways. Education and support about the caregiving role helps the older children understand the need for balance in their lives and their need to attend to self-care. The father is encouraged to maximize his functioning. The family benefits from being able to identify and communicate their feelings directly to each other. Emotional problem solving begins with the ability to identify feelings and communicate them as a family. The next step is to seek solutions. In the Jetson family, this includes the development of new individual coping skills as well as communal family coping skills.

Cultural differences exist in coping styles and coping preferences. For example, the Korean culture is typically patriarchal, with an emphasis on controlling emotions, so the above strategies for helping the Jetson family express feelings would be less appropriate in a Korean family. In Korean families, the emphasis is on maintaining an optimistic outlook. Hope and less frequent use of information-seeking are significantly associated with lower psychological distress and better family relationships in Korean mothers of children with cancer (Han, Cho, Kim, and Kim, 2009). These mothers reported that they coped by "believing that my child is receiving the best medical care possible," "believing that my child will get better," and "believing that things will work out." There is no single correct way of coping and a family interviewer must ask, "How does this style of coping work for your family?"

Communication

Sometimes, the major issue is that the family is so busy that they do not have time to interact with each other. If people work shifts, then they may not be able to spend much time together. The next questions focus on the quality of communication: "For the time you do spend together, do you communicate clearly with each other? Do you sometimes have to guess what other people in the family mean? Is communication OK or is it a problem? Has this changed since you became ill? How much time do you spend talking about illness? Is this enough time or too much time? Do family members want to spend more time away from their sick relative? Do family members communicate about feelings? Is it clear how everyone is feeling? Does the person with the illness try to hide when they are not feeling well? How does the family respond to this?

Communication is affected by culture. At the end of life, Latino families tend to communicate indirectly with less emphasis on discussing dying, compared to white families. Language is important and care providers must recognize that "hospice" translates to "hospicio" in Spanish, which means orphanage or place for poor people. Latino caregivers may feel that telling the truth about prognosis is harmful to the patient and cruel to the family. Latino caregivers may feel that it is their responsibility to protect the patient from the knowledge of his or her illness, to deny that death is imminent, and to act as if the patient is getting well. In many Latino families, discussion about the family member's death is minimal because they do not want to "hurt" each other. One family member stated, "Well, as a Latino the fact that they tell you straightforward that your husband is dying ... the doctor tells you 'he is at the end of his life;' it sounds a little cruel ... I knew there was no cure for him. Everything they were doing for him was palliative, that all the medicine that was used for nausea and vomiting was palliative only. However, still it made me angry when the doctor told me he was dying." (Kreling, Selsky, Perret-Gentil, Huerta, and Mandelblatt, 2010: 431.)

Asking a family how they would like to communicate about end of life issues is respectful and helps the family discuss their feelings and plans for their dying relative. Asking specifically about family beliefs, past experiences of the current and prior generations can help a family control the communication process around end of life issues. It is important not to assume that the treatment team knows best how a family should be discussing end-of-life care.

Roles

Families usually divide up responsibilities so that each family member has a designated role such as the breadwinner, homemaker, nurturer, universal babysitter or fixer-of-all-things-broken etc. Traditional families divide up roles by gender, but this does not have to be the case. Families can negotiate any arrangement that suits them. Questions to ask include: Who works and for how many hours? Who handles the money? Who buys the groceries and prepares the meals? Who looks after the home and car? Who oversees the children's education? Who is involved in major decisions? Who has the final say? Do any of you feel overburdened by your roles? Are the responsibilities fairly shared between family members? If not, how would you like to see it done?

Illness-related questions include: Who helps with medications and transportation to appointments? Who provides emotional support? How have things changed since you became ill? Are you intimate with each other? Has that changed since your illness? Who is the primary caregiver? Some people like being caregivers and others do not, how do you feel? Are there alternative caregivers in this family? Do you feel guilty that someone has to care for you? In what other ways has the illness changed your roles in the family? Do you expect your family to take care of you?

There are cultural differences in the expectations about the caregiver role (Gallant, Spitze, and Grove, 2010). African-American (AA) elders have stronger expectations for intergenerational co-residence and filial responsibility, than white elders. Older AA women have larger, more intricate social networks with children especially daughters as caregivers, than older AA men. AA women frequently exchange services such as childcare or elder services. Older AAs, especially women, are more religious than whites and churches play a central role in the AA community providing spiritual comfort, and practical and emotional support. However, AA women do not necessarily utilize their social supports because of the strong cultural value placed on independence.

The role of elders in Latino cultures is to educate younger generations and pass along cultural values. Elders are generally held in high esteem and aging well is associated with involvement in a social network. Latinos, like AAs, are more likely to live in multi-generational households compared to whites, although most elders would prefer to live independently. Mexican-American (MA) family systems are in closer contact with their adult children than either AAs or whites. MA women, like AAs, provide more childcare and assistance to extended family members, compared with whites.

In Chinese cultures, caring for the sick is considered a family responsibility and caregiving is an important role. When elderly Chinese migrate to the USA, they may modify their values to correspond to their children's independence. However, Chinese values can be stronger among the adult children than their immigrant parents. Elderly Chinese first practice self-care, before seeking help from their spouses. Friends and neighbors, as well as adult children are turned to next. Older Chinese adults often rely on neighbors and friends for practical help, such as transportation, language assistance, and decision-making. Older Samoan women seek care from kin networks for chronic-illness related health behaviors, and seek support from non-kin networks for broader lifestyle behaviors, like exercise and losing weight. Medical help is only sought when health become significantly poor.

Native American (NA) values include a strong emphasis on group identity. Elders are highly respected and play an important role in native culture. NAs place great responsibility on caring for family and extended tribal members. Elders, particularly women, play a central role in maintaining cultural norms and in caring for children and grand-children. They, in turn, are cared for by younger members of the family and the tribe, particularly by adult women. The elders view the needs of their family and community as more important than their own.

This attitude is shown by a Native American patient who presented to be considered as an altruistic kidney donor. He had no specific trade or income but performed tasks, such as childcare, for tribal members who were working or needed to be away from home. He would stay in their homes and would receive food and clothing from the family in exchange for his services. He stating that he wished to give one of his kidneys to a distant relative. He did not fit the profile of a "good donor" as he did not attend medical appointments, did not know if he had any illnesses and had no one place that he lived. However, he felt that he could provide a service that was consistent with his role in the community. This service was to donate a kidney.

Meal preparation is an important family role that usually falls to the maternal figure. Men with special dietary needs are well cared for by their spouses who plan and cook their meals. It is more challenging for women to balance their own dietary self-care needs with the family's expectations of traditional meals. For many women, their role as household manager and meal preparer frequently trumps their ability to attend to their own dietary needs.

Affective Responsiveness

This dimension focuses on how each person experiences their feelings and how they communicate feelings to other family members. Questions to ask include: Are you a family that responds to situations with a lot of feeling? Do any of you feel that you are a family who under-responds in terms of emotions? Which kinds of emotions do you think you over- or under-respond to? Are there any feelings that you experience more intensely than reasonable given the situation? Is your spouse mostly happy/sad/angry/critical? Does your spouse agree with that assessment? Have things changed since you became ill? If so, how have they changed? Do you have specific fears? Do you feel angry about how things have changed? Are you able to express your feelings and talk openly about how you feel? Are there feelings that you cannot express or talk about?

When someone is ill or dying, family members may hide their sad or angry feelings, in order to protect the ill family member. Family members want to appear strong to provide support for the ill member. In Latino cultures, this brave stance is typical of how families present.

Affective Involvement

This dimension assesses the family's emotional commitment and involvement with each member. Questions to ask include: Who cares about what is important to you? Do you think other family members are interested in you? Do they ever show too much interest? Do you feel that they are truly interested in you because it is important to you, or only because they think they should be? Do you feel that other members of the family go their own way and do not care or notice what happens to you? Does the family spend time together? Does the illness prevent the family from doing things together? Are there alternative activities that the family can do together when the illness is getting in the way? Is the primary caregiver managing well and can the caregiver take time out for themselves?

Illness frequently forces a family to develop new hobbies and interests. Unfortunately, many family members say that they are not interested in other activities and insist that their previous activities like skiing or hiking are the only things that hold their interest. Anger at these limitations may be a barrier to family closeness. A Narrative Therapy technique can be helpful: "This illness is not only robbing you of what you like, but also stopping your whole family from being close. Are there ways that you, as a family, have been able to prevent this illness from having control over your lives?"

Chinese families, like Korean families, want an emphasis on the positive in order to protect patients' hope. "Protective truthfulness" maintains an atmosphere of confidence in treatment and hope in recovery. Family members express caring for each other by protecting each other from physical and mental hurt. Patients express appreciation of this protectiveness, even when they learn about their diagnosis (Liu, 2005). One patient noted that his family members did not say much, but diligently cooked various kinds of nourishing food and soup, and that these actions were more powerful than any word could be. The questions to ask are: "Do you feel that your family cares? How do you know this? How does your family show they care?" Each family has its own way of caring and showing caring feelings; there is no right or wrong way.

Working hard at helping the family identify new interests is worth the time and effort. Who knew that Mr Lionel would like to cook or that the family would enjoy building birdhouses together? Sending the family on an outing to the library to look at books on hobbies can be an effective homework task.

Behavior Control

This dimension is most important when the identified patient is a child or adolescent. Questions to ask include: Do you have rules in your family about how to handle different situations? How do you handle dangerous situations? Do you allow hitting or yelling at each other? Do you know what is expected of you in terms of behavior with people outside the family? Do you let people know where you are when you are away from home? Are the rules clear? Are the rules the same for everybody? Can you discuss the rules? Are there rules about smoking, drinking, or curfews? Do the rules get enforced or do things slide? What about exercise and diet? How have things changed since you became ill? Does anyone try to stop you enjoying the things you used to enjoy, because of your health? Are there new rules about what you can do and what you can eat? Who nags you the most?

For adolescents with diabetes, the struggle over "what is best for your heath" can conflict with their drive for independence. Questions about meal times, how blood sugars are monitored, and rituals around administering insulin illuminates the family dynamics about diabetic care. A positive framework works best: How do you keep such good control most of the time? What accounts for the episodes of lack of control? What prevents you from managing your diabetes well, on those days? What happens in the family when you have a bad day? How many times a day does your mother/father ask if you have checked your blood sugar? How many times do they ask about what you ate or did not eat each day? Does their worrying and caring about you feel like too much nagging? Does anyone express such concern for you at school? Do your parents' concerns about your illness affect other aspects of your life?

Case Example: John and Susan Han Negotiate Illness Behavior

John and Susan Han are newly married young executives who are focused on establishing themselves in their respective careers. John develops severe anxiety symptoms in the context of an undiagnosed gastrointestinal illness. He feels unable to go to work; he cannot concentrate, is getting chest pain, feels anxious and is unable to sleep. He feels that his life is falling apart and perceives his wife telling him "to shape up and get a grip" as callous and uncaring. She is currently working from home and states that she cannot deal with him "lying around all day complaining." He says his wife is not sympathetic and that their marriage is falling apart. He wants his wife to be more sympathetic. The psychiatrist explains to Mr Han that he has generalized anxiety disorder, starts nortryptyline 50mgs at night, and schedules a family systems interview.

Dr A: Welcome, thank you for coming in. This meeting is to talk about how you, as a couple, have been coping with this illness. Susan, why don't you start?

Susan: Well, I know he is in pain but I don't really have much patience. I don't know how to help him. It is frustrating. He is just laying around and not doing anything but moaning. It is making me very upset. I don't know what to do!

John: She starts yelling at me, and then she cries a lot.

Dr A: So, John what happens? You get up in the morning, feel chest pain, then what do you do? What happens next?

John: I tell her.

Dr A: What do tell her and what are you expecting from her?

John: I tell her I am in pain. I expect her to rub my back or something. Make me feel better.

Susan: Oh, is that what you expect? It seems to me that you are like a child and want me to be your mother!

Dr A: Is that right John?

John: Well, some sympathy would be nice.

Dr A: What would your mother do if she were there?

John then describes, with the therapist's support, how his mother, a nurse, took care of all his ills as a child. He has never learned self-care skills. When Susan is asked about her expectations when she is ill, she talks about her mother never being there and that she learned as a child how to care for herself and that she sees John's deficiencies in this area as "quite repulsive" to her. She then yells at him to "get a grip," he gets more chest pain and a vicious cycle ensues.

At the end of this 40 minute exchange, the couple is asked how they would like things to be different. John says he would like Susan to rub his back and say something comforting. Susan says she can do that for ten minutes but after that, he needs to do things to care for himself. She is able to offer concrete examples of skills that she thinks would help him, such as take a walk, read a book, or call a friend. If he does this, then she is willing to return to him later in the day and offer more soothing touching to him. He agrees to this plan. The rest of the family assessment is completed. The family works well in all other areas. The therapist remarks on the health of their relationship except for problem solving around emotional difficulties trying to manage Mr Han's illness.

One month later, the patient returns for follow-up. He is improved and notes that his relationship is also improved. He states that since he saw his wife cry in the office, he had no idea that she actually cared about him so much. He remarks on how their upbringings have been so different. Now, when she sees him in pain, she will approach him and try to divert him. They will then do something together, like watching a movie.

This is an example of a young couple understanding their individual coping styles and learning a new dyadic coping style. A healthy family adapts and makes changes: an unhealthy family gets stuck in patterns that are maladaptive and hurtful. This couple is able to change their relational dysfunction early in their marriage, before dysfunctional transactions become entrenched and more difficult to shift.

Conclusion

A family systems assessment has common factors, regardless of the family therapy model used. New approaches to families are continually being developed but family systems models can be recognized by the presence of these common factors. A structured family assessment helps differentiate a well-functioning family that is having current adjustment difficulties, from a poorly functioning family which has become more dysfunctional in the presence of chronic illness. It is important to recognize that families may have one area of difficulty and many areas of strength. Not all families will need therapy and simply identifying areas of concern can help some families make changes.

Good family relationships become temporarily dysfunctional in the face of stress. In fact, when a child is born into a family, the family becomes dysfunctional for about three months, then most families reorganize to function well with its additional member (Gustafsson, Bjorksten, and Kjellman, 1994). There are several models that have been tested and found to be effective in assessing and treating families with medical illnesses. Family systems treatments are presented in Chapter 10.

References

Bateson, G. (1972). *Steps to an Ecology of Mind: Collected Essays in Anthropology, Psychiatry, Evolution, and Epistemology.* Chicago: University of Chicago Press.

Bertalanffy, L.V. (1968). *General System Theory: Foundations, Development, Applications.* New York: Braziller.

Bowlby J. (1982). *Attachment and loss. Vol. 1: Attachment* (2nd Edition), Basic Books, New York.

Danielson, C. B., Hamel-Bissell, B., and Winstead-Fry, P. (1993). *Families, Health and Illness.* St Louis. Missouri: Mosby.

Epstein, N. B., and Bishop, D. S. (1981). Problem Centered Systems Therapy of the Family. *Journal of Marital and Family Therapy,* 7 (1), 23–31.

Epstein, N. B., Bishop, D. S., and Levin, S. (1978). The McMaster model of Family Functioning. *Journal of Marital and Family Therapy,* 4(4), 19–31.

Frank, J. D., and Frank, J. B. (1991). *Persuasion and Healing: A Comparative Study of Psychotherapy.* (3rd Edition) Johns Hopkins University Press, Baltimore.

Gallant, M. P., Spitze, G., and Grove, J. G. (2010). Chronic Illness Self-care and the Family Lives of Older Adults: A Synthetic Review Across Four Ethnic Groups. *Journal of Cross Cultural Gerontology,* 25, 21–43.

Gold, J. I., Treadwell, M., Weissman, L., and Vichinsky E. (2011). The mediating effects of family functioning on psychosocial outcomes in healthy siblings of children with sickle cell disease. *Pediatric Blood & Cancer,* 57(6), 1055–61.

Gostecnik, C., and Repic, T. (2009). Relational Marital Paradigm. *American Journal of Psychotherapy*, 63(1), 1–12.

Gustafsson, P. A., Bjorksten, B., and Kjellman, N. I., (1994). Family dysfunction in asthma: a prospective study of illness development. *Journal of Pediatrics*, 125(3), 493–8.

Han, H. R., Cho, E. J., Kim, D., Kim, J. (2009). The report of coping strategies and psychosocial adjustment in Korean mothers of children with cancer. *Psycho-Oncology*,18, 956–64.

Heru, A. M., and Ryan, C. E. (2006). Family functioning in the caregivers of patients with dementia: one-year follow-up. *Bulletin of the Menninger Clinic*, 70(3), 222–31.

Keitner, G. I., Heru, A. M., and Glick, I. (2009). *Clinical Manual of Couples & Family Therapy*. Washington DC: APPI Press.

Kreling, B., Selsky, C., Perret-Gentil, M., Huerta, E. E., and Mandelblatt, J. S. (2010). 'The worst thing about hospice is that they talk about death': contrasting hospice decisions and experience among immigrant Central and South American Latinos with US-born White, non-Latino cancer caregivers. *Palliative Medicine*, 24(4), 427–34.

Liu, J. E., Mok, E., and Wong, T. (2005). Perceptions of supportive communication in Chinese patients with cancer: experiences and expectations. *Journal of Advanced Nursing*, 52(3), 262–70.

McCubbin, M. A., and McCubbin, H. I. (1989). Families coping with illness: The resiliency model of family stress, adjustment and adaptation. In, C. B. Danielson, B. Hamel-Bissel, and P. Winstead-Fry, *Families, health & illness: Perspectives on coping and intervention*. St. Louis: Mosby.

McCubbin, H. I., Thompson, A. I., and McCubbin, M. A. (1996). *Family assessment: Resiliency, coping and adaptation: inventories for research and practice*. Madison, WI: University of Wisconsin Publishers.

McDaniel, S. H., Hepworth, J., and Doherty, W. J. (1992). *Medical Family Therapy: a biopsycho-social approach to families with health problems*. Basic Books; New York.

McGoldrick, M., Gerson, R., and Petry, S. S. (2008). *Genograms: Assessment and intervention* (3rd Edition). New York: W. W. Norton & Co.

Minuchin, S., Baker, L., Rosman, B. L., Liebman, R., Milman, L., and Todd, T. C. (1975). A conceptual model of psychosomatic illness in children. Family organization and family therapy. *Archives of General Psychiatry*, 32, 1031–8.

Olsen, D. H., Russell, C. S., and Sprenkle, D. H. (1983). Circumplex model VI: Theoretical update. *Family Process*, 22, 69–83.

Rohrbaugh, M. J., and Shoham, V. (2011). Family Consultation for Couples Coping with Health Problems: A Social Cybernetic Approach. In H. S. Friedman (Ed.), *Oxford Handbook of Health Psychology*, pp. 480–501. New York: Oxford University Press.

Scharff, J. S., and Scharff, D. E. (1997). Object relations couple therapy. *American Journal of Psychotherapy*, 51(2), 141–73.

Sprenkle, D. H., Davis, S. D., and Lebow, J. (2009). *Common Factors in Couple and Family Therapy: The Overlooked Foundation for Effective Practice*. New York: Guilford Press.

Rolland, J. (1994). *Families, Illness, and Disability: An Integrative Treatment Model. New York*: Basic Books.

White, M., and Epston, D. (1990). *Narrative Means to Therapeutic Ends*. New York: Norton.

Wood, B. L. (2001). Physically manifested illness in children and adolescents. A biobehavioral family approach. *Child and Adolescent Psychiatric Clinics of North America*, 10(3), 543–62.

10 Three Levels of Family Intervention

- Family inclusion brings families into the treatment decision-making process.
- Family psychoeducation provides patients and their families with skills for disease management and aims to improve the health and well-being of all family members.
- Family systems therapy targets dysfunctional relational patterns for change and promotes healthy relational patterns.

Introduction

Family Attitudes Toward Illness Matters

A supportive attitude generally results in supportive behavior. Unsupportive family attitudes and behaviors often result from a lack of understanding of the illness, how to manage illness symptoms and behaviors and/or a lack of resources. At a deeper level, family conflict contributes to poorer illness outcome and increased difficulties for all family members. Knowing how to assess and intervene with families is an important skill in caring for patients with medical illness.

This chapter differentiates three levels of family intervention: family inclusion, family psychoeducation, and family systems therapy. All clinicians can begin with family inclusion which requires no special training, just a willingness to "think family." The clinician can then progress to family psychoeducation, if needed. Clinicians with basic family skills can provide psychoeducation. Basic family skills include being able to handle emotional reactions such as anger, sadness or frustration that might occur in the psychoeducational family setting. Helping families process these feelings also helps them adjust to the presence of illness. These basic family skills can be acquired through a short series of didactics and some case supervision. The highest level of family intervention is family systems therapy which requires specific training (Berman et al., 2006).

This chapter describes each level of family treatment and describes family systems therapies in depth. This provides the reader with a solid understanding of this specialized and sophisticated therapy. The chapter concludes with a case example that illustrates how to move from family inclusion through family psychoeducation to family systems therapy.

Family Inclusion

Family inclusion means "thinking family." Including the family and especially the primary caregiver, in the patient's visit allows you to ask both the patient and caregiver about psychological symptoms as well as physical symptoms. Physicians can positively influence the health and well-being of the primary caregiver by recognizing their contribution and assessing their needs (physical, psychological, and spiritual). Providing resource material and screening tools in the waiting room shows the clinic's openness to providing family-oriented patient care.

A useful and easily available screening tool is the American Medical Association (AMA) caregiver tool (see Appendix, p. 230), which can be completed in the waiting room, prior to the visit. Asking the caregiver to self-report normalizes the caregiving experience and helps the caregiver understand the rationale for a caregiver intervention, if needed (Chapter 5 outlines the caregiver perspective in detail).

Marital satisfaction is an important variable that can be measured in the medical office. Good marital quality is associated with better outcomes in many medical illnesses, especially for women (Heru, 2010). A one-item screening tool: "On a scale of 1 to 10 rate your overall satisfaction with your marriage, with 1 being very unsatisfied and 10 being extremely satisfied" has been used successfully in primary care to identify marital difficulties (Bailey, Kerley, and Kibelstis, 2012). In this study, patients were invited at check in to complete a survey that included basic demographics, health screen questions and the one-item screening question. Inclusion criteria were being English speaking, age ≥18, and married. The number of surveys completed was 159 (76%), with six patients refusing to fill out the survey, most commonly because they felt the topic was too personal. On the one-item scale, a cut-off of ≥8 for those satisfied and ≤7 for those who were unsatisfied, maximized sensitivity and specificity.

The one-item question had adequate psychometric properties when tested against the Dyadic Adjustment Scale (DAS) (Spanier, 1976). The DAS is a 32 question, well validated tool used to measure marital satisfaction (Graham, Liu, and Jeziorski, 2006). Patients can have a score between 0–150 with a score of < 100 as a cut-off for dissatisfaction (Sher and Baucom, 1993). The average DAS score of the patients in the study was 111 ± 21.5, similar to the national average of 114 ± 17.8. In this study, following the completion of the survey, patients expressed pleasure that they were being asked about their relationships because they felt it was an important part of who they were. Using a one-item screen is certainly acceptable to patients and feasible for many clinics. What should be done for those patients who identify marital dissatisfaction?

In a follow-up to this study, five couples with low scores who agreed to work on their relationship were given a copy of John Gottman's "5 times and traits" (Gottman and Silver, 1999). Gottman describes the ability to make the most of times spent together (partings, reunions, admiration and appreciation, affection), and a weekly date, as predictors of better marital satisfaction. A three- to five- minute brief explanation was given to the couples and follow-up appointments were made for two and four weeks. By the second visit, all five couples expressed improvement in their relationships and by six months, all five couples expressed that they were happy or very happy with their relationship (Bailey, 2007). This is very small pilot study but it shows how relational quality can be attended to with a very brief assessment and intervention. The tool and the intervention did not require any training so can easily be incorporated into busy clinic settings.

Another easy to use tool is the genogram which is a visual diagram of family interactions across generations (McGoldrick, Gerson, and Petry, 2008). A genogram provides a patient with a perspective on the intergenerational transmission of illness behaviors and attitudes. Genograms are especially helpful in families where there are members of different cultures or immigrant families with differing integration into the dominant culture. Understanding the family context helps the patient and the clinician understand what "being ill" means in a specific family, how family members respond to people with illness and what messages children receive from their parents about "being ill."

Family Psychoeducation

Psychoeducation focuses on illness education, explores the meaning of the illness for each family member and promotes the development of a broad repertoire of coping skills. Psychoeducation can be given to a single family or provided to several families in a group setting. In multifamily group psychoeducation, families have access to other families' successes and failures, which benefits all families (see Chapter 12 for discussion of multifamily groups). Family psychoeducation is effective for many illnesses, and can improve both patient and family outcomes.

Family psychoeducation can be simple and time efficient. Three weekly diabetes psychoeducational sessions improved beliefs about diabetes, psychological well-being, diet, exercise, and family support (Keogh et al., 2011). The first two sessions occurred in the patient's home with their family member, and the last session was a phone call to the person with diabetes. Each session lasted 40 minutes. At six-month follow-up, the intervention group had lower mean A1C levels than the control group ($p = .04$), especially for those with the poorest control at baseline ($p = .01$).

Family psychoeducation can improve parental management of children with medical illnesses. Cognitive-behavioral techniques help parents manage their children's complaints more effectively. Two hundred children with functional abdominal pain, and their families, were entered into a randomized controlled trial of Social Learning and Cognitive Behavior Therapy (SLCBT) (Levy et al., 2010). Three weekly sessions consisting of relaxation training, modification of the family responses to illness and wellness behaviors, and cognitive restructuring were given. The educational support control group (ES) included comparable therapist contact time and homework assignments. Children who received SLCBT showed a reduction in pain and GI symptom severity (as reported by parents) compared to children who received ES ($p < 0.01$). Parents in SLCBT had less solicitous responses to their child's symptoms compared with parents in ES ($p < 0.0001$).

Family Systems Therapy

The most sophisticated family interventions are the family systems therapies. Family systems interventions require clinicians to have specific training. This training can be in any type of family systems therapy as these therapies share common factors (see p. 173). In a meta-analysis, family systems therapies were defined as "any couple, family, group, multifamily group, or individual focused therapeutic intervention that refers to either one of the following systems-oriented authors (Anderson, Boszormeny-Nagy, de Shazer, Haley, Minuchin, Satir, Selvini-Palazzoli, Stierlin, Watzlawick, White, Zuk) or specified the intervention by use of at least one of the following terms: systemic, structural, strategic, triadic, Milan, functional, solution-focused, narrative, resource/ strength oriented, McMaster model." Using this definition, 38 randomized controlled trials (RCTs) were identified for inclusion in the meta-analysis (Von Sydow, Beher, Schweitzer, and Retzlaff, 2010).

A variety of outcome measures were used in the meta-analysis. In terms of patient symptoms, family systems interventions resulted in improved outcome for patients with conversion symptoms (Ataoglu, 2003) and reduced psychological distress in chronic pain studies (Saarijarvi, 1991; Saarijarvi, Alanen, Rytokoski, and Hyppa 1992; Saarijarvi, Lahti, and Lahti, 1989; Saarijarvi, Rytokoski, and Alanen, 1991). Patients given family systems interventions after orthopedic surgery, had improved adaptation and a higher percentage had returned to work at two months (Cockburn, Thomas, and Cockburn, 1997). Combined with medical routine treatment (MRT), family systems therapy was more effective in reducing acute postoperative anxiety and depression in breast cancer patients, compared with MRT alone (Hu et al., 2007). Family members' burden, depression, and anxiety were also reduced in family systems interventions (Martire, Lustig, Schulz, Miller, and Helgeson, 2004).

Family systems therapies used in research protocols are highly manualized to ensure good adherence to the model. These therapy models are usually specifically tailored to match the patient population and disease studied and it may be difficult to use these protocols in the clinic setting. The following family systems therapies include evidence-based family system therapies that can be adapted for use in the clinic setting.

Goals of Family Systems Therapy

- Help families manage stresses as a team
- Mobilize patient's natural support system
- Enhance family closeness
- Increase mutually supportive interactions
- Build extra-familial support
- Minimize intra-familial hostility and criticism
- Reduce adverse effects of external stress and disease-related trauma.

(Adapted from Weihs, Fisher, and Baird, 2002)

Family Systems Therapies

FAMCON Therapy

FAMCON therapy: FAMCON stands for "family consultation" and is a family systems therapy that focuses on resolving problems using strategic pattern interruption and communal coping (Rohrbaugh, Kogan, and Shoham, 2012). After the assessment, interventions focus on changing sequences of interaction that maintain the target symptom. This family intervention, like most family interventions, emphasizes communal coping i.e. viewing problems as a family problem rather than an individual problem. The treatment team actively works to promote a sense of "we-ness."

FAMCON is ideally suited for couples who are having difficulty with smoking cessation. Couple transactions and behaviors that maintain smoking are targets of this family systems intervention. FAMCON has three treatment phases; the preparation phase, quit phase and the consolidation phase. In the preparation phase, the factors that contribute to problem maintenance i.e. that keep the person smoking, are identified and preparation for change is made. These factors include ironic processes and symptom-system fit (see Chapter 9, p. 170 for a fuller discussion of this assessment). Ironic processes are family interactions that have the opposite result from their intention. Symptom-system fit refers to the experience of closeness when couples smoke together. In the quit phase, two to three sessions focus on setting a quit date, and discuss how to cope with urges and withdrawal symptoms. Strategies to reduce ironic processes are promoted. A non-blaming disengaging stance is emphasized for family members who are not smokers. The therapist emphasizes positive interactions using phrases like "just observe" or "admit helplessness." The consolidation phase, which can last up to five sessions, begins as soon as a smoker has quit. During this phase, the new transactions and behaviors that support abstinence are supported.

The FAMCON intervention in 20 couples reached a 50% rate of stable abstinence at six months (Shoham, Rohrbaugh, Trost, and Muramoto, 2006). The FAMCON approach is particularly well suited to female smokers and smokers whose partner also smoked; two groups at high risk for relapse. The FAMCON approach has also been used for couples struggling to cope with chronic health difficulties (Rohrbaugh et al., 2012).

FAMCON Techniques for Smoking Cessation

Engage patient and spouse in order to

- Identify ironic processes that promote smoking
- Discuss ways that spouse can be supportive
- Discuss a new ritual to keep the couple close, instead of smoking together.

Brief Systemic Family Therapy for Children and Adolescents

Brief Systemic Family Therapy (BSFT) is an integration of structural (Minuchin and Fishman, 1981) and strategic (Haley, 1976) models and is an empirically validated family therapy for children and adolescents. BSFT is a short-term intervention model designed to treat substance abuse and associated behavior problems and to restructure problematic family interactions. BSFT has been able to engage and retain a significantly larger number of children and adolescents than other forms of treatment. It is associated with improvement in self-concept, parental involvement, conduct, and family functioning and with a reduction in substance abuse, emotional problems, and association with antisocial peers (www.promoteprevent.org/publications/ebi-factsheets/brief-strategic-family-therapy-bsft).

BSFT was originally developed at the University of Miami, with Hispanic/Latino families but has been expanded for use with African-American and white families. It was selected by the National Institute of Drug Abuse to be the adolescent treatment model to be tested as part of the National Clinical Trials Network at eight sites throughout the country. The model is also successful with foster families of varied ethnic backgrounds. This model is included here because it has proven effectiveness and follows the same principles as other family systems models. Its principles can be applied to children and adolescents with medical illness, and their families. BSFT consists of 12 to 16 sessions over a four-month period, and allows for up to eight booster sessions.

The Three Steps of BSFT

1. Joining: establishing a therapeutic alliance with each family member and with the family as a whole.
2. Diagnosis: identifying family strengths and weaknesses and problematic relationships that are associated with the presenting problem. The assessment occurs across five domains: family structure, conflict resolution, resonance, family developmental stage, and identified patienthood.
3. Restructuring: restructuring strategies include reframing family interactions, changing communication patterns, changing family alliances, and helping families develop effective behavior management skills.

Family systems therapies are effective for treating adolescents with anorexia nervosa. In one study, 121 participants were randomized to either family-based treatment (FBT) or adolescent-focused individual treatment (AFT) (Lock et al., 2010). FBT is a three-phase treatment. In the first phase, therapy focuses on "absolving the parents from the responsibility of causing the disorder" and compliments them on the positive aspects of their parenting. Families are encouraged to work out for themselves how best to help restore the weight of their child with anorexia nervosa. In the second phase, parents are helped to transition eating and weight control back to the adolescent in an age-appropriate manner. The third phase focuses on establishing a healthy adolescent relationship with the parents. Although both treatments were similarly effective in producing remission at the end of treatment, FBT was more effective in facilitating full remission at twelve months' follow-up.

FBT for Adolescents with Anorexia Nervosa

Phase One: develop a positive relationship with parents, support them and empower them to seek solutions that work for them.
Phase Two: support parents' transition control of eating back to their adolescent.
Phase Three: development of age-appropriate relationship between adolescent and her parents.

Brief Family Intervention for Managing Somatic Complaints

Brief Family Intervention (BFI) is a cost-efficient treatment for patients with somatic symptoms (Schade, and Torres, 2007). In the primary care setting, BFI significantly reduced health-care costs, when compared to the control group (effect size of 0.8) (Schade, Torres, and Beyebach, 2011). BFI includes a variety of therapeutic approaches, including problem-focused brief therapy (Watzlawick, Weakland, and Fisch, 1974), and solution-focused therapy (de Shazer, 1994, de Shazer et al., 1986). These results have been replicated in the primary care setting where professionals, who had no previous psychotherapeutic training, easily learned this treatment (Real, Rodrıguez-Arias, Cagigas, Aparicio, and Real, 2000).

BFI allows the patient to choose an informative, counseling, or a strategic approach to care. In each of the three options, homework tasks are given. In the informative approach, illness information is provided and available treatment options are discussed. In the counseling approach, the patients and their families receive advice and education about managing somatic complaints. The strategic approach is indirect, and aims at changing their usual way of dealing with problems. Several strategies were employed. "Seeking out exceptions" means discussing instances where the somatic complaint did not happen. This strategy was used in 35% of the BFI cases (de Shazer et al., 1986). "Pretreatment changes" were explored in 31% (Weiner-Davis, de Shazer, and Gingerich, 1987) and the "Miracle Question" was asked in 19% (de Shazer, 1988). "Attempted, ineffective solutions" were explored and reverted to effective solutions in 15% of cases. "Progress scaling questions" (de Shazer, 1994) were used in each session to monitor progress. Any difficulties that arose during treatment were discussed in a collaborative way.

In this study, the patients and their families were offered a choice of treatments and they overwhelmingly chose the strategic approach (80.4%). Only 13% chose the counseling approach and only 7% chose the delivery of medical information. The average number of sessions with the strategic and the counseling approach was three sessions. The patients who chose the informative approach received one session. In the control condition, participants received treatment as usual, which consisted of a varying mixture of interventions, from direct advice giving to Rogerian active listening and home visits.

BFI was designed by Schade and Torres (2007) to implement family counseling with somatoform patients. Brief systemic therapy (BST) is a variant of BFI that has been developed in Chile. In primary care in Chile, the framework of the biopsycho-social Family Health Model that the Chilean government has embraced as part of its recent health reform, has created a network of Family Health Centers. These centers are in charge of primary health care and promote personal and family well-being. BST integrates the main concepts of brief systemic therapy into a broader, cooperation-based approach adapted to the Chilean social and cultural environment. Patients with somatoform disorder (n = 256) from seven Chilean health centers benefited from BST in a randomized controlled trial. The sample was mostly women (95%) with a mean age of 45 years, and who were living with a partner (70%). Participants had an elementary education (44%), secondary education (46%), and one had a university education. The first session lasts one hour, and subsequent sessions lasted 30–45 minutes. BFI helps patients activate their own personal and interpersonal resources to improve their problem solving with the goal of helping them function autonomously again.

Medical Family Therapy (MedFT)

Susan McDaniel and colleagues (1992) use a biopsychosocial approach to families with health problems. Developed in the primary care setting, MedFT strives for collaboration between the medical profession and family systems therapists (McDaniel, Hepworth, and Doherty, 1992). "Both–And" thinking emphasizes mind–body interaction and promotes attending to each domain (the mind and the body) equally. The "Both–And" approach is promoted during intake assessments by asking about both psychological and biological symptoms, regardless of the presenting problem (McDaniel et al., 1992, p. 1068). This approach is successful with somatizing patients, where working with the family helps resolve somatic symptoms.

Watson and McDaniel's Treatment Strategies for Somatizing Patients

- Validate the reality of the problem
- Involve the family
- Work closely with the health-care team
- Enhance curiosity
- Actively attend to somatic symptoms
- Link the somatic and the psychological
- Use physical interventions
- Tolerate uncertainty and practice patience
- Terminate gently.

(Watson and McDaniel, 2000).

Problem-Centered Systems Therapy of the Family (PCSTF) for Families Managing Family Illnesses

PCSTF is the model used in most clinical examples throughout this book (Epstein and Bishop, 1981). The assessment occurs over one to two sessions and reviews family functioning in six dimensions: problem-solving, communication, roles, affective responsiveness, affective involvement, and behavior control. At the end of the assessment with the family's agreement on the information gathered, a problem list is generated. The problem list will include difficulties with managing the medical illness as well as other family difficulties that may have pre-dated or are a consequence of the presence of the illness. The family reviews the problem list and, if they wish, the family chooses to enter into a treatment contract. The family may also decide to work on the problem list themselves. A problem-solving approach teaches the family the steps of problem solving so they have skills to solve future problems.

Case Example: Managing Somatic Complaints: Progressing from Family Inclusion to Family Therapy

Nina is a 45-year-old married white female with fibromyalgia (FMA), who is referred to an outpatient psychosomatic medicine clinic for help with her chronic pain. She presents with her husband, Juan, for her first appointment. Juan is quiet through most of the evaluation, but nods affirmatively at specific points when he agrees. During her psychiatric evaluation, the psychiatrist asks her to rate her pain.

"On a scale of 1–10, it is about a 9!" she exclaims.

"What would be a level that you would consider your pain manageable?" asks Dr Thom.

"I would be happy with a 5."

"So the way it works," says Dr Thom, "is that depression and emotional stress contribute to the experience of pain. Psychiatric care can reduce your experience of pain quite a bit. I don't think it is unreasonable that with medication for depression and with psychotherapy, you could expect to have a pain level of about 5 in a few weeks."

Nina and Juan look pleased. Dr Thom prescribes citalopram 10mgs and asks Nina to set up a series of six appointments.

"Should my husband be coming to all of these appointments?"

"Let's agree on one more session with your husband and then we will see where things stand." Both agree.

The following session takes place two weeks later and Nina presents alone. She is tolerating the medication well. She wants to talk about infidelity that had occurred two years ago. She also wants to talk about her feelings of alienation from her mother and sister. Growing up, she states that her sister was the "good sister" and she was the "bad sister." She wants to be able to visit her mother and sister without experiencing conflict. Nina says that she feels that her body is reacting badly to the stress of negative events and that "letting the feelings out" will be helpful. She believes that her body is telling her that it is "time to try to resolve these issues rather than carry them around." The session includes learning relaxation techniques and reinforcing her motivation to talk about the issues that are concerning to her.

At the following appointment, Nina and Juan attend together. Her husband has some questions about how he should respond to his wife's complaints of pain and sadness. He asks about fibromyalgia and its relationship with depression. Psychoeducation is given, including support, stating that chronic pain can alter family interactions. Dr Thom asks if they want to come back for a couple's session to specifically address the relationship difficulties that Nina had brought up. The husband agrees. The fourth session is a couple assessment.

Couple Assessment

Orientation

This session begins with an orientation to the purpose of the session: to identify all family problems. The first two problems identified are managing chronic pain and Juan's Internet affair and its effects on the relationship. The affair had lasted a few months and Nina states that she trusted Juan that the affair is over. She states she understood why he had the affair (because they had drifted apart) and feels that their relationship needs to be stronger in order to prevent that from happening again. She states that the infidelity is now "causing me to raise a wall between us, to keep him from hurting me again." Juan talks about his repentance and his attempts to make things up to her. He states that he cannot think of what else to do but wants very much to repair the relationship and regain her trust.

Problem Solving

The couple is good at solving practical problems but poor at emotional problem solving. They have drifted apart since Juan's affair and still retain the same pattern of poor identification of emotional problems. Nina has not expressed her anger at her husband, has blamed herself for the affair, and has become sad. She has not communicated these feelings to her husband.

Communication

They can communicate well around practical problems but do not communicate about emotional problems. When they do communicate, it is clear and direct: meaning that they speak directly to each other and that the other person clearly understands what has been said.

Affective Responsiveness

Both are sad, withdrawn, and guilty about the affair. They have minimal time together and their relationship is not affectionate. There is no intimacy. They focus on their children's activities. They agree that they are "paralyzed" by the problem. Both have limited capacity to recognize what feelings they are having and are unable to express the feelings that they do recognize to each other.

Affective Involvement

They spend little time together as a couple. They spend a great deal of time with their children. Nina often withdraws and spends time in bed, because she is in pain. She also has stopped seeing her friends and reduced her work to part-time. Juan is unsure if he should be trying to spend time with her or if he should leave her alone. This pattern has been present over the past two years.

Roles

Juan has taken over many of the household chores, as well as working full time. They both still split the childcare responsibilities. Nina has reduced her work schedule. An older daughter from her previous marriage is having emotional difficulties and Nina spends time on the phone in the evenings providing support to her.

Behavior Control

After Nina learned of the affair, Juan stayed home each evening and tried to please his wife by cooking for her. There was much discussion about how she had found out about the affair and how she can no longer trust him. Juan states over and over again that he is sorry and wants the marriage to work. He also has begun to drink more heavily in the evenings when Nina and the children have gone to bed.

Both agree to this assessment and state they are motivated for change. The following problem list is generated.

Problem List for Nina and Juan

1. Nina's chronic pain and the limitations the pain places on her activity
2. Juan's affair and the meaning of it for the couple
3. Nina's lack of trust and her anger towards her husband
4. Juan's guilt about the affair and his "frustration" because he does not know how to help them get over the affair
5. The couple spend little time together
6. They had difficulty expressing feelings to each other
7. Juan's increased alcohol use.

The initial homework task is focused on the identification of feelings. Nina chooses to write down how she is feeling in a daily journal. Juan says he will reflect on his feelings in the evening instead of drinking.

At the follow-up session, each was able to talk about their feelings of frustration that the affair still takes up such a large part of their relationship. Dr Thom helps them discuss the barriers to resolving what had happened and explores what might help them "to get past it." Nina says she wants a quit date sometime in the future when they would stop thinking about it. Getting ready to quit would mean doing things to rid the house of that memory. Juan and Nina had been exposed to quit smoking tactics recently and liked the format and the rituals associated with quitting. They work together to discuss redecorating the living room and their bedroom, discussing moving furniture, and buying new curtains etc. The quit date would be marked by a special event. They plan a dinner together and a romantic evening when the children would stay at a relative's house.

They both discuss what they need to do emotionally to move on. Juan says he needs to recognize that he is vulnerable to flattery and not to get so easily distracted from his family. He says that he needs to feel that he matters to his wife and would welcome some caring comments. Nina says she will spend more time caring for him, including welcoming him home with a hug each evening. She says she needs to express how angry and hurt she has been and that he needs "to really listen and not get angry." He agrees. Dr Thom suggests one future session could be devoted to this. They set a session date when this would happen. Part of the agreement is that once Nina has expressed herself fully, there will be no mention of the affair again.

At that session, Nina reads a prepared statement to him. It includes several ways that he has hurt her from the beginning of the marriage and how she has turned away from him as a result. She feels resentful and has punished him by not being affectionate and making cutting remarks. She thinks that her anger contributes to her FMA. She tells him that she feels angry with him but has not expressed it and that from now on, she will tell him to his face, whenever she feels angry with him.

At the following session one month later, Nina and Juan report that they had a great romantic evening and that things are better all around. Nina's pain has dropped to a five, and she is more engaged in her work and social activities. Nina is able to tell her husband how she feels when he makes her angry, by writing it out and then asking him to sit and listen. For his part, Juan listens and they try to resolve whatever the issue is. If they cannot resolve it, they shelve it to bring to a therapy session.

Commentary

This example shows how family inclusion progressed to family psychoeducation then to family systems therapy. If at the point where the affair is disclosed, and the psychiatrist is unsure how to proceed, a referral can be made to a family therapist. However, if the psychiatrist is able to use a family systems approach, treatment can proceed quickly. This case is presented here to illustrate how to move from simple levels of family intervention to more skilled family systems intervention.

One of the most interesting aspects of this case is how the patient tied her emotional difficulties to her experience of pain. The patient's conceptualization of her bodily pain as being emotional pain helped speed the process along. Her belief that she could express her emotions and therefore rid her body of pain certainly helped the treatment process. It is acceptable to both the patient and her husband, to think about emotions as affecting her body in this way. She further commented that tension and stress affect her body by stiffening her muscles and giving her a headache. While FMA is not conceptualized by the medical profession as being caused by emotions, the role of emotions in making the perception of pain worse was acceptable to the patient and her husband. Having the husband present while this explanation was discussed, also helped to smooth the way for her recovery. Patients may not wish to consider emotional or psychological factors as "causes" for their illnesses but can readily accept that stress, anxiety, and depression make the experience of symptoms worse. The patient accepted that the pain could be reduced to manageable levels, and did not insist that it be eliminated.

Conclusion

Family interventions for medical illnesses aim to help family members agree on a program of disease management; help them manage stress by preventing the disease from dominating family life and sacrificing normal developmental and personal goals; help the family deal with the losses that chronic illness can create and mobilize the family's natural support system. Education and support in disease management reduces social isolation and resulting anxiety and depression.

In addition, family systems therapy helps the family adjust their roles and expectations, improves relational patterns, and helps resolve relational conflict. Helping families make the transitions through the stages of chronic illness is an important developmental step in managing chronic illness (see Chapter 3).

The three levels of family interventions presented here are associated with an increasing level of clinician skills. The case example shows how a psychiatrist can start with family inclusion, move through family psychoeducation and into family systems therapy. The next chapter describes a couple as they go through the assessment and treatment phase of family systems therapy.

References

Ataoglu, A., Ozcetin, A., Icmeli, C., and Ozbulut, O. (2003). Paradoxical therapy in conversion reaction. *Journal of Korean Medical Science*, 8(4), 581–4.

Bailey, J. (2007). Diet, exercise and marriage? Presented at the 2007 Uniformed Services Academy of Family Physicians Scientific Assembly, Portland, OR.

Bailey, J., Kerley, S., and Kibelstis, K. (2012) A Brief Marital Satisfaction Screening Tool for Use in Primary Care Medicine. *Family Medicine*, 44(2), 105–9.

Berman, E. M., Heru, A. M., Grunebaum H., Rolland. J., Wood, B., and Bruty, H. Group for the Advancement of Psychiatry Committee on the Family (2006). Family skills for general psychiatry residents: meeting ACGME core competency requirements. *Academic Psychiatry*, 30 (1), 69–78.

Cockburn, J. T., Thomas, F. N., and Cockburn, O. J. (1997). Solution-focused therapy and psychosocial adjustment to orthopedic rehabilitation in a work hardening program. *Journal of Occupational Rehabilitation*, 7, 97–106.

Gottman, J., Silver, N. (1999). *Seven Principles to Make Marriage Work*. New York: Three Rivers Press.

Graham, J. M., Liu, Y., and Jeziorski, J. (2006) The Dyadic Adjustment Scale: a reliability generalization meta-analysis. *Journal of Marriage and the Family*, 68 (3), 701–17.

Haley, J. D. (1976). *Problem-solving Therapy*. Jossey-Bass: San Francisco.

Heru, A. (2010). Improving marital quality in women with medical illness: integration of evidence-based programs into clinical practice. *Journal of Psychiatric Practice*, 16 (5), 297–305.

Hu, D., Wu, H., Dong, Y., Chen, D., Li, Y., and Hu, L. (2007). Study on the effect of family therapy on social support and mental status in peri-operative patients with breast cancer. *Journal of Nursing Administration*, 7 (9), 9–11.

Keitner, G. I., Heru, A. M., and Glick, I. D. (2009). *Clinical Manual of Couples and Family Therapy*. Arlington, VA: American Psychiatric Publishing.

Keogh, K. M., Smith, S. M., White, P., McGilloway, S., Kelly, A., Gibney, J., and O'Dowd, T. (20110) Psychological family intervention for poorly controlled type 2 diabetes. *American Journal of Managed Care*, 17(2), 105–13.

Levy, R. L. et al. (2010). Cognitive-Behavioral Therapy for Children With Functional Abdominal Pain and Their Parents Decreases Pain and Other Symptoms. *American Journal of Gastroenterology*, 105(4), 946–56.

Lock, J., Le Grange, D., Agras, S. W., Moye, A., Bryson, S.W., and Booil, J. (2010). Randomized clinical trial comparing family–based treatment with adolescent-focused individual therapy for adolescents with anorexia nervosa. *Archives of General Psychiatry*, 67(10), 1025–32.

Martire, L. M., Lustig, A. P., Schulz, R., Miller, G. E., and Helgeson, V. S. (2004). Is it beneficial to involve a family member? A meta-analysis of psychosocial interventions for chronic illness. *Health Psychology*, 23, 599–611.

McDaniel, S. H., Hepworth, J., and Doherty, W. J. (1992) *Medical Family Therapy: A Biopsychosocial Approach to Families*. New York: Basic Books.

McGoldrick, M., Gerson, R., and Petry, S. S. (2008). *Genograms:Assessment and Intervention* (3rd Edition). New York: W. W. Norton & Co.

Minuchin, S., and Fishman, H. C. (1981). *Family Therapy Techniques*. Cambridge, MA: Harvard University Press.

Real, M., Rodrıguez-Arias, J., Cagigas, J., Aparicio, M., and Real, M. (2000). Terapia Familiar Breve: Ahorro en el gasto sanitario de la patología somatomorfa [Brief Family Therapy: Cost reduction in the treatment of somatoform pathology]. *Cuadernos de terapia familiar*, 14, 167–73.

Rohrbaugh, M. J., Kogan, A. V., and Shoham, V. (2012). Family consultation for psychiatrically complicated health problems. *Journal of Clinical Psychology*, 68(5), 570–80.

Rolland J. (1994). *Families, illness, and disability: An integrative treatment model*. New York: Basic Books.

Saarijärvi, S. (1991). A controlled study of couple therapy in chronic back pain patients. Effects on marital satisfaction, psychological distress and health attitudes. *Journal of Psychosomatic Research*, 35, 265–72.

Saarijärvi, S., Alanen, E., Rytökoski, U., and Hyppä, T. (1992). Couple therapy improves mental well-being in chronic back pain patients. A controlled, five year follow-up study. *Journal of Psychosomatic Research*, 7, 651–6.

Saarijärvi, S., Lahti, T., and Lahti, I. (1989). Time-limited structural couple therapy with chronic low back pain patients. *Family Systems Medicine*, 7, 328–38.

Saarijärvi, S., Rytökoski, U., and Alanen, E. (1991). A controlled study of couple therapy in chronic back pain patients. No improvement of disability. *Journal of Psychosomatic Research*, 35, 671–7.

Schade, N., and Torres, P. (2007). *Manual de Consejerı á familiar en salud.* [Family Health Counseling Manual]. Concepcion, Chile: Cosmigenon.

Schade, N., Torres, P., and Beyebach, M. (2011). Cost-Efficiency of a Brief Family Intervention for Somatoform Patients in Primary Care. *Families, Systems, & Health*, 29 (3), 197–205.

de Shazer, S. (1988). *Clues: Investigating solutions in brief therapy.* New York, NY: Norton.

de Shazer, S. (1994). *Words were originally magic.* New York, NY: Norton.

de Shazer, S., Berg, I. K., Lipchik, E., Nunnally, E., Molnar, A., Gingerich, W., and Weiner-Davis, M. (1986). Brief therapy: Focused solution development. *Family Process*, 25, 207–21.

Sher, T. G., and Baucom, D. H. (1993). Marital communication: differences among maritally distressed, depressed, and non-distressed non-depressed couples. *Journal of Family Psychology*, 1, 148–53.

Shoham, V., Rohrbaugh, M. J., Trost, S. E., and Muramoto, M. (2006). A family consultation intervention for health-compromised smokers. *Journal of Substance Abuse Treatment*, 31, 395–402.

Spanier, G. B. (1976). Measuring dyadic adjustment: New scales for assessing the quality of marriage and similar dyads. *Journal of Marriage and the Family*, 38, 15–28.

Von Sydow, K., Beher, S., Schweitzer, J., and Retzlaff, R. (2010). The efficacy of systemic therapy with adult patients: a meta-content analysis of 38 randomized controlled trials. *Family Process*, 49 (4), 457–85

Watson, W. H., and McDaniel, S. H. (2000). Relational therapy in medical settings: working with somatizing patients and their families. *Journal of Clinical Psychology*, 56(8), 1065–82.

Watzlawick, P., Weakland, J. H., and Fisch, R. (1974). *Change, principles of problem formation and problem resolution.* New York: Norton.

Weihs, K., Fisher, L., and Baird, M. A. (2002). Families, health and behavior: A section of the commissioned report by the committee on Health & Behavior: Research, Practice & Policy Divison of Neurosciences & Behavioral Health and Division of Health Promotion & Disease prevention, Institute of medicine. *Families, Systems and Health*, 20 (1), 7–47.

Weiner-Davis, M., De Shazer, S., and Gingerich, W. (1987). Building on pretreatment change to construct the therapeutic solution: An exploratory study. *Journal of Marital and Family Therapy*, 13, 359–64.

11 Family Assessment and Treatment
The Case of Mr and Ms Dewey

- A family assessment occurs over one to two sessions.
- The assessment is a collaborative process with the family.
- The assessment is comprehensive and captures the family difficulties as well as the family strengths.
- The assessment results in a problem list which generates the treatment goals.
- Treatment occurs when the family negotiates how to manage each problem on the list.
- The therapist facilitates the negotiation and suggests homework that helps them reach their goals.
- Successful treatment often means that the family learns a better way of identifying and communicating about problems which, in turn, leads to better problem solving.

Introduction

Mark and Mary Dewey attend two sessions of family assessment, then decide to enter treatment and subsequently participate in five treatment sessions. The seven sessions each last one hour and take place over three months. The case report has had key details changed to maintain patient confidentiality. The sessions are documented at the end of each session, as treatment proceeds, giving the narrative "a real-time feel." In this way, decision-making is based on the information obtained at that time. Treatment begins easily but by the fifth treatment session, the main difficulties emerge strongly. The adjustment of each person to Mr Dewey's illness arises from time to time but does not really get addressed until the last session. This discussion coincides with his illness worsening. Not all problems get dealt with evenly, and the process is choppy. Therapy ends prematurely when the patient cites financial concerns.

Inpatient Consultation to Psychiatry

Mr Dewey is a 60-year-old married white male with serious lung disease, who is admitted to an inpatient medical floor. On the day of admission, he states that he is frustrated with his lack of progress. He had stopped wearing his oxygen mask the previous weekend, and said, "Screw it." His current worsening state is the result of this frustration. The clinic RN notes that he is "somewhat angry," and in her opinion, he is depressed about his situation and she recommends a psychiatric evaluation.

During his inpatient stay, he is treated aggressively, his dyspnea decreases, and he notes significant improvement in his exercise tolerance. His lung condition stabilizes and he feels positive again. During his stay, he is seen by the transplant service for a possible lung transplant. A psychiatric consult is called to assess and treat his depression.

During the initial interview, the psychiatric resident makes a diagnosis of depression secondary to a general medical condition. The patient is noted to say that he is "the strong one in the family," and keeps emotional issues away from his wife because she "couldn't handle it." The resident describes a man who is supportive and caring of his family whom he tries to protect from the consequences of his illness. The resident helps him with individual coping skills, so that he can talk more openly about his feelings about his illness. The resident helps him focus on future goals such as his children graduating from high school. The resident reports that the patient is improving with support and had identified additional ways to cope with the stress of his illness. The resident recommends signing off on the case as the patient is now symptomatically improved.

The attending, however, wants to evaluate the patient's comments about his wife. The attending asks the resident to set up a family assessment. In the family meeting, underlying relationship difficulties are identified. The patient and his wife have very different coping strategies that cause significant relational conflict, worsening the patient's ability to manage his symptoms. The husband's perceived role as the "strong one" is contrasted with his wife's view that he is unable to manage his emotions. The patient agrees to an outpatient family assessment, citing his desire to help his wife.

Session One: Family Assessment

At this first outpatient visit, Mr and Ms Dewey are asked to identify what concerns they have and what they hope to achieve by coming to the family meeting. Mr Dewey states he is having a hard time coping with being on oxygen and states that the medications make him more irritable. "Progress is too slow," he states. He and his wife agree that he has been more irritable and angry as the disease progresses, especially over the past six months. He does not endorse sad mood, concentration, or energy changes. He denies anxiety symptoms and denies any past psychiatric history. He used to drink heavily but does not drink any more. He does not use tobacco or other substances. He has no previous psychiatric history and no family psychiatric history. He was diagnosed with chronic lung disease in 2006 and has been "very compliant with his clinic appointments and his medical care," able to identify his medications and he is considered a good surgical candidate for lung transplant.

His developmental history is significant for a stepfather who, he states, was not interested in parenting. He has two sisters. He describes his mother as coping well with all situations and having a "positive attitude and outlook on life." She never complains and he admires her very much. He was on the football team in high school, and attended college, graduating with a business degree. He and his wife own a hardware store and work together. He complains that her bookkeeping skills are not acceptable as she makes basic mistakes. She states that this is only recent, since she became depressed. She begins to cry. She states that she is being treated for depression and is on ecitalopram 10mgs prescribed by her primary care physician.

He met his wife in college and they have been together since then. They have two sons, aged 16 and 17 years. They describe their marriage as "it has always been difficult." Their relationship has worsened since his illness began. She states that she feels "bad that he won't get to live to see his children grow up and won't get to meet his grandchildren."

He states that he is a practical person and that he "has come to terms" with his illness. He states he has talked with his doctors and is aware of what his life expectancy is without the transplant. He states, "Realistically, my wife is emotionally limited." When asked to elaborate, he describes that she is too emotional and can't handle stress. They do not talk about his illness. He also says that there is a lack of affection and that she does not seem to care. She agrees that she has "put a wall up" because she "can't deal with his illness." She states, "I do best if I just don't think about it." He states, "I think that she hates me." She is crying throughout this whole interchange.

Currently he likes to stay home because he can manage his symptoms better at home, rather than at work. They cannot enjoy their usual hobbies, as he is unable to be outdoors or go on trips. They identify no indoor hobbies or mutual home interests.

At the end of the first session, the following problems are identified:

1. They are both at different stages of adaptation to his illness and his shortened life expectancy.
2. Their relationship is overrun by anger and sadness.
3. There are work conflicts.
4. They lack common interests
5. They do not communicate about the illness.

They make a commitment to return to complete the couple's assessment. They agree to the following homework task: to write down what they would like from their relationship in the coming year.

Commentary

The patient's open and degrading comments about his wife are remarkable. He is not supportive of her difficulty adjusting to his illness and is openly disgusted by her tearfulness and emotionality, seeing her as "weak and defective." Setting the homework task therefore needs to be an individually based exercise, as it appears unlikely that they would be able to work together at this time. A reflective exercise might help set the stage for future difficult discussions about end of life issues. The homework task is to write down "what they both consider to be important for them in the next year, in terms of their relationship." This task also allows the therapist to see what possible areas of mutuality they might have, what they want from their relationship, what their commitment to the relationship is and what areas they most want to change. They are to do this individually, not to share their notes with the other person before the next session. At the next session, they will be asked to read their notes to each other.

Setting homework tests the couple's motivation to engage in the process of treatment and can set the stage for change. The homework must be easy to complete. For couples who find it difficult to communicate verbally with each other, a written script about their hopes can help them focus on the future. If they do not do their homework, then the conclusion is that there is little motivation for change.

Session Two

The couple has done their homework and each come with a written list. They look pleased and read the lists in turn. They have clearly been thoughtful about the homework.

Mark's wish list for their future relationship:

1.   Learn to love Mary again in a way that is apparent to her.
2.   Get affection and the love back in our lives.
3.   Learn to manage my stress so that I am not putting Mary and the kids on edge.
4.   Work with Mary better around the business so as not blame her so much for mistakes.
5.   Phrase things thoughtfully so I don't come across as condescending.
6.   Mary to learn to listen before responding.
7.   Mary to admit when she is wrong.

Mary's wish list for their future relationship:

1.   Get back the love and the hugs will follow.
2.   Happy household with no yelling.
3.   Conversations without fear I will set him off.
4.   Travel.
5.   Be a better listener.
6.   Entertain more.

It is remarkable that their lists are so similar. Mark is most surprised how similar they are but Mary says she is not surprised. The remainder of the session is spent completing the family assessment. The issues they identify in their lists are incorporated into the assessment. The following is the result of the first two sessions.

Family Assessment

Problem Solving. Practical problem solving is excellent. Both identify practical problems, communicate them well, and reach easy resolution. However, emotional problems are not identified and therefore not discussed. They each have different thresholds for identifying emotional difficulties. Mark has a high threshold and "lets many feelings just wash over me." He states that he tends not to react too much. Mary describes that she is the opposite and has a low threshold, identifying and expressing her feelings easily. There has always been poor communication about emotional issues. Mary would express hurtful feelings and Mark would "let it go in one ear and out the other." They both agreed that they had never been good at identifying or resolving emotional problems.

Communication. Both describe their difficulties in a similar way. Mark states that Mary does not take the time to listen to him and give a thoughtful answer. "She will just say something before I have even finished talking. How can that be thoughtful?"

Mark dismisses Mary's communications about feelings. He states he has always done this saying, "It's just Mary." He wants to be less condescending and sarcastic towards her. She wants to be more patient and listen more.

Roles. Mark has the final say about the business and Mary has the final say about things at home. Mary is more involved in the education and discipline of the children. There is little affection between them and they both want to have a more intimate relationship. Mary goes to her friends for support. Mark does not go to anyone, feeling like he can manage adequately on his own. They disagree about how much support they should give each other.

Affective Involvement. They both want to spend more quality time together at home in the evening. Currently, in the evening, they each go to separate areas in the house. They also want to think about traveling more and entertaining their friends at home, as they used to do. They talk about how Mark's illness makes these things difficult, but emphasize that it is not impossible. They say they can try to do some of these things on a smaller scale. They enjoy shopping and cooking on the weekends. Mary goes out with her friends a couple of times a month. Mark would like to see his friends more but feels his illness impedes this as he cannot go to the bar or out for a meal. He has not considered having his friends visit him at home.

Affective Responsiveness. Mark experiences and expresses anger more than other feelings. He experiences fear and happiness but rarely sadness. Sometimes Mark will talk to his friend Corey about feelings. Mark used to drink alcohol heavily and in secret (four rum and cokes) at night after the family went to bed. Mary thinks that his anger is covering up his sad feelings. Mary experiences and expresses a full range of feelings but over the past three years has had predominately sad feelings. She is currently on ecitalopram 10mgs but is not yet back to baseline. Mary agrees that in the past few years, since his diagnosis, she has "put a wall up between them." She says this is because of difficulty coming to terms with the need for a transplant.

Behavior Control. No current issues. Mark is no longer drinking alcohol. The children are obedient: know the rules and the couple have no concerns about them.

Homework. At the end of session two, the therapist asks the couple what homework they would like. The therapist reinforces the great job they had done with the previous homework. They do not know what homework to do and ask for suggestions. The therapist suggests a daily hug. They both readily agree. The therapist asks them to identify when it should occur. Mark says he would like to have a hug in the morning, before he goes to work.

Commentary. It is very positive that their wish list for their relationship is so similar. This was a good homework task because they can be successful merely by completing a list, regardless of what is on the list. The fact that their lists are similar brings them immediately together in terms of their understanding and view of the problem. On reflection, this homework also tests their ability to identify problems.

Choosing a homework task at the end of the first session when you have not yet completed a full family assessment is challenging. It is important to choose a task that can be completed successfully with little stress. Choosing a task that does not require change is helpful. Other homework examples that might be effective would be to ask them to write down or notice when a particular problem or behavior occurs.

So, in summary, this homework worked well for three reasons; it was a test of their motivation to work between the sessions; it assessed their ability to identify problems; and it helped them consider the other person's perspective. It is significant that neither of them brought up his illness or the future transplant.

After the second session, it is again important to make sure that any assigned homework will be successful. Both had identified a lack of affection on their wish list. Although Mary had said that "get back the love and the hugs will follow," behavior change often occurs first and then the feelings follow. A daily hug in a couple who want more affection and who readily agree to this can be successful. Mark asked for a kiss as well as a hug, but Mary hesitated and the task was kept to the hug. Limiting the task is preferable as there is more likelihood of success. While it is unlikely that this simple prescriptive task will result in change, the daily hug task can still help show each person how motivated for change the other person is, and help them each face the need for behavioral change on a daily basis.

It is clear from the assessment that their emotional difficulties pre-date his illness. They both agree that they had never been good at identifying, communicating, and solving emotional problems. Astute clinicians and family members can see that this might have origins in his childhood, with a stepfather who was not warm or affectionate. This may become a topic of discussion in later sessions as the couple struggle to understand their patterns of interaction. His illness has clearly exacerbated their difficulties identifying, communicating, and solving emotional problems. The emotional impact of his chronic illness has not yet been identified by either of them.

Each person has had to come to terms with what the illness means for each of them as individuals, before coming to terms with what the illness means for other family members and for the family as a unit. How Mark has come to terms with his illness is not yet clear. In response to the emotional impact of her husband's illness, Mary has developed a depressive illness and withdrawn from him. Mark has become angry, as she has withdrawn her affection. At this point, there has been no discussion between them about this pattern. This dysfunctional relational pattern is a cycle that gets repeated between them: Mark's anger leads to Mary withdrawing which leads to Mark's anger etc.

The following problem list was drawn up to present to them at the next session. The first paragraph is a summary of the main problem with its dysfunctional transaction described. The first paragraph ties their difficulties to the effect of Mark's illness on their relationship. It is a short statement intended to provide the couple with a brief way of understanding their difficulties. The problem list that follows describes their difficulties in more detail.

Problem List for Mark and Mary Dewey

Throughout their marriage, Mark and Mary have been very good practical problem solvers but poor emotional problem solvers. After Mark became ill, both members of the couple adapted to his illness in their own way. They did not adapt together as a couple. This has resulted in Mary getting depressed and withdrawing from Mark who then gets angry which leads Mary to withdraw more and a vicious cycle is set up.

1. Poor emotional problem solving is based on their different thresholds for experiencing and expressing emotion. Mark has felt that Mary's emotional concerns were not worthy of attention.
2. Communication is characterized as "dismissive" on her part and "inattentive" on his part. Their communication about emotional problems lacks meaning for them both. However, communication about practical aspects is clear and direct.
3. The experience of emotions is essentially different for both of them. Mary is more emotional. Mark tends to be more angry than sad. It is unclear if anger is a substitute for sadness.
4. They both want a more affectionate and intimate relationship.
5. They both acknowledge that the quality of their time together could be improved. Mark wants more time with his friends.
6. Each person has come to adapt and emotionally process Mark's illness and future transplant in their own way, resulting in an imbalance of adaptation.

This is the first draft of the contract. It is important that the contract is accurate because the treatment plan is dependent on the contract. At the next session, the couple will be asked to comment and make changes to ensure its accuracy.

Session Three

The couple is seen after six weeks absence, due to the therapist's vacation and canceled appointments. Mary is especially distraught. Regarding the homework task, they had done it for a few days but then they had a fight and did not do it anymore. Mary feels like they are "both broken" and asks about individual therapy for each of them.

She goes on to say that "Mark is controlling, and that the children agree." Mary says that she thinks that he is controlling of others because he cannot control his illness. He denies this and says that he feels that he is managing his illness well. He asks Mary for examples of his controlling behavior. Mary is unable to come up with an example that he feels is a satisfactory example. She eventually comes up with one, but it turns out to be a bad example. Mark says; "See this is what she does all the time! She complains then cannot back it up. What am I supposed to do with that?" Mary is crying. They want the therapist to take sides. The therapist, in response, says that many factors go into these types of arguments and asks them to look at the problem list and pick which area they think their current fight in the office falls under. Mary picks problem No. 3 and Mark picks problem No. 1. The therapist agrees and also adds problem No. 6, saying that they are having trouble because of the illness; that they both are managing the illness in different ways.

The therapist then asks them to review the problem list for accuracy. They agree with the problem list. The therapist introduces the idea of coping skills to manage his illness. "Do you have couple coping skills that you use together?" They seem puzzled by the idea. They are each asked what their individual coping styles are like. Mark states that he copes by "being strong" and "pushing through" any difficulties. Mary states that she copes by "expressing feelings." Mark thinks that his wife wants him to become "weak and passive" like her father. She says that her father is not weak and passive and that because Mark did not have a father growing up, to show how you can be a man and be kind, that this has stopped him from developing. She states that he thinks that showing feelings means being weak.

The session is drawing to a close. The therapist summarizes by explaining that many issues are involved in this interaction and that "we need to pull each strand apart and work on each one individually." In setting the homework, after the prior failed attempt, the therapist tries to balance it out, so that each person feels that they are getting something they want from the other person. The couple settles, with the therapist's guidance, on the following homework:

1.   Mary will bring in examples of his "controlling behavior" so that they can discuss the specifics, and how it affects Mary and the other family members.
2.   Mark agrees to tell her each morning how he is feeling. She will then ask, "What can I do for you?" and he will give her something to do that might make him feel better and cared for. He suggests bringing the newspaper, a drink, or something to eat.
3.   Mark requests that she say, " How are you doing?" when he comes home and not start with bad news.

Commentary

Their previous homework had not been successful for more than a few days. It was clear that their arguments would need to diminish and there be more of a reservoir of good feelings before any physical intimacy, even a basic gesture such as a hug, could occur.

Their spat in the office is typical of their interactions. The multiple layers become obvious as the quarrel continued. The therapist has little hope of disentangling the threads in the midst of a fight. It is important to stop the fight, and to help the couple reflect on the transactional process.

In setting the homework, Mary's concerns are validated: she will have time to bring examples of Mark's controlling behavior. Mark is very supportive of this as he feels frustrated by her accusations that fall apart when he tries to examine them. He expresses a desire to work on these issues. The other tasks are focused on building couple skills, in helping them manage the illness together. The first step is to have a simple daily transaction about the illness. Mary wants to be emotionally involved and Mark wants her to be more caring. At this stage in their conflict, a simple acknowledgement of how the illness is affecting him, can provide a starting point for Mary, by doing something practical. Homework tasks should, whenever possible, be measureable behaviors.

Session Four

The couple has completed their homework as agreed. Mark has let Mary know when he was not feeling well, he then asked her to do something for him and she did as he requested. Both are pleased with this result. He says he feels like she cares about him and she feels that he expressed his feelings more and let her be closer to him.

The therapist moves on to the next part of the homework. Mary brought an example of when Mark is "angry and controlling." They had spent ten to fifteen minutes writing a comprehensive shopping list. Mary left to go shopping but forgot the list. When she returned she had all the items on the list but Mark was still angry she had forgotten the list. Mark agrees this is a good example and they discuss it. Mark is angry with Mary because he sees her lapse as "stupid" and "disorganized" and he "is not like that" and it annoys him. He feels he is "super-organized and efficient" and is proud of these traits. Mary said, "he was never like this before he became ill, now he is angry a lot." Mark says he "gets very annoyed when she says this because it is not true." She continues, "it is true and the children agree."

The therapist asks them to look at the problem list and pick out what area this difficulty falls under. Mark picks problem No. 2. Mary picks problem No. 3. The therapist picks problem No. 6, adding that most fights involve so many layers that it can be difficult to disentangle. This seems an exact repeat of the previous spat in the office.

When they are asked to think about how to resolve this conflict, Mark suggests that they both stop saying negative things to each other. Mary agrees. Mary also will stop talking about how he "is angry because of the illness and stop bringing the kids into fights." Mark says that he will stop calling her stupid. They write this agreement down. They then discuss, with prompting, how they will interrupt each other when they transgress. Mark wants to use a stop signal, like a red flag. They laugh and enjoy this part of the discussion. Mark then reflects that his super-organized personality has a negative aspect to it. This allows the therapist to suggest that Mark spend some time on this negative aspect, thinking how he would like to change.

Mark now had a written homework task: to write about his anger; what it means, how he currently manages his anger, how he would like to manage his anger, how he sees other people that he aspires to be like, manage their anger. The goal is for him to explore his feelings. The writing is not for anyone other than himself. He agrees. The other homework task is to use the red flag to alert each other to their new way of interacting.

Commentary

This session went very well. They both participated in problem solving, making suggestions, and working together with pleasure. They still are avoiding dealing with the impact of Mark's illness and their likely foreshortened future together.

Session Five

They cancel the next appointment because Mark is admitted into the hospital. They request that the therapist meet with them on the inpatient medical floor. Mark is feeling well and about to be discharged, when the meeting takes place. They both report that the homework had gone well. Mark had made two small red flags. They placed one in the living room and one in the kitchen. They waved the flag each time the other transgressed, as agreed in the previous session. Mary did not like the flag being waved, so she monitors what she says to prevent this. Both are pleased with this intervention.

Mark has worked on anger and been thinking about the reasons for his anger. He has come up with several ways he wants to be able to handle his anger better. He talks about several businessmen he knows who he thinks handle their anger and disappointments well. He sees them as good role models. The therapist asks him how he could involve Mary in helping him manage his anger. Mark mentions how effective it had been when his physician had placed a hand on his shoulder and said to him, "I understand." Mary agrees that she will place her hand on his shoulder and say, "I understand, but calm down." Mark expresses skepticism that she will be able to help him with this, but she is adamant that she can do this. He then continues to describe how she is not an affectionate person and does not like to hug or touch others. She agrees that this is her nature but that she can change.

The therapist helps the couple look over the problem list to see what they want to talk about next. They choose "their adaption to the transplant process." This will be the priority for the next session. The therapist commends them on their good progress and they both agree that they are doing well. Mark states that raising awareness of issues is the first step towards change. He identifies ways that he has been working on the contract on his own, pointing out problem No. 1 and giving an example from this morning where he had given Mary's emotional response his full attention. He is pleased with how he had been effective in helping her calm down. She is pleased also and says, "It worked!"

Commentary

This couple is actively working on problem resolution. The therapist's interventions are to make sure they set goals that are easily within reach. It is unclear how much change they are making and whether or not they are making superficial efforts without any real substantial change occurring. The major issue concerning his illness has yet to be tackled. The therapist wonders if they are tackling easy things first and purposely avoiding this major and significant problem.

Session Six

Mary begins the session by stating that Mark did not want his family to know he had been hospitalized. Mary does not agree with this as it places "a heavy burden" on her. After discussing this briefly, the therapist asks about the homework.

Mary had attempted to intervene when Mark got heated, but Mark had not noticed. The couple then discusses how they would like the intervention to go. Mark describes himself as "a pit-bull" in the confrontation which had occurred with one of his sons. This discussion of how to manage his interactions with his son, takes up most of the session. The couple then begins to disagree about how they should parent their children but cannot reach an agreement, just firing missiles at each other. Mark does say that he wants to be able to look in the mirror first and not everything is Mary's fault.

Commentary

The couple avoid dealing with adaptation to illness, which had been on the agenda to discuss at that day's session. The difficulty with the homework task has taken up most of the session.

Session Seven

Mark has again been admitted to hospital but has allowed his wife to let people know and has in fact told his father-in-law himself. He agreed that the family could text him. He states, "I do not want sympathy." Mary exclaims, "But why not! Don't you think you are sick?" Mark responds, "Yes, but I don't like sympathy." The therapist easily moves on to discuss coping skills.

Mark states that he uses avoidance and he wants Mary to respect that style. Mary says she talks to her friends about how she is feeling. She adds that she does not like Mark's style and that he should talk to someone too. He again asks that she respect his style. Mary states angrily, "But it doesn't work! You get angry and explode on us! It's not fair!" Mark replied, "Well, you should understand that is how I cope!" Mary challenges him. "Why should I accept that? That just gives you a free rein to be angry and blow up at us. That is not right!"

This argument continues for some time. The therapist enquires if either of them wants to change their styles. The therapist emphasizes that it is their choice if they choose to cope as individuals or as a couple. The therapist gives them a handout on a variety of coping styles and asks them to read it and discuss this topic more at the next visit.

Commentary

This session was difficult but got to the crux of their problem. Mary is concerned about Mark's anger and that he is coping poorly but Mark wants her to respect that this is his choice. Mary cannot accept this, as she and the family are suffering from his angry outbursts. They left with a list of coping skills that they agreed to discuss. At the very least, they will be able to see a range of coping skills and understand that there are many ways to cope with stress of illness.

Conclusion

This patient called to say that they would have to stop coming because of a lack of further insurance coverage. Mr Dewey also stated that his wife had a new job so that they no longer worked together and that this separation during the day was helping to improve their relationship. Mr Dewey discussed how he was actively engaged with the transplant team and hopeful that he would be placed on the transplant list soon.

While this couple continue to struggle with Mr Dewey's illness and its implications, these seven couples sessions brought them to a clearer understanding of their difficulties. They chose to work together to resolve some issues such as their communication styles, emotional problem solving with a preliminary discussion of coping strategies. Mr Dewey's angry outbursts remain a difficult topic for them, as he sees this as his coping style and does not want to make changes in this area. Their individual ways of coping with his illness remain an area of disagreement and conflict between them.

Looking back over the sessions, it seems that one thing the therapist did repeatedly was to help them stand back from their fights, reflect on the process, and understand how several difficulties were contributing to the conflict. Helping them become aware of their patterns of interactions, was, as Mr Dewey said, the first step to change. One technique used in couples therapy is to "slow down the interaction," helping each person step back and observe. This helps each person understand the other person better. Experiencing their partner differently can make it easier for each person to take responsibility for their role in the conflict. As the couple learned to step back, they became more relaxed with each other, thus opening up the possibility to change.

If the therapist had continued to see them, the focus would have continued to be on adaptation to illness. Mr Dewey's anger and denial of grief, is his way of managing his symptoms. He asks his wife to respect this stance. The therapist could have worked more on helping them understand each other's point of view more fully. Ultimately, Mr Dewey would manage his emotions however he decided, regardless of the opinion of his wife. The therapist wondered if Mr Dewey chose to gracefully end the therapy before this next and most difficult phase was begun. This case can be used to generate discussion when teaching family therapy.

Questions that can be asked

- Why did the therapist start where she did?
- What mistakes were made?
- Would it have been better if the therapist had started with the main issue of adjustment to illness?
- Are the other problems somewhat irrelevant if the underlying issue of his adjustment to illness is not addressed?
- Should they have been given individual therapy when Ms Dewey asked?
- What is the role of understanding versus their ability to change?
- What ability or energy does Mr Dewey have to focus on psychological change when he is literally "fighting for his life"?

12   Multifamily Group (MFG) Interventions

- Multifamily support groups are usually open to all families, community-based, ongoing, and led by a volunteer.
- Multifamily psychoeducational groups are short-term, highly structured, often with didactics, manualized and replicable.
- Multifamily systems therapy groups are short-term, focus on relational aspects of coping with illness, develop a shared language to talk about illness and may use "group within a group" technique.
- All multifamily groups include education about illness and its effect on the family, frequently using a coping with stress paradigm, and focusing on developing resilience.

Introduction

Families want to know how best to manage chronic illness in the family. Families seek out educational material wherever they can find it, often on the Internet. Internet information can provide helpful information but cannot provide a good context for learning how to manage chronic illness. Managing chronic illness means understanding many of the factors discussed in previous chapters, such as life stage of the family, the family role of the person who is ill, the type of illness, and the stage of the illness. Multifamily groups (MFGs) are excellent ways to provide education and support with the assistance of a professional (or a knowledgeable volunteer in the case of community-based support groups). Families who attend MFGs can ask questions that pertain to their specific situation and receive help from other families who have first-hand knowledge of their difficulties. The group leader provides a context for questions and additional information and resources where needed.

The rationale for MFGs is that all families experience similar difficulties in managing chronic illness. MFGs allow families to share feelings and attitudes about managing illness and learn that their responses are common to all families and not the result of individual family deficiencies. Family members provide support to each other and encourage the use of effective coping strategies. Like other family interventions, MFGs can be of increasing sophistication, ranging from family support, through family psychoeducation to family systems interventions which are the most sophisticated type of family intervention. Each level of intervention is associated with specific expertise in the group facilitator, from minimal training for community-based family support groups, to basic group and family training for the psychoeducational groups, to family systems training which is required to facilitate family systems groups.

Historically, patients were excluded from family support groups because it was thought that open and honest discussion would not occur if patients were present. However, "family-only" groups can reinforce barriers between patients and family members by validating complaints about "bad patients." Most clinician-run MFGs include both patients and family members which allow the sharing of perspectives, reduction of blame and self-critical attitudes, and the promotion of family problem solving. As MFG research has progressed, it has been found that some situations do merit the exclusion of either patients or family members (see p. 219).

Traditionally, MFGs have been offered at the time of diagnosis and during the terminal phase of illness, with less emphasis on the daily stress of living with chronic illness. As people live longer with chronic illness, the family's need for help with the management of chronic illness has increased. Most MFGs focus on one specific illness and are usually accessed through specialty clinics.

Psychoeducational and family systems MFGs have become more and more short-term, often condensed into a single one-day workshop. Families like this format because it is easier to commit to a one-day workshop, especially on a weekend, rather than a series of weekly meetings. Families like the emphasis on education and coping because they carry less stigma than meeting with a mental health professional for family therapy.

Family Support Groups

Family support groups for families and patients are often community-based, open-ended, and function as a drop-in resource. These groups are usually free, with donations paying for room rental, coffee, snacks, and guest speakers. The volunteers who facilitate these groups are often family members who have a relative with that specific illness. Some community support groups may be advocacy groups with fund raising or legislative change as an additional goal. The National Family Caregivers Association (NFCA) and the National Alliance for Caregiving (NAC) provides guidance for family members who are looking for support groups (www.familycaregiving101.org). Informal support for patients and families is also available through local churches and community centers. Online groups, Facebook etc. can also be helpful.

Family support packets for patients and families can form the basis of a support group. These packets can be offered through clinics and in hospital waiting rooms. DVDs that include patient and family testimony are useful educational tools that can also serve as a stimulus for group discussion. Cultural barriers to care can be addressed with specifically designed support packets.

One such support packet or toolkit is designed specifically for the American Indian cancer survivors in the Southwest USA (Hodge, Itty, Cadogan, and Martinez, 2012). American Indian cancer survivors and their family members participated in 13 focus groups to identify cultural barriers to care and to make recommendations for self-management techniques. They developed a toolkit which consists of a guide, resource directory, video, and other supportive materials. Southwest American Indian imagery is used in the toolkit's design. A woven blanket is used for the book's border to symbolize the "Weaving Balance into Life" theme of the toolkit. Large print and colorful imagery with warm colors and pictures of families illustrate "balance and strength" which are the themes of the book.

The focus group participants identified poor communication as a major barrier for American Indian families. They commented; "We don't talk about it" and "We don't bring our burdens home." The focus group participants recommended using story-telling, a traditional way of communicating in American Indian communities, in the making of the video. American Indian cancer survivor testimonies illustrate the main themes of the book. Effective self-management techniques for common symptoms, such as pain, depression, and fatigue are emphasized. Family members are given tangible ways to provide support. The resource directory includes clinic locations, websites, and treatment facilities where cancer care services are offered, e.g. support groups, stores for wigs, rehabilitation materials. The toolkit was developed to bring "balance" back into survivors' lives and is an example of how patients and families can create the resources that they need in their community.

How effective are family support groups? A significant positive effect on caregivers' psychological well-being, depression, burden, and social outcomes is found for caregivers who attend dementia support groups (Chien et al., 2011). This meta-analysis of 30 studies, from 1998 and 2009, included groups of all types (family support, psych-oeducational, and educational groups), making it difficult to parse out the effective components of the intervention. However, it was found that psychological well-being and depression are most improved when the support groups are longer, more intense and use a theoretical model.

Family Psychoeducation Groups

Family psychoeducation was first used in the family treatment of schizophrenia (Hogarty et al., 1991). The premise of psychoeducational groups is that family members who understand illness symptoms and the disease process adjust better to the presence of illness. This, in turn, allows the patients to do better. Psychoeducational groups also address family conflict that arises from misunderstandings about illness and illness symptoms, and actively teaches the identification and management of difficult emotions.

Family members often feel guilty about negative feelings, such as blame or anger, that they have towards the person with the chronic illness. Families benefit from understanding that these feelings are common and can learn new ways of coping with these feelings. Information concerning the illness and illness symptoms help patients and families anticipate future disruptions caused by the illness. Another goal of family psychoeducation is to move the responsibility for managing the illness from the individual to the family.

The format and process of all family psychoeducational groups are similar, with the content being specific to that illness. One of the strengths of psychoeducational groups is that the format is highly structured, frequently manualized, and therefore replicable. The use of a curriculum is common. The list below describes a curriculum used in MFGs for managing adolescent obesity.

The Psychoeducational Curriculum for Adolescent Obesity

Session 1: Getting started, a typical day, and environmental contributions to obesity
Session 2: Substituting healthful alternatives, basics of healthful eating, lifestyle log
Session 3: Benefits and problem-solving barriers
Session 4: Goal setting and rewarding
Session 5: Communication skills and Fruit Group (fitting fruit into your diet)
Session 6: Social support, recruiting supports and Vegetable Group
Session 7: Energy balance
Session 8: Body image
Session 9: Media literacy, All Foods Can Fit discussion
Session 10: High-risk situations, relapse prevention
Session 11: Stress and time management, celebration and wrap-up.

(Adapted from Kitzman-Ulrich et al., 2009)

This study of obesity compared MFG-plus-psychoeducation, psychoeducation-only, and control wait list group (Kitzman-Ulrich et al., 2009). The study occurred over 16 weeks. Adolescents in the psychoeducation-only group demonstrated a greater decrease in energy intake compared to the MFG-plus-psychoeducation, or the control groups (p < 0.01). Positive changes in family nurturance were associated with lower levels of adolescent energy intake (p < 0.05). The MFG-plus-psychoeducation group consisted of an additional 45 minute MFG session where families discussed implementing the psychoeducational curriculum and shared their experiences. This single 45 minute session does not really qualify as a multifamily systems group intervention, although the study describes it as MFG. In this study, the psychoeducational intervention was the effective component.

A psychoeducational MFG was compared to a patient-only group program with the goal of improving functioning in patients with arthritis (van Lankveld, van Helmond, Naring, de Rooij, and van den Hoogen, 2004). The patient-only group treatment was called "Working on Arthritis." It combined education about arthritis, with cognitive-behavioral techniques that focused on restructuring disease-related cognitions and teaching effective coping styles. Patients met for eight sessions of one and a half hours, with four educational sessions and four sessions focusing on cognitive-behavioral change. In the MFG comparison, 56 couples were enrolled and there was additional focus on the effect of the illness on their relationship. In both conditions, similar positive changes in disease activity, cognitions, coping, and physical and psychological functioning were found. There was no additional benefit for the patients who attended the MFGs. At baseline, these couples had good marriages, with high levels of marital satisfaction and low levels of criticism. It may be that if couples with poor marital functioning had been selected, then MFG treatment would have been of benefit.

Similar findings were found in a comparison of a patients-only psychoeducational group, a psychoeducational group with partners and the provision of educational materials. In this study of 218 patients, rheumatoid arthritis patients who attended **with** partners developed more fatigue and a decrease in self-efficacy (Riemsma, Taal, and Rasker, 2003). Passive involvement of partners without teaching them how to manage specific situations or without addressing specific relational difficulties worsened patient outcome. Referring caregivers to psychoeducational groups may be deleterious for some patients, so it is important to assess family and caregiver needs before recommending treatment.

There is a place for "family-only" psychoeducational groups. Mothers of children newly diagnosed with cancer were taught problem-solving skills to decrease their symptoms of depression and anxiety (Sahler et al., 2005). This study consisted of an eight-session intervention. Evaluated in two randomized clinical trials, these mothers reported significant improvements in problem-solving skills and improved mood up to three months after the intervention. Improvements in problem-solving skills accounted for 40% of the variance in changes in mood. Mothers who were single and younger benefitted most. This program has been successfully adapted to Spanish-only speaking mothers.

A family-only six-session psychoeducational MFG was provided to spouses of patients with breast cancer patients (n = 34) and compared to treatment as usual (TAU) (Bultz, Speca, Brasher, Geggie, and P., 2000). The first two sessions of the group provided partners with information on medical and psychosocial aspects of the illness, using videotapes featuring men talking about the impact of their wives' breast cancer. At the second session, an oncologist provided information and responded to questions. The following four sessions helped partners explore their feelings and confront their fears and anxieties, with the intent of strengthening their relationships. Three months after the intervention, partners had less mood disturbance than did controls (p = .07) and patients reported less mood disturbance (p = 0.10), and greater confidant support (p = 0.06). For those receiving TAU, patients' marital satisfaction and perceived support had deteriorated. This suggests that a psychoeducational MFG intervention for spouses has a protective effect. This may be especially so when illnesses have a significant impact on relationships.

In summary, psychoeducational MFGs are helpful for some people but not so helpful for others. These studies show the need for screening of families in order to tailor the interventions to their needs. Couples and families that are functioning well need information, inclusion in decision-making, and to be treated as team members. Couples and families who have conflict or dysfunction will likely benefit more from a focused intervention, either a psychoeducational intervention that addresses emotional difficulties and family conflict, or a multifamily systems group (MFSG) intervention.

Multifamily Systems Groups

MFSGs explore illness beliefs and emotions in more depth than psychoeducational MFGs. The looser structure of MFSG sessions allows for a deeper exchange and sharing between families, although the goals are still clear and well defined. MFSGs use specific family systems techniques to clarify family processes and to help families make changes in relational patterns.

The early work on MFSGs included patients and families with all types of chronic illness. One of the early articles was called "Putting the Illness in Its Place: Discussion Groups for Families with Chronic Medical Illnesses" (Gonzalez, Steinglass, and Reiss, 1989). Steinglass (1998) developed the Multiple-Family Discussion Group (MFDG), an eight-week structured workshop, with four to six families. It assessed family rituals, daily routines, and family problem-solving strategies, using metaphors to understand the role of the illness in the family. The first three educational sessions focused on the family stresses generic to chronic illnesses. The second three sessions focused on coping strategies. The last two sessions focused on emotional style and expressiveness. The MFDG was conceptualized as a preventative intervention to help the patient and family learn to live well with chronic illness.

The leaders of MFSGs are trained family therapists. They promote a positive non-judgmental stance for all members, they maintain the group structure, and they synthesize the perspectives of the different subgroups of family members. The leaders' philosophy is that "every family is doing its best" to manage the demands of the illness. Direct criticisms or attacks on individual family members are interrupted and redirected. Families are asked to examine their current coping styles and emotional style. Family change occurs as the group process unfolds. MFSGs have several stages.

Stage one: the therapist identifies the illness roles (patients, primary caregivers), family roles (spouses, children), and developmental roles (teenager, career-oriented adults) in the families. Specific subgroups are identified for the "group with a group" or fishbowl technique.

The fishbowl technique is a therapeutic intervention that is effective in increasing empathy for others in the family. Using this technique, one subset of the family e.g. the patients, sit and discuss their experience of the illness within an inner circle, while the other family members sit and listen in an outer circle. A therapist facilitates the patient discussion within the inner circle. The patients discuss their experiences together and the therapist facilitates a synthesis of the "patient perspective" on the impact of illness on family life. The other family members e.g. family caregivers, who are listening to this perspective, then give their feedback. Next, the family members take their turn in the inner circle to discuss the impact of the illness from the "family perspective." The patients become the listening observer group. After the patients give their feedback, a general discussion occurs. This technique is a powerful way for subsets of families to develop a collective voice. The therapist normalizes the impact of chronic illness on the family and shows the universal themes that all families experience.

Family metaphors are used to help the family develop a new language to describe their experiences. Useful family metaphors are identified and built on throughout the sessions. Family identity, family rituals, family routines, and problem solving are examples of family metaphors. Family identity is unique to a particular family and frequently gets eroded by the presence of chronic illness. Each family has its own identity separate from the illness. The illness can derail family rituals, family routines, and problem solving, previously valued activities and priorities get neglected or abandoned. Chronic illness disrupts families and is characterized as a "two-year-old terrorist with excessive and unpredictable demands." The therapist moves the responsibility for managing the illness from the individual to the family. The family becomes motivated to work toward the common goal of improved functioning for all family members.

Stage two: this stage focuses on the development of effective coping strategies. Each individual family assesses their coping skills. The "group within the group" or fishbowl technique separates out one family as the subgroup. The other families sit in the outer circle and listen. Each family takes its turn. The individual family presents a selected topic and discusses the topic with one of the co-leaders. The observer families give their feedback, followed by a general discussion. Useful metaphors at this stage include "keeping the illness in its place" and "preserving family identity." The therapist discusses the allocation of family resources between illness needs and the needs of normal family development.

Stage three: the last two sessions focus on the impact of chronic illness on the emotional life of the family. Typically, with chronic illness, the experience of emotions is intensified but the expression of emotions is reduced. All family members experience negative emotions. Patients are expected to complain about their illness and their symptoms and the other family members are expected to give sympathy. Family members usually do not complain, as this would be seen as adding to the burden of the patient. The expression of positive feelings, such as caring, warmth, and concern are reduced. This general constriction of feelings may be the result of fear of inadvertently expressing negative feelings but also may reflect a fear of the loss of a loved one.

The emotional styles of individual family members and of the whole family are reviewed. Using the "group within a group" format, subgroups are composed of individuals from different families who have similar emotional styles. A useful metaphor is "family emotional style," emphasizing the family as an "emotional unit." The role of other family members is described as being the "emotional thermostat" that maintains the overall family emotional climate. A family's emotional style is discussed as a feature of each family's unique identity. The role of illness in enhancing or disrupting the family's emotional style is discussed.

Basic Principles for MFSGs

- Therapist maintains a positive non-judgmental stance
- No criticalness or blaming attitudes allowed
- Use of "group within a group" technique
- Education about normal responses of families dealing with chronic illness
- Assessment of coping styles and skills
- Attention to emotional responses of individual family members and the family unit.

Metaphors

- Family identity
- Keeping the illness in its place
- Allocation of family resources
- Preserving family identity
- Family emotional style.

Group within a Group

- One therapist within each group keeps boundaries clear and summarizes themes
- Subgroup perspective has a specific role in developing the overall goals
- Inner circle of chairs for subgroup
- Observer feedback group in outside circle responds when inner subgroup has finished.

- Whole group has general discussion with everyone participating
- Therapist(s) summarizes the important themes.

The MFSG model can be adapted for particular cultural groups. One successful adaptation occurred in a low-income Harlem community. After assessing the community with questionnaires and focus groups, Lavelle (2007) identified three key components of the MFSG format that needed to be changed. The first change is that the definition of family needs to be expanded to include all the people involved with the patient. This is described as a "kinship network." The kinship networks include neighbors, friends, and even family members who live elsewhere. Secondly, the format of the MFSG needs to acknowledge the presence of multiple chronic illnesses in the family and a fluid changing of caregiver and patient role. Thirdly, the notion of family identity needs to be expressed in a culturally appropriate way. In the Harlem setting, identity was found to be best expressed as a family song title. This accommodated the many different ethnic groups that were present. Each ethnic group could identify a particular song that resonated for them and that gave them a strong sense of family identity.

MFSGs are all structured in similar ways with the content tailored to specific areas of concern associated with specific illnesses, the life stage of the family etc. For example, family conflict over autonomy is common in adolescence and therefore MFSG that focus on the management of diabetes and eating disorders in adolescence have similarities in content. Childhood cancer has significant repercussions for parents and the associated MFSGs focus on parenting concerns. Breast cancer has specific psychological repercussions for spouses and the content includes a focus on intimacy. The following examples show how the MFSG structure is similar but the content differs by population.

Behavioral Family Systems Therapy For Diabetes (BFST-D)

Behavioral Family Systems Therapy for Diabetes focuses on better diabetic control in families with adolescents who have poorly controlled Type 1 diabetes. BFST-D targets diabetes-specific behavioral problems and helps families develop better behavioral techniques. BFST-D provides parental simulation of living with diabetes which improves empathy for patients living with diabetes. BFST-D consists of ten sessions that focus on problem solving, communication, cognitive restructuring, and redefining parental coalitions. The structure is as follows:

- Problem-solving training teaches families about the steps of problem identification, communication etc. and how to use a behavioral contracting approach to problem resolution.
- Communication skills training include giving instructions, providing feedback, the use of role modeling, and rehearsal for common parent–adolescent communication problems.
- Cognitive restructuring identifies and focuses on changing any family members' irrational beliefs, attitudes, and attributions.
- Redefining parental coalitions. Weak parental coalitions or cross-generational coalitions are identified and addressed as part of the therapy process.

BFST-D resulted in better AIC results compared to an Educational Support group (a ten-week multifamily comparison group) or standard care. A significantly higher percentage of BFST-D youth achieved improvement in treatment adherence which correlated significantly with improvements in A1C at each follow-up (Wysocki et al., 2007).

MFSG for Eating Disorders

A 20-session MFSG treatment for eating disorders was tested against three other conditions: inpatient treatment, outpatient (with individual/family psychotherapy for twelve sessions), and no treatment (Crisp et al., 1991). The MFSG treatment consisted of ten sessions with the patients and the families together and ten sessions with the families alone. The structure was as follows:

• Problem-solving. Parental discord and conflict that occurred about how to manage the eating disorder is addressed as a group problem-solving exercise.
• Communication and relationship skills.
• Cognitive strategies including identification of moods and their attachments and origins, sense of self, the meaning of weight and shape, management of impulses.
• Dietary counseling and advice was offered on four occasions to both the MFSG treatment and to the individual/family psychotherapy treatment.

All of the three treatment regimes were highly effective at one year in terms of weight gain, return of menstruation, and aspects of social and sexual adjustment. A Spanish study that replicated this study, found that systemic family therapy worked as well as the combination of peer group and parent support groups (Espina Eizaguirre, Ortego Saenz de Cabezon, and Ochoa de Alda Martinez-de-Appellaniz, 2000).

MFSG and Multiple Sclerosis

"Resilient Partners" is a four-week discussion group aimed at helping couples focus on their strengths when coping with multiple sclerosis (Rolland and McPheters, 2008). The MFSG is based on the Family Systems Illness Model (Rolland, 1994) (see Chapter 3). Couples are helped to develop resilience and relationship stability. Themes emerging from group discussions include uncertainty and the need to balance being realistic and pessimistic, and understanding taboo topics. Taboo topics were: Does addressing topics like caregiver burden, loss, and fears for the future make things worse? How does role change affect the relationship and one's sense of one's self? How do you balance caregiver and romantic partner role? The format is described in the list below and illustrates how the structure of MFSG is adapted for specific illnesses.

Resilient Partners MFSG

Session 1. Introductions and group format: participants share topics they hope to cover in the group. Purpose of group: (1) Family prevention-oriented psychoeducation and discussion, (2) Relational orientation, (3) Reduce isolation/network couples, (4) Explore meaning of MS to family and psychosocial challenges over time, (5) Normative, resilience-oriented mindset, (6) Keeping MS "in its place." Family as primary unit/system. Psychosocial demands of MS over time. Symptoms of MS and treatments. Thinking developmentally; individual and family development in relation to MS.

Session 2. Communication and problem solving: (1) Couple relationship (role flexibility and gender norms, protection and growth of relationship, co-parenting, balancing work and family), (2) Parent/child relationships, (3) Relationship between the MS patient, family and the health-care providers.

Session 3. Living with uncertainty and future caregiving: family planning, raising children, other family/personal/work life-cycle goals. Minimizing couple relationship skew: putting MS in its place, we are partners, not just patient and caregiver.

Session 4. Belief Systems: making meaning of adversity, spirituality, positive outlook (what to look forward to). Professional and Community Resources. Ongoing monthly group and feedback.

Dialysis and MFSG

MFSGs allow exploration of the effect of dialysis on the patient and their quality of life. This MFSG was tested with four families in 90-minute sessions, delivered over six weeks (Díaz Rodríguez et al., 2004). High levels of satisfaction were reported, with improvement in the quality of life and the adjustment of the participants to the illness. The patients developed more support from their families, changed their view of the illness, and learned new ways to resolve the difficulties. This example of MFSG is presented here because dialysis is a relatively neglected area for psychosocial interventions. The list below outlines the session content.

Summary of Dialysis MFSG

Sessions 1 and 2. Chronic illness impact component. These sessions identify the problems and family perspectives related to dialysis and facilitate connections between participants.

Sessions 3, 4 and 5. Family development component. These sessions focus on feelings and sharing experiences and problems. The useful categories and metaphors are "putting the illness in its place," describing and clarifying each family's vision about the impact of dialysis on the family. These sessions use visual aids to construct the shape of the families before and after dialysis. The goal is to reconstruct each family story, paying attention to family values that have been affected by dialysis. Future strategies for managing illness symptoms are visually explored.

Session 6. Family illness integration component. The group participants bring "physical reminders" that represent dialysis. These are used to describe the impact of dialysis in the family interaction patterns and the method of coping used by the family. At the end, a symbolic ritual helps the family "find the illness place" and facilitate a way of coping for the family.

Heart Failure and the Family Partnership Intervention

Patients with heart failure have special lifestyle management needs. The Family Partnership Intervention (FPI) can promote healthy autonomy in these patients (Clark and Dunbar, 2003). This brief intervention consists of an introductory educational session focusing on the importance of self-care. The two follow-up meetings have separate patient and caregiver components. The caregiver group focuses on helping the caregiver show empathy and understanding to the patient and encourage healthy choices in diet and exercise. Case scenarios, exercises and role-playing help the caregiver develop techniques to support the patient without demanding the patient change their behavior or attitude. For example, one caregiver joined a weight-loss group and invited the patient to go with them, saying that, "It is up to you if you want to come." Thus, the caregiver reduced her controlling behavior and demonstrated that she could success-fully use "the autonomy-supportive" approach.

Childhood Cancer and the Surviving Cancer Competently Intervention Program (SCCIP)

A traumatic stress framework helps family members understand their reactions to pediatric illness and reduces their symptoms of distress (Pai and Kazak, 2006). A traumatic stress framework intervention called the Surviving Cancer Competently Intervention Program (SCCIP) helps parents and caregivers of children who are newly diagnosed with cancer. The three-session SCCIP program helps parents identify their beliefs about their child's cancer, evaluate the consequences of those beliefs, and restructure dysfunctional beliefs. The intervention was done with one family, and the presence of other family members was simulated through media. A DVD showed four parents of children with cancer discussing common thoughts, feelings, and beliefs about their child's cancer.

Adolescent Cancer Survivors and the Adversity–Beliefs–Consequences (ABC) Model

The adversity–beliefs–consequences (ABC) model was tested with 150 adolescent cancer survivors and their parents, in a one-day intervention. This model integrates cognitive-behavioral and family therapies. Adversity refers to the common experience of having cancer or a family member with cancer. Beliefs are identified as thoughts about these adversities. Consequences are defined as emotions and behaviors in response to the adversity. Reframing involves the participants restructuring thoughts and beliefs about cancer such as accepting the uncontrollable and focusing on the controllable. The inter-vention group reported fewer arousal symptoms and fathers reported significantly greater reductions in intrusive thoughts, compared to the control group (Kazak et al., 2004).

Adult Head and Neck Cancer and MFSG

Adult head and neck cancers are very suitable for MFSG because family conflicts are common in this population. Family conflicts are common because smoking and alcohol, which are voluntary activities, are significant causal factors in the development of head and neck cancers. The MFSG intervention was given as a one-day intervention. Patients and families were educated about the ways typical family life is affected by the diagnosis and treatment. The discussion included coping styles of the families in the posttreatment adjustment phase of cancer recovery and ways of balancing the illness with other priorities in their lives (Steinglass, Ostroff, and Steinglass, 2011). The families (n = 15) who participated in the intervention rated the MFSG experience positively, endorsing the content of the workshop, and the value of holding it as a one-day, weekend workshop, rather than consecutive, weekly sessions. They liked the small size of the groups and sharing with others who were coping with similar situations. They noted that the group format reduced their isolation, and helped them see how others were coping and normalized many of their reactions.

This intervention followed the typical MFSG format using the "group within a group" exercise. Family members in this cancer group developed a new appreciation of the impact on patients of posttreatment sequelae like chronic low-level pain and disruption of salivation and swallowing. Patients, on their part, began to appreciate the confusion experienced by caregivers when patients kept symptoms and worries to themselves. During subgroup discussions, assumptions about cancer reoccurrence that had remained silent, were expressed.

A family collage representing the cancer experience was constructed. The family collage component is a variation of the family identity exercise. Families draw on their core beliefs and values, then generate ideas about change. The family has to step back to organize its thoughts and look at the problems it has experienced in adapting to cancer, its treatment, and its aftermath. The collages, when viewed as a collection, help all families think about future directions for their family. Creating the collage is a fun activity that contrasts with the serious group discussions that surround cancer. The family collage component concludes with a group discussion about the themes and ideas that have emerged about future directions for managing and balancing cancer issues in family life. The therapists emphasize that each family will determine the right balance for themselves, based on their own identity, values, and priorities.

Breast Cancer and MFSG for Couples

An MFSG intervention of two different lengths was piloted for families and patients with breast cancer. The first group (n = 12) consisted of two sessions, each of four hours duration, for a total of eight hours. The second group (n = 21) consisted of a single four-hour session. A third group served as the control group (n = 15). Both the eight-hour and the four-hour MFSG focused on comparing and contrasting patients' and spouses' experiences with cancer. The "group within a group" technique was used. Both groups used communication exercises to strengthen the couples' communication about emotion. To help couples find meaning and perspective on the cancer, couples make a timeline of their life together. The two-session eight-hour format showed the most promise for producing positive change in mental health functioning and cancer-related stress (Shields and Rousseau, 2004). The content of these sessions are described below.

Summary of Breast Cancer and MFSG for Couples

Session 1. Illness Story-Telling

A five-minute introduction draws a distinction between cognitions and emotions. The patients and spouses are divided into groups for the "group within a group" exercise. This exercise allows the memories, thoughts, and feelings that patients and partners have been avoiding to be openly discussed.

Patients talk about their fears and frustrations and the support they receive from their spouses. The patient subgroup actively processes traumatic memories of the cancer experience and the observer group gains new insights on their loved one's experience.

Spouses talk about their own fears at the time of diagnosis, their desire to help, and the helplessness they experience when they do not know how to support or comfort their loved one. When patients and partners hear the stories of others in similar situations, their experience seems less aversive, and they begin to work through the experience. Patients and spouses are separated and make lists of bridges and barriers to communication. This task provides data to use when teaching about communicating emotions and responding to emotional disclosure.

Session 2. Couple Communication

The section opens with a short talk about the role of communication in coping with stressful events and gives examples of how to respond supportively to emotional disclosures. In the two-session format, the bridges and barriers identified by patients and spouses are discussed. Each participant identifies emotions and cognitions that they experienced during treatment. They then sit together as couples to discuss. A short talk on cognitive restructuring and finding meaning in difficult experiences is followed by the making of a timeline of their life together. They plot significant events in their life together and plan the trajectory of their life post-cancer. Couples share and discuss these timelines with the larger group.

A second study of MFSG was tested with women with early stage breast cancer and their spouses (n = 238) (Manne et al., 2005). Women who rated their partners as more unsupportive and women with more physical impairment benefited most from the MFSG intervention. Only 33% of eligible women accepted the offer of treatment. The most common reason for refusal being that it would take "too much time." Study participants were younger and sicker than those that refused. Those who refused reported being fully active and able to carry on all pre-disease performance without restriction. There were no differences between participants and refusers in terms of ethnicity or cancer stage. One conclusion that can be derived from this study is the need to adequately screen for level of family dysfunction or distress before offering resources to patients who may not need or want them.

Conclusion

As the number of people with chronic illness increases and the practice of medicine shifts to the management of chronic illness, MFGs become more accepted in the health-care system. MFGs are cost-effective interventions and once the protocols have been developed, MFGs are easy to implement. Psychoeducational groups are the easiest to implement as they usually have a well-developed, manualized format that can be taught to new facilitators. MFSGs require more extensive training, but these groups also run according to a specific format that is easily taught and implemented.

From the above review of MFG studies, it is clear that families and couples should be screened for family conflict before they are enrolled. It is also clear that families need to be taught specific skills rather than just be passive participants in educational groups. Psychoeducational groups must tailor their teaching to illness-specific needs of the family caregivers.

Trials of MFSGs continue to occur with other populations of patients e.g. families with relatives with traumatic brain injury (Charles, Butera-Prinzi, and Perlesz, 2007). Adaptations of the MFG content are needed for specific illnesses, specific cultural and ethnic groups, and for different family stage, life stage and perhaps for specific subgroups of patients. One very important study examined the experience of adolescents who had a parent with breast cancer (Davey, Gulish, Askew, Godette, and Childs, 2005). The adolescents had additional roles and responsibilities in the family and suggested that intervention programs target coping skills that are sensitive to girls and boys of different ethnic and racial backgrounds. They also wanted MFGs to focus on a shared family understanding and open communication between parents and adolescents. Refinements of MFGs will continue and we can look forward to MFGs becoming a greater part of the health-care system in the future.

References

Bultz, B. D., Speca, M., Brasher, P. M., Geggies, P. H., and P., S. A. (2000). A randomized controlled trial of a brief psychoeducational support group for partners of early stage breast cancer patients. *Psycho-Oncology*, 9, 303–13.

Charles, N., Butera-Prinzi, F., and Perlesz, A. (2007). Families living with acquired brain injury: A multiple family group experience. *NeuroRehabilitation*, 22, 61–76.

Chien, L. Y., Chu, H., Guo, J. L., Liao, Y. M., Chang, L. I., Chen, C. H., and Chou, K. R. (2011) Caregiver support groups in patients with dementia: a meta-analysis. International *Journal of Geriatric Psychiatry*, 26(10), 1089–98.

Clark, P. C., and Dunbar, S. B. (2003). Family partnership intervention. A guide for a family approach to care of patients with heart failure. *American Association of Critical Care Nurses Clinical Issues*, 14(4), 467–76.

Crisp, A. H. et al. (1991). A controlled study of the effect of therapies aimed at adolescent and family psychopathology in anorexia nervosa. *British Journal of Psychiatry*, 159, 325–33.

Davey, M., Gulish, L., Askew, J., Godette, K., and Childs, N. (2005). Adolescents coping with mom's breast cancer: developing family intervention programs. *Journal of Marital & Family Therapy*, 31, 247–58.

Díaz Rodríguez, C. et al. (2004). A preliminary report on multiple family discussion groups for patients with chronic medical illness and its repercussions in the management of the hemodialysis process. *Therapeutic Apheresis and Dialysis*, 8(6), 492–96.

Espina Eizaguirre, A., Ortego Saenz de Cabezon, M. A., and Ochoa de Alda Martinez-de-Appellaniz, I. (2000). Un ensayo controlado de intervenciones familiares en trastornos alimentarios (A controlled trial of family interventions in eating disorders). *Anales de Psicatria*, 16(8), 322–36.

Hogarty, G. E., Anderson, C. M., Reiss, D. J., Kornblith, S. J., Greenwald, D. P., Ulrich, R. F., and Carter, M. (1991). Family psychoeducation, social skills training and maintenance chemotherapy in the aftercare treatment of schizophrenia: II. Two-year effects of a controlled study on relapse and adjustment. *Archives of General Psychiatry*, 48, 340–7.

Hodge, F. S., Itty, T. L., Cadogan, M. P., and Martinez, F. (2012). "Weaving Balance into Life": Development and cultural adaptation of a cancer symptom management toolkit for Southwest American Indians. *Journal of Cancer Survivorship*, 6(2), 182–8.

Gonzalez S., Steinglass P., Reiss D. (1989). Putting the illness in its place: discussion groups for families with chronic medical illnesses. *Family Process*, 28, 69–87.

Kazak A. E., *et al.* (2004). Treatment of posttraumatic stress symptoms in adolescent survivors of childhood cancer and their families: A randomized clinical trial. *Journal of Family Psychology*, 18, 493–504.

Kitzman-Ulrich, H., Hampson, R., Wilson, D. K., Presnell, K., Brown, A., and O'Boyle, M. (2009). An adolescent weight-loss program integrating family variables reduces energy intake. *Journal of American Diet Association*, 109(3), 491–6.

van Lankveld, W., van Helmond, T., Naring, G., de Rooij, D. J., and van den Hoogen, F. (2004). Partner participation in cognitive-behavioral self-management group treatment for patients with rheumatoid arthritis. *Journal of Rheumatology*, 31, 1738–45.

Lavelle, L. (2007). The healthy families project. In Linville, Deanna (ed); Hertlein, Katherine M. (ed.). *The therapist's notebook for family health care: Homework, handouts, and activities for individuals, couples, and families coping with illness, loss, and disability* (pp. 59–63). New York: Haworth Press.

Manne, S. M. et al. (2005). Couple-Focused Group Intervention for Women with Early Stage Breast Cancer. *Journal of Consulting and Clinical Psychology*, 73 (4), 634–46.

Pai, A. L., and Kazak, A. E. (2006). Pediatric medical traumatic stress in pediatric oncology:

Riemsma, R., Taal, E., and Rasker, J. (2003). Group education for patients with rheumatoid arthritis and their partners. *Arthritis and Rheumatism*, 49, 556–66.

Rolland, J. S. (1994). *Families, Illness, and Disability: An Integrative Treatment Model*, New York: Basic Books.

Rolland, J. S., and McPheters, J. K. (2008). Resilient Partners: A collaborative project with the MS Society. Collaborative Family Health Association Annual Conference, November 2008, Denver, CO.

Shields, C. G., and Rousseau, S. J. (2004). A pilot study of an intervention for breast cancer survivors and their spouses. *Family Process*, 43, 95–107.

Sahler, O. J. et al. (2005). Using problem-solving skills training to reduce negative affectivity in mothers of children with newly diagnosed cancer: report of a multisite randomized trial. *Journal of Consulting and Clinical Psychology*, 73(2), 272–83.

Steinglass, P. (1998). Multiple family discussion groups for patients with chronic medical illness. *Families, Systems and Health*, 16, 55–70.

Steinglass, P., Ostroff, J. S., and Steinglass, A. S. (2011). Multiple family groups for adult cancer survivors and their families: a 1-day workshop model. *Family Process*, 50, 393–409.

Wysocki, T., Harris, M. A., Buckloh, L. M., Mertlich, D., Lochrie, A. S., Mauras, N., and White, N. H. (2007). Randomized trial of behavioral family systems therapy for diabetes maintenance of effects on diabetes outcomes in adolescents. *Diabetes Care*, 30(3), 555–60.

Appendix

Family Life Stages

Couplehood
Birth of child/children
Raising young children
Families with teenagers
Launching children
Middle years
Retirement
Aging and Death.

Assessment of the Caregiver Experience

Self-rating screens: some self-rating screens can be provided in a waiting room or handed out by clinic staff as part of a routine visit. One such tool is the AMA caregiver screen which is aimed to help caregivers recognize their need for support.

AMA Caregiver Self-AssessmentQuestionnaire: How are YOU?

Caregivers are often so concerned with caring for their relative's needs that they lose sight of their own well-being. Please take just a moment to answer the following questions. Once you have answered the questions, turn the p. to do a self-evaluation.

During the past week or so, I have ...

1.	Had trouble keeping my mind on what I was doing	Yes/No
2.	Felt that I could not leave my relative alone	Yes/No
3.	Had difficulty making decisions	Yes/No
4.	Felt completely overwhelmed	Yes/No
5.	Felt useful and needed	Yes/No
6.	Felt lonely	Yes/No
7.	Been upset that my relative has changed so much from his/her former self	Yes/No
8.	Felt a loss of privacy and/or personal time	Yes/No
9.	Been edgy or irritable	Yes/No

10. Had sleep disturbed because of caring for my relative Yes/No
11. Had a crying spell Yes/No
12. Felt strained between work and family responsibilities Yes/No
13. Had back pain Yes/No
14. Felt ill (headaches, stomach problems, or common cold) Yes/No
15. Been satisfied with the support my family has given me Yes/No
16. Found my relative's living situation to be inconvenient or a barrier to care Yes/No
17. On a scale of 1 to 10, with 1 being "not stressful" to 10 being "extremely stressful," please rate your current level of stress _____
18. On a scale of 1 to 10, with 1 being "very healthy" to 10 being "very ill," please rate your current health compared to what it was this time last year _____
    Comments: (Please feel free to comment or provide feedback.) _____

Self-evaluation: To determine the score:
1. Reverse score questions 5 and 15. (For example, a "No" response should be counted as "Yes" and a "Yes" response should be counted as "No.")
2. Total the number of "yes" responses.

To interpret the score:
Chances are that you are experiencing a high degree of distress:

If you answered "Yes" to either or both Questions 4 and 11; or if your total "Yes" score = 10 or more; or if your score on question 17 is 6 or higher; or if your score on question 18 is 6 or higher.

Next steps:

• Consider seeing a doctor for a check-up for yourself
• Consider having some relief from caregiving (Discuss with the doctor or a social worker the resources available in your community)
• Consider joining a support group.

Valuable resources for caregivers:

• Eldercare Locator (a national directory of community services) (800) 677–1116 www.eldercare.gov
• Family Caregiver Alliance (415) 434-3388 www.caregiver.org
• Medicare Hotline (800) 633–4227 www.medicare.gov
• National Alliance for Caregiving (301) 718-8444 www.caregiving.org
• National Family Caregivers Association (800) 896-3650 www.nfcacares.org
• National Information Center for Children and Youth with Disabilities (800) 695-0285 www.nichcy.org

"Family Caregiving … It's is not all up to you."

This is the name of the national outreach program that aims to connect family caregivers to information and services that can help improve their lives and the level of care they can offer their loved ones: <www.familycaregiving101.org>.

Handouts for Patients and Families

There are several good resources for patients and their families. There are several good websites: up to date (http://www.uptodate.com), the Mayo Clinic (http://www.mayoclinic.com/health/DiseasesIndex/DiseasesIndex) and the Merk Manual (http://www.merck-source.com/pp/us/cns/cns_merckmanualhome.jsp). However, many of these lack a "What can the family do to help" section.

There are many good books as resources for caregivers of patients with dementia such as *American Medical Association Guide to Home Caregiving* by the American Medical Association, Angela Perry (Editor), 2001, Wiley, and *The 36 Hour Day. A Family Guide to Caring for People with Alzheimer Disease, Other Dementias, and Memory Loss in Later Life*, 4th Edition, by Nancy L. Mace, Peter V. Rabins, 2007., Johns Hopkins University Press.

One organization/website that has grown tremendously in the past decade focuses on family awareness and depression and suicide is <www.familyaware.org>.

Coping well with Illness

Carver, C. S. (1997). You want to measure coping but your protocol's too long: Consider the Brief COPE. *International Journal of Behavioral Medicine*, 4, 92–100.

The Brief COPE is available in Spanish, French, Greek and Korean and is offered for free download on the website: <http://www.psy.miami.edu/faculty/ccarver/sclBrCOPE.html>.

Brief COPE

These items deal with ways you have been coping with the stress in your life since you found out you were going to have to have this operation/you have this illness. There are many ways to try to deal with problems. These items ask what you have been doing to cope with this one. Obviously, different people deal with things in different ways, but I am interested in how you have tried to deal with it. Each item says something about a particular way of coping. I want to know to what extent you have been doing what the item says. How much, or how frequently. Do not answer on the basis of whether it seems to be working or not—just whether or not you are doing it. Use these response choices. Try to rate each item separately in your mind from the others. Make your answers as true FOR YOU as you can.

1 = I have not been doing this at all
2 = I've been doing this a little bit
3 = I've been doing this a medium amount
4 = I've been doing this a lot

1. I've been turning to work or other activities to take my mind off things.
2. I've been concentrating my efforts on doing something about the situation I'm in.
3. I've been saying to myself "this isn't real."
4. I've been using alcohol or other drugs to make myself feel better.
5. I've been getting emotional support from others.
6. I've been giving up trying to deal with it.
7. I've been taking action to try to make the situation better.
8. I've been refusing to believe that it has happened.
9. I've been saying things to let my unpleasant feelings escape.
10. I've been getting help and advice from other people.
11. I've been using alcohol or other drugs to help me get through it.
12. I've been trying to see it in a different light, to make it seem more positive.
13. I've been criticizing myself.
14. I've been trying to come up with a strategy about what to do.
15. I've been getting comfort and understanding from someone.
16. I've been giving up the attempt to cope.
17. I've been looking for something good in what is happening.
18. I've been making jokes about it.
19. I've been doing something to think about it less, such as going to movies, watching TV, reading, daydreaming, sleeping, or shopping.

20. I've been accepting the reality of the fact that it has happened.
21. I've been expressing my negative feelings.
22. I've been trying to find comfort in my religion or spiritual beliefs.
23. I've been trying to get advice or help from other people about what to do.
24. I've been learning to live with it.
25. I've been thinking hard about what steps to take.
26. I've been blaming myself for things that happened.
27. I've been praying or meditating.
28. I've been making fun of the situation.

Family Systems Assessment

McMaster model of Family Functioning

Problem solving: The ability to resolve problems to maintain effective family functioning. Instrumental problems are problems of everyday life, such as managing money, obtaining food, clothing, and housing and affective problems concerning emotions such as anger or depression. Families whose functioning is disrupted by instrumental problems rarely deal effectively with affective problems. Stages of effective problem solving are: identification of the problem and communication of the problem with an appropriate person; developing alternatives; deciding on an alternative; acting upon that decision and monitoring outcome.

Questions: Who first notices problems? What did you do after you noticed the problem? Did you discuss it with anybody? What did you decide to do about the problem? Did you think of any alternatives? Did you discuss how you dealt with the problem once you had taken care of it? How do you handle practical problems? How do you handle emotional problems?

Roles: How the provision of resources, nurturance and support, sexual gratification, personal development and maintenance and management of the family system are divided between members, including decision-making, boundaries, household finances and management.

Questions: Who works and for how many hours? Who handles the money? Who buys the groceries and prepares the meals? Who looks after the home and cars? Who oversees what happens with the children's education? Who is involved in major decisions and who has the final say? Do any of you feel overburdened by your jobs? Are the responsibilities fairly shared between family members? If not, how would you like to see it done?

Communication: The verbal exchange of information within a family. Families can have marked difficulties with the affective component of communication but can function very well in the instrumental area. Communication can be clear or masked (camouflaged). Communication can be direct or indirect (comments delivered to someone else rather than the intended person).

Questions: Do people in this family talk with one another? Can you talk about practical things with each other? Can you talk about emotional issues with each other? Do you feel that you can talk things through with others in the family, or do you have to be guarded about what you say? Can you tell things to each other directly, or do you go through someone else?

Affective involvement: How the family shows interest in and values the activities of other family members. Families who lack involvement with each other merely coexist in the same space without connection. Family members who are narcissistically involved are invested in others only in terms of what they can get, without real concern for others. Empathic involvement means that family members demonstrate true concern for others, even though these concerns are peripheral to their own interests. Over-involvement and symbiotic involvement are over-intrusive, over-protective, with blurred boundaries between family members.

Questions: Who cares about what is important to you? Do you think other family members are interested in you? Do they ever show too much interest? Do you feel that they are truly interested in you because it is important to you, or only because they think they should be? Do you feel that other members of the family go their own way and do not care or notice what happens to you?

Affective responsiveness: Ability to respond with a full range of feelings, and whether or not the emotion experienced is consistent with the context. Welfare emotions consist of affection, warmth, tenderness, support, love, consolation, happiness, and joy. Emergency emotions are fear, anger, sadness, disappointment, and depression.

Questions: Are you a family that responds to situations with a lot of feeling? Do any of you feel that you are a family who under-responds in terms of emotions? Which kinds of emotions do you think you over- or under-respond to? Are there any feelings that you experience more intensely than reasonable given the situation?

Behavior control: How a family establishes rules about behavior, such as parental discipline, and standards and expectations of behavior that adults set for each other. There are several styles of behavior control: rigid behavioral control, flexible behavior control, laissez-faire behavior control (where there are no standards or direction), and chaotic behavior control where standards shift in a random unpredictable fashion.

Questions: Do you have rules in your family about how to handle different situations? How do you handle dangerous situations? Do you allow hitting or yelling at each other? Do you know what is expected of you in terms of behavior with people outside the family? Do you have rules about drinking? Driving too fast? Letting people know where you are when you are away from home? Are the rules clear? Are the rules the same for everybody? Can you discuss the rules to change them? Do you know what to expect if the rules are broken?

(Adapted from Keitner, Heru, and Glick, *Clinical Manual of Couples and Family Therapy* (2009). APPI Press, p. 74–8)

Global Assessment of Relational Functioning

The Global Assessment of Relational Functioning (GARF) provides a score of the functioning of a family or other relationship on a continuum ranging from competent, optimal relational functioning to a disrupted, dysfunctional relationship. It is analogous to Axis V (Global Assessment of Functioning Scale) provided for individuals in DSM-IV. Three areas are assessed:

A. Problem solving—skills in negotiating goals, rules, and routines; adaptability to stress; communication skills; ability to resolve conflict.
B. Organization—maintenance of interpersonal roles and subsystem boundaries; hierarchical functioning; coalitions and distribution of power, control, and responsibility.
C. Emotional climate—tone and range of feelings; quality of caring, empathy, involvement, and attachment/commitment; sharing of values; mutual affective responsiveness, respect, and regard; quality of sexual functioning.

81–100 SATISFACTORY: Relational unit is functioning satisfactorily from self-report of participants and from perspectives of observers.
61–80 SOMEWHAT UNSATISFACTORY: Functioning of relational unit is somewhat unsatisfactory. Over a period of time, many but not all difficulties are resolved without complaints.
41–60 MOSTLY UNSATISFACTORY: Relational unit has occasional times of satisfying and competent functioning together, but clearly dysfunctional, unsatisfying relationships tend to predominate.
21–40 RARELY SATISFACTORY: Relational unit is obviously and seriously dysfunctional; forms and time periods of satisfactory relating are rare.
1–20 CHAOTIC: Relational unit has become too dysfunctional to retain continuity of contact and attachment.
(Abbreviated from DSMIV 1994. American Psychiatric Publishing, Inc.)

Further Resources for Chapter 7: Parenting with Life-Threatening Illness

Website

The website for the PACT Program at Massachusetts General Hospital <www.mghpact.org>.

Books and Articles

Harpham, W. (2004). *When a Parent Has Cancer: A Guide to Caring for Your Children*. Harper Collins.

Heiney, S., Hermann, J., Bruss, K., and Fincannon, J. (2001). Cancer in the Family: Helping children cope with a parent's illness. American Cancer Society, Atlanta, GA.

McCue, K. (1994). *How to Help Children Through a Parent's Serious Illness*. St. Martin's Griffin.

Moore, C. W. (2007). Helping children cope with breast cancer. Patient education pamphlet published by the Young Survival Coalition.

Muriel A. C. (2004). Delivering the News. In Stern T., and Sekeres M. (Eds). *Facing Cancer: A Complete Guide for People with Cancer, Their Families, and Caregivers*. New York, NY: McGraw-Hill, pp. 55–61.

Muriel, A. C., and Rauch, P. K. (2003) Suggestions for patients on how to talk with children about a parent's cancer. *Journal of Support Oncology*. 1(2), 143–5.

Rapaport, W. S. (1998).*When diabetes hits home*. American Diabetes Association, Alexandria, VA.

Rauch, P. K., and Durant, S. (2003). Helping Children Cope with a Parent's Cancer. In Stern T., Sekeres M. (Eds). *Facing Cancer: A Complete Guide for People with Cancer, Their Families, and Caregivers*. New York: McGraw-Hill Professional, pp. 125–36.

Rauch, P. K., and Muriel, A. C. (2003). Delivering the News. In Stern T., and Sekeres M. (Eds). *Facing Cancer: A Complete Guide for People with Cancer, Their Families and Caregivers*. New York: McGraw-Hill Professional, 55–62.

—and Cassem, N. H. (2003). Parents With Cancer: Who's Looking After the Children? *Journal of Clinical Oncology*, 21(9) (Suppl), 117–21.

—(2006). *Raising an Emotionally Healthy Child When a Parent Is Sick*. New York (NY), McGraw-Hill.

Rauch, P. K., Muriel, A. C., and Cassem, N. H.(2002). Parents with cancer: who's looking after the children? *Journal of Clinical Oncology*, 20(21), 4399–402.

Shuman, R., and Schwartz, J. (1994). *Living with Multiple Sclerosis: A Handbook for Families*. New York: Collier Books.

Books and Resources for Children

Blake, C., Blanchard, E., and Parkinson, K. (1998). *The Paper Chain*. Albuquerque, New Mexico: Health Press.

Clifford, C. (1998). *Our Family Has Cancer Too!* Duluth, Minnesota: Pfeifer-Hamilton Publishers.

DePaola, T. (1973). *Nana Upstairs and Nana Downstairs. A storybook about death*. New York: Puffin Books.

Fitzgerald, H. (2000). *The Grieving Teen: a Guide for Teenagers and Their Friends*. New York: Fireside Books.

Glader, S. (2010). *Nowhere Hair*. Mill Valley, CA: Thousand Words Press.

Lewis, A. (2005). *When Someone You Love Has Cancer*. Meinrad, Indiana: One Caring Place, Abbey Press.

Meiners, C. J. (2003). *When I Feel Afraid*. Minneapolis, MN: Free Spirit Publishing.

Miles, M., and Parnell, P. (1985). *Annie and the Old One*. New York, NY: Little, Brown Books for Young Readers.

Sachedina, S. (2006). *Metu and Lee*. Dr Shenin Sachedina Medical Educational Products, c/o The Central Florida Breast Center, Winter Park, FL.

Viorst, J. (1988). *The Tenth Good Thing about Barney. A storybook about death*. New York: Aladdin Paperbacks.

When Someone You Know Has Cancer: An Activity Booklet for Families available at www.pbs.org and at The Lance Armstrong Foundation website www.livestrong.org.

When Your Parent Has Cancer, A Guide for Teens available at <http://www.cancer.gov/cancertopics/coping/when-your-parent-has-cancer>.

Index

This index covers all chapters and the appendix. Tables and figures are indicated by page numbers in **bold** type.

asthma *continued*
    disparities 32–3, 34–5; inhaler usage 35; life-threatening attacks and 36; limitations 32, 33; listening on 36–7); symptoms 23; telephone information 78; uncertainty on 25
Asthma-Specific Coping Scale 155

back pain 13
Bailey, J. et al. 190
basal cell carcinoma 52
BBFM (biobehavioral family model) 149
behavior care plans 89–91, 96, 103–4; coercion and 89; containment and 98, 101; ethics and 98; expectations and 94, 96, 101; extra-therapeutic goals 92, 96, 105; extra therapeutic pain relief 105–6; on goals 90; language in 90; patient care plans and 93; signatures on 91
behavior modification 88, 91–2, 93, 108
Behavioral Family Systems Therapy for Diabetes (BFST-D) 222–3
Benefit-Finding Scale in Multiple Sclerosis (BFiMSS) 158
BFI (Brief Family Intervention) 194–5
BFiMSS (Benefit-Finding Scale in Multiple Sclerosis) 158
BFST-D (Behavioral Family Systems Therapy for Diabetes) 222–3
biobehavioral family model (BBFM) 149
Bishop, D. S. 178
blame 61; depression and 61
blood pressure (BP) 7; low 88–9, 103–4
blood tests 89
borderline personality disorder 106
Boston Medical Center 74–5
Boston University Medical Center 78
BP (blood pressure) 7; low 88–9, 103–4
brain injury 162; life structures and autonomy 56
breast cancer: immune systems and 8; MFGs 219; MFSGs 226–7, 228
Brief COPE 233–4; on avoidance and denial 233
Brief Family Intervention (BFI) 194–5
Brief Systemic Family Therapy (BSFT) 193–4
brief systemic therapy (BST) 195
Brigham and Women's Hospital 73
BSFT (Brief Systemic Family Therapy) 193–4
BST (brief systemic therapy) 195
Bultz, B. D. et al. 219
burns 93; pain 88, 93–6

CABG (coronary artery bypass graft) 12–13
Camberwell Family Interview 5

Campbell, T. L. xi
cancer 130, 162; basal cell carcinoma 52; breast cancer 8, 219, 226–7, 228; control over 60; distress thermometer 125; faith and 157; fatality and 48; head and neck cancer 225–6; leukemia 61; lung cancer 143; MFGs 216–17, 219; MFSGs 222, 225; pain 118; palliative care 121, 122–3; PAT2.0 125; PFCC 73–4; SCCIP 225; *see also* PACT
Captains of Kindness 141
cardiovascular conditions *see* blood pressure; heart conditions
Caregiver Briefcase xiii, 81
Caregiver Health Effects Survey 81
caregiving 109, 153, 230, 232; age factors 109; constraint 81; disparities 83, 109–10; 115; disruption and 99; ethics and 82, 110; fatality and 126 (grief and 119; home-based/hospital care 64; loss and 119; self-transcendence and 119; time factors 119); financial factors 80; goals 114; problem solving 115, 116; scope xiii, 42, 80–2, 114, 115–16, 126; self-care and 109; time factors 80; understanding on 115; *see also individual terms*
Centers for Disease Control and Prevention 34
CFHA (Collaborative Family Healthcare Association) xv
Chien, L. Y. et al. 217
child abuse xii
children xi, 131–2, 142, 161–2; age factors 117, 123–5, 132–4, **135**, 136, **144**, 162, 185, 193–4, 218, 222–3, 225, 228; box of records for 142; as caregivers 80–1; challenges on 140; delays 136; emotional factors 135–6, 142; expectations and 142; family time for 140–1 (absence and 141; expectation and 141; understanding and 141); fatality and 143, 145 (challenges 143; disclosure 143–4; funerals 145–6; goodbyes 145; home-based/hospital care 145; legacy gifts 145; memorials 145; safety and 144; time factors 145; understanding and 144, **144**); genetic factors on 50; life structures for 140 (autonomy and 55); mental health support for 142–3; on pain 116–17, 191; school contacts for 141–2; substance abuse and 193–4; temperament factors 135 (inhibition 135, 136; reactivity 135, 136; understanding and 135–6); understanding and 136, 142; video calling for 142; visual factors 142; *see also individual terms*
Chinese-American families 110; age factors 183

Chinese families 184–5
Christ, G. H. and Christ, A. E. 123
chronic conditions 3, 33–4, 41, 42, 215; acute
    factors and 4; control over 42; reassurance
    on 42; time factors 4, 43; trauma of
    diagnosis 17; understanding 43; *see also*
    individual terms
Cincinnati Children's Hospital Medical Center
    73
cognitive appraisal 154
cognitive-behavioral therapy: on arthritis 218;
    on cancer 227; DBT 92, 106–7; on pain
    116–17, 191
Collaborative Family Healthcare Association
    (CFHA) xv
collages 226
Community Development Model 37
Concord Hospital 74
confidentiality 79–80
contrasting for accusations 102–3
COPE model 121, 122; on problem solving
    121
coping strategies: as automatic behaviors 153;
    autonomy and 162; avoidance and denial as
    6, 7, 11, 156 (adaptive avoidance 154, 156);
    benefit-finding as 158; challenges 165–6;
    disparities 161–2; emotional factors 155,
    156–7 (acceptance in 6; depression and
    157); language on 154; learned 158, 160–1;
    problem solving as 13, 155; repression as
    157; resource information 233; scope 6,
    17, 153, 154, 155, 156, 161, 162, 166; space
    on 153; time factors 155, 162; uncertainty
    161; understanding and 153, 154; *see also*
    individual terms
coronary artery bypass graft (CABG) 12–13
couples *see* married and unmarried couples
Cox, S. 158
Crisp, A. H. 223
customer recovery 97
cybernetics 171
cystic fibrosis 83; MFGs 51

Dana-Farber Cancer Institute (DFCI) 73–4
Danielson, C. B. et al. 175
DAS (Dyadic Adjustment Scale) 5–6, 190
Davey, M. et al. 228
DBT (Dialectical Behavior Therapy) 92, 106–7
DBT-Ways of Coping Checklist (DBT-WCCL)
    6
dementia 7, 12, 118; Alzheimer's disease 45,
    82–3, 119; depression and 118; MFGs 217;
    resource information 232
depression 15, 16, 118, 157, 192, 197, 204;
    blame and 61; disparities 15, 110, 123

DFCI (Dana-Farber Cancer Institute)
    73–4
diabetes 191; autonomy and 185; control over
    185; disruption on 117; McMaster model
    185; MFGs 51; MFSGs 222–3; problem
    solving on 117; time factors 191
diabetic ketoacidosis 149
Dialectical Behavior Therapy (DBT) 88, 91,
    92, 106, 108
dialysis 224
Díaz Rodríguez, C. et al. 224
diet *see* nutrition and dietary factors
disability 41, 42, 45; disparities 45; heart
    conditions 53, 56; time factors 45;
    uncertainty on 45–6
distress thermometer 125
Doherty, W. J. xiv
Dyadic Adjustment Scale (DAS) 5–6, 190

eating disorders 223; anorexia 194
EE (expressed emotion) 5
egocentrism 132–3
elderly people xi, 7, 111; age factors 173;
    dementia 118–19; ethics and 113; HHCS
    110–11; McMaster model 183; nursing
    homes and 111
empathy 177, 179
energy efficiency 36
epilepsy *see* seizures
Epstein, N. B. 178
ethnic and cultural factors 63, 110, 111–12,
    113–14, 155; ADLs 114; asthma 23, 30,
    31–2, 37; cancer 60, 216–17; depression
    110; disparities xi, 3–4, 10, 17, 62–3,
    110, 111, 155; EE 5; faith 112; family
    experiences and 177; gender issues 111, 112
    (socioeconomic factors 111); genograms
    191; heart conditions 56; HHCS 110–11;
    language 113; McMaster model 181, 182,
    183, 184–5; MFSGs 222; nursing homes
    111; PACT 137; PFCC 83–4; seizures
    163–5; self-care 113; socioeconomic factors
    8; uncertainty 112–13; visiting restrictions
    and 63–4
expressed emotion (EE) 5
extra-therapeutic goals 97, 99; extra
    therapeutic pain relief 104–5

FAAS (Family and Asthma Study) 25, **26**;
    disparities 30; on environmental factors 30;
    on inhaler usage 26–7, **27**, 28, **28**, 29, **29**,
    30 (FMSS 29; time factors 31); listening in
    30–1; time factors 31
FAD (Family Assessment Device) 6, 126
fairness 133